Chicago Sun-Times

METRO CHICAGO ALMANAC

Chicago Sun-Times

METRO CHICAGO ALMANAC

Fascinating Facts and Offbeat Offerings about the Windy City

Don Hayner
and
Tom McNamee

Bonus Books, Inc., Chicago, and Chicago Sun-Times, Inc.

95 94 93 92 91   5 4 3 2 1

Library of Congress Catalog Card Number: 91-73573

International Standard Book Number: 0-929387-38-4

Bonus Books, Inc.
160 East Illinois Street
Chicago, Illinois 60611

Chicago Sun-Times, Inc.
401 North Wabash
Chicago, Illinois 60611

Norm Schafer, cover design

Susan Randstrom, cover illustration

Rich Cahan, picture research

Elizabeth Novickas, computer support services

Ken Kozak, editing support

Composition by Point West Inc., Carol Stream, IL

Printed in the United States

CONTENTS

FOREWORD

Until now, Metropolitan Chicago has had almost everything. Sixteen-inch softball. The most beautiful skyline in the world. Irv Kupcinet. Nonpareil hot dogs and pizza.

Clearly, we have the most livable urban/suburban environment in the United States in which prospers the nation's best aquarium, its most popular zoo and the most magnificent cluster of museums anywhere.

But something was missing. Until now. And you have it in your hand. The first ever—and, thus, indisputably the best—almanac on Metropolitan Chicago produced by the *Chicago Sun-Times!*

We know you'll have fun with it, learn a great deal from it and come to rely on it as the authoritative source for information on this fabulous area in which we live.

Enjoy!

Dennis A. Britton
Editor
Senior Vice President
Chicago Sun-Times

INTRODUCTION

Deadline.

Our science reporter is digging through drawers jammed with files in search of the deepest depth of Lake Michigan.

Our religion writer is on the phone in search of a good count on Zoroastrians in the Chicago area.

Our chief political writer is rooting through stacks of papers in search of the exact date of that infamous City Council session where Eugene Sawyer was elected mayor.

And then there's the young intern in the corner, assigned to write the day's weather story. He hasn't got a clue about where to find the record for the hottest day in Chicago.

Well, he can look here. Because this is the *Chicago Sun-Times Metro Chicago Almanac*, a convenient one-stop depository for all those quirky, funny and fundamental facts about the Chicago area that *Sun-Times* and *Daily News* reporters have been trolling about and collecting for more than 100 years. They were squirreled away in all those crowded desk drawers and thick skulls. Now they're here.

Hey, this isn't the history of the world, but it hopefully provides the flavor and aroma of a city born of clout, crooks and the Columbian Exposition. Within these pages you'll find when spitting on the L was first outlawed and about the family buried in a suburban parking lot.

Care to know what were the ten most devastating fires in Chicago history? Check under "Disasters." Care to know what a violinist is paid in the Chicago Symphony Orchestra? Check under "Music." Ever wonder how Romeoville got to be Romeoville? Okay. Probably not. But it's a good story all the same.

You won't find absolutely everything about Chicago and the burbs in this book. Let's face it. The Chicago area is far too complex, too complicated and too rich in history to be squeezed within the covers of one book. Or a library full of books. But you will find a fascinating and authoritative cross section of the stuff that makes Chicago shake, the stuff that makes it home.

CHICAGO OPENERS

TALKING CHICAGO

There's one quick way to spot a real Chicagoan. Ask him to open his mouth and say "Chicago."

Ask that question around the *Sun-Times* newsroom and you'll hear "Chi-cah-go" from the downstater. And you'll hear "Chi-cah-go" from the guy who grew up in Waukegan, which is like being a downstater.

"Chi-caw-go," says the guy from Cleveland. Clevelanders always get it right. They're notorious chameleons, eager to conceal their true identity.

But what about all those people who pronounce it "Chi-cah-go"?

"No greater sign of an amateur," says Al Parker, chairman of Columbia College's radio department. "I don't care what the hell Sinatra says in 'My kind of Town Chi-cah-go Is.' It's 'Chi-caw-go.'"

Longtime WBBM radio commentator John Madigan has also registered shock over Sinatra's ability to "get away unapprehended." When Sinatra played the Chicago Theatre in 1986, Madigan asked Mayor Washington "to please tell Sinatra to try and get it right this one time: Chi-caw-go."

But hold on. Are we being fair? *Webster's Ninth New Collegiate Dictionary* has it both ways. And Mary Berger, a Chicago-based speech coach, won't say Chi-cah-go is wrong, although she teaches her students to say: "Chi-caw-go."

"She-caw-gu," says Sam Keahna, a board member of the American Indian Center, 1630 W. Wilson. The name is Potawatomi and probably means wild onion or skunk grass. When it's spoken at prayer ceremonies, Keahna said, it's always pronounced with the "caw."

Hey, what more do you need?

A WORD ON TEN CHICAGO WORDS

They say "vacant lot," but we say "prairie."
They say "soda," but we say "pop."

They say "going to," but we say "going by."
They say "hardball," but we say "league."
They say "sneakers," but we say "gym shoes."
They say "walkway," but we say "gangway."
They say "sack," but we say "bag."
They say "downtown," but we say "the Loop."
They say "he said," but we say "he goes."
They say "pull," but we say "clout."

FOR OUT-OF-TOWN WRITERS:
A CHEAT SHEET TO CLICHE NICKNAMES

- The City that Works
- The City of Neighborhoods
- That Toddlin' Town
- The Windy City
- City of Big Shoulders
- Hog Butcher to the World
- Chi-town
- The Second City
- City on the Make
- Jewel of the Prairie
- My Kind of Town
- Sweethome Chicago
- Crossroads of the Nation
- Hub of the Nation
- City of Clout
- Beirut by the Lake
- The Gem of the Lakes
- Convention Capital of the World

FOR OUT-OF-TOWN WRITERS:
A CHEAT SHEET TO CULTURAL CLICHES

- Deep-dish pizza
- 16-inch softball
- Aldermen with pinky rings

- Cigar-chomping pols
- The Cubs, those "lovable losers"
- Scarface Al Capone
- "Front Page" journalism
- Second City Theater Company
- Chicago blues
- Mrs. O'Leary's cow
- "The most segregated city in America"
- "It's a great newspaper town"
- "State Street, that Great Street"
- The "Magnificent Mile"
- The "aroma" of the stockyards
- The Democratic Machine

CHICAGO FLAG AND SEAL

Seal: The shield, designed in 1837, represents the national spirit of Chicago. The Indian represents the first discoverers of Chicago, and celebrates their contributions. The ship signifies the approach of modern civilization. The sheaf of wheat signifies activity and natural abundance. The babe in the shell is the ancient classical symbol of the pearl, signifying Chicago as "the gem of the lakes." The motto, "Urbs in Horto," means "City in a Garden." The date, March 4, 1837, is when Chicago incorporated as a city.

Flag: The two bars of blue signify the Chicago River's two branches. The three white strips, from top to bottom, represent the North, West and South sides. The four stars signify Fort Dearborn, the Chicago Fire of 1871, the Columbian Exposition of 1893 and the Century of Progress Exposition of 1933.

Charges of Racism: Some folks say Chicago's city seal is racist. In 1987, two aldermen, Robert Shaw and Allan Streeter, charged that the ship on the seal—signifying European settlement—represents "institutionalized racism" and should be replaced with a cameo of Jean Baptiste Point DuSable, a black man who was the city's first settler. When the seal was created in 1837, Mayor William B. Ogden's design committee said the ship symbolized "the approach of white man's civilization and commerce."

STATE AND COUNTY FLAGS AND SEALS

STATE SYMBOLS

- **State Animal:** White-tailed deer.
- **State Bird:** Cardinal
- **State Fish:** Bluegill
- **State Flower:** Violet
- **State Insect:** Monarch butterfly
- **State Mineral:** Fluorite
- **State Slogan:** Land of Lincoln
- **State Tree:** White oak
- **State Prairie Grass:** Big bluestem
- **State Fossil:** The Tully Monster, a soft-bodied marine animal that lived 280 million to 340 million years ago.

Mysterious Shifting Baby: For years the city seemed uncertain of the symbolism of the naked baby. Originally, city officials said, the baby symbolized tranquility and peace. Then, in 1854, the City Council ordered that the seal be changed to lay the baby in a shell, symbolizing the idea of "plenty." Ten years later, without official permission, somebody redrew the seal, placing the baby on its stomach. In 1881, the shell was removed and the baby was left floating without a background. In 1887, the baby was placed back on its stomach. And ten years later, the baby rolled over on its back again. In 1905, the city commissioned a dentist, Dr. B.J. Cigrand, to redesign the seal. Cigrand made the baby sit up in the shell. Cigrand never explained the change, but an early mayor, John Wentworth, had once predicted that when "barbarism gave way to civilization" in Chicago, the baby would "wake up." Evidently, civilization had arrived.

STATE SEAL AND FLAG

State Seal: Adopted in 1867, it shows a free and noble eagle perched on a shield of U.S. stars and stripes, holding a banner bearing the words, "State Sovereignty, National Union."

Flag: Consists of the word "Illinois" and a replica of the state seal on a white background. It was adopted as the state's flag on July 1, 1970.

I Will: Chicago's official slogan is "Urbs in Horto"—meaning city in a garden, adopted in 1833. It is included in the city seal. But Chicago's unofficial slogan is "I Will," which was the motto of the Columbian Exposition of 1893. In 1892, a Chicago newspaper, the *Inter-Ocean*, sponsored a contest to find an appropriate motto and image for the fair. The winning entry, from more than 300 submitted, was by Charles Holloway, thirty-three, a Chicago painter best known for his mural in the Auditorium Theatre. Holloway had submitted a drawing of a strong and dignified woman wearing the leather wristband of an athlete and carrying a carpenter's square. On her head was a crown bearing the words, "I Will." Where'd Holloway get the idea? "Into my head came the old saying, 'When a woman will, she will, you may depend on't.'" Actually, the correct quote, from eighteenth century English writer Aaron Hill was, "First then, a woman will, or won't—depend on't."

COUNTY FLAGS AND SEALS

Cook County: The seal illustrates the geographic essence of the county—a ship, signifying Lake Michigan, and a city skyline. A banner, unfurled before an outline of a county map, bears the date of founding, 1831. The county flag consists of a white field with red and yellow trim, and the words "Cook County" in blue letters. In the center of the flag is the seal. Thirty-eight stars around the seal represent the county's thirty suburban townships and original eight city townships.

Will County: The seal presents, in a single picture, some of the most important elements in the development of the county—an Indian in a canoe representing the contributions of Native Americans, the Illinois & Michigan Canal, the railroads, agriculture, factories and forest preserves. A rising sun in the background, county officials say, alludes to the county's "bright future." The county's gold-fringed flag displays the county seal on a background of white.

Lake County: The county seal features a city skyline on a lake shore, a rifle and an ax—tools of the pioneers—and a banner stating, "Lake County 1839." The flag displays the county seal on a background of blue.

Du Page County: The seal celebrates the county's rural roots, displaying a bundle of wheat and several farm tools, and the words, "County of Du Page, Wheaton, Illinois." Du Page County has no official flag.

Kane County: One seal consists of a circle with the words "Seal of Kane County, State of Illinois" and the words "Organized Jan. 16, 1836." A second, newer seal, one used on many county documents, consists of a circle colored green and yellow-orange, with a blue strip down the middle. The green is for the rural areas and small towns. The yellow-orange is for the urban areas. The blue stripe is for the Fox River. The county flag consists of sixteen gold stars—one for each township—and a white banner stating "Kane County" on a field of blue.

McHenry County: The seal is almost exactly the same as that for the state of Illinois—the shield, the eagle and the banner bearing the words "State Sovereignty, National Union." The county flag, based on a design submitted in 1979 by Theresa Smith, then a second-grade student from Harvard, Illinois, celebrates rural life. It includes the year McHenry County was founded—1837—and depicts a cow, a corncob and a jumping fish.

Sister Cities: One of Chicago's nine sister cities is Casablanca, Morrocco; the others are Kiev, USSR; Warsaw, Poland; Milan, Italy; Osaka, Japan; Prague, Czechoslovakia; Accra, Ghana; Gothenburg, Sweden; Shenyang, China.

A CHICAGO
TIME LINE

1779—Chicago's first settler, Jean Baptiste Point DuSable establishes a trading post on the north bank of the Chicago River.

1795—Gen. "Mad Anthony" Wayne overruns Indians and forces them to cede huge tracts of Midwestern land, including "six miles square at the mouth of the Chickago River."

1796—Antoine Ouilmette and his Potawatomi wife, Archange, settle in a log cabin to the west of DuSable. Lakefront land later is granted to Archange by the U.S. government in gratitude for her husband's assistance in securing an Indian treaty. It becomes suburban Wilmette.

1803—Blue-coated U.S. soldiers, under the command of Captain John Whistler, arrive from Detroit and build Fort Dearborn at what is now Lower Wacker and Michigan. It is named for Henry Dearborn, secretary of war. Whistler was the grandfather of the famous artist James A. McNeill Whistler.

1812—In the so-called Fort Dearborn Massacre, Indians ambush the fort's settlers as they attempt to flee during times of frontier tensions. Fifty-two of the fort's men, women and children are slain.

1816—Fort Dearborn rebuilt.

1818—Illinois admitted to the Union as the twenty-first state.

1825—Erie Canal opened, creating a new water route between Chicago and the East.

1826—Mark Beaubien, a fiddle-playing French Canadian with a wild streak, arrives in Chicago on a visit to his brother Jean, decides to stay, and opens the most famous tavern and hotel of his time, the Sauganash.

1829—Plainfield, Will County's oldest community, is settled by Reverend Jesse Walker, a pioneer Methodist circuit rider, and his son-in-law, James Walker.

1830—Surveyor James Thompson plots out the town of Chicago so that parcels can be sold off to finance the digging of the Illinois and

Michigan Canal. The town is bounded by Madison, Kinzie, State and Desplaines streets.

1831—John and Joseph Naper settle Du Page County's oldest town, Naperville, then known as the Naper Settlement.

1832—Sauk warrior Black Hawk and his band wage war to regain their homelands. They are defeated at the Bad Axe River in Wisconsin, and all of northern Illinois is opened for pioneer settlement.

1833—Chicago votes to incorporate as a village on about August 5, by a vote of 12 to 1. Qualified voters are white males, over age twenty-one, who have lived in the settlement at least six months or own property.

1834—George W. Dole opens a slaughterhouse and makes the first shipment of beef from Chicago, 287 barrels.

1835—Indians gather in Chicago for the last time, to collect treaty-arranged payoffs before moving to lands west of the Mississippi River.

1836—Kane County's first officials elected by 180 men at Herrington's Tavern on June 4.

1837—The village of Chicago incorporates as a city with 4,170 residents, but has no gas, basements, paved streets or buildings taller than two stories. William B. Ogden defeats John Kinzie to become first mayor.

1838—First McHenry County election held, with 115 voters casting ballots to elect county officials.

1839—The firm of Newberry and Dole ship 1,678 bushels of wheat on the ship *Osceola*, marking the beginning of Chicago's leading role in grain export trade.

1846—First newspaper in McHenry County, the *Illinois Republican*, is published in Woodstock.

1847—Illinois and Michigan Canal is completed, linking the Gulf of Mexico with the Atlantic and making Chicago, indisputably, the nation's crossroads. It opens the next year.

1848—Chicago area's first railroad, the Galena and Chicago Union, completes its first ten-mile run on Nov. 20, 1848, between the city and the Des Plaines River. It will evolve into the Chicago & North Western Railroad.

1850—Passage of the Fugitive Slave Act, establishing penalties for anyone caught harboring a slave, ironically fuels development of the Underground Railroad in Du Page County. Once slaves reached the Tremont Hotel in Chicago, black barbers there acted as conductors on the last leg of the trip through Detroit into Canada.

1856—Chicago Historical Society organized.

1857—Mayor John Wentworth, tired of dog fights and sex shows in the city's red light district, The Sands, personally leads thirty cops and hundreds of citizens on a clean up crusade. They demolish every disreputable house.

1860—Abe Lincoln nominated for president at Republicans' first national convention, held in Chicago's Wigwam on May 18.

1865—Body of Abraham Lincoln arrives May 2 aboard a black-draped Illinois Central funeral train and lies in state in the courthouse while an estimated 125,000 citizens pay their last respects.

1871—Great Chicago Fire sparked on October 8 in Mrs. O'Leary's barn.

1874—Woman's Christian Temperance Union founded in Evanston. Frances E. Willard is first president.

1886—Seven policemen killed in the Haymarket Affair on May 4.

1889—Jane Addams founds Hull House, the nation's most respected settlement house, on Halsted Street on the Near West Side. She fights for the minimum wage, factory inspections and an end to child labor.

1890—Kane County Court House destroyed by fire. Records, locked in fire-proof vaults, survive.

1891—First performance of the Chicago Symphony Orchestra, on October 16 in the Auditorium Theatre.

1892—University of Chicago opens its doors.

1893—World's Columbian Exposition held in Chicago.

1894—Sleeping car manufacturer George Pullman cuts workers' wages in his company town south of Chicago, but not rents or food costs. Employees, led by Eugene V. Debs, go on strike. Federal soldiers try to operate the trains, but strikers rip up tracks and overturn cars. Debs is jailed and the strike is broken—but not forgotten.

1897—Rapid transit lines that form the actual Loop are built.

1900—Chicago makes the Chicago River run backward to Mississippi River, via the Illinois River.

1903—Iroquois Theater Fire on December 30 kills 596. And first Ford in America sold to a Chicago dentist.

1906—Upton Sinclair's *The Jungle* published.

1909—Architect Daniel H. Burnham produces his famous Plan of Chicago, which serves as a blueprint for the city's physical development.

Children from Hull House wait in the rain to get a glimpse of Jane Addams' body on May 22, 1935, one day after her death. Addams founded Hull House, one of the nation's most respected settlement houses, in 1889. *(Photo by Emme)*

1914—Mayor Fred A. Busse dies, leaving behind a mysterious safe-deposit box full of stock in a company that sold the city its manhole covers.

1915—The Eastland, packed with 2,000 men, woman and children on a company outing on July 24, rolls over in the Chicago River, drowning 812.

1919—A black youth drifts into a white swimming area and drowns when a white man on shore hits him with a stone. The ensuing riots leave thirty-seven more dead.

1922—Lottie Holman O'Neil of Downers Grove becomes the first woman to be elected to the Illinois General Assembly.

1924—North Side gangster Dion O'Banion shot dead in his flower shop. One hit man shook O'Banion's hand. The other gunned him down.

1929—Seven gangsters killed in the St. Valentine's Day Massacre.

Chicago in about 1912. The population had just passed the two-million mark, and only a few office buildings had attained a height of 300 feet. *(Photo by Alvina Lenke Studio)*

1930—James Dewar of Schiller Park invents the Twinkie.

1933—Chicago hosts another world's fair, a Century of Progress, and gives the world a sexy sensation—Sally Rand.

1933—Mayor Anton Cermak fatally shot March 6 by bullet meant for President Franklin D. Roosevelt.

1934—John Dillinger, Public Enemy Number One, is shot dead by federal agents and local police as he strolls out of the Biograph Theater on July 22.

1937—Ten Republic Steel strikers killed when they clash with police outside the plant on Memorial Day. A congressional report accuses police of using "excessive force."

1938—Samuel Insull, once the most powerful and unscrupulous businessman in Chicago—holding control of major utilities and streetcar lines—dies, leaving behind $14,000 in debts.

1939—Saul Alinsky and Joe Meegan organize the Back of the Yards Council, a model for modern grassroots community organizations.

1942—A team of physicists at the University of Chicago achieve the first nuclear chain reaction.

1943—Billy Graham graduates from Wheaton College in Wheaton.

1944—Mayor William "Big Bill" Thompson dies, leaving behind mysterious safe deposit boxes containing $1,578,000 in cash, stocks and bonds.

1947—Park Forest, the first packaged community in America, planned right down to the number of saloons, is founded.

1955—Richard J. Daley elected mayor April 5. The world's first McDonald's opens in Des Plaines on April 15.

1959—Chicago White Sox win the American League pennant.

1965—Lucky Debonair, a horse trained at the elegant Danada Farms outside Wheaton, wins the Kentucky Derby.

1966—Richard Speck murders eight student nurses in Chicago on July 14.

Housing marchers start their fourteen-block hike through the Ashburn section of the Southwest Side in August 1966. *(Photo by Fred Schnell)*

1967—U.S. government builds Fermilab, a center for energy research and development, on a 6,800-acre site outside Batavia.

1968—Dr. Martin Luther King, Jr., is shot in Memphis, and Chicago's West Side, like inner-cities across America, goes up in flames. In August, riots return to Chicago, this time led by anti-war protesters during the Democratic National Convention.

1971—Union Stockyard closes in August.

1972—In the wake of Watergate, a record four Democrats are elected to the county board in Republican Du Page County. One—Jane Spirgel of Elmhurst—survives and is reelected into the 1980s. People point and say, "There's the Democrat."

1976—Mayor Richard J. Daley dies on December 20.

1979—Jane Byrne elected mayor on February 27, stunning the Regular Democratic Organization and most of the city.

1980—John Wayne Gacy locked up on Death Row for the murder of thirty-three men and boys.

A horse-drawn wagon moves through the deserted Chicago stockyards area around 42nd and Exchange. A few minutes later, this scene was lost forever as workmen dynamited the chimney on the left during a landclearing project. *(Photo by Larry Nocerino)*

1982—Eight persons killed by cyanide-laced Tylenol capsules on September 29 and 30.

1983—Harold Washington elected first black mayor on February 22.

1984—John J. Devine becomes the first Cook County Circuit Court judge convicted in the Operation Greylord court corruption investigation on October 8. At least eighty-five convictions would follow, including those of twelve more judges and forty-nine lawyers.

1985—Cathleen Crowell Webb on March 25 recants her story that Gary Dotson, of Country Club Hills, raped her in 1977. Gov. James R. Thompson on May 12 commutes Dotson's sentence, and Dotson is paroled.

1986—Council Wars rage. Police have to restore order at a September 24 Chicago City Council meeting after Ald. Bernard L. Stone (50th) shrieks to Ald. Luis V. Gutierrez (26th), "How dare you come in here, you little pipsqueak!" Mayor Washington comments, "Stone's got a stone head."

1987—Eugene Sawyer elected mayor at wild ten-and-a-half-hour overnight City Council session.

1988—Laurie A. Dann opens fire in a Winnetka school on May 20, killing eight-year-old Nicholas Corwin and injuring five of his classmates. She wounds a college athlete before fatally shooting herself.

1988—Scott and Carolyn MacLean of Wheaton discovered missing April 2, their red BMW abandoned in a downtown alley. The worst is feared, but they turn up many weeks later, married, in San Diego. "We want to be totally different," Carolyn had told a friend. "We want to be kind of like, noticed."

1989—In Cook County, three out of every ten black men in their twenties do time in County Jail, according to a study.

1990—Tornado sweeps through Plainfield on August 28, killing twenty-nine and leaving hundreds homeless.

1991—Kane County Cougars, Chicago area's new minor league baseball team, open home season on April 13 with a 13-0 loss to South Bend White Sox.

GEOGRAPHY

NORTH SIDE, SOUTH SIDE

It's true in every city. The most revealing question you can ask somebody is: "What part of town are you from?"

Where you're from defines who you are.

In Chicago, South Siders generally think North Siders are from nowhere, while North Siders view South Siders as the intellectual allies of Indiana. Many North Siders believe there is no mail delivery south of Roosevelt Road.

That's Chicago's classic division—North Side vs. South Side.

North Siders see themselves as cutting-edge, ambitious and envied. To them, a South Sider's idea of getting dressed up is a dry-cleaned bowling shirt.

South Siders see themselves as the real people, the workers, the brawn of the city. To them, the North Side is a place where you go to the ballpark wearing a tie.

Baseball has a role here, too. North Siders are Cub fans. South Siders root for the Sox. Sure, there's some cross-pollination, but it's not easy.

But a sense of where you are in Chicago goes beyond North Side/South Side. There is, for example, the West Side, viewed suspiciously by South Siders and not at all by North Siders.

There are also nuances of geography. Consider the Near North Side, where self-worship is an art form. Or the Southwest and Northwest Sides, simplistically portrayed by the media as lands of white people, mostly firemen and cops.

And how do you know, for example, whether Twenty-sixth Street and, say, California Avenue is on the South Side, West Side or Southwest Side.

"Easy," replied *Sun-Times* police reporter Jim Casey. "If it's in [Police] Area 4, it's the West Side."

And then there is that other breed of place: the much maligned suburbs.

Everybody knows the score here: Du Page County is rich. The North Shore is rich and smart. The south suburbs are forgotten. The northwest suburbs are an airport, a place where people move apparently to complain about the noise.

Suburbia's image is one of black socks, white shoes, Bermuda shorts and a backyard barbecue run by a guy with a goofy smile and a big chef's hat. If the suburbs were a decade they would be the 1950s.

North Siders view the suburbs as a land of unsophisticated boobs. South Siders view it as land where people lack street smarts but dress nice. And the suburbs view the city as a rabid, junkyard dog.

Everybody's right, of course. And everybody's wrong. It's just a question of where you're from.

PREHISTORY

More than 400 million years ago, a tropical sea covered the heart of North America. As it receded from what now is the Chicago area, it left behind a bedrock of Niagara limestone. On top of the stone, it smeared a thick layer of impermeable clay, making it difficult for ground water to run off and—consequently—creating some tremendously muddy streets in early Chicago.

Later, a series of glaciers—beginning with one more than 1 million years ago—repeatedly advanced and receded over the Great Lakes region, gouging out the landscape, creating new ridges and troughs. Ancient river valleys were widened and deepened and became the basins of the Great Lakes. The glaciers left behind a series of concentric rings of debris—sand, silt, clay and boulders—called moraines.

The last glacier was the Wisconsin, which pushed halfway down the state of Illinois some 50,000 years ago. As it receded, melting in warming weather, it formed Lake Chicago—an oversized version of Lake Michigan.

Palos-Area Moraines: Water from Lake Chicago drained to the south through what are now the rolling moraines of the southwest suburbs. The moraines' greatest height is about sixty feet, near Palos Hills. The Palos moraines marked a low-elevation sag in Lake Chicago's dam, so water gushed out there, headed downhill toward the Mississippi River. Today, the Chicago Sanitary and Ship Canal follows this path through the moraines. A second path—or "sag"—for escaping Lake Chicago water was the valley through which the Calumet Sag Channel today runs.

Blue Island, Stony Island and Thornton Island: As ancestral Lake Chicago receded, knobs of the hardest terrain stood up to the escaping waters, forming islands. As late as 4,500 years ago, suburban Blue Island and Thornton, and the high ground of Chicago's Stony Island Avenue, all were islands. That hard Thornton limestone that stood up so well to the forces of erosion today is quarried and used as a building material.

Spits: As the glaciers slowly receded, the meltwater also formed beaches, bars and spits—fingers of beach jutting out from the land. These sandy stretches of dry high ground were used as trails by the Indians and roads by the early European settlers. Many of the Chicago area's oldest streets—the ones running on diagonals—follow the lines of these glacial spits. Among them are Chicago's Ridge Avenue, North Clark Street, Blue Island Avenue, Vincennes Avenue and Longwood Drive, north suburban Skokie's Niles Center Road and the south suburbs' Glenwood-Dyer Road.

Chicago Portage: Near what is today Harlem Avenue just north of the Stevenson Expressway, the Chicago River and the Des Plaines River flow within eight miles of each other and once were connected by a continuous swampy tract. In wet seasons, Indians and early explorers were able to travel by canoe, without portaging, between Lake Michigan and the Mississippi River by way of this swamp. In dry weather, they portaged by foot between the two rivers, hiking through mud and swamp, their boats on their shoulders, over an eight-mile trail now followed by U.S. 66 and Joliet Road. The Chicago portage opened the West to commerce and settlement. Louis Jolliet and Jacques Marquette, returning from their first voyage on the Mississippi in 1673, were the first white men to use the Chicago portage.

Railroad representatives, meeting in Chicago in 1883, pioneered the current national system of standard time zones. Before then, individual towns reckoned their own times by the sun, giving Illinois alone twenty-seven different local times in 1883. Determined to end the confusion, a majority of the nation's railroads, meeting at a General Time Convention in Chicago in November 1883, agreed to accept England's Greenwich mean time as their standard and divided the continent into four one-hour times zones—known today as Eastern, Central, Mountain and Pacific. Almost immediately communities across the nation voluntarily adopted this new system and, a year later, the U.S. Congress followed suit.

SIX-COUNTY METRO GEOGRAPHY

Square miles: 3,740.

Greatest Length and Breadth: 90-by-56 miles.

Highest Elevation: In excess of 900 feet above sea level at various points.

Lowest Elevation: 577 feet above sea level at the Lake Michigan shore.

Acres of Farmland: 977,286 as of 1987, the last federal count (46,907 in Cook, 25,432 in Du Page, 227,961 in Kane, 82,349 in Lake, 265,908 in McHenry, 328,729 in Will).

CHICAGO GEOGRAPHY

Square miles: 228.1.

Greatest Length and Breadth: 25-by-15 miles.

Highest Elevation: 93.5 feet above the level of Lake Michigan, on the 9400 block of South Claremont.

Shoreline: 30 miles.

Average Size of a City Block: 660 feet long and 330 feet wide (5 acres).

City-owned Movable Bridges: 50.

Viaducts: 81.

Pedestrian Underpasses: 26.

Miles of Street: 3,676 miles.

Geographic Center: 37th and Honore Street. Fittingly, it's a neighborhood mix: a house, a two-flat, a church and a school. St. Andrew Lutheran Church has been at the intersection's northwest corner for 100 years.

LAKE MICHIGAN

Age: 10,300 years.

Length: 307 miles.

Width: 118 miles.

Average depth: 279 feet.

Maximum depth: 923 feet.

Volume: 1,180 cubic miles.

Gallons of Water: 1,350 trillion (enough to give 270,000 gallons to every person on Earth).

How Long Water Stays in Lake Before Draining Out: 99 years.

Area: 22,300 square miles (about 40 percent of the area of Illinois).

Shoreline: Around lake: 1,638 miles. In Chicago: 30 miles (all but 4 miles publically owned).

Elevation: 577 feet above sea level.

Population: Around lake: 14 million. In Chicago's lakefront census tracts: 212,000.

Water Removed from Lake at Chicago: Average of 24,000 gallons per second.

Concentration of Toxic PCBs in Lake: One part per trillion (comparable to one second in 32,000 years).

Commercial Fishing Licenses: Wisconsin, 100; Indiana, 20; Michigan, 6; Illinois, 3.

Property Value of Chicago's Lakefront: $7.4 billion.

Percent of Chicago's Economy that Depends on Lake: 20.

Number of Chicago Beaches: 29.

Man-made Landfill on Chicago's Shoreline: 3,000 acres (4.7 square miles).

Number of Annual Lakefront Users Counted by Chicago Park District: 61.5 million.

Percent of Lake within Illinois' Jurisdiction: 7.

Fish Population: About 70 species of fish, including 12 not indigenous to these waters. But others are thought to be extinct: original lake trout, greyling, muskie, blackfin cisco, longjaw cisco, shortjaw cisco, shortnose cisco, deepwater cisco, spoonhead sculpin.

CHICAGO-AREA RIVERS

Calumet River: 8½ miles, all in Cook County, 11 feet deep.

Calumet Sag Channel: 16½ miles, all in Cook County, 11 feet deep.

Chicago River: The North Branch through Cook and Lake counties is 35 miles, and deepest—17 feet—between Lake Michigan and North Avenue. The South Branch, from where it separates from the North Branch to the Chicago Sanitary & Ship Canal, is 4 miles long and as deep as 21 feet.

Des Plaines River: 97 miles through Cook, Du Page, Lake and Will counties. Maximum depth: 15 feet.

Du Page River: Main channel through Will County is 27 miles long, 7 feet deep. East Branch through Du Page and Will counties is 32 miles long, 5 feet deep. West Branch through Du Page County is 26 miles long, 10 feet deep.

Fox River: 69 miles through Kane, Lake and McHenry counties, 12 feet deep.

Kankakee River: 19 miles, all in Will County, 18 feet deep.

Little Calumet River: 24 miles, all in Cook County, 11 feet deep.

North Shore Channel: 7.63 miles through Cook County, 7.3 feet deep.

Salt Creek: 35 miles through Cook and Du Page counties, 4 feet deep.

TEN BIGGEST LAKES IN THE CHICAGO AREA

1) Fox Lake in Lake County (1,700 acres)

2) Pistakee Lake in McHenry County (1,700)

3) Lake Calumet in Cook County (1,600)

4) Grass Lake in Lake County (1,360)

5) Commonwealth-Edison's Nuclear Lake in Will County (865)

6) Wonder Lake in McHenry County (730)

7) Busse Lake in Cook County, (590)

8) Lake Marie in Lake County (480)

9) Wolf Lake in Cook County (419)

10) Saganashkee Slough in Cook County (325)

Note: The biggest lake in Du Page County is Mallard Lake (75 acres). The biggest in Kane County is Nelson Lake (201 acres). The biggest body of water in Illinois is the man-made Carlyle Reservoir in Clinton County (24,580).

Lake Calumet and Wolf Lake on Chicago's Southeast Side are remnants of Lake Michigan's prehistoric predecessor, Lake Chicago. Hundreds of other lakes in the six-county Chicago area also were formed by glaciers, but are not part of the Lake Chicago glacial trough.

LAKES, PONDS, RIVERS AND STREAMS

	No. Lakes and Ponds	Acres Lake/Ponds	Miles Rivers/Streams	Acres River/Streams	Total Acres
Cook County	1,302	7,835	421	3,479	11,314
Du Page County	613	1,431	150	695	2,126
Kane County	510	896	291	1,622	2,517
Lake County	1,060	13,851	188	1,093	14,944
McHenry County	818	4,137	301	1,429	5,566
Will County	1,074	6,975	478	5,821	12,796

INDIAN RESERVATIONS

Much of the northwest Cook County Forest Preserves, as well as eastern Wilmette and the northern portion of Evanston, once were Indian reservations.

As part of the Treaty of Prairie du Chien on July 29, 1829, in which several Midwest tribes surrendered claims to various Illinois lands, land reserves in the Chicago area were set aside for certain Indians who helped secure the tribes' assent to the treaty. Specifically:

Alexander Robinson, also known as Che Che Pinqua, an adopted Pot-awatomi of Ojibwa and Scottish parentage, was awarded two square miles along the Des Plaines River near Lawrence Avenue. He lived on the reserve until his death at age eighty-nine on April 22, 1872. His daughter, Mary Robinson, lived there until 1927. And a granddaugh-ter, Katherine Toettcher, lived in the family home there with her son, Herbert, until it was destroyed by fire on May 25, 1955. Herbert, a welfare recipient and heavy drinker, died at age seventy-two on July 3, 1973. Robinson, his wife, Catherine, and other family members are buried on the reservation, which now is part of the Cook County Forest Preserves.

Billy Caldwell, also known as The Sauganash or Englishman, an adopted Potawatomi of Irish and Mohawk parentage, was awarded 1,600 acres of land—2 1/2 square miles—along the North Branch of the Chicago River. Caldwell, who migrated to Iowa with his Potawat-omi tribe in 1835, never lived on the land. With permission from Presi-dent Martin Van Buren, he sold the land in 1841 to Captain Seth Johnson of Chicago. Half of Caldwell's reserve is owned today by the Cook County Forest Preserve District.

Archange Chevalier Ouilmette and her children were awarded roughly 1,200 acres along Lake Michigan. The land was given to them as an in-direct reward to Chevalier's French-Canadian husband, Antoine Ouilmette, who was not himself eligible for a U.S. land grant because he was not an Indian. Suburban Wilmette stands today on 900 acres of the reserve. The remaining 300 acres are part of north Evanston. The family lived on the reservation until 1838, when Antoine moved to a farm near Racine, Wisconsin. The children sold the land in bits and pieces in the middle 1840s and resettled on the Potawatomi reservation in Iowa.

Claude La Framboise, an interpreter and brother of an Indian chief, was granted a one-square-mile reserve along the Des Plaines River im-mediately to the south of Robinson's reserve. It is owned today by the forest preserve district.

Victoire Pothier and Jane Miranda, two sisters who had served in the household of early settler John Kinzie, were granted small reserves im-mediately adjacent to Caldwell's reserve. Pothier received roughly one half of a square mile, and Miranda received a quarter square mile. Both agreed to sell their land and move west to Iowa with their Pota-watomi tribe after the Treaty of Chicago on Sept. 27, 1833.

INDIAN BOUNDARIES

Most of the diagonal streets in the Chicago area were once Indian trails (see "Spits," page 17), but a few were drawn from scratch by cartographers establishing the local limits of Indian territory. When the U.S. government decided to build the Illinois and Michigan Canal, it negotiated a treaty with the Indians in 1816 that ceded to the government a wide strip of land straddling the canal's proposed route from Lake Michigan to the Illinois River. The north boundary line of the strip began at Lake Michigan ten miles north of the mouth of the Chicago River and ran southwest, with two minor bends, to the Fox River ten miles above Ottawa. The south boundary line began at Lake Michigan ten miles south of the mouth of the Chicago River and ran southwest to the Kankakee River ten miles above its junction with the Des Plaines River. Among the roads that came to be developed along these boundary lines are Rogers Avenue in Rogers Park, from Sheridan Road to Ridge Boulevard; Forest Preserve Drive just north of River Grove, from Montrose Avenue to Thatcher Avenue; and Brennan Highway in south suburban Markham—now the route for a stretch of I-57.

COUNTY BOUNDARIES

County boundaries in Illinois changed almost constantly in the 1700s and early 1800s. The Virginians, who claimed rights to the Illinois territory under their colonial charter, created the County of Illinois on Dec. 9, 1778. It included all land between the Wabash and Illinois rivers, north from the Ohio River. Virginia surrendered its western claims to the United States in 1784.

Illinois was made a part of the newly organized Northwest Territory and, in 1790, the first territorial governor, Arthur St. Clair, established Downstate St. Clair County and Knox County, which included what are today Cook, Du Page, Lake and Will counties.

From 1801 to 1821, as the population exploded and new counties were formed, the entire Chicago area became part of St. Clair County (1801), Madison (1812), Edwards (1815), Crawford (1816), Clark (1819) and Pike (1821).

In 1823, most of the Chicago area was attached to Fulton County, but present-day southern Cook and eastern Will were attached to Edgar County.

In 1825, the entire Chicago region was made part of Putnam County. The individual Chicago-area counties then were formed as follows:

Cook County: 954 square miles; created on Jan. 15, 1831, from the northeastern part of Putnam County. It originally included what are now Du Page, Lake and part of Will counties.

Kane County: 516 square miles; created on Jan. 16, 1836, it originally included DeKalb County and a northern chunk of Kendall

County. DeKalb separated from Kane in 1837, and Kendall separated in 1841.

McHenry County: 610 square miles; created in 1836 from the northwest part of Cook County, it originally also included what is now Lake County.

Will County: 845 square miles; created Jan. 12, 1836, from parts of Cook and Iroquis counties.

Du Page County: 332.1 square miles; created on Feb. 28 1839, from the western part of Cook County.

Lake County: 457 square miles; created March 1, 1839, from the eastern part of McHenry County.

Sources: Chicago Sun-Times science reporter Jim Ritter; Don McKay of the Illinois Geological Survey; Illinois Secretary of State, Bill Scott, public relations; *Counties of Illinois: Their Origin & Evolution*, 1974, published by the State of Illinois; *Indians of the Chicago Area*, 1990, by Virgil J. Vogel, Ph.D.; *Illinois Fishing Guide* and the *1989 Inventory of Illinois Surface Water Resources*, publication of the Illinois Department of Conservation; Wilmette Public Library; the Lake Michigan Federation; The Wilmette Historical Museum; *Charts of the Illinois Waterway*, 1990, U.S. Army Corps of Engineers, Chicago; Illinois Department of Transportation; Mark Thomas of the Northeastern Illinois Plan Commission; Ron Losew of the Chicago Park District; M.H. Clay of the Chicago Metropolitan Water Reclamation District; Friends of the Chicago River.

THIS IS NOT CHICAGO (SUBURBAN CURIOSITIES)

Curiosities about the many towns of metropolitan Chicago.

THE FIRST SUBURBAN BOOM: Chicago's suburban collar experienced its first land rush when the U.S. Government in 1820 began selling off public lands at $1.25 an acre—a bargain price even then—and, fifteen years later, opened a conveniently located land office in Chicago. Land speculators bought up large tracts of suburban lands and resold them at higher prices to new settlers.

- Gambling on suburban pinball machines got so bad in 1965 that Cook County Sheriff Richard B. Ogilvie threatened to seize 167 machines in twenty-one towns—mostly in small restaurants and taverns. The machines, he said, were generating about $2.3 million a year for the crime syndicate. Ogilvie listed the offending suburbs as: Burnham, Calumet City, Calumet Park, Chicago Heights, Cicero, Elmwood Park, Forest View, Hanover Park, Lyons, McCook, Melrose Park, Oak Forest, Phoenix, Posen, River Grove, Rosemont, South Chicago Heights, Steger, Stickney, Stone Park and Summit.

- Frank Earl Herrick, a justice of the peace in the 1930s, wrote a poem celebrating Du Page County, although few have heard of it. In "Song of Du Page," Herrick describes Du Page as "A star upon the breast of the Great Chicagoland, a jewel in the crest of Illinois the grand." Those words also explain why nobody has ever heard of Frank Earl Herrick.

- One reason Alsip incorporated was to avoid becoming a place for the dead. Cemeteries were digging in throughout the area, and there was concern graves would be everywhere unless something was done. Among Alsip's first official acts after incorporation was to prohibit further cemetery expansion.

- Luther Bartlett, founder of suburban Bartlett, heard about the Chicago Fire in 1871 and rushed to the city with food and concern for a daughter who lived there. After seeing the devastation, he informed his wife that Chicago "had ceased to exist" and "could never amount to anything commercially," according to a newspaper interview later given by his wife.

- One ordinance passed in Bartlett after incorporation in 1891 gave the village board power to brand a person a "drunkard" and ban him from patronizing local taverns.

- Some 17,767 people live in Bensenville, but by day the population more than triples to 60,000 people because of industrial employment in the village. Bensenville is one of the ten largest industrial communities in Illinois.

- They call it the "Bensenville Pause"—that automatic halt in conversation in every Bensenville school, business and home each time a low-flying jet headed to or from nearby O'Hare Airport buzzes overhead.

- In Channahon it is illegal for property owners "to refuse or neglect to cut, remove, pull or destroy weeds when such weeds have reached a height in excess of 12 inches."

- Du Page County was named for a French trader named Du Page or "DuPahze," or something like that. Nobody seems sure of his full name, and he didn't even live in the county, but rather four miles south of Naperville in Will County.

- The sundae was invented in Evanston, a sweet and proper town where seltzer water—let alone evil alcohol—was considered a wicked indulgence on Sundays. So Deacon Garwood, the owner of an ice cream parlor in town, complied with a law forbidding ice cream sodas on Sundays by serving ice cream and syrup without the soda. It was called a sundae—rather than a Sunday—so as to avoid being sacrilegious.

- Flossmoor Country Club, founded in 1898, helped make Flossmoor a golfing town. Ten trains made the round trip daily from Chicago in the early 1900s to bring golfers to the various country clubs in this area. Some of the older frame houses in Flossmoor used to be summer houses for golfers and many of the streets are named for famous golfers or bear golf-related names such as Caddy or Bunker. There were even, at one time, a Tee Street and a Loftie Street.

- The idea to incorporate Flossmoor came up in 1924 when a couple of men left a PTA-sponsored Leap Year party to have a smoke in the school basement.

- Forest View once was known as "Caponeville," "the mystery village," and "the town that Al built" because of the influence and control of mob boss Al Capone. The village was incorporated in 1924, and shortly thereafter Capone built his largest brothel (the sixty-girl Maple Inn) in Forest View. By 1926, the chief of police was ex-convict William "Porky" Dillon. At one point, detectives came looking for Porky after he lost a U.S. Supreme Court appeal, but Dillon showed them a pardon from the governor. Forest View's police magistrate reportedly didn't live in the village, preferring instead a place at Eighteenth and Ashland in Chicago. And detectives investigating Capone's control of the town were able to locate only three of the six village trustees. When interviewed, those three trustees were unable to name the other three. Said one: "They are foreigners, and we don't know their names. Oh sure, they come to village board meetings—when we have them."

● Indian graveyards uncovered on Point Comfort Hill in Fox Lake indicate the area was inhabited by a prehistoric race of "Mound Builders." Skeletons have been exhumed of men more than seven feet tall.

● Great America amusement park in Gurnee attracts 2.5 million visitors a year and provides 3,000 part-time summer jobs.

● In the middle 1800s, before the railroads were built, a one-way trip to downtown Chicago from Lincolnwood over planked roads could take as long as five hours.

● Manhattan incorporated in 1886 for one good reason—everybody wanted a saloon. By Illinois law, a saloon could not operate in an unincorporated area.

● Morton Grove in June 1981, passed the first village ban on handguns in the United States, gaining international attention.

● The governmental seat of Du Page County was moved from Naperville to Wheaton in 1867, but not without considerable grief from folks in Naperville. A referendum calling for the move carried in 1867, but Naperville refused to turn over the records. So a band of Civil War veterans from Wheaton made a midnight raid on the Naperville courthouse in 1868 and seized the records. As they were making their escape, an alarm was sounded and, in their rush, the raiders dropped a few of the books. These books were taken to Chicago for safekeeping, where they were destroyed in the Chicago Fire of 1871.

● When folks in Park Ridge decided to shuck their town's old name—Brickton—they did it in style. On the Fourth of July, 1873, everybody gathered in a park and watched the release of a twenty-foot-high helium balloon labeled "Brickton." As it drifted into the distance, they waved good-bye.

● During World War II, when unused beef fat was recycled into weapons' parts, patriotic housewives stored fat in old cans and returned it to butcher shops. But in Park Ridge, one harassed butcher put up a sign that read: "Ladies, do not bring your old fat cans in here on Saturdays."

● Lumber milled in Plainfield—then called Walker's Grove—was hauled to Chicago by Reuben Flagg in 1832 to build Chicago's first frame house.

● A small shopping center on the northeast corner of Camp McDonald and Elmhurst roads in Prospect Heights is said to be the first one-stop shopping center built in the Midwest, the forerunner to the modern shopping mall. Built in the late 1930s, it introduced the then-novel idea of set-back stores and parking spaces for several cars in front of each store.

● Betty Robinson, who became the first woman in history to win an Olympic gold medal in track when she won the 100-meter dash in the 1928 Olympics, grew up in Riverdale.

- The suburbs once had a Romeo and Juliet. Romeoville was called Romeo in pioneer days because neighboring Joliet was called Juliet. Cute. In 1845, Juliet was renamed Joliet. And in 1895, Romeo was renamed Romeoville.

- In Round Lake, the meatpacking Armour family in 1901 opened what was said to be the largest icehouse in the world. When it burned down in 1917, some observers blamed it on the International Workers of the World. Nobody could prove it was the Wobblies, but everybody knew they felt no fondness for such as the Armours. The icehouse made 100,000 tons of ice each winter.

- Schiller Park has two unofficial town songs. The first, "Song of Schiller Park," by Rose Schmidt, includes the lyrics:

  > We'll always be true Schiller Park
  > We're glad that we're here
  > So we'll stand up and cheer.

The second song, "The Little Town of Schiller Park," by Charles Koskie, includes the lyrics:

  > There's a little town called Schiller Park,
  > Where the Des Plaines River flows,
  > Where the flies and mosquitoes
  > In the summertime repose.
  > Anytime you're looking for scenery,
  > Take a look at our beautiful beanery.

- If a few folks had not bad-rapped Holland, Michigan, suburban South Holland might not exist today. South Holland's original Dutch settlers, seeking religious freedom in the New World, were destined for Holland, Michigan, in 1847 when a terrible storm on Lake Michigan forced them to stop in Chicago. While in town they heard bad reports on Holland and decided to go no further.

- When the Great Depression hit in 1929, Tinley Park real estate developer Grover C. Elmore survived in business by giving free chickens to anybody who bought one of his homes. The homeowner would sell eggs and chickens back to Elmore to earn money to pay off his mortgage.

- Pioneers who dealt with Indians honorably usually had nothing to fear. When John and Jane Fulton came to Tinley Park—then called New Bremen—in 1844, they were visited by an old Indian who conversed in sign language. He asked for, and was given, a bowl of buttermilk. On a later visit he returned the favor by giving them a full hindquarter of venison.

- The last one-room schoolhouse in Du Page County, the McAuley School in West Chicago, closed for keeps on June 7, 1991, because all six of its students graduated or moved away. The school opened in 1914.

- The oldest standing structure in Du Page County is thought to be the house of Warrenville founder Julius Morton Warren. The house, on the northwest corner of Main Street and Batavia Road in Warrenville, was built in 1834.

- The bones of a mammoth were found in 1977 in the Blackwell Forest Preserve near Warrenville. A carbon dating showed the remains to be 13,130 years old, give or take a century. It's the only mammoth ever found in the region.

- Wheaton Wars. Both *Washington Post* editor Bob Woodward and comedian John Belushi grew up in Wheaton and attended Wheaton High School. But hometown and school loyalties didn't stop Woodward from exposing Belushi's dirty druggy secrets in his biography, *Wired*.

- Orson Welles got his theatrical start at the Woodstock Opera House. Welles was a student at the Todd School, a boys academy near Woodstock, when he put on a series of Shakespearean dramas in 1934 at the opera house.

- In Zion, a town founded by religious zealots, everything once went by the book—the Good Book. But then in 1921, a war of words, fists and billboards broke out between loyalists to church leader Wilbur Glenn Voliva and upstarts who dared suggest that maybe a ban on nicotine, movies, oysters, silk stockings, modern science and stepping out after 10 p.m. was a bit much. "We are not all fanatics!" stated one billboard put up by the anti-Volivas. "Come and see. Help us redeem and civilize this city." In the end, the rebels won out, and Zion shook free of zealotry.

POLITICS

FIRSTS

Chicago City Hall: For five years after Chicago incorporated in 1837, the Common Council met in the Saloon Building, at the southeast corner of Clark and Lake streets. It was not a tavern, but contained a spacious third-floor meeting hall—or "salon." The word saloon is derived from this French word.

Chicago City Council: On May 2, 1837, Josiah C. Goodhue (1st), a physician; Frances C. Sherman (1st), a merchant, brickyard owner and future mayor; John S.C. Hogan (2nd), a storekeeper and postmaster; Peter Bolles (2nd), who served as the first finance committee chairman; John D. Caton (3rd), a lawyer and future justice of the Illinois Supreme Court; Asahel Pierce (4th), a blacksmith credited with making the first plows in Chicago; Frances H. Taylor (4th); Bernard Wood (5th); Hiram Pearsons (6th), a real estate developer; and Samuel Jackson (6th), who built the first lighthouse in the Chicago Harbor were elected aldermen. The lighthouse had three-foot-thick walls and stood fifty feet high and fell down before it was completed. Jackson said the problem was quicksand. His critics said the problem was bad workmanship.

Acting Mayor in Chicago: Ald. Lester Bond (10th) became Chicago's first acting mayor when the incumbent, Joseph Medill, took an extended European vacation in 1873.

Woman Mayor in Chicago: Jane Byrne was elected April 3, 1979.

Black Mayor in Chicago: Harold Washington was elected April 12, 1983.

Black Alderman in Chicago: Oscar DePriest (1871-1951), the son of ex-slaves from Alabama, was elected alderman of the South Side's 2nd Ward in 1915. Thirteen years later, he became the first black from the North to be elected to Congress. In June 1929, DePriest's wife created a national stir when she accepted Mrs. Herbert Hoover's invitation to tea at the White House. The Texas House of Representatives voted 99 to 10 to rebuke Mrs. Hoover.

Oscar DePriest, Chicago's first black alderman. His wife created a national stir when she accepted Mrs. Herbert Hoover's invitation to tea at the White House.

Hispanic Alderman in Chicago: William E. Rodriguez, a Near North Side alderman from 1915 to 1918, was the son of a Mexican father and a German mother, and was born in Naperville on Sept. 15, 1879. Rodriguez was a member of the Socialist Party and ran unsuccessfully for mayor in 1911. He was alderman of the old 15th Ward for two terms and lived near Kedzie and Division Street in what is now the 31st Ward. Rodriguez was graduated from Chicago's John Marshall Law School in 1912, and served in the U.S. Army during the Spanish American War.

When Abe Played the Wigwam: The new Republican Party chose Abraham Lincoln as its presidential nominee on May 18, 1860, at the Wigwam in Chicago. The Wigwam, a large two-story hall of rough pine boards, was built in a hurry for the convention on the southeast corner of what are now Lake Street and Wacker Drive. On the first ballot, former New York governor William H. Seward led. On the second ballot, Lincoln gained. On the third ballot, Lincoln won the nomination. Bonfires were lit all over town. The city—greatly fond of this loping lawyer who was a man of the prairie like themselves—partied all night. Lincoln himself was in Springfield.

EXTREMES

■ Lincolnwood claims the longest-ruling mayor in the Chicago area's history: Henry Proesel, village president from 1931-1976.

■ The most votes cast in a single Chicago mayoral election was 1,565,832 in 1947. Martin H. Kennelly won with about 59 percent of that vote. The most votes cast in history for a mayor was 919,593—for Kennelly in 1947.

■ Chicago's longest-term mayor was Richard J. Daley. He held office from 1955 to 1976.

■ Chicago's shortest-term mayor was David D. Orr, who served as acting mayor from Nov. 25 to Dec. 2, 1987.

The "Smoke-filled" Room: Chicago is the home of the original smoke-filled room. On Feb. 21, 1920, President Warren G. Harding's campaign manager, Harry Daugherty, predicted in the *New York Times* that the Republican convention in Chicago would be deadlocked and ultimately decided at about 2 a.m. by a small group of men sitting "around a table in a smoke-filled room." He was right. The exact room was suite 804-805 in the Blackstone Hotel.

POLITICIANS' NICKNAMES

These are common nicknames, bandied about by press and pols alike, more often than not by a critic.

● Former Cook County Sheriff John Babb: *Two-Gun Babb.*

● Ald. Edward M. Burke: *Flashy Eddie; The Other Eddie.*

● Mayor Jane M. Byrne: *Lady Jane; Attila the Hen; Crazy Jane; Fighting Jane; the Snow Queen.*

● Anton *"Pushcart Tony"* Cermak, so called by his critics because he once worked as a teamster with a horse and wagon.

● Former state senator and 42nd Ward committeeman William Connors: *Botchy.*

● *"Bathhouse"* John Coughlin, the crooked 1st Ward alderman in the late 1800s, once worked in a public bathhouse.

● Former Assessor P.J. Cullerton: *Parky.*

● Mayor Richard J. Daley: *Boss, Hizzoner, The Man on Five, The Great Dumpling, Da Mare, Oscar.*

● Mayor William Dever: *The Calvin Coolidge of Chicago.*

● Former Cook County Board President George W. Dunne: *Gentleman George, The Silver Fox.*

● Louis *"El Supremo"* Farina, former 39th Ward alderman, so called because he designed himself a special braided uniform while supervisor of the city's meter maids.

Hizzoner Was a GOP: Richard J. Daley was first elected to the Illinois General Assembly as a Republican, winning as a Republican write-in candidate when the incumbent, Republican David Shanahan, died fifteen days before the Nov. 3, 1936, election. Daley had to sit on the Republican side of the House for one morning before he was allowed to cross the aisle to the Democrats.

- Former Cook County Circuit Court Clerk Morgan Finley: *Buddy.*

- Michael *"Hinkey Dink"* Kenna, the crooked alderman of the 1st Ward in the late 1800s, was unusually short.

- Cook County Board Commissioner Ted Lechowicz: *Well-Fed Ted.*

- Mayor Martin Kennelly: *Marty the Mover.*

- Former Du Page County Coroner R.K. *"Tiny"* Matthews. He was huge.

- Robert D. McCormick, former president of the Metropolitan Sanitary District: *The Colonel.*

- Former Judge James *"Big Jim"* McDermott.

- Sen. Bernard Neistein, former 29th Ward committeeman: *Senator Stradivarius.*

- Cook County Board President Richard J. Phelan: *North Shore Dick.*

- State Senate Minority Leader James *"Pate"* Phillip. It's a shortened version of his middle name—Peyton.

- Cook County Circuit Court Clerk Aurelia M. Pucinski: *Cherry Blossom Princess.* She was Illinois' representative one year in the Washington, D.C., Miss Cherry Blossom Pageant when her dad, Roman, was a congressman.

- Former Ald. Roman C. Pucinski (41st): *Pooch.*

- Mayor Eugene "Mayor Mumbles" Sawyer.

- U.S. Rep. Gus Savage (D-Chicago): *Gashouse Gus.*

- Ald. Niles *"Pot O' Gold"* Sherman (21st). Refers to his momentous jump to the Ed Vrdolyak faction of the Democrat Party in 1982 because, as he explained, he wanted to "reach over the rainbow to the pot of gold."

- James *"Bulljive"* Taylor, former 16th Ward Democratic committeeman, earned his name after two women said he demanded sexual favors in exchange for a tavern license. Confronted with the accusation, Taylor said he was just "bulljiving."

- Gov. James R. Thompson: *Big Jim, His Tallness, Governor for Life.*

- Mayor William H. Thompson: *Big Bill the Builder.*

- Ald. Dorothy Tillman (3rd): *The Hat.* She always wears one.

William Hale Thompson, three-time mayor of Chicago, was known to be just a little corrupt. While mayor, he provided police protection to Al Capone, and when he died, he left behind safe deposit boxes containing $1,578,000 in cash, stocks and bonds.

- Edward *"Fast Eddie"* Vrdolyak—fast with his tongue, fast at making money, fast at cutting deals. The moniker was hung on him by former *Daily News* reporter Jay McMullen. Also: *Past Eddie.*

- Mayor John *"Long John"* Wentworth.

- Edward H. *"The Iron Master"* Wright was Chicago's first black committeeman (Republican, 1920, 2nd Ward).

- Commissioner of the Cook County Water Reclamation District Harry *"Bus"* Yourell. Named for Buster Brown, the little boy with the old-fashioned clothes in the logo for Buster Brown Shoes. "That's how my mother dressed me," Bus said.

ALL IN THE FAMILY

Some politicians are self-made. They choose the work. Others are born or married into it. It is not their fault.

Balanoff: State Rep. Clement Balanoff is the son of Cook County Circuit Court Judge Miriam Balanoff.

Burke: 14th Ward Ald. Edward M. Burke is the son of former 14th Ward Ald. Joseph Burke.

Clark: Supreme Court Justice Bill Clark is the son of former Cook County Assessor John Clark.

Richard J. Daley is greeted by his family the day after winning his first mayoral election. Twelve-year-old Richie is third boy from left.

Crane: U.S. Rep. Philip M. Crane (R-12th) is the brother of Du Page County Board member Judith Crane Ross.

Cullerton: The first Cullerton, Edward, was elected to the City Council months before the Chicago Fire of 1871 and stuck around for 48 years—a council record. A second Cullerton—P.J. "Parky" Cullerton—was elected alderman of the 38th Ward in 1935. When Parky was elected county assessor in 1958, his brother William took over in the council. And when Bill died in 1973, his nephew, Thomas, took over.

Daley: Mayor Richard J. Daley. His son, Mayor Richard M. Daley. Another son, State Sen. John Daley (D-Chicago). And his first cousin, former 18th Ward Democratic Committeeman John Daley.

D'Arco: State Sen. John A. D'Arco, Jr., (D-Chicago) is the son of former 1st Ward alderman and Democratic committeeman John D'Arco.

Dunne: Cook County Circuit Court Judge Arthur Dunne is the son of former Judge Robert Jerome Dunne and the grandson of former mayor/governor Edward Dunne.

Elrod: Cook County Circuit Court Judge Richard J. Elrod, the former sheriff, is the son of former 24th Ward Democratic committeeman Arthur Elrod.

Fawell: U.S. Rep. Harris W. Fawell (R-13th) is the ex-brother-in-law of State Sen. Beverly Fawell (R-Glen Ellyn). Beverly Fawell's ex-husband is former Du Page County Circuit Court Chief Judge Bruce Fawell.

Carter Harrison: Mayor Carter Harrison I was the father of Mayor Carter Harrison II.

Hartigan: Judge Matthew Hartigan is the uncle of, and former city treasurer David Hartigan is the father of, former attorney general Neil F. Hartigan.

Hoellen: Former Ald. John Hoellen (47th) is the son of the former alderman and Republican ward committeeman.

Howlett: Former Secretary of State Michael J. Howlett is the father of former Cook County Circuit Court Judge Michael J. Howlett, Jr.

Igoe: Former County Board Secretary Michael Igoe is the son of former U.S. District Judge Michael Igoe.

Keane: Five members of the Keane family have served as alderman of the 31st Ward. Tom Keane, serving as Mayor Richard J. Daley's floor leader until convicted in a moneymaking scheme, was the best known. But his maternal grandfather, an uncle, his father and his wife also served as the alderman.

Kucharski: 18th Ward GOP Committeeman Ed Kucharski is the son of former county treasurer and county GOP chairman Ed Kucharski, who is the son of former 12th Ward GOP committeeman Felix Kucharski.

Laurino: Ald. Tony Laurino (39th) is the father of State Rep. William Laurino. (D-Chicago).

Madigan: House Speaker Michael J. Madigan is the son of former 13th Ward streets superintendent Michael J. Madigan, Sr.

Marovitz: State Sen. William Marovitz (D-Chicago) is the son of former Chicago Park District commissioner Sydney Marovitz, and the nephew of U.S. District Judge Abraham Lincoln Marovitz.

Pucinski: Cook County Circuit Court Clerk Aurelia Pucinski is the daughter of former 41st Ward Alderman Roman C. Pucinski.

Rostenkowski: U.S. Rep. Daniel Rostenkowski is the son of former 32nd Ward alderman and Democratic committeeman Joseph Rostenkowski.

Roti: Former 1st Ward alderman Fred Roti is the son of former 1st Ward alderman Bruno Roti.

Ryan: Former Cook County Board President Dan Ryan was the father of future County Board President Dan Ryan, whose wife Ruby served as a Cook County commissioner.

Shaw: Ald. Robert Shaw (9th) and State Rep. William Shaw (D-Chicago) are identical twin brothers who wear toupees.

Stevenson: Former Sen. Adlai E. Stevenson III is the son of former Gov. Adlai E. Stevenson II and the great grandson of former Vice President Adlai E. Stevenson.

Swinarski: Former State Sen. Theodore Swinarski (D-Chicago) was the father of Donald Swinarski, former 12th Ward alderman and state senator.

Touhy: Former 28th Ward committeeman John J. Touhy was the father of John M. Touhy, Illinois house speaker and state Democratic party chairman.

Vrdolyak: Brothers Victor and Edward were 10th Ward aldermen.

CHICAGO MAYORAL ELECTIONS
OF THE 20TH CENTURY

Year	Candidates	Party	Votes Received
1901	Carter H. Harrison	Democratic	156,756
	Elbridge Hanecy	Republican	128,413
	John Collins	Socialist	5,384
	Others		7,078
1903	Carter H. Harrison	Democratic	146,208
	Graeme Stewart	Republican	138,548
	Charles L. Breckon	Socialist	11,124
	Thomas L. Haines	Prohibition	
	Daniel L. Cruice	Independent Party	13,635
	Henry Sale	Socialist Labor	
1905	Edward F. Dunne	Democratic	163,189
	John M. Harlan	Republican	138,548
	John Collins	Socialist	23,034
	Oliver W. Stewart	Prohibition	3,294
1907	Fred A. Busse	Republican	164,702
	Edward F. Dunne	Democratic	151,779
	George Koop	Socialist	13,429
	William A. Brubaker	Prohibition	6,020
1911	Carter H. Harrison	Democratic	177,997
	Charles E. Merriam	Republican	160,672
	William E. Rodriguez	Socialist	24,825
	Anthony Prince	Socialist Labor	
	William A. Brubaker	Prohibition	3,297
1915	William Hale Thompson	Republican	398,538
	Robert M. Sweitzer	Democratic	251,061
	Seymour Stedman	Socialist	24,452
	John H. Hill	Prohibition	3,974
1919	William Hale Thompson	Republican	259,828
	Robert M. Sweitzer	Democratic	238,206
	Maclay Hoyne	Independent	110,851
	John Fitzpatrick	Labor	55,990
	John Collins	Socialist	24,079
	Adolph S. Carm	Socialist Labor	1,848
1923	William Dever	Democratic	390,413
	Arthur C. Lueder	Republican	285,094
	William C. Cunnea	Socialist	41,186

CHICAGO MAYORAL ELECTIONS
OF THE 20TH CENTURY

Year	Candidates	Party	Votes Received
1927	William H. Thompson	Republican	515,716
	William E. Dever	Democratic	432,678
	John Dill Robertson	People's Ownership-Smash Crime Rings	51,347
1931	Anton J. Cermak	Democratic	671,189
	William H. Thompson	Republican	476,922
1935	Edward J. Kelly	Democratic	798,150
	Emil C. Welten	Republican	166,571
	Newton Jenkins	The Third	87,726
1939	Edward J. Kelly	Democratic	822,469
	Dwight H. Green	Republican	638,068
	Arthur P. Reilly	The Third	4,921
1943	Edward J. Kelly	Democratic	685,567
	George McKibbin	Republican	571,547
1947	Martin H. Kennelly	Democratic	919,593
	Russell W. Root	Republican	646,239
1951	Martin H. Kennelly	Democratic	697,871
	Robert L. Hunter	Republican	545,326
1955	Richard J. Daley	Democratic	708,660
	Robert E. Merriam	Republican	581,461
1959	Richard J. Daley	Democratic	778,712
	Timothy P. Sheehan	Republican	311,940
1963	Richard J. Daley	Democratic	679,497
	Benjamin Adamowski	Republican	540,705
1967	Richard J. Daley	Democratic	792,238
	John L. Waner	Republican	272,542
1971	Richard J. Daley	Democratic	740,137
	Richard E. Friedman	Republican	315,969
1975	Richard J. Daley	Democratic	542,817
	John J. Hoellen	Republican	139,335
	Willie Mae Reid	Socialist Workers	16,693
1977	Michael A. Bilandic	Democratic	490,683
	Dennis H. Block	Republican	135,282
	Dennis Brasky	Socialist Workers	5,546
	Gerald Rose	U.S. Labor	2,497
1979	Jane Byrne	Democratic	700,874
	Wallace D. Johnson	Republican	137,664
	Andrew Pulley	Socialist Workers	15,625
1983	Harold Washington	Democratic	668,176
	Bernard E. Epton	Republican	619,926
	Ed Warren	Socialist Workers	3,756
1987	Harold Washington	Democratic	600,290
	Edward R. Vrdolyak	Ill. Solidarity	468,493
	Donald H. Haider	Republican	47,652
1989	Richard M. Daley	Democratic	577,141
	Timothy C. Evans	H. Washington Party	428,105
	Edward R. Vrdolyak	Republican	35,998
1991	Richard M. Daley	Democratic	450,581
	R. Eugene Pincham	H. Washington Party	160,302
	George S. Gottlieb	Republican	23,421
	James Warren	Socialists Workers	3,581

A TIME LINE:
MAYOR RICHARD M. DALEY

April 24, 1942—Born to Richard J. Daley, then an Illinois state senator, and Eleanor "Sis" Daley, the fourth child and first of four sons.

Aspirations of a professional baseball career soon gave way to politics for this future Chicago mayor—Richard M. Daley. *(Photo by Ellingsen Photos)*

1960—Graduates from De La Salle Institute.

1961-67—Serves in the Marine Corps reserves; takes two summers of officer's training, but turns down a commission.

1965—Graduates from DePaul University with a bachelor's degree in history after transferring from Providence College in Rhode Island.

1968—Graduates from DePaul School of Law.

1969—Passes the bar exam on his third try and works as assistant corporation counsel under Mayor Richard J. Daley.

1970—Enters private law practice with former Corporation Counsel Raymond F. Simon, where he works for one year; elected a delegate to the Illinois Constitutional Convention.

TG - SWS Dec. 30

RF Jan. 12

Sacred Heart Fri a.m.

PLEASE LEAVE AT THE FRONT DESK. (   )

M 200 _____

M 201 _____

M 202 _____

M 203 _____

M 204 _____

M 205 _____

M 207 _____

M 208 _____

M 210 _____

M 212 _____

M 213 _____

M 214 _____

M 215 _____

M 216 _____

M 217 _____

1971—Enters law partnership with his brother, Michael, and Francis J. Reilly.

1972—Marries Margaret Ann Corbett, moves out of his parents' home to a nearby house in Bridgeport; elected to the Illinois Senate.

1975—Named chairman of the state Senate Judiciary Committee.

1976-80—Serves as 11th Ward Democratic committeeman.

1980—Elected Cook County state's attorney, defeating Ald. Edward M. Burke (14th) in the Democratic primary and Republican incumbent Bernard J. Carey.

1981—His son, Kevin, dies at the age of thirty-three months of spina bifida. Other children are Nora, born Aug. 9, 1973; Patrick, born June 10, 1975; and Elizabeth, born Nov. 17, 1983.

1983—Finishes third in the Democratic mayoral primary behind Harold Washington and Mayor Jane M. Byrne.

1984—Reelected state's attorney over Republican Richard J. Brzeczek.

1988—Reelected state's attorney over Republican Terry Gainer.

Feb. 28, 1989—Defeats Mayor Eugene Sawyer in the Democratic mayoral primary for a special election called as a result of the death of Mayor Harold Washington on Nov. 25, 1987.

April 4, 1989—Defeats Harold Washington Party candidate Timothy C. Evans and Republican Edward R. Vrdolyak to become the forty-fifth mayor of Chicago—and the eighth of Irish descent.

April 2, 1991—Reelected mayor, defeating Cook County Commissioner Danny Davis and Byrne in the Democratic primary and Republican George Gottlieb and Harold Washington Party candidate Eugene Pincham in the general election.

Daley Digressions: He likes cigars, but never smokes in public. Drinks moderately. Pays a visit every Election Day morning to his father's grave at Holy Sepulchre Cemetery in Chicago Ridge. Dislikes comparisons to his dad. Went by the nickname of "mayor" at De La Salle. Works out regularly at the East Bank Club.

THE BASICS

HOW BIG IS A CHICAGO WARD? State law requires that each of Chicago's fifty wards has a population equal to about 1/50th of the city's total population. In 1980, that meant about 60,101 residents per

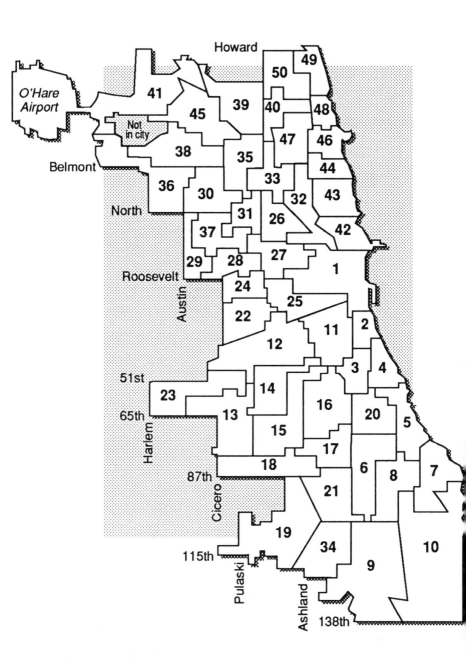

A map of the fifty Chicago wards.

ward. With a new 1990 Chicago population count of 2,783,726, that means—after remapping—about 55,674 residents per ward.

WHAT IS A PRECINCT? The precinct system is designed is make voting as convenient as possible by putting a polling place within walking distance of all voters. By law, a precinct is supposed to have about 400 voters and no more than 600. But that's often impractical. In Chicago, where there are close to 3,000 precincts, some have as few as 200 and as many as 1,000 people. It's often a question of geography. For example, an entire apartment building could be one precinct by itself or maybe two. Some wards have more precincts than others, because they have more registered voters. The more registered voters, the more precincts.

COUNTY VOTES
IN 1988 PRESIDENTIAL ELECTION:*

County	Plurality	Republicans Bush/Quayle	Democrats Dukakis/Bentsen
Cook	251,411 Dem.	878,562	1,129,973
Du Page	123,622 Rep.	217,907	94,285
Kane	29,917 Rep.	66,283	36,366
Lake	49,788 Rep.	114,115	64,327
McHenry	27,216 Rep.	46,135	18,919
Will	23,313 Rep.	73,129	49,816

*Does not include Libertarian or Solidarity parties

WHERE ELEPHANTS ROAM
Du Page County

In 1972, a *Sun-Times* reporter, posing as an applicant for a job with the Du Page County Probation Department, was told he would have to prove he voted in the last Republican primary, contribute $25 to the Republicans' annual golf outing, and distribute Republican campaign literature.

Those days are gone. Or so folks say. But Du Page County remains the most Republican county in all Illinois, the suburban elephant playing tug of war with the Chicago donkey. Since 1952, only one Republican presidential candidate—Barry Goldwater—has failed to carry at least 60 percent of the county's vote. More typically, Republican candidates walk away with 70 percent of the vote or more.

DU PAGE COUNTY PRESIDENTIAL VOTES

1952			1972		
Eisenhower:	71,134	(76%)	Nixon:	172,341	(75%)
Stevenson:	22,489		McGovern:	57,043	
1956			1976		
Eisenhower:	91,834	(79.9%)	Ford:	175,055	(70.8%)
Stevenson:	23,103		Carter:	72,137	
1960			1980		
Nixon:	101,014	(69.5%)	Reagan:	182,308	(72.6%)
Kennedy:	44,263		Carter:	68,991	
1964			1984		
Goldwater:	98,871	(59.9%)	Reagan:	227,141	(76.1%)
Johnson:	66,229		Mondale:	71,430	
1968			1988		
Nixon:	124,893	(72%)	Bush:	217,907	(69.8%)
Humphrey:	48,492		Dukakis:	94,284	

BAD MOVES

Occasionally, a politician makes a move so dumb or so brave that it haunts him for life. Politically, it's a bad move. Chicago and its suburbs have known more than a few.

1. **Governor John Peter Altgeld.** If he pardoned the seven anarchists convicted in the May 4, 1886, Haymarket Affair, he knew he would never win reelection. He did. And didn't.

2. **Anton Cermak.** The Chicago mayor had just stepped up to talk to President Franklin D. Roosevelt on the evening of March 6, 1933, when a gunman, Giuseppe Zangara, lunged forward and shot him. The usual assumption is Zangara was aiming for FDR, so it was just bad luck that Cermak chose that moment to chat with the president. Others, even to this day, suspect Zangara was aiming for Cermak all along, acting on orders from Al Capone.

3. **Bernard Epton** was reputed to be a thoughtful man and progressive Republican. But then he adopted that infamous slogan—"Before it's too late"—in his 1983 mayoral race against Harold Washington, and thousands of potential lakefront supporters accused him of playing on racial fears. Epton faced an uphill climb to begin with, but after that he never stood a chance.

4. **Edward V. Hanrahan.** At about 4:40 a.m. on Dec. 4, 1969, Cook County State's Attorney Hanrahan led fourteen Chicago police officers on a raid of the five-room apartment of Chicago Black Panther leader Fred Hampton. The police fired between 83 and 99 shots into the apartment. Black Panther Mark Clark fired once. Hampton and Clark were killed. Much of Chicago was outraged, and Hanrahan's political career was destroyed.

5. **James Murray.** In the early 1960s, Mayor Daley ordered Murray, then alderman of the 18th Ward, to draft Chicago's first fair-housing ordinance. Murray knew it would ruin him among Southwest Side voters, but did as he was told. The outcry was so intense—"Daley had a little lamb, his name was Jimmy Murray!"—that he didn't even bother to run for reelection. As a consolation prize, Daley made him a circuit court judge.

6. **Governor Richard Ogilvie.** If he pushed through the state's first income tax in 1969—a tax badly needed—he knew he would never win reelection. He did. And didn't.

7. **Roman Pucinski.** He had a safe seat in Congress, but gave it up in 1972 to go for the Senate. Friends and political pundits warned him that Republican incumbent Charles Percy would stomp him. They were right. As a consolation prize, Mayor Richard J. Daley found a place for him in the City Council.

8. **Edward R. Vrdolyak.** He jumped from the Democratic to the Republican Party after Harold Washington was reelected mayor and was never heard from again. On the other hand, Vrdolyak, a former alderman and county Democratic chief, made so many earlier bad moves that maybe he was a goner anyway.

9. **Joseph Vogrich.** He stumbled with his tongue. In 1990, Vogrich, an Oak Lawn trustee, told a local newspaper that he opposed subsidized housing in the village for racial minorities because poor people had nothing to contribute. In the ensuing firestorm, two Chicago aldermen threatened to cut off the suburb's supply of lake water, the village board officially censured him, and the voters turned him out of office.

10. In December 1987, four black aldermen sided with the City Council's white majority and elected Eugene Sawyer mayor over Tim Evans. Three of them—**Marlene Carter** (15th), **William C. Henry** (24th) and **Sheneather Butler** (27th)—paid for it in the spring of 1991 when their constituents voted them out of office. The fourth, Ald. **Robert Shaw** (9th), managed to rebuild a political base by posturing as Mayor Daley's harshest critic in the council.

CROOKED POLS

Chicago's City Hall has always had its share of politicians on the take.

■ When **Mayor Fred A. Busse** died, he left behind a safe-deposit box full of stocks in the company that sold the city its manhole covers.

■ **John Patrick Hopkins**, the city's first Irish Catholic mayor, established a nonexistent gas company and used it to blackmail utilities by threatening to compete with them. He retired from politics after selling his dummy corporation for more than $6 million.

■ **William Hale Thompson** ripped off the city's schools by awarding contracts to his buddies and provided police protection to Al Capone. His yacht sank in Belmont Harbor when too many people crowded aboard to celebrate his reelection in 1927.

■ In 1988, the U.S. attorney's office indicted fifty-two city employees, including forty-five police officers. In 1987, the feds indicted thirty-eight, and in 1986 they indicted twenty-three. Many of those indicted were consumer services, sewer, building and fire inspectors.

■ Since 1972, fifteen aldermen have been convicted on federal corruption charges, mostly some form of bribery, extortion, mail fraud or income tax evasion. They are Thomas E. Keane (31st), Paul T. Wigoda (49th), Louis Farina (36th), Edward T. Scholl (41st), William Carothers (28th), Frank W. Kuta (23rd), Donald Swinarski (12th), Joseph Jambrone (28th), Joseph Potempa (23rd), Casimir J. Stasczuk (13th), Fred D. Hubbard (2nd), Clifford Kelley (20th), Wallace Davis, Jr. (27th), Marian Humes (8th) and Perry Hutchinson (9th).

■ **Biggest Catch:** Squinty-eyed Tom Keane was Chicago's most powerful alderman for decades. As alderman of the North Side's 31st Ward, he was Mayor Richard J. Daley's closest political associate and City Council floor leader, ruling the council with an iron fist. He was a shifty and secretive sort of fellow who once said, "Daley wanted power, and I wanted to make money, and we both succeeded." But in October 1974, after a *Sun-Times* investigation unearthed most of the dirt, it all caught up with him. He was convicted on eighteen counts of federal mail fraud and conspiracy. Keane had engaged in a complex scheme involving the purchase and resale of hundreds of tax-delinquent properties. His politically inexperienced wife, Adeline, who took over as alderman, tried to curry favor with Hispanic voters by announcing she supported the teaching of Latin in public schools.

THE CHICAGO CITY COUNCIL
(ELECTED 1991)

WARD 1

	1980	Percent	1990	Percent	% Change
Total Population	61,716		64,677		+ 4.8
Black	26,475	42.9	24,814	38.4	− 6.3
Hispanic	11,633	18.8	10,903	16.9	− 6.3
Asian	6,108	9.9	7,948	12.3	+ 30.1
White, Other	16,974	27.5	20,927	32.4	+ 23.3

Ted Mazola—First elected: 1991

Residential builder and community activist; replaces twenty-three-year Ald. Fred Roti, who retired to fight federal corruption charges that tainted the entire 1st Ward Democratic organization.

WARD 2

	1980	Percent	1990	Percent	% Change
Total Population	60,141		45,409		− 24.5
Black	54,938	91.3	42,577	93.8	− 22.5
Hispanic	463	.8	307	.7	-33.7
Asian	952	1.6	858	1.9	− 9.9
White, Other	3,546	5.9	1,643	3.6	− 53.7

Bobby L. Rush—First elected: 1983

Former official of the Black Panther Party, now deputy chairman of the Illinois Democratic Party but says he often will vote with independents; agent and lobbyist for an insurance company.

WARD 3

	1980	Percent	1990	Percent	% Change
Total Population	62,396		43,682		− 30.0
Black	61,332	98.3	43,192	98.9	− 29.6
Hispanic	617	1.0	254	.6	− 58.8
Asian	71	.1	62	.1	− 12.7
White, Other	283	.5	165	.4	− 41.7

Dorthy Tillman—First elected: 1985

Nominated by Mayor Harold Washington in 1983 but not confirmed by the council for a year, then elected in 1985; ward committeeman.

WARD 4

	1980	Percent	1990	Percent	% Change
Total Population	60,051		44,797		− 25.4
Black	47,120	78.5	33,451	74.7	− 29.0
Hispanic	810	1.3	734	1.6	− 9.4
Asian	1,037	1.7	1,451	3.2	+ 39.9
White, Other	10,634	17.7	9,072	20.3	− 14.7

Toni Preckwinkle—First elected: 1991

Director of Chicago Jobs Council; succeeded in her third attempt to oust Timothy C. Evans, eighteen-year alderman and 1989 mayoral candidate.

WARD 5

	1980	Percent	1990	Percent	% Change
Total Population	60,215		51,679		− 14.2
Black	45,160	75.0	39,155	75.8	− 13.3
Hispanic	579	1.0	790	1.5	+ 36.4
Asian	1,082	1.8	1,684	3.3	+ 55.6
White, Other	12,870	21.4	9,979	19.3	− 22.5

Lawrence S. Bloom—First elected: 1979

Lawyer: promoter of progressive agenda; though white, easily won reelection in a majority black South Side ward; made mayoral bid in 1989.

WARD 6

	1980	Percent	1990	Percent	% Change
Total Population	60,576		53,500		− 11.7
Black	59,220	97.8	52,778	98.7	− 10.9
Hispanic	470	.8	285	.5	− 39.4
Asian	168	.3	91	.2	− 45.8
White, Other	558	.9	319	.6	− 42.8

John O. Steele—First elected: 1989

Lawyer; former chairman of City License Appeal Commission, fought to control proliferation of liquor licenses in parts of the ward.

WARD 7

	1980	Percent	1990	Percent	% Change
Total Population	59,906		50,152		− 16.3
Black	34,318	57.3	34,681	69.2	+ 1.1
Hispanic	18,025	30.1	12,739	25.4	− 29.3
Asian	215	.4	153	.3	− 28.8
White, Other	6,786	11.3	2,492	5.0	− 63.3

William M. Beavers—First elected: 1983

Former cop, chairs Police and Fire Committee; was bodyguard for former alderman and city treasurer Joseph Bertrand.

WARD 8

	1980	Percent	1990	Percent	% Change
Total Population	59,928		50,872		− 15.1
Black	57,311	95.6	49,747	97.8	− 13.2
Hispanic	594	1.0	338	.7	− 43.1
Asian	200	.3	122	.2	− 39.0
White, Other	1,519	2.5	642	1.3	− 57.7

Lorraine L. Dixon—First elected: 1991

Appointed by Mayor Richard M. Daley last year to replace the late Ald. Keith Caldwell. Helped residents file class-action suit against city and Metropolitan Water Reclamation District over sewer backup.

WARD 9

	1980	Percent	1990	Percent	% Change
Total Population	60,469		53,059		− 12.3
Black	53,530	88.5	48,470	91.4	− 9.5
Hispanic	2,897	4.8	2,576	4.9	− 11.1
Asian	107	.2	97	.2	− 9.3
White, Other	3,743	6.2	1,871	3.5	− 50.0

Robert Shaw—First elected: 1979

Tossed out of office in 1983 for supporting Mayor Jane M. Byrne over Harold Washington; reclaimed seat in 1987, won 1991 runoff by a whisker. Fierce Daley critic, twin brother of state Rep. William Shaw.

WARD 10

	1980	Percent	1990	Percent	% Change
Total Population	60,140		55,699		− 7.4
Black	16,149	26.9	15,753	28.3	− 2.5
Hispanic	10,075	16.8	16,329	29.3	+ 62.1
Asian	170	.3	180	.3	+ 5.9
White, Other	33,348	55.5	23,359	41.9	− 30.0

John J. Buchanan—First elected: 1967.

Returns to council after twenty years; defeated in 1971 by onetime powerhouse Edward R. Vrdolyak; later worked for Vrdolyak and his brother, Victor, alderman from 1987 to 1991.

WARD 11

	1980	Percent	1990	Percent	% Change
Total Population	58,439		54,181		−7.3
Black	7,318	12.5	6,997	12.9	−4.4
Hispanic	12,689	21.7	15,160	28.0	+19.5
Asian	675	1.2	5,299	9.8	+685.0
White, Other	37,457	64.1	26,598	49.1	−29.0

Patrick M. Huels—First elected: 1977

From Daley's home ward, he is the mayor's floor leader; former paid secretary for the ward Democratic organization; works quietly behind the scenes.

WARD 12

	1980	Percent	1990	Percent	% Change
Total Population	60,674		62,351		+2.8
Black	8,350	13.8	7,975	12.8	−4.5
Hispanic	10,817	17.8	22,995	36.9	+112.6
Asian	650	1.1	1,070	1.7	+64.6
White, Other	40,390	66.6	30,209	48.4	−25.2

Mark J. Fary—First elected: 1987

Nephew and onetime aid to former U.S. Rep. John Fary; also was aide to former state Sen. Timothy Degnan, who is now a top Daley aide.

WARD 13

	1980	Percent	1990	Percent	% Change
Total Population	61,249		59,567		−2.7
Black	57	.1	115	.2	+101.8
Hispanic	2,093	3.4	8,067	13.5	+285.4
Asian	235	.4	567	1.0	+141.3
White, Other	58,541	95.6	50,795	85.3	−13.2

John S. Madrzyk—First elected: 1973

Regular Democratic stalwart, former purchasing supervisor for city Health Department: a chief advocate of an aldermanic pay raise.

WARD 14

	1980	Percent	1990	Percent	% Change
Total Population	61,240		68,773		+12.3
Black	317	.5	15,093	21.9	+4661.2
Hispanic	14,548	23.8	28,407	41.3	+95.3
Asian	470	.8	721	1.0	+53.4
White, Other	45,215	73.8	24,387	35.5	−46.1

Edward M. Burke—First elected: 1969

Lawyer; for twenty-two years one of the most powerful aldermen; as Finance Committee chairman knows the budget inside out; ward committeeman.

WARD 15

	1980	Percent	1990	Percent	% Change
Total Population	61,710		55,637		− 9.8
Black	45,452	73.7	45,359	81.5	− .2
Hispanic	3,309	5.4	3,217	5.8	− 2.8
Asian	253	.4	456	.8	+ 80.2
White, Other	12,245	19.8	6,578	11.8	− 46.3

Virgil E. Jones, Jr.—First elected: 1991

Police officer; won runoff after Ald. Marlene Carter lost primary; seeks better cooperation between police and residents; opposed neighborhood referendum for a private security force to help police.

WARD 16

	1980	Percent	1990	Percent	% Change
Total Population	57,581		47,880		− 16.8
Black	56,310	97.8	47,271	98.7	− 16.1
Hispanic	653	1.1	300	.6	− 54.1
Asian	93	.2	108	.2	+ 16.1
White, Other	409	.7	178	.4	− 56.5

Shirley A. Coleman—First elected: 1991

Department of Human Services official; supported by retiring Ald. Anna Langford; squelched political comeback bid for former state Sen. James C. Taylor in a runoff.

WARD 17

	1980	Percent	1990	Percent	% Change
Total Population	58,234		51,671		− 11.3
Black	57,390	98.6	50,800	98.3	− 11.5
Hispanic	350	.6	223	.4	− 36.3
Asian	92	.2	99	.2	+ 7.6
White, Other	343	.6	533	1.0	+ 55.4

Allan Streeter—First elected: 1982

Real estate salesman and former deputy sheriff; ward committeeman; among leaders of aldermanic charge against notorious painting of Washington at the School of the Art Institute in 1988.

WARD 18

	1980	Percent	1990	Percent	% Change
Total Population	60,705		54,673		− 9.9
Black	30,226	49.8	30,221	55.3	− .0
Hispanic	729	1.2	1,371	2.5	+ 88.1
Asian	207	.3	279	.5	+ 34.8
White, Other	29,334	48.3	22,787	41.7	− 22.3

Thomas W. Murphy—First elected: 1991

Lawyer and former Democratic precinct worker, but didn't have regular party support to replace retiring Ald. Robert T. Kellam; won runoff by a hair.

WARD 19

	1980	Percent	1990	Percent	% Change
Total Population	59,786		57,011		− 4.6
Black	8,715	14.6	11,729	20.6	+ 34.6
Hispanic	622	1.0	1,003	1.8	+ 61.3
Asian	213	.4	326	.6	+ 53.1
White, Other	50,109	83.8	43,913	77.0	− 12.4

Virginia A. Rugai—First elected: 1991

Appointed by Daley last December to replace Michael Sheahan, who was elected Cook County sheriff; former high school teacher; was aide to state Sen. Jeremiah Joyce.

WARD 20

	1980	Percent	1990	Percent	% Change
Total Population	59,981		42,581		−29.0
Black	58,187	97.0	41,409	97.2	−28.8
Hispanic	389	.6	202	.5	−48.1
Asian	155	.3	198	.5	+27.7
White, Other	1,100	1.8	751	1.8	−31.7

Arenda Troutman—First elected: 1991

Appointed by Daley in 1990 to replace the late Ald. Ernest Jones; former precinct captain who helped organize for Washington in 1983.

WARD 21

	1980	Percent	1990	Percent	% Change
Total Population	59,336		52,197		−12.0
Black	58,062	97.9	51,551	98.8	−11.2
Hispanic	342	.6	187	.4	−45.3
Asian	96	.2	70	.1	−27.1
White, Other	740	1.2	368	.7	−50.3

Jesse J. Evans—First elected: 1987

Postal worker for twenty-nine years, now a union steward at main post office; ward committeeman; community activist who fought proposed Crosstown Expressway.

WARD 22

	1980	Percent	1990	Percent	% Change
Total Population	59,803		64,684		+8.2
Black	2,622	4.4	2,231	3.4	−14.9
Hispanic	46,710	78.1	58,605	90.6	+25.5
Asian	162	.3	68	.1	−58.0
White, Other	9,908	16.6	3,621	5.6	−63.5

Jesus G. Garcia—First elected: 1986

Community activist; elected committeeman in 1984, first Hispanic to hold that office: former deputy water commissioner.

WARD 23

	1980	Percent	1990	Percent	% Change
Total Population	58,596		53,942		−7.9
Black	52	.1	80	.1	+53.8
Hispanic	2,143	3.7	4,022	7.5	+87.7
Asian	250	.4	434	.8	+73.6
White, Other	55,881	95.4	49,391	91.6	−11.6

James J. Laski, Jr.—First elected: 1991

Appointed by Daley in December, 1990, when Ald. William F. Krystyniak quit to take a county job; ex-aide to U.S. Rep. William O. Lipinski, became a lawyer, alderman and husband in the past few months.

WARD 24

	1980	Percent	1990	Percent	% Change
Total Population	63,308		48,795		− 22.9
Black	61,235	96.7	47,307	97.0	− 22.7
Hispanic	1,370	2.2	1,085	2.2	− 20.8
Asian	61	.1	58	.1	− 4.9
White, Other	554	.9	327	.7	− 41.0

Jesse L. Miller—First elected: 1991

Former director of the Lawndale Peoples Planning and Action Council, defeated Ald. William C. Henry, who is facing federal corruption charges; wrested the committeeman's post from Henry in 1988.

WARD 25

	1980	Percent	1990	Percent	% Change
Total Population	60,075		59,922		− .3
Black	4,570	7.6	3,824	6.4	− 16.3
Hispanic	43,824	72.9	50,246	83.9	+ 14.7
Asian	343	.6	167	.3	− 51.3
White, Other	11,037	18.4	5,543	9.3	− 49.8

Ambrosio Medrano—First elected: 1991

Former director of the City Commission on Latino Affairs for Daley; succeeded in his second attempt to oust Ald. Juan Soliz.

WARD 26

	1980	Percent	1990	Percent	% Change
Total Population	60,612		56,108		− 7.4
Black	6,081	10.0	6,726	12.0	+ 10.6
Hispanic	38,919	64.2	39,057	69.6	+ .4
Asian	986	1.6	557	1.0	− 43.5
White, Other	13,911	23.0	9,602	17.1	− 31.0

Luis V. Gutierrez—First elected: 1986

Former social worker; helped Washington score with Hispanic voters and later helped Daley do the same, chairman of Council's Housing Committee.

WARD 27

	1980	Percent	1990	Percent	% Change
Total Population	60,891		43,053		− 29.3
Black	49,094	80.6	34,053	79.1	− 30.6
Hispanic	5,912	9.7	4,831	11.2	− 18.3
Asian	655	1.1	614	1.4	− 6.3
White, Other	4,884	8.0	3,542	8.2	− 27.5

Rickey R. Hendon—First elected: 1991

Independent filmmaker and secretary-treasurer of Cook County Forest Preserve District; defeated Ald. Sheneather Y. Butler in her bid for a second term; ward committeeman.

WARD 28

	1980	Percent	1990	Percent	% Change
Total Population	58,613		42,236		− 27.9
Black	57,455	98.0	41,728	98.8	− 27.4
Hispanic	572	1.0	253	.6	− 55.8
Asian	94	.2	47	.1	− 50.0
White, Other	436	.7	198	.5	− 54.6

Ed H. Smith—First elected: 1983
Former salesman and management counsultant; ward committee-man; defeated Senate President Philip J. Rock (D-Oak Park) for seat on state Democratic committee in 1990.

WARD 29

	1980	Percent	1990	Percent	% Change
Total Population	61,446		47,558		− 22.6
Black	51,627	84.0	43,862	92.2	− 15.0
Hispanic	2,275	3.7	854	1.8	− 62.5
Asian	1,144	1.9	275	.6	− 76.0
White, Other	6,140	10.0	2,551	5.4	− 58.5

Sam Burrell—First elected: 1991
Electrical contractor; ex-aide to Danny K. Davis; took his boss's seat in December with Daley's appointment after Davis was elected to County Board; won runoff after second-place showing in primary.

WARD 30

	1980	Percent	1990	Percent	% Change
Total Population	59,968		67,132		+ 11.9
Black	142	.2	10,344	15.4	+ 7184.5
Hispanic	10,734	17.9	27,019	40.2	+ 151.7
Asian	1,431	2.4	1,532	2.3	+ 7.1
White, Other	47,108	78.6	28,134	41.9	− 40.3

Carole Bialczak—First elected: 1991
Worked for Metropolitan Water Reclamation District and ward Committeeman Ted Lechowicz; appointed by Daley in 1989 to succeed the late Ald. George J. Hagopien.

WARD 31

	1980	Percent	1990	Percent	% Change
Total Population	59,555		62,319		+ 4.6
Black	3,153	5.3	13,747	22.1	+ 336.0
Hispanic	35,403	59.4	41,547	66.7	+ 17.4
Asian	1,289	2.2	673	1.1	− 47.8
White, Other	19,094	32.1	6,206	10.0	− 67.5

Regner 'Ray' Suarez—First elected: 1991
Former Streets and Sanitation employee; replaces retiring Ald. Raymond A. Figueroa; a Vietnam veteran who has held various city positions since 1974.

WARD 32

	1980	Percent	1990	Percent	% Change
Total Population	61,459		56,059		− 8.8
Black	3,072	5.0	3,112	5.6	+ 1.3
Hispanic	27,497	44.7	28,533	50.9	+ 3.8
Asian	1,028	1.7	870	1.6	− 15.4
White, Other	28,568	46.5	23,268	41.5	− 18.6

Theris M. Gabinski—First elected: 1969
Former high school teacher; loyal to his political sponsor, U.S. Rep. Dan Rostenkowski, and to Daley; came close to being tabbed by Council as acting mayor after Washington died in 1987.

WARD 33

	1980	Percent	1990	Percent	% Change
Total Population	58,693		59,071		+ .6
Black	953	1.6	2,278	3.9	+ 139.0
Hispanic	21,068	35.9	31.003	52.5	+ 47.2
Asian	1,695	2.9	2,203	3.7	+ 30.0
White, Other	34,327	58.5	23,478	39.7	– 31.6

Richard F. Mell—First elected: 1975

Affluent businessman known for his antics the night the Council selected a successor to Washington; as Rules Committee chairman, will oversee drawing new ward map; ward committeeman.

WARD 34

	1980	Percent	1990	Percent	% Change
Total Population	60,092		52,538		– 12.6
Black	57,855	96.3	51,531	98.1	– 10.9
Hispanic	786	1.3	412	.8	– 47.6
Asian	114	.2	85	.2	– 25.4
White, Other	1,225	2.0	484	.9	– 60.5

Lemuel Austin, Jr.—First elected: 1987

Former ward sanitation superintendent; brooks no criticism from black colleagues for his support of Daley, who named him Budget Committee chairman.

WARD 35

	1980	Percent	1990	Percent	% Change
Total Population	58,648		61,682		+ 5.2
Black	88	.2	425	.7	+ 383.0
Hispanic	6,851	11.7	19,290	31.3	+ 181.6
Asian	1,992	3.4	3,277	5.3	+ 64.5
White, Other	49,202	83.9	38,590	62.6	– 21.6

Mike Wojcik—First elected: 1991

Former precinct captain for Ald. Joseph S. Kotlarz, Jr., who retired, resigned from city job and lived off savings while campaigning; led campaign to reclaim neighborhood park from gangs.

WARD 36

	1980	Percent	1990	Percent	% Change
Total Population	58,942		58,338		– 1.0
Black	37	.1	2,693	4.6	+ 7178.4
Hispanic	1,565	2.7	7,413	12.7	+ 373.7
Asian	503	.9	1,683	2.9	+ 234.6
White, Other	56,506	95.9	46,518	79.7	– 17.7

William J. P. Banks—First elected: 1983

Lawyer and former aide to the late U.S. Rep. Morgan F. Murphy; quiet, methodical head of powerful Zoning Committee; ward committeeman.

WARD 37

	1980	Percent	1990	Percent	% Change
Total Population	60,736		50,441		– 17.0
Black	48,735	80.2	46,042	91.3	– 5.5
Hispanic	5,615	9.2	2,864	5.7	– 49.0

WARD 37 (continued)

	1980	Percent	1990	Percent	% Change
Asian	833	1.4	311	.6	− 62.7
White, Other	5,178	8.5	1,213	2.4	− 76.6

Percy Giles—First elected: 1986

Former Walgreens assistant manager; headed nonprofit Westside Business Improvement Association, 1980 to 1986; ward committeeman.

WARD 38

	1980	Percent	1990	Percent	% Change
Total Population	59,784		58,796		− 1.7
Black	219	.4	247	.4	+ 12.8
Hispanic	1,125	1.9	3,860	6.6	+ 243.1
Asian	569	1.0	1,690	2.9	+ 197.0
White, Other	57,660	96.4	52,982	90.1	− 8.1

Thomas W. Cullerton—First elected: 1973

Former manager of city electricians; ward committeeman; member of a family that has had a Council member for 120 years, easily survived his first runoff challenge.

WARD 39

	1980	Percent	1990	Percent	% Change
Total Population	60,669		64,042		+ 5.6
Black	318	.5	1,131	1.8	+ 255.7
Hispanic	6,760	11.1	12,871	20.1	+ 90.4
Asian	6,454	10.6	12,984	20.3	+ 101.2
White, Other	46,123	76.0	36,934	57.7	− 19.9

Anthony C. Laurino—First elected: 1965

"Dean" of Council; associated with real estate and insurance firm; worked his way up from city inspector and aldermanic secretary; ward committeeman; heads Traffic Committee.

WARD 40

	1980	Percent	1990	Percent	% Change
Total Population	58,685		59,919		+ 2.1
Black	403	.7	1,624	2.7	+ 303.0
Hispanic	7,826	13.3	14,527	24.2	+ 85.6
Asian	6,288	10.7	10,624	17.7	+ 69.0
White, Other	42,850	73.0	32,998	55.1	− 23.0

Patrick J. O'Connor—First elected: 1983

Lawyer; made bid for Democratic nomination for state's attorney in 1990; ward committeeman; his father works for the Finance Committee.

WARD 41

	1980	Percent	1990	Percent	% Change
Total Population	60,579		57,077		− 5.8
Black	170	.3	331	.6	+ 94.7
Hispanic	771	1.3	1,629	2.9	+ 111.3

WARD 41 (continued)

	1980	Percent	1990	Percent	% Change
Asian	657	1.1	1,113	1.9	+ 69.4
White, Other	58,788	97.0	53,981	94.6	− 8.2

Brian G. Doherty—First elected: 1991

Engineer for state Transportation Dept., aid to state Rep. Roger McAuliffe (R-Chicago) and only Republican on Council; ousted eighteen-year Ald. Roman C. Pucinski on an anti-tax platform.

WARD 42

	1980	Percent	1990	Percent	% Change
Total Population	60,173		56,135		− 6.7
Black	21,728	36.1	14,425	25.7	− 33.6
Hispanic	1,841	3.1	1,733	3.1	− 5.9
Asian	971	1.6	1,714	3.1	+ 76.5
White, Other	35,346	58.7	38,238	68.1	+ 8.2

Burton F. Natarus—First elected: 1971

Lawyer; regular Democratic sidekick of former County Board President George W. Dunne; dilgent housekeeper in ward that ranges from the Gold Coast to Cabrini-Green.

WARD 43

	1980	Percent	1990	Percent	% Change
Total Population	60,156		64,051		+ 6.5
Black	4,559	7.6	2,982	4.7	− 34.6
Hispanic	4,294	7.1	2,553	4.0	− 40.5
Asian	1,749	2.9	1,556	2.4	− 11.0
White, Other	49,215	81.8	56,925	88.9	+ 15.7

Edwin W. Eisendrath—First elected: 1987.

Former teacher whose 1987 campaign was most expensive ward race in city history; reelected despite tough opposition after failed challenge to U.S. Rep. Sidney R. Yates in 1990 primary.

WARD 44

	1980	Percent	1990	Percent	% Change
Total Population	60,163		55,831		− 7.2
Black	3,414	5.7	2,611	4.7	− 23.5
Hispanic	10,684	17.8	6,110	10.9	− 42.8
Asian	2,919	4.9	2,368	4.2	− 18.9
White, Other	42,472	70.6	44,673	80.0	+ 5.2

Bernard J. Hansen—First elected: 1983

Former sanitation superintendent; successfully sponsored ordinances on hate crimes and human rights, twice won reelection over gay-activist opponent.

WARD 45

	1980	Percent	1990	Percent	% Change
Total Population	58,818		56,667		– 3.7
Black	16	.0	110	.2	+ 587.5
Hispanic	1,324	2.3	3,464	6.1	+ 161.6
Asian	1,096	1.9	2,195	3.9	+ 100.3
White, Other	56,189	95.5	50,867	89.8	– 9.5

Patrick J. Levar—First elected: 1987

Teacher; became precinct captain at age eighteen for Thomas G. Lyons, now the county Democratic chairman; also has worked for Circuit Court clerk's office.

WARD 46

	1980	Percent	1990	Percent	% Change
Total Population	59,848		57,949		– 3.2
Black	8,466	14.1	11,738	20.3	+ 38.6
Hispanic	13,275	22.2	11,057	19.1	– 16.7
Asian	5,175	8.6	4,860	8.4	– 6.1
White, Other	31,689	52.9	30,208	52.1	– 4.7

Helen Shiller—First elected: 1987

Liberal community activist nudging toward the mainstream; overcame strenuous efforts by Daley for her runoff opponent.

WARD 47

	1980	Percent	1990	Percent	% Change
Total Population	60,005		57,823		– 3.6
Black	326	.5	1,685	2.9	+ 416.9
Hispanic	11,663	19.4	16,390	28.3	+ 40.5
Asian	4,195	7.0	4,432	7.7	+ 5.6
White, Other	42,757	71.3	35,152	60.8	– 17.8

Eugene C. Schulter—First elected: 1975

Former deputy county assessor, now an independent appraiser; a regular Democrat who broke with his ward committeeman, Edmund L. Kelly, in 1987 to endorse Washington.

WARD 48

	1980	Percent	1990	Percent	% Change
Total Population	60,135		62,366		+ 3.7
Black	9,170	15.2	14,947	24.0	+ 63.0
Hispanic	9,055	15.1	9,985	16.0	+ 10.3
Asian	6,877	11.4	9,172	14.7	+ 33.4
White, Other	33,321	55.4	28,120	45.1	– 15.6

Mary Ann Smith—First elected: 1991

Appointed by Daley in 1989 when Ald. Kathy Osterman was named special events director; passed ordinance aimed at preventing shoulder-to-shoulder lakefront high-rises.

WARD 49

	1980	Percent	1990	Percent	% Change
Total Population	60,231		63,615		+ 5.6
Black	5,813	9.7	16,057	25.2	+ 176.2
Hispanic	6,603	11.0	10,874	17.1	+ 64.7
Asian	4,270	7.1	5,915	9.3	+ 38.5
White, Other	42,291	70.2	30,655	48.2	– 27.5

Joe Moore—First elected: 1991

Lawyer for city; ran Network 49, independent organization led by David D. Orr, the county clerk and former alderman; defeated Daley's candidate in runoff.

WARD 50

	1980	Percent	1990	Percent	% Change
Total Population	59,916		65,529		+ 9.4
Black	595	1.0	3,462	5.3	+ 481.8
Hispanic	2,894	4.8	7,378	11.3	+ 154.9
Asian	4,604	7.7	10,458	16.0	+ 127.2
White, Other	50,753	84.7	44,083	67.3	– 13.1

Bernard Stone—First elected: 1973

Outspoken lawyer who helped bury proposed World's Fair; switched to Republicans in 1987, made failed bid for recorder of deeds in 1988, switched back to Democrats in 1990.

Sources: U.S. Census Bureau; Chicago Planning Department.

CHICAGO MAYORS

	Tenure	Grave Site	Date of Death	
William Ogden	1837-38	New York	3 Aug.	1877
Buckner Morris	1838-39	Rosehill	16 Dec.	1879
Benjamin Raymond	1839-40	Graceland	6 Apr.	1883
Alexander Lloyd	1840-41	Rosehill	7 Apr.	1871
Francis Sherman	1841-42	Graceland	7 Apr.	1870
Benjamin Raymond	1842-43	Graceland	6 Apr.	1883
Augustus Garrett	1843-44	Rosehill	30 Nov.	1848
Alson Sherman	1844-45	Oakwood, Waukegan	27 Sept.	1903
Augustus Garrett	1845-46	Rosehill	30 Nov.	1848
John Chapin	1846-47	Graceland	27 June	1864
James Curtiss*	1847-48	City Cemetery	2 Nov.	1859
James Woodworth	1848-50	Oakland, Dolton	26 Mar.	1869
James Curtiss	1850-51	City Cemetery	2 Nov.	1859
Walter Gurnee	1851-53	New York	18 Apr.	1903
Charles Gray	1853-54	Graceland	17 Oct.	1885
Isaac Milliken	1854-55	Rosehill	2 Dec.	1885
Levi Boone	1855-56	Rosehill	24 Jan.	1882
Thomas Dyer	1856-57	Connecticut	6 June	1862
John Wentworth	1857-58	Rosehill	16 Oct.	1888
John Haines	1858-60	Rosehill	4 July	1896
John Wentworth	1860-61	Rosehill	16 Oct.	1888
Julian Rumsey	1861-62	Graceland	20 Apr.	1886
Francis Sherman	1862-65	Graceland	7 Nov.	1870
John Rice	1865-69	Rosehill	17 Dec.	1874
Roswell Mason	1869-71	Rosehill	1 Jan.	1892

	Tenure	Grave Site	Date of Death	
Joseph Medill	1871-73	Graceland	16 Mar.	1899
Lester Bond**	1873 2	Rosehill		1903
Harvey Colvin	1873-75	Rosehill	16 Apr.	1892
Thomas Hoyne	1876		27 July	1883
Monroe Heath	1876-79	Oak Woods	21 Oct.	1894
Carter Harrison	1879-87	Graceland	28 Oct.	1893
John Roche	1887-89	Rosehill	10 Feb.	1904
DeWitt Cregier	1889-91	Rosehill	9 Nov.	1898
Hempstead Washbourne	1891-93	Graceland	13 Apr.	1918
Carter Harrison	1893	Graceland	28 Oct.	1893
George Swift	1893	Rosehill	2 July.	1912
John Hopkins	1893-95	Calvary	13 Oct.	1918
George Swift	1895-97	Rosehill	2 July	1912
Carter Harison II	1897-1905	Graceland	25 Dec.	1953
Edward Dunne	1905-07		24 May.	1937
Fred A. Busse	1907-11		9 July	1914
Carter Harrison II	1911-15	Graceland	25 Dec.	1953
William Thompson	1915-23	Oak Woods	18 Mar.	1944
William Dever	1923-27	Calvary	3 Sept.	1929
William Thompson	1927-31	Oak Woods	19 Mar.	1944
Anton Cermak	1931-33	Bohemian	6 Mar.	1933
Frank Corr	1933	Holy Sepulchre	3 June	1934
Edward Kelly	1933-47	Cavalry	20 Oct.	1950
Martin Kennelly	1947-55	Cavalry	29 Nov.	1961
Richard Daley	1955-76	Holy Sepulchre	20 Dec.	1976
Michael Bilandic	1976-79	Living		
Jane Byrne	1979-83	Living		
Harold Washington	1983-87	Oak Woods	25 Nov.	1987
David Orr	1987	Living		
Eugene Sawyer	1987-89	Living		
Richard M. Daley	1989-	Living		

*No records are available indicating the present cemetery for James Curtiss. His son is buried in Graceland.

**Lester Bond was the first acting mayor appointed by the City Council while Medill took an extended European vacation.

PAST TENSE

He Had the Common Touch
By Harlan Draeger
(*Chicago Daily News*, Dec. 21, 1976—
the day after Richard J. Daley died)

Chicago without Mayor Daley.

For most people in his city, the idea is hard to grasp.

For some, it is frightening.

Richard J. Daley was more than a veteran mayor to the 3.3 million people inside Chicago's borders.

He was the symbol of the city, its undisputed leader, father-figure, protector and provider, the indispensable man, the irreplaceable part.

Now he is gone.

Nearly all Chicagoans—even those who disliked his brand of politics—feel a sense of loss. And many are undergoing a difficult mental adjustment.

Their words at his death revealed a special relationship between man and city, where the lines often blurred.

Daley was admired, yes, and respected for 21 robust years at the helm of the nation's second largest city.

Most of all, though, the stocky man from Bridgeport was appreciated for certain human qualities.

In the end, Chicago's six-term mayor may be best remembered for something he didn't do.

Richard J. Daley, political powerhouse and adviser to Presidents, never lost the common touch.

It's Washington
Huge Vote Is Key; Epton Exits on Bitter Note
By Basil Talbott, Jr.
(*Chicago Sun-Times*, April 13, 1983)

Rep. Harold Washington was elected Chicago's first black mayor Tuesday after a mean race that ended with a pledge from the victor to "heal divisions" and a bitter post-mortem from the vanquished Republican, Bernard E. Epton.

With 99 percent of the city's 2,914 precincts counted, Washington had 656,727 votes, or 51.4 percent of the vote, to Epton's 617,159, or 48.3 percent. The Socialist Workers Party candidate, Ed Warren, had 3,725.

The 60-year-old congressman was carried to victory by a huge outpouring from black wards, an extra push from Hispanics and a white lift from the north lakefront.

He had to overcome a huge vote from white ethnic precincts on the Southwest Side, where State's Attorney Richard M. Daley scored best in the Feb. 22 primary elections, and the Northwest Side white base of outgoing Mayor Jane Byrne.

CLASSIC QUOTES

"Around the turn of the century we used to be known as gray wolves and boodlers. But under your leadership, Mr. Mayor, the image of an alderman has risen a great deal."

—Ald. Ed Burke (14th) in 1970

In the following seventeen years, fifteen aldermen were convicted on federal bribery charges.

Kissing the mistletoe:
"Mayor Daley's administraton is the finest in all the world and outer space"

—Ald. Claude W.B. Holman (4th) in 1970.

Sources: Steve Neal, columnist for the *Chicago Sun-Times*; William Braden, Ray Hanania, Fran Spielman and Harlan Draeger of the *Sun-Times*; Chicago Board of Election Commissioners; Village of Lincolnwood; State Board of Elections; Jim Tamm of the Du Page County Board of Elections; *History of Chicago*, by A.T. Andreas.

DISASTERS

FIRSTS

Recorded Fire in Chicago: A man carrying a shovel full of hot coal from one building to another on a day in October 1834, accidently set afire a building on the corner of Lake and La Salle streets. As the fire raged, nobody took charge of dousing it. As a result, Chicago's leaders passed an ordinance that gave the town's four fire wardens—the first building inspectors—authority to draft men right off the streets to fight fires. Any man refusing to help would be fined $5.

Shipwreck in Lake Michigan: The Hercules, a small schooner bound for Chicago, sank near Burns Harbor, Indiana, between Michigan City and Gary, in 1817.

Fire Pole: The Chicago Fire Department invented the fire pole. In 1878, David Kenyen, captain of Engine Company 21, noticed one day that several of his men working in the firehouse's third-floor hayloft were responding remarkably fast to fire alarms by sliding down a hay-binding pole and leaping aboard the fire wagon. So, with permission from Chief Fire Marshall Matt Benner, Kenyen and his men installed a permanent fire pole, anchoring it on the first floor and running it through a hole in the ceiling. Other firefighters scoffed at the "sliding pole," but it soon became obvious Engine 21 was getting to fire scenes faster than anybody else. Benner issued an order to install fire poles in all firehouses.

Pickax and Fireplugs: The Chicago Fire Department also claims to have invented the pickax and coined the phrase "fireplug." According to Fire Department historians, Chicago firefighters at the scene of a fire in the middle 1800s had to dig into the ground below the freeze line to locate wooden water mains. They would punch a hole in the line with the pickax, allow the dirt pit to flood, and syphon off the water to fight the fire. When the fire was doused, the firefighters would plug the hole in the main, recover it and mark the site. The next time there was a fire in the same area, the firefighters would seek out the original fireplug.

A Hero's Handprint Never Fades: Chicago Firefighter Francis X. Leavy was washing windows in a firehouse on Good Friday, April 18, 1924, when an alarm interrupted his work. A building was ablaze at Fourteenth and Blue Island. Leavy ran off to fight the fire, but never returned. He was killed when the building collapsed on him. The next morning, another firefighter took up Leavy's cleaning chores at the firehouse (at 2258 W. Thirteenth St.) and discovered the dead man's handprint smugged on the unfinished window. From that day on, firefighters claimed that nothing could remove the print. The window was broken in 1946 when a newspaper boy threw a paper through it.

LIST OF TEN
AVIATION DISASTERS

1. **May 25, 1979:** It remains the deadliest crash in the history of U.S. aviation—273 killed. American Airlines Flight 191 lost its left-wing engine on takeoff from O'Hare, banked sideways out of control, slammed into a field and exploded. Everybody on board and two people on the ground were killed. The plane itself virtually disintegrated. It had taken off shortly after 3 p.m., on a sunny day. Its tail dropped and its silver nose pointed skyward. Seconds later, a controller in the O'Hare tower shouted, "Look at that! Look at that! He blew an engine!" The plane plowed into a grassy area about a half mile northwest of the runway. In the wake of the crash, more than 200 lawsuits were filed, and an estimated $70 million in damages was paid out by American and the aircraft's maker, McDonnell Douglas.

2. **Dec. 8, 1972:** A United Airlines 737 jetliner dropped out of an overcast sky and crashed about one and a half miles southeast of Midway Airport, killing forty-five. Two of those killed were trapped inside one of three homes the plane demolished, near Seventieth Street and Lawndale. The others were passengers on the Washington-to-Midway flight. A possible explanation for the crash, investigators concluded, was icing on the elevator sections of the tail. One victim was the wife of convicted Watergate burglar E. Howard Hunt. Mrs. Hunt was carrying more than $10,000 in cash in her purse, for reasons never fully explained.

3. **Dec. 27, 1968:** It was two days after Christmas when a twin-engined North Central Convair 580 crashed into an O'Hare hangar, killing twenty-seven people and injuring twenty-six others. The airliner, carrying forty-one passengers from Minneapolis–St. Paul, veered 90 degrees left on landing and slammed into a hangar on the northwest end of the field, 400 feet from the runway. The National Transporation Safety Board re-

ported that the glare of lights through fog had confused the pilot as the plane came out of the clouds toward the runway.

4. **Sept. 17, 1961:** A Northwest Orient Electra bound for Miami zoomed out of O'Hare Airport on a sunny Sunday morning, banked sharply west and—sixty seconds after takeoff—crashed in Bensenville, killing all thirty-seven passengers. An engine oil valve mistakenly left in the closed position was blamed for the accident.

5. **Sept. 1, 1961:** For lack of a 2½-inch bolt, seventy-eight people died. A TWA plane was flying out of Midway when that bolt dropped from the plane's elevator booster system, causing it to crash near Clarendon Hills. In essence, one investigator later said, the pilot had lost his power steering and had no time to react manually. One Clarendon Hills resident, still sleeping when the plane crashed at 2 a.m., said, "I was shaken out of bed. It sounded like an atomic explosion." Another resident said, "I could see nothing but bodies. They were past help."

6. **July 27, 1960:** A helicopter carrying thirteen passengers crashed into a cemetery between Maywood and Forest Park at 10:40 p.m., while on an eleven-minute, eighteen-mile flight from Midway to O'Hare. All thirteen persons were killed. Investigators said the blade of the helicopter's main rotor came off in flight.

7. **Nov. 24, 1959:** A Trans World Airlines freight plane fell like a flaming bomb into seven small houses southeast of Midway Airport, killing eleven. Investigators later said the four-engine plane probably was crippled by fire in its No. 2 engine as it attempted to return to Midway shortly after takeoff. As a result of the crash, ruled accidental by a coroner's jury, runway lighting at Midway was improved.

8. **July 17, 1955:** A Braniff Airways twin-engine Convair, swooping in for a landing at Midway Airport at 7:22 a.m., on a Sunday, clipped a service station sign, plunged through a fence and cartwheeled onto the airfield. Twenty-two passengers were killed. Investigators blamed the crash on human error, saying the pilot had swerved sixty to eighty feet below the proper flight path as he flew into Midway from the northwest in heavy fog.

9. **May 20, 1943:** Twelve crewmen of an Army bomber plane were killed when their four-engine B-24 crashed into a huge gas storage tank while trying to land at Midway Airport. The bomber, originating from Fort Worth, Texas, flew into the rain and murk of Chicago shortly before noon. As it circled the airport, manuevering into landing position, it crashed into the gas tank at Seventy-third Street and Central Park Avenue, sparking a massive explosion.

Tail fin of United Airlines 737 is still intact after crashing into home on the Southwest Side on Dec. 8, 1972. *(Photo by Edmund Jarecki)*

10. **Dec. 4, 1940:** A United Airlines plane crashed late in the afternoon within two blocks of Midway—then called Chicago Airport or Municipal Airport—killing all three crewmen and seven of thirteen passengers. The pilot of the plane, which was flying in from New York, was blamed. Investigators said he apparently failed to fly with enough speed to prevent engine stall while coming in for a landing in dangerously icy weather.

LIST OF TEN
FIRE DISASTERS

1. **Iroquois Theater Fire:** The worst theater fire in United States history—602 killed—took place on Dec. 30, 1903, in Chicago's Iroquis Theater, a building advertised as "absolutely fireproof." The musical that afternoon was "Mr. Blue Beard," starring Eddie Foy and Annabelle Whitford. The audience was big—1,900. Shortly after the second act began, a footlight ignited a curtain. Foy rushed to center stage and called for calm. But the fire quickly spread, and the stage's asbestos curtain became stuck as it was lowered. Several doors leading out of the theater were locked. Worse yet, many doors opened only inward—against the press of bodies trying to exit. The crowd panicked. Hundreds were trampled. As a result of the Iroquis fire, Chicago's fire code for theaters was completely revamped. Among the changes: all exit doors would have to swing outward.

2. **The Great Chicago Fire:** Chicago was destroyed. A more magnificent Chicago was born. The great fire raged from October 8 to October 10 and almost completely leveled four square miles of the city, including the teeming downtown. It started about 9 p.m., on the Near Southwest Side, probably in Mrs. O'Leary's barn—now

Looking southwest from Randolph and Wabash after the Chicago Fire of 1871. *(Gift of Herman Kogan)*

the site of the Chicago Fire Department Training Academy at 558 W. DeKoven—and swept northeast to Lincoln Park at Fullerton Avenue, then the city limit. Chicago was a tinderbox—dry wood buildings in a season of drought. It succumbed easily to the flames carried on dry thirty-mile-an-hour winds. The fire's toll: 250 or more dead, 100,000 homeless, 18,000 buildings destroyed, $200 million in property damage. But that story about the cow and lantern? It was probably nothing more than a newsman's tall tale.

3. **Our Lady of the Angels Fire:** It was called "the fire that couldn't happen." At 2:25 p.m., on Dec. 1, 1958, just thirty-five minutes before school was to be dismissed for the day, a fire broke out at Our Lady of the Angels Catholic School. Ninety-two children and three nuns were killed. The fire, of unknown origins, started in a pile of paper stored illegally at the bottom of a rear stairway in the two-story school at 3820 W. Iowa Ave. The teachers smelled the smoke, but told their students to remain in their seats. By the time they realized the severity of the situation, it was too late. Children on the first floor were able to escape when the alarm finally sounded, but many on the second floor were trapped by the smoke and heat. As a result of the fire, Chicago's fire code for schools was strengthened greatly.

4. **La Salle Hotel Fire:** Maybe it was a discarded cigarette. Or maybe an electrical short circuit. Nobody really knows. But when a fire broke out in the La Salle Hotel shortly after midnight on the morning of June 6, 1946, sixty-one guests were killed. It stands as the worst hotel fire in Chicago history.

5. **Skid Row Fire:** On Feb. 12, 1955, a fire razed the Barton Hotel, on West Madison Street, Chicago's old Skid Row, killing twenty-nine men. The fire allegedly was started at about 1:30 a.m., on the hotel's second floor by a seventy-year-old man who dropped cigarette ash into the alcohol solution he was using to massage his legs. About twenty residents survived, some fleeing in their underwear into the sub-zero cold night.

6. **Stockyards Fire:** On Dec. 22, 1910, Chief Fire Marshal James Horan, twenty-one of his firefighters and three civilians were killed by an explosion in a South Side stockyards fire. It was—and remains—the Fire Department's greatest loss of life in a fire. The firefighters were standing beneath a metal canopy on a platform used as a loading dock for rail cars when an explosion rocked a six-story brick building nearby. The canopy fell on the firefighters, crushing many of them, and part of the building collapsed onto the loading dock. A buildup of gases, heat and smoke inside the building, located on Forty-third Street between Loomis and Packers, apparently triggered the explosion. A plaque honoring the

dead firefighters hangs in Room 105 in City Hall, the department's headquarters. A second huge stockyards fire hit on May 19, 1934, spreading over eight blocks.

7. **Lake Street Fire of Oct. 19, 1858:** Twenty-two people were killed when a fire that started in a brothel swept through a big chunk of Chicago's old business district, Lake and South Water streets, destroying all stores, warehouses and rooming houses. At a mass funeral for the victims, the Rev. W.W. King said, "What we have just witnessed is but a slight breaking out of the volcanic fires burning under our feet. It is shameful to witness that complicity between authority and vice and crime by which our city is cursed and degraded."

8. **The Cold Storage Building Fire:** Icemaker to the Columbian Exposition of 1893, it was called the "greatest refrigerator on earth." It was 130-by-255 feet and had a skating rink on an upper story. Fire struck the building on July 10, 1893, when exposed wooden elements of its smokestack ignited. Seventeen firefighters were killed when the tower collapsed with them on it. A monument to the firefighters stands in Oak Woods Cemetery on the South Side.

Last But Not Least: The last home destroyed by the Chicago Fire of 1871 was that of Dr. John H. Foster. His home was on land bounded by Lincoln Park, and Belden, Fullerton and Clark streets.

---

9. **Goodyear Blimp Fire:** The Goodyear blimp *Wingfoot* was coasting over the Loop one day—July 21, 1919—when flames from burning engine oil ignited it's hydrogen-filled envelope. Boom! The blimp exploded. Thousands in the Loop watched in horror as the flaming ship crashed through a skylight and into the main banking room of the Illinois Trust and Savings Bank, at LaSalle and Jackson (now part of the Continental Illinois National Bank & Trust Co.). Twelve people were killed, nine of them bank employees and three of them blimp passengers.

10. **614 W. Hubbard Street Fire:** On Jan. 28, 1961, nine Chicago firefighters were killed when one outer wall of this burning six-story building collapsed and tumbled onto the roof of an adjacent two-story building. Several firefighters standing on the lower roof were trapped by the falling rubble. When other firefighters rushed to their aid, the roof caved in from the weight of the debris and all were killed. "My God, my people are under there," shouted a deputy fire marshal, Harry Mohr. A baking supply company and a glass company occupied the six-story building. Three other Chicago fires—the 419 W. Superior St. fire on July 8, 1943, the South

Side's Mickleberry Food Products Co. fire on Feb. 7, 1968 and the Rosenbaum Brothers fire on May 11, 1939—also resulted in nine deaths each.

Air Raid? What Air Raid? Chicago's air raid sirens have never been sounded in an emergency, which is a darn good thing because most of them don't work anyway. More than half of the city's ninety-three emergency warning sirens were found to be broken in 1991. The problem is so bad, in fact, that the Chicago Fire Department has a contingency plan to pull their trucks into the streets and turn on the truck sirens during a disaster. City officials say state and federal funds needed for repairs have dried up.

McCORMICK PLACE FIRE

Chicago's first McCormick Place, an exposition center recognized nationally for its state-of-the art design, burned to the ground on Jan. 16,

McCormick Place after the Jan. 16, 1967, fire that destroyed the $120 million "fireproof" building. *(Photo by Bob Kotalik)*

1967. A watchman, Kenneth Goodman, thirty-two, was killed. The ten-acre lakefront building, described by its designers as fireproof, was only six years old. The tremendous blaze started at about 2 a.m., in a drapery and spread with explosive violence, destroying the $120-million building and 1,236 exhibits set up for the National Houseware Manufacturers Association show. The hall had no sprinkler system in its main exhibit area and no fireproofing around its overhead steel beams. In addition, several crucial fire hydrants were frozen. Mayor Richard J. Daley vowed the same day to rebuild a bigger and better McCormick Place, and he did.

THOSE LEERY O'LEARYS

More than a century after the Chicago Fire of 1871, the descendants of Mrs. O'Leary are still leery. They don't pose for pictures much, do interviews or in other ways trade on their famous name. They have been burned, they say, in more ways than one. "We don't say too much," says one great-granddaughter. "It's something Grandpa instilled in us. It's just that the family was hurt."

The shame of it all, contemporary historians generally agree, is that Mrs. O'Leary and her cow likely got a bum rap. The fire almost undoubtedly started in the family barn, but there is little evidence that Mrs. O'Leary was milking her cow at the time. To the contrary, in the only two interviews Mrs. O'Leary ever gave—both under oath—she said that she and her husband, Patrick, had gone to bed early that night. The legend of the cow may have been concocted by an imaginative newspaper reporter, and the fire's real cause remains unknown.

Fed up with the unrelenting notoriety, Catherine and Patrick O'Leary fled the old neighborhood to the Back of the Yards, where they hoped nobody would know them. Within days a carnival manager came calling. He offered Mrs. O'Leary big money to exhibit herself with a cow. She slammed the door in his face. The family moved on to Canaryville, hoping to lose themselves among fellow Irish immigrants. But one day, an agent sent by P. T. Barnum dropped by to ask Mrs. O'Leary to join the circus. She threatened him with a broomstick.

Catherine O'Leary died July 3, 1895. A reporter stopped by the house to ask questions. "You are mistaken," said the person who answered the door, before slamming it shut. "The Mrs. O'Leary who died here today only came to America from Cork six years ago."

The O'Learys had five children, but only one was well known—Big Jim, a famous stockyards gambler. Overlooked was Cornelius, known as "Pudge," who on a Saturday night in 1885 got drunk in Canaryville and shot his girlfriend, Mary Ann Snyder, thirty, and his own sister, Mary O'Leary Scully, twenty-eight.

LIST OF TEN
SHIPPING DISASTERS

1. **The Eastland:** On the sunny morning of July 24, 1915, some 2,500 employees and families of the Western Electric Company crowded aboard the *Eastland* for a holiday cruise and picnic in Michigan City, Indiana. The steamer was drifting away from a dock on the Chicago River at La Salle Street when it began to list to port, leaning toward the north side of the river. It righted itself, but then listed again. Hundreds of frantic passengers rushed to the listing side. This act decided their fate, for now the boat completely rolled over on its side. Hundreds of passengers penned in below deck were drowned. Many more were crushed to death in the rush to escape by a staircase. Death toll: 812 men, women, boys and girls. The Eastland, renamed the USS Wilmette, was later used as a Navy training vessel. In 1946, it was sold for $2,500 to a scrap iron firm.

Passengers scramble for safety after the steamboat *Eastland* suddenly turned on its side in the Chicago River. Within minutes, 812 people had died.

2. **The Lady Elgin:** It was the worst disaster in the history of the Great Lakes. Death toll: 287. On Sept. 8, 1860, the *Lady Elgin*, a 300-foot all-wood luxury sidewheel steamboat, sank in a storm ten miles off Wilmette. The steamer, enroute from Chicago to Milwaukee on a party cruise, was cutting through deadly fogs and frigid waves at about 2:30 a.m., when it was struck by a two-masted lumber schooner, the *Augusta of Oswego*. The *Lady Elgin* was split nearly in half. In 1989, an adventurous salvage diver, Harry Zych, discovered the wreck of the ship on the lake's bottom.

3. **The Seabird:** A sidewheel steamer, the *Seabird* made her first run of the spring season to Chicago on April 9, 1868, after wintering

at Manitowoc, Wisconsin. In the early hours of dawn, the ship caught fire after a coal porter tossed smoldering ashes into the lake. One ember landed on the straw-packed freight, instantly touching off a blaze. The ship sank seven to eight miles east of Waukegan. Money, jewelry and gold bullion in the ship's safe would today, by some estimates, be worth $100,000 or more. All but one of the 100 passengers perished.

Lake Cemetery: Lake Michigan is one of the Midwest's great ship grave-yards because the capricious wind over the narrow lake blew ships into low water, where they capsized. An estimated 8,500 vessels sank in Lake Michigan from 1679 to 1947. Most of those ships carted supplies and raw materials to the early settlers of Lake Michigan's shores, as well as ore, coal, iron and grain to new Midwestern industries. Only rarely did a ship haul a truly precious cargo, although some treasure hunters claim there is as much as $1 billion in gold, silver, copper and jewelry littering the Great Lakes.

---

4. **The Alpena:** A 653-ton passenger steamer, she was last seen in a storm on Lake Michigan on Oct. 16, 1880, thirty miles from Chicago, on her way from Grand Haven, Michigan, to Chicago. Some wreckage of the ship was found near Holland, Michigan. The ship's safe, though never recovered, was reported to have contained gold and silver now worth as much as $100,000. Ninety-seven lives were lost. In the same storm, the David A. Wells, a 311-ton schooner, also was lost, about seven miles northeast of Chicago. Eight lives were lost.

5. **The Hippocampus:** This ship, sailing from St. Joseph, Michigan, to Chicago, rolled over in a storm just north of Michigan City, Indiana. Apparently, her crew had loaded too much of its cargo—peaches—on deck, making the ship top-heavy. Twenty-five lives were lost.

6. **The Globe:** On the morning of Nov. 8, 1860, the steamer *Globe* exploded at Hale's dock, Clark and Wells streets, killing the crew of twenty-five and blasting debris eight blocks away.

7. **The L.R. Doty:** A 2,056-ton steamer, the *Doty* chugged north out of Chicago in the fall of 1898, loaded with corn and towing a small schooner. As best as can be determined, the tow line broke in a storm and the *Doty* was broached when it tried to turn and recover the schooner. Seventeen died.

8. **Material Service:** This specially designed self-propelled motor ship worked a route between Muskegan and suburban Lemont, hauling gravel, limestone and other building material for the Material Service Corp. On July 29, 1936, it was caught in a cross wave 1,900

feet outside Calumet Harbor and went under. At least fifteen were killed.

Captured Sub: Lake Michigan's most exotic shipwreck is a captured World War I German submarine brought to Chicago as part of a local war bond drive. In 1921, the U.S. Navy intentionally sank the submarine a few miles offshore from the Great Lakes Naval Training Center near Waukegan. The ship that "killed" the sub, ironically, was the notorious Eastland, which had been salvaged by the Navy and renamed the USS Wilmette.

---

9. **The David Dows:** She was the only five-mast schooner and the largest schooner ever to sail the Great Lakes. The David Dows was wrecked Nov. 8, 1889, in Lake Michigan off Ninety-fifth Street. Fourteen crewmen died.

10. **The Wells Burt:** A 756-ton schooner with a cargo of coal, she was lost off Evanston on May 20, 1883. Ten died.

Smoke on the Water: While building a tunnel below Lake Michigan at Seventy-third Street in 1909, the city erected a wooden temporary crib on the line of the tunnel about one mile from shore. Scores of workmen lived in the crib to save the time and trouble of ferrying to and from shore each day. On the morning of January 8 in that year, the crib caught fire and there were no boats at hand to rescue the trapped workmen. Seventy men were burned or drowned. A few survivors leaped into the lake and clung to ice floes until tugs from shore rescued them.

KILLER TORNADOES

Oak Lawn Twister: On a Friday afternoon, April 21, 1967, several tornadoes spun like raging dervishes through northeastern Illinois, tearing up parts of suburban Oak Lawn, Hometown, Chicago's Southwest Side and—eighty miles to the northwest—the little town of Belvidere. The Oak Lawn twister touched down first on a house at 103rd Street and 83rd Avenue in Palos Hills, then traced a sixteen-mile course to Lake Michigan at 79th Street in exactly sixteen minutes. It carved out a half-block-wide section through Palos Hills and ripped through a 95th Street drive-in theater. Moving into Oak Lawn, it dropped directly on one of the town's busiest intersections—95th Street and Southwest Highway. Autos were thrown through the air, the Fairway supermarket was leveled and a motel, restaurant and bus station were destroyed. In Oak Lawn, thirty-three people perished. The tornado moved on through Evergreen Park and Homewood, doing huge damage to property but killing nobody, and hurled down 79th Street. Two more victims—both Chicagoans—were claimed. On that same day, another tornado ripped through Belvidere in Boone County, killing twenty-four—mostly children caught running to school buses.

Plainfield Twister: On Aug. 28, 1990, a twister ripped through the heart of Plainfield, one of the Chicago area's oldest towns, destroying the public high school, a Catholic church and elementary school, most of a new subdivision and an apartment complex. Hundreds of homes were lost and twenty-nine people died. The tornado touched down first in the late afternoon on a tiny white duplex in the cornfields northwest of Plainfield, on U.S. 30. It roared for fifteen miles southeast straight through Plainfield, whipped through the Lily Cache subdivision on the outskirts of town, tore up part of unincorporated Crest Hill, and fizzled to a stop just before hitting Joliet.

Worst Illinois Twister: The so-called Tri-State Tornado of March 18, 1925, lasted an unprecedented four hours. It ripped across Missouri, Illinois and Indiana, killing a record 600 people, 400 of them in Illinois. A study of Illinois tornadoes in the last fifty years found that their average length on the ground was fifteen minutes.

County-by-County Death Count: Since 1916, according to the National Weather Service, fifteen killer tornadoes have claimed fifty-nine lives in Cook County, three in Du Page, two in Lake, seven in Kane, one in McHenry and thirty-five in Will.

EXTREMES

Worst Bus Disaster: Seven Joliet teenagers were on their way to a Bruce Springsteen concert in Soldier Field on Aug. 9, 1985, when their car collided with a CTA bus on Lake Shore Drive near McCormick Place. All seven teens were killed. A team of Northwestern University investigators concluded that the car had turned sharply in front of the bus, making the accident unavoidable.

Worst Car Crash: Seven people, including four children, were killed on Sept. 3, 1984, when a southbound auto jumped a concrete median on Lake Shore Drive and plunged into an oncoming car, sparking an explosion and fire. In all, five cars were involved in the 9 p.m., accident in the 1800 north block of the Outer Drive.

Worst L Disaster: It was rush-hour on a Friday afternoon, 5:29 p.m., on Feb. 4, 1977. An eight-car Lake-Dan Ryan L train squealed around the Lake-Wabash curve at no more than ten miles an hour. Directly ahead was a stopped Ravenswood train. The conductor slammed on his emergency brakes, but too late. His train churned into the train ahead, and four cars fell slowly off the track and into the street below.

The worst L disaster occurred on Feb. 4, 1977, when four cars of a Lake-Dan Ryan L train derailed at Lake and Wabash during the evening rush hour. *(Photo by Jack Lenhan)*

Eleven people were killed. The National Transporatation Safety Board blamed the motorman for going past a red signal without permission from the control tower. The motorman was fired.

Worst Streetcar Disaster: On May 25, 1950, a streetcar and a jack-knifed gasoline truck collided at Sixty-third and State streets, killing thirty-three people. The streetcar, truck, several autos and eight buildings all burst into flames. Contributing to the high death toll were the "safety bars" placed across the streetcar windows to keep children from poking their arms or heads out the windows.

Wooden L Wreck: Nov. 24, 1936, marked the beginning of the end for wooden L cars in Chicago. It was on that day that an all-steel North Shore-bound L train plowed the entire length through the wooden last coach of an Evanston Express at the Granville station, killing eleven and injuring fifty-nine. In the days that followed, the public demanded the city abolish wooden cars. But the Chicago Rapid Transit Company— forerunner to the Chicago Transit Authority—owned thousands of wooden cars, so the transition to steel cars came slowly. In 1956, four of the wooden cars went up in flames, killing two more passengers. Chicago's last wooden L car, Car 2925, made its final run on a Sunday afternoon twenty-one years after the fatal wreck—Dec. 1, 1957.

Worst Train Disaster. On Monday, Oct. 30, 1972, an Illinois Central Railroad express commuter train, packed to rush-hour capacity, slammed into the rear of a local commuter train at the Twenty-seventh

Street station. Forty-five people were killed and sixty-six were seriously injured. The train, equipped with a new kind of brake "softened" for the comfort of passengers, overshot the station, backed up to let off passengers, and was struck from behind by an older, smaller train, which telescoped into the first train. As firefighters worked for six hours with blowtorches, trying to free survivors, a Catholic priest moved among them, administering the church's last rites.

Deadliest Explosion: Thirty-five employees of a Haber Corp. plant, 908 W. North Ave., were killed on April 16, 1953, when the place exploded like a bomb. The explosion in the manufacturing plant, unofficially accepted by city officials as the most deadly in Chicago history, was started by sparks flying from a polishing machine into an exhaust vent.

PAST TENSE

90 Die in Fire
By Hugh Hough
(Chicago Sun-Times, Dec. 2, 1958)

87 children.

And three of the nuns who were their teachers.

That, as near as any informed person could tell, was the terrible arithmetic of the fire that swept Our Lady of Angels school at 3820 W. Iowa Monday just 18 minutes before the day's final schoolbell.

It was the worst fire toll since the Iroquois Theater disaster of 1903, which claimed 602 lives.

Monday's school blaze, like the Iroquois fire, stunned the city and the nation.

Sources: Tom Seibel and Hugh Hough of the *Chicago Sun-Times;* Herb Hoffman, tornado expert for the National Weather Service; Mike Cosgrove, public relations for the Chicago Fire Department; Harry Zych of the American Diving and Salvage Company; The National Transportation Safety Board; City of Chicago Department of Aviation; Bill Utter of the Chicago Transit Authority.

MEDICINE

FIRSTS

■ The first recorded epidemic in Chicago came in 1832 when troops arrived to fight the Black Hawk War and brought cholera with them.

■ The first city hospital in Chicago was built for smallpox cases in 1843 near North Avenue and the lake.

Clout Kills: Dr. Theodore B. Sachs, director of the city's first tuberculosis sanitarium, committed suicide in 1916 to protest political interference in the management of medical institutions. Mayor William Hale "Big Bill" Thompson's political machine looked at city hospitals and clinics as places to put political pals instead of medical professionals. After Sachs' death, Thompson claimed Sachs killed himself because his financial accounts turned up short—a charge later proven to be unfounded.

■ Dr. David Jones Peck was the first black American to receive a degree from a U.S. medical school—in 1847 at what is now Rush-Presbyterian-St. Luke's Medical Center.

■ Dr. Amante Rongetti, who operated the Ashland Boulevard Hospital during the 1920s, was the first Illinois physician to be convicted of murder relating to an abortion case. In 1928, he was sentenced to the electric chair for the murder of a nineteen-year-old woman who died after he performed an abortion on her. The Illinois Supreme Court later reversed the conviction, but Rongetti eventually was sentenced to prison for manslaughter.

■ The first heart transplant was performed on a dog in 1904 by the University of Chicago's Dr. Alexis Carrel. The dog survived for two hours. Carrel won the Nobel Peace Prize in 1912—America's first in physiology.

■ Dr. James Bryan Herrick discovered sickle cell anemia in 1908 at what is now Rush-Presbyterian-St. Luke's Medical Center.

■ Dr. William D. Shorey was the first in the U.S. to reattach a severed hand (1962), at Rush-Presbyterian-St.Luke's Medical Center.

■ The world's first successful living-donor liver transplant was done in November 1989 by Dr. Christoph Broelsch, professor of surgery at the University of Chicago.

> **Women Doctors:** The Women's Medical College of Chicago was founded in 1870 and closed in 1902, but not before it opened the door to the medical profession for women. Mary E. Bates, a graduate of the college, was the first woman to win an appointment as an intern in a Chicago hospital. Slowly, more followed.

■ A dieting Elgin man who lost 170 pounds donated his extra skin to the University of Chicago Hospitals' burn unit in June 1988. This is thought to be the first case of a living non-related skin donor.

■ Nathaniel Kleitman first identified REM (Rapid Eye Movement) sleep, the period of dreaming, in 1953 at the University of Chicago.

■ In experiments done in Oak Park and Evanston from 1946 to 1961, Dr. James Roy Blaney and Dr. Iden Hill paved the way for the fluoridation of water as a way to prevent tooth decay.

■ The nation's first blood bank was established in 1937 by Dr. Bernard Fantus at Cook County Hospital

Dr. Daniel Hale Williams, founder of the first black hospital in the U.S., was the first surgeon to successfully operate on the heart.

■ The nation's first trauma center, designed to give specialized treatment to victims of accidents and violence, was established at Cook County Hospital in 1966.

■ Cook County Hospital in 1973 became the first hospital to use an all-frozen blood bank system.

■ Dr. Austin M. Curtis (1868-1939) was the first black doctor at Cook County Hospital (1896).

■ Dr. Daniel Hale Williams (1856-1931) was the first black member of the American College of Surgeons,. He also founded the first black hospital, Provident, in the U.S. and was the first surgeon to successfully operate on the heart.

EXTREMES

■ The most babies born in one year in Illinois was 239,871 in 1959.

■ The most deaths in Illinois in one year was 112,905 in 1918.

■ Spitting on the L ended in 1918 during what is believed to have been the worst epidemic in Chicago history. From Sept. 21 to Nov. 23, 1918, 8,510 people died of influenza and pneumonia. At its worst, 381 died on one day (Oct. 17). "Vigorous measures were taken to combat this epidemic. Influenza was made reportable on Sept. 16. Public funerals were prohibited on Oct. 12. Smoking on street and elevated railroad cars was prohibited on Oct. 13. This order was not rescinded after the epidemic with the result that smoking together with the accompanying spitting nuisance on these cars has been abolished in Chicago since that date," reads a publication of the state Department of Public Health.

■ The world's largest dental library — 40,000 books, journals and references — is in Chicago at the American Dental Association, according to the ADA.

■ The Journal of the American Medical Association (JAMA), published by the Chicago-based American Medical Association, is the world's most widely read medical journal, according to the AMA. JAMA is printed in seven languages and circulated in 132 countries.

■ The University of Illinois at Chicago College of Medicine is the largest medical school in the country in terms of enrollment, with 1,269 students. It also has the largest minority enrollment (African-American, Asian-American and Hispanic) of any medical school in the country except for traditionally African-American medical schools.

■ Nearly 17,000 Illinois people were diagnosed with salmonella in 1985 was the largest outbreak of salmonella in United States history.

Deep Freeze Woman: Dorothy Mae Stevens Anderson, a South Side woman whose *Sun-Times* obituary referred to her as the "deep freeze" woman, was once known through headlines around the world. On Feb. 8, 1951, she was found in 12-below-zero weather lying in a South Side alley. Her body temperature had dropped to 64 degrees and her pulse was twelve. Her blood had turned to mudlike sludge and her blood pressure couldn't be read. Despite this, she was revived by doctors at Michael Reese Hospital and lived until 1974, although both her legs and most of her fingers were amputated because of the exposure. Since Anderson had been drinking that night, doctors theorized the alcohol acted as antifreeze and saved her life. Mrs. Anderson once said a man later told her he had given her knockout drops. She also said originally a DOA (dead on arrival) tag was put on her big toe, but fortunately the morgue attendant was out for lunch and left her on a stretcher instead of shoving her into a freezer compartment. While she was lying there, a young intern happened to notice her eyelids moving.

BIRTHS AND DEATHS (1990)

Births—in Illinois: 191,735.

Deaths—in Illinois: 100,880.

Births—Chicago, 58,533; Cook (excluding Chicago), 43,234; Du Page, 13,030; Lake, 9,294; Kane, 6,948; Will, 3,301; McHenry, 1,787.

Deaths—Chicago, 24,993; Cook (excluding Chicago), 21,901; Du Page, 4,402; Lake, 3,293; Kane, 2,028; Will, 1,912; McHenry, 981.

LIST OF TEN LEADING CAUSES OF DEATH (1988)

The top ten lists for Chicago and the rest of the state are the same:

1. Heart disease

2. Cancer

3. Cerebrovascular (diseases of the vascular system)

4. Accidents (motor vehicle and accidents of all kinds)

5. Pneumonia and influenza

6. Pulmonary diseases (such as emphysema)

7. Diabetes

8. Birth defects and other problems at birth

9. Cirrhosis of the liver

10. Suicide

President's Doctor: Dr. Roswell Park (1852-1914), a onetime intern at Cook County Hospital and medical school professor at Rush Medical College and Northwestern University Medical School, operated on President William McKinley after the president was shot in 1901. McKinley didn't recover.

TEN INFECTIOUS DISEASES MOST REPORTED TO THE ILLINOIS DEPARTMENT OF PUBLIC HEALTH IN 1990

Illinois

1. Strep throat	40,170
2. Chicken pox	31,189
3. Salmonella	3,231
4. Scarlet fever	2,645
5. Hepatitis A	1,726
6. Giardia[1]	1,454
7. Measles	1,356
8. Shigellosis[2]	1,126
9. Aseptic meningitis[3]	934
10. Hepatitis B[4]	596

[1]Giardia: generally an infection of the upper small intestine. It affects children and it's most often associated with poor sanitation and hygiene.

[2]Shigellosis: most common in children aged one to four, it's a bacteria affecting the intestinal tract that is often associated with poor hygiene and sanitation.

[3]Aseptic meningitis: spread by discharges from the nose and throat, mostly due to viruses that attack the membranes that cover the brain and spinal cord.

[4]Hepatitis B: liver ailment that can be spread by sexual contact or by blood to blood contact.

Chicago

1. Strep throat	1,523
2. Chicken pox	1,345
3. Salmonella	1,137
4. Hepatitis A	1,119
5. Measles	645
6. Shigellosis	532
7. Hepatitis B	285

8. Giardia	169
9. Scarlet fever	110
10. Aseptic meningitis	100

Cook (including Chicago)

1. Strep throat	10,746
2. Chicken pox	8,125
3. Salmonella	1,759
4. Hepatitis A	1,391
5. Measles	937
6. Shigellosis	729
7. Giardia	374
8. Hepatitis B	357
9. Aseptic meningitis	300
10. Haemophilus influenzae[1]	102

[1]Haemophilus influenzae is a bacteria that can attack different parts of the body; a vaccine is available and recommended for all young children. Vaccines are available for measles and haemophilus influenzae.

Other Five Counties (Will, Lake, Du Page, McHenry, Kane)

1. Strep throat	10,077
2. Chicken pox	8,315
3. Scarlet fever	672
4. Salmonella	590
5. Giardia	462
6. Aseptic meningitis	372
7. Measles	312
8. Shigellosis	221
9. Hepatitis A	139
10. Pertusis[1]	57

[1]Pertusis: Whooping cough. There is a vaccine.

All the above tables do not include sexually transmitted diseases.

Patented Life: In 1980, the U.S. Supreme Court ruled that living things produced by "genetic engineering" can be patented. The justices ruled in the case of Ananda M. Chakrabarty, who developed a bacterium one-ten-thousandth of an inch long that eats crude oil. He invented it for General Electric Company, but worked for the University of Illinois at Chicago when the ruling was made.

SEXUALLY TRANSMITTED DISEASES, 1990

	Gonorrhea	Early Syphilis	Chlamydia
State	38,195	3,598	24,145
Chicago	24,390	3,057	10,626
Cook	27,315	3,357	11,903
DuPage	157	20	555
Will	681	10	248
Lake	756	20	1,202
McHenry	13	0	43
Kane	454	30	326

AIDS

In 1990 there were 1,214 reported cases of AIDS in Illinois. Cook including Chicago (849) had 972 cases, Lake County: 15; McHenry County: 6; Kane County: 25; Du Page County: 37; Will County: 11.

Total cases through March 31, 1991: 5,029.

Deaths through March 31, 1991: 3,262.

DOCTORS IN ILLINOIS AND SIX COUNTY AREA

Number of doctors (not working for the government): Illinois: 26,349; Cook: 16,110; Du Page 2,218; Kane 501; Lake 1,139; McHenry 170; Will 339.

What are doctors paid? In 1989 the average physician income nationwide was $155,800 (median income was $125,000). Chicago area doctors were below that, with an average income of $138,000 and a median income of $114,000.

HOSPITALS

LIST OF TEN LARGEST GENERAL COMMUNITY HOSPITALS IN THE CHICAGO AREA
(by number of all services staffed beds)

Hospital	City	Number of Staffed Beds
1. Cook County Hospital	Chicago	898
2. Rush-Presbyterian-St. Luke's Medical Center	Chicago	853
3. Christ Hospital and Medical Center	Oak Lawn	800
4. Northwestern Memorial Hospital	Chicago	676
5. Michael Reese Hospital and Medical Center	Chicago	675
6. Lutheran General Hospital	Park Ridge	616
7. Ingalls Memorial Hospital	Harvey	571
8. University of Chicago Hospitals	Chicago	546
9. Loyola University Medical Center	Maywood	516
10. St. Francis Hospital of Evanston	Evanston	478

NUMBER OF HOSPITALS AND BEDS IN SIX COUNTY AREA

County	No. of Hospitals	No. of Staffed Beds
1. Cook County	65	20,727
2. Lake County	7	1,481
3. Du Page County	6	1,698
4. Kane County	6	1,210

County	No. of Hospitals	No. of Staffed Beds
5. McHenry County	3	319
6. Will County	2	721

COOK COUNTY HOSPITAL
1835 W. HARRISON AVE.

There are thirteen buildings in the Cook County Hospital complex at 1835 W. Harrison Avenue. The oldest was built in 1910, the newest in 1982. In 1990 there were 33,841 admissions, 115,672 adult emergency room visits and 61,463 pediatric emergency room visits. The hospital has a staff of over 500 physicians.

M.E.: Cook is the only county in Illinois to have a medical examiner. How is that different from a county coroner? A coroner is elected while the medical examiner is appointed by the county board president. A medical examiner also has to be a forensic pathologist, a coroner does not. Cook County decided on a medical examiner in a 1972 referendum. The first appointment came in 1976.

OFFICE OF THE COOK COUNTY MEDICAL EXAMINER

Medical Examiner: Dr. Robert J. Stein. Salary: $124,000 a year.

Budget: 1991, $5.5 million.

Employees: 118, including 30 full-time investigators.
The medical examiner's office is called into about 12,000 death cases a year and "takes jurisidiction" on about 6,000 deaths. The office performs about 4,500 autopsies a year. About three bodies a year go unidentified.

THE BIG FOUR IN CHICAGO

American Medical Association
Headquartered in Chicago at 515 N. State St., the AMA is a service organization of physicians with 287,659 members, or more than 48 percent of the nation's 600,789 physicians. Founded in 1847, it has grown to an organization with 1,143 employees and a 1991 operating budget of $186 million. Its library of 110,000 books and subscriptions to 2,500 journals is one of the nation's largest medical libraries.

American Hospital Association

Headquartered in Chicago at 840 N. Lake Shore Drive. Founded in 1899, it now has 800 Chicago-based employees and a budget of $85 million. Hospitals representing 85 to 95 percent of the nation's hospital beds are members. This includes most of the 6,500 hospitals nationwide. It also has 60,000 personal members.

American Dental Association

Headquartered in Chicago at 211 E. Chicago Ave. Founded in 1859, it now has 400 full and part-time employees and a budget of $42 million. The professional association, dedicated to the science and art of dentistry, has 140,000 members, or about 75 percent of the nation's dentists.

American College of Surgeons

Headquartered in Chicago at 55 E. Erie St. Founded in 1913, the American College of Surgeons is a "scientific and educational association of surgeons" with 180 employees and a budget of $23.3 million. It has about 50,000 members or "Fellows" and 2,000 "Associate Fellows."

Sources: *Chicago Sun-Times* medical writer Howard Wolinsky; *Sun-Times* and *Daily News* clips, *History of Chicago* by A.T.Andreas; University of Chicago; The Illinois State Medical Society and its Great Moments in Illinois Medicine series; the local medical schools and professional associations named above; Illinois Department of Public Health; Metropolitan Chicago Healthcare Council; *Chicago and Its makers;* Office of the Cook County Medical Examiner; The state's Department of Public Health's *The Rise and Fall of Disease in Illinois* (1927).

GREAT FEATS

FIRSTS

■ Wearing a skintight "Spiderman" costume, Daniel Goodwin, a mountain climber and actor, was the first person to scale the outside of the 110-story Sears Tower—the tallest building in the world. He made his ascent on May 25, 1981, with a ladder to the first floor. He used suction cups and straps to travel the 1,454 feet. It took less than seven and a half hours. In preparation for the climb he ran, lifted weights and ate little or no meat. His diet included grain and lots of sea algae. The costume cost him $450. In November 1981, Spiderman tried to climb the John Hancock Center. Trying to stop him, firemen poured water on Spiderman, which prompted an onlooker to say, "That was the most stupid thing I ever saw."

■ The original Ferris wheel was built on the Midway of the 1893 Columbian Exposition. Built by George Washington Gale Ferris, its diameter was 250 feet and it could spin as many as 1,400 passengers.

■ On Oct. 12, 1960, Commonwealth Edison dedicated the nation's first investor-owned commercial nuclear power plant (Dresden I) near Morris, Illinois.

Tower of Power: Commonwealth Edison generates more electricity from nuclear power than any other utility in the country. Of the 115 or so nuclear power plants running nationwide, Commonwealth Edison has 12. It generates 80 percent of its power from nuclear reactors—the nation as a whole generates about 20 percent. Edison generates about 11.5 percent of the nation's nuclear energy. It also temporarily stores more nuclear waste fuel on site than any of the nation's other utilities.

■ Chicago's first water system began sending water through wooden pipes beneath city streets in 1842.

■ A Henry Moore sculpture at about Fifty-seventh and Ellis (in the 5600 block) marks the site where Italian physicist Enrico Fermi headed a team of physicists who achieved the first controlled nuclear chain reaction on Dec. 2, 1942.

EXTREMES

■ Fermilab boasts the world's most powerful atom smasher. The particle accelerator at Fermilab, forty miles west of Chicago near Batavia, has an energy of 1.8 trillion electron volts, about three times the power of its closest competititor, the Cern atom smasher in Switzerland. The superconducting super collider scheduled to be built in Texas will be more powerful, but it won't be operable for another ten years.

Disppearing Town: On Nov. 26, 1969, the far west suburban town of Weston died for the sake of science. At first the 421 residents of Weston thought bringing Fermilab into the area would help their economy. But the state kept promising more land to the federal government in an effort to outbid other states. Eventually the state offered 6,800 acres, including Weston. On that November night, the village board approved a resolution that cleared the way for the dissolution of their community. Fermilab now employs 2,300 people, including 326 scientists and 184 engineers.

■ The world's largest waste water treatment plant is the West-Southwest plant in Stickney, which treats 800 million gallons a day, according to the Metropolitan Water Reclamation District of Greater Chicago. It's designed to treat up to 1.2 billion gallons a day.

■ Chicago's James W. Jardine Water Purification Plant, 1000 E. Ohio, is the largest such plant (that uses a filtration process) in the world, according to the city. It pumps, on average, about 620 million gallons a day.

■ The most water ever pumped in a day by Chicago was on June 29, 1971, when the city pumped 1.76 billion gallons.

■ Argonne National Laboratory is trying to make the world's brightest light. Argonne, twenty-five miles southwest of the Loop, is building a $456 million lab that can examine matter with X-rays brighter than light from the sun's surface. Called the Advance Photon Source, it will be 10,000 times more powerful than existing X-ray sources. If it were in use today, it would be the world's brightest light.

■ Material Services Division of General Dynamics Corp.'s limestone quarry in south suburban Thornton lays claim to being the world's largest commercial quarry. It is 1 mile wide and 260 feet deep. Limestone has been quarried there since the 1830s.

Nose Holder: For 105 years the Union Stockyards, a square mile of stench and livestock running from Thirty-ninth to Forty-seventh street and from Halsted to Ashland, was a major supplier of meat to the nation. It went out of business in August 1971. Its first shipment—fifteen railroad cars of hogs—arrived on Dec. 26, 1865, and by the time it closed some 1 billion creatures had been slaughtered. Its peak year was 1924, when it received 18,653,539 head of livestock. For most Chicagoans, the most invigorating memory of the stockyards was its overpowering odor.

■ In 1893, the then world's largest telescope was on display at the Columbian Exposition. After the fair, it was moved to the Yerkes Observatory in Williams Bay, Wisconsin.

■ The world record for tunneling was set by a crew working on the Deep Tunnel flood control project in the summer of 1990. They dug 160 feet in twenty-four hours.

■ McCormick Place, which has a total of 1.6 million square feet of exhibit space, is the largest convention center in North America.

Nobel Winner: Charles G. Dawes, of Evanston, won the Nobel Peace Prize in 1925 along with Sir Austen Chamberlain. The award recognized his drawing of the so-called Dawes Plan, which provided for Germany's payment of reparations for its liability for World War I. Dawes was vice president (1925-29) under Calvin Coolidge.

CHICAGO'S SEVEN WONDERS

1. THE ILLINOIS AND MICHIGAN CANAL

Background: This huge project made Chicago. Yet all that's left of it in the city is an archeological dig near Ashland and the Chicago River in Bridgeport. The project was the Illinois and Michigan Canal. This, the first of many massive public works projects connected to Chicago, was built to link Lake Michigan to the Mississippi River.

Statistics: It took twelve years to build, ran ninety-six miles (almost twice the length of the Panama Canal), cost $6.5 million and required the efforts of 5,000 workers a year (many of them Irish immigrants). About 30,000 people traveled it annually in the early 1850s. The most cargo ever shipped on the canal was about a million tons in 1888. It was about six feet deep and sixty feet wide.

What's there now? The canal connected Lake Michigan to the Mississippi via the Illinois River. It started in Bridgeport and ran to La Salle-Peru. It's now the backbone of the Illinois and Michigan Canal National Heritage Corridor. Most of its Chicago length is covered by the Stevenson Expressway.

History: Even in 1836, when construction began, the idea for this canal was nothing new. Explorers Louis Jolliet and Father Jacques Marquette thought it was a great idea when they came to Chicago in 1673—only they thought it could be done with a canal running about half a league (1.5 miles).

Benefit: The canal helped Chicago avoid being in Wisconsin. Some historians argue that when state lines were drawn, Chicago was kept in Illinois so if a canal was built it would all be within one state's jurisdiction. It gave Chicago some good, early publicity, brought settlers here, and helped make Chicago a major transportation center. It also helped map out the city. In 1830, Chicago was surveyed so lots could be sold to help finance the canal. Few people, however, were willing to pay the $50 a lot for what is now downtown Chicago. Why should they when lots a mile a way were going for $1.50?

Detriment: It didn't really work well. It never brought that huge commercial trade promised by a linking of Lake Michigan and the Mississippi River.

Classic Quote: A 1923 *Daily News* article called the canal "Chicago's most colossal and tragic blunder—and one of her greatest achievements."

Pullman Lifts: Using 5,000 jackscrews, George Pullman, before he became known for his Pullman sleeping car, jacked up the Tremont House hotel in 1861 and raised it onto a higher foundation because street levels had been raised downtown to combat flooding and mud. The hotel was raised six feet, and not one pane of glass was cracked in the process.

---

2. CHICAGO IS A JACKED UP CITY

Sewage was a major problem for early Chicago. It spread disease and generally made rain a health hazard. In 1855, Ellis Sylvester Chesbrough, an engineer who is the father of Chicago sewers, hit upon the idea of making the Chicago River one huge city sewer. To do this the city needed to build sewers to flow into the river. To do that, the sewers had to be high enough to flow into the river. That meant raising virtually all the city streets, some by as much as twelve feet. As the sewers were raised, street levels started rising above the first floors

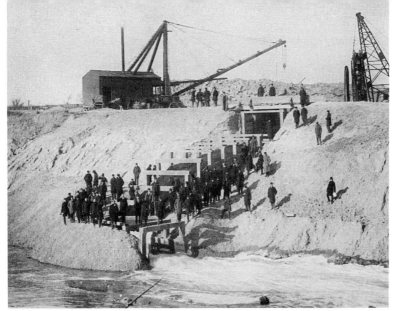

On January 2, 1900, Needle Dam was opened, allowing the Chicago River to flow into the newly completed Sanitary and Ship Canal. This was the first step to reversing the flow of the Chicago River and diverting sewage away from Lake Michigan.

of many Chicago buildings. That meant a good many buildings needed to be jacked up or have their first floor become their basement. Many owners chose to jack up their buildings and plop them down on new foundations. After street grades were raised in 1855 and 1857, the city had to fill in the streets around the sewers. That still wasn't done by the time of the Chicago Fire, so some of the debris from the fire was used to finish the job.

3. REVERSING THE RIVER

A six-inch rain hit Chicago in August 1885, filling the Chicago River and sending sewage far out into the lake past the water intake cribs. The city's water was fouled, and some 80,000 people died from typhoid, cholera and dysentery. This scared everybody enough to come up with a plan. The completion of the Illinois and Michigan Canal reversed the river when the conditions were right, but it wasn't permanent. Digging the I & M deeper in the early 1870s was an unsuccessful attempt to reverse the Chicago River and divert sewage water away from the lake. After the catastrophe of 1885, it was time to try it again.

By 1889 the Metropolitan Sanitary District had been formed to dig a new drainage ditch (the Sanitary & Ship Canal) and make it and the Chicago River flow away from the lake. That way the lake wouldn't be polluted, and the sewage would be diluted with fresh lake water. It took $40 million, eight years (1892 to 1900) and a work force of about

8,500 to finish the job. The crews blasted over 12 million cubic yards of rock and dug out close to 30 million cubic yards of earth. The twenty-eight-mile canal was dug twenty-four feet deep. And right before it was to open, Missouri went to court to stop it, arguing that the flow of sewage water through Illinois rivers into the Mississippi would threaten the St. Louis water supply. But before the suit was filed, the MSD board, some say hurriedly, opened the gates in Lockport for the new canal and the reversal took place.

Biggest misconception: The lock at the mouth of the Chicago River has nothing to do with reversing the flow of the river. It was put there in the 1930s because other states and Canada were worried Chicago would drain Lake Michigan by reversing the flow (even though that happened thirty years before). The amount of water that Chicago siphons from the lake is monitored.

- From 1908 to 1910, the 8 mile North Shore channel was dug.
- From 1911 to 1922, the 16.2 mile Calumet-Sag Canal was built.

4. BUILDING THE LAKEFRONT

From 1830 to 1933, Chicago created 5.6 square miles of new shoreline with landfill from such places as sand dunes and the rubble of the Chicago Fire. Some of that landfill was used to fill in parts of Lake Calumet and Wolf Lake, but most of it (about 3,000 acres or 4.7 square miles) was added to the shoreline of Chicago—twenty-four of the city's twenty-nine miles of shoreline are public parks and beaches. The landfill was deposited gradually.

History: As early as 1851, Chicagoans were concerned about the lake getting out of hand. One day that year, it came crashing onto Michigan Avenue. Mayor Walter Gurnee, who lived on the corner of Michigan and Monroe, hit the street to make repairs. This kind of pummelling prompted residents to encourage the Illinois Central Railroad to build its tracks east of Michigan Avenue, because then the railroad would have to build a breakwater to halt the waves. The IC did, and gradually filled in the area west of the breakwater. Lake Park—the beginning of Grant Park—was the result.

In 1890, Aaron Montgomery Ward filed suit to make sure nobody could build on the lakefront. Surveys as old as 1836 and 1839, which indicated no buildings should be built on the lakefront, were used to support his efforts. By 1895, the city had convinced the IC to lower its tracks, which improved sightlines. The landfills kept pushing north, south and east. Additions were made for the 1893 and 1933 world's fairs and for park projects, and there might be more land filling in the lakefront's future.

5. WORLD'S COLUMBIAN EXPOSITION OF 1893

This was a world's fair held to honor the 400th anniversary of the landing of Christopher Columbus, but it was a year late and hundreds of miles from where Columbus landed. Still it wowed the country with its clean white buildings dubbed the "White City."

Attendance: Total paid attendance: 21,480,141; estimates of who got in go as high as 27.5 million, equal to about half the population of the U.S. in 1893.

Cost: $19 million.

How did it start: On May 1, 1893, President Grover Cleveland pushed a button. Lights went on and motors hummed and the fair began.

Size: It was built on 633 to 753 acres. The site was swampy, sandy land described as having an "air of nakedness and poverty of vegetation." It was transformed into a beautiful park of lagoons, gardens, a Midway filled with entertainment, and a city of over 200 buildings. Frederick Law Olmsted, the same guy who designed New York City's Central Park, designed the world's fair park, although he once called the site "forbidding." The so-called White City was the main part of the fair, and these buildings were mostly neo-classical in design—in other words, they looked like the Greeks and Romans built them. The fair was masterminded by Chicago architect and city visionary Daniel Burnham—but not everyone approved of the East Coast architects calling a lot of the shots on the building designs.

What's there now: Jackson Park and the Museum of Science and Industry, which was the Fine Arts building during the fair.

How much was there to see: To see the whole fair and stop at all the sites, a visitor had to walk over 150 miles. There were exhibits from sixty countries, transported on 8,000 railroad cars

Admisssion: Adults—50 cents; children under 12—25 cents; children under six got in free.

6. THE 1933 CENTURY OF PROGRESS

This fair commemorated the first 100 years of Chicago (1833-1933), but stayed open for 1934, too. Because that century brought such inventions as the telephone, automobile, airplane and motion picture, it was called the Century of Progress. The fair was a showcase of everything modern. Many of the buildings didn't have windows, befitting their futuristic styles. Tricks and feats of electricitry and illumination were everywhere. Even the Aurora Borealis was faked by shining lights on fog created by chemicals dropped from airplanes.

Biplanes fly over the 1933 Century of Progress World's Fair, which stretched along the lakefront.

Location: From Twelfth Street south to Thirty-ninth Street. It spanned three and a half miles, much of it landfill used to create additional shoreline.

Attendance: 39 million paid—more than any fair up to that time. The closest to the record was the 21 million who paid to attend the 1893 Columbian Exposition in Chicago.

Fly Guy: Italian aviator General Italo Balbo and his flying armada flew direct from Italy to Chicago for the 1933 Century of Progress world's fair. Although the city named a street in his honor, he fought on the wrong side in World War II.

How did it start: A light beam from Arcturus, a star 225 million miles away, was caught by a telescope and focused onto a photoelectric cell that provided enough juice to turn on the lights for the entire fair.

What's there now: Park land, boat harbors and Meigs Field, which is on Northerly Island—created by landfill.

Exhibits: New advances in science and technology were emphasized, such as the twelve-story Travel and Transport Building that was topped with a dome 206 feet in diameter and suspended from cables. The sky-ride, a trip through the air on cable cars 200 feet off the ground, was one of the more popular attractions. Fort Dearborn was recreated, as was a group of buildings that played a role in Abraham Lincoln's life.

7. DEEP TUNNEL

Hundreds of feet below Chicago a network of tunnels 22 to 36 feet wide snake along a route that will ultimately run for 131 miles—if the funding holds up. It is called the Deep Tunnel or TARP (Tunnel and Reservoir Plan). Begun in 1975, the first phase of the project is for water pollution control and the second phase is for flood control (both have been started). So far, 51 miles of tunnel have been completed at a cost of about $1.8 billion (contracts completed or committed). Since its completion in 1985, the main tunnel, which runs 31 miles from the North Shore to the west suburbs, has captured over 136 billion gallons of combined sewage and floodwater. The total cost of both phases is estimated at about $3.7 billion.

WATER

The city provides Lake Michigan water for more than $4^{1}/_{2}$ million residents of Chicago and 95 suburbs. Chicago uses about 291 billion gallons a year, and the suburbs use 86 billion gallons. The water is sent out to an area that covers 596 square miles.

The Landmark: The Water Tower, which everyone knows was one of the few structures to survive the Chicago Fire of 1871, was finished in 1869. It was built to conceal a standpipe that was 138 feet high and 3 feet wide. The standpipe helped keep the water system flowing evenly by absorbing pumping surges.

How do we get it? Lake Michigan water first comes to the city through the shore intakes of water purification plants or through intake cribs two miles out in the lake and thrity-five feet down. It flows through the purification plant, where it is treated with chlorine for sterilization and other chemicals to remove impurities, bad tastes and odors and to prevent corrosion in the system. Flouride is added to prevent tooth decay. Water takes about eight hours to go through the plant. Then it flows downhill to the city's eleven pumping stations and then to the tap.

Mouthing Off: The U.S. government made the largest expenditure in its then young history in 1834 when it paid $25,000 to build a pier and dig a channel to relocate the mouth of the Chicago River. Prior to that, the river meandered south to Randolph Street (some say as far as Madison Street) where it opened onto Lake Michigan. The channel basically placed the mouth in its present location—although there have been many improvements over the years. The pier extended the north shore of the river and eventually sand built up along it, creating what is now Streeterville.

METROPOLITAN WATER RECLAMATION DISTRICT OF GREATER CHICAGO

Founded: 1889 by the legislature as the Chicago Sanitary District. In 1955 the name was changed to the Metropolitan Sanitary District. In 1989, it received its present name.

Purpose: It was founded to stop pollution to the lake, which provides drinking water. The MWRD also cleans up waterways and controls flooding.

Governing body: Nine-member Board of Commissioners, elected at large within the district. Three commissioners are elected every two years, for six-year terms.

Locks were built: Wilmette Harbor: 1910; Calumette River: 1922; mouth of Chicago River: 1938.

Service Area: For wastewater treatment: 124 municipalities; 860 square miles

Water: 1.5 billion gallons of wastewater are treated a day.

Treatment Plants: There are seven treatment plants: West-Southwest in Stickney; North Side in Skokie; Calumet on the South Side; Hanover Park; John E. Egan in Schaumburg; O'Hare in Des Plaines; and Lemont.

Sewers: Fifty-three municipalities have combined sewers—meaning they handle both wastewater and floodwater. Chicago has over 4,300 miles of sewer pipes, 191,000 catch basins and 146,000 manholes.

Straightening the River: In the 1920s the south branch of the Chicago River, which at one point ran as far east as Clark Street, was straightened between Harrison and Eighteenth streets. This allowed streets such as Wells and Franklin to run straight through north and south without being blocked by the river. Although the river was straightened, the railroad tracks, which also blocked the streets, weren't moved.

Source: *Chicago Sun-Times* Science and Environmental writer Jim Ritter; *Chicago Sun-Times* clips; *Construction Digest* (Feb. 4, 1991); Alison Zehr director of prgrams for Friends of the Chicago River; Metropolitan Water Reclamation District of Greater Chicago; *Fair Management, The Story of a Century of Progress Exposition* by Lenox R. Lohr; Metropolitan Pier and Exposition Authority; *Illinois Central Magazine,* Dec. 5, 1923; "A History of the World's Columbian Exposition, edited by Rossiter Johnson; City of Chicago Department of Water; *The Chicago World's Fair of 1893, A Photographic Record* with text by Stanley Appelbaum; *Chicago Growth of a Metropolis* by Harold M. Mayer and Richard C. Wade; *Chicago Highlights of Its History*—Chicago Historical Society; *The Final Official Report of the Director of Works for the World's Columbian Exposition*" by Daniel H. Burnham; *The New Encyclopaedia Britannica.*

BIG BUCKS

FIRSTS

■ The first company incorporated in Illinois was the Illinois & Mississippi Telegraph Company—May 2, 1849. Headquartered in Ottawa, it was authorized to run a telegraph line to Chicago and other cities. It was dissolved Feb. 13, 1917.

■ The first permanent Board of Trade building was on the second floor of the Chamber of Commerce Building at La Salle and Washington (built in 1865).

■ The first Chicago telephone book was printed by R.R. Donnelly in 1886. It was printed for the Chicago Telephone Company, predecessor of Illinois Bell.

■ The first time every business in Chicago closed was April 15, 1865—the day Abraham Lincoln died.

■ The first McDonald's restaurant opened on April 15, 1955, at 400 Lee Street, Des Plaines. It's now a museum.

THINGS INVENTED IN CHICAGO

■ The Hostess Twinkie was invented in Schiller Park in 1930 by James Dewar, manager of Continental Baking Company's Hostess Bakery. He came up with the name after seeing a sign advertising Twinkle Toe Shoes. Dewar ate two Twinkies a day and lived to be eighty-eight.

■ Cracker Jack was invented by F.W. Rueckheim, a late 1800s Chicago popcorn vendor. He first sold it at the 1893 Columbian Exposition. The prizes were added in 1912 (and more than 17 billion have been given out since then) and the red, white and blue colors and Sailor Jack and his dog, "Bingo," were added as a patriotic gesture after World War I started. Sailor Jack was modeled after Rueckheim's grandson, Robert, who died shortly after the caricature was created.

■ The Weber Grill was invented by a suburban man whose name wasn't Weber. It was George Stephens. He didn't like the 1950s way of barbecuing, so he made something more to his liking and more efficient at the Weber Brothers Metal Works, where he worked. That was 1951. His neighbors liked it, too. Now Weber-Stephen Products Co. of Palatine estimates there are 9.5 million of its charcoal grills and 3.2 million of its gas grills dotting American backyards.

■ Spray paint was invented in Chicago in the late 1940s by a new groom with some help from his bride. Edward Seymour's wife was spraying air freshener in their new apartment and said it would be great to be able to paint a room that way—the idea light went on, and Seymour of Sycamore became the nation's first manufacturer of spray paint. Seymour, along with other companies, makes Chicago the world's spray paint capital.

■ The zipper was invented in Chicago by Whitcomb L. Judson, who patented his invention in 1896. It was then called a hookless fastener.

■ The window envelope was invented by Chicagoan Americus F. Callahan, who patented it in 1902. He called the window an "outlook,"

Now a museum, the first McDonald's restaurant was opened in 1955 by Ray Kroc in Des Plaines. *(Photo by Gene Pesek)*

but the outlook has become gloomy because window envelopes often contain bills.

■ Allen Pinkerton established the first private detective agency in Chicago around the mid 1800s. His logo was a huge eye. His motto: The Eye That Never Sleeps.

■ Pinball started here with the Whoopee Game. The ten-balls-for-a-nickel game was made by In & Outdoor Games Company in 1930.

■ Levant M. Richardson invented roller skates in Chicago. He got the patent in 1884.

NUMBER OF COMPANIES

About 210,000 companies are incorporated in Illinois and another 30,000 companies do business in the state. Some 50,000 non-profit corporations operate in the state. There are about 213,309 businesses in the six-county Chicago area.

THE JOBS PEOPLE DO
(1990, eight counties)

Total employment in the eight Illinois counties nearest Chicago (Lake, Will, Cook, Du Page, McHenry, Kane, Kendall, Grundy) is 3.7 million. Most people work in the service industry—990,000; wholesale and retail trade—929,000; manufacturing—657,000; state, federal and local government—439,000; financial/insurance/real estate—292,000; transportation and utility—227,000; construction—154,000.

UNEMPLOYMENT

The lowest rate of unemployment in Illinois since 1970 was 3.6 percent, with 171,000 people unemployed in 1970. The highest rate of unemployment was in 1983: 11.4 percent with 640,000 people unemployed.

■ Unemployment in the Chicago metro area (defined by the federal government as Cook, Du Page and McHenry counties):

Year	Rate of Unemployment	Number of Unemployed
1983	10.3%	310,367
1984	8.4%	254,989

Year	Rate of Unemployment	Number of Unemployed
1985	8.2%	255,705
1986	7.3%	228,574
1987	6.7%	210,604
1988	6.2%	199,443
1989	5.5%	182,758
1990	5.9%	195,479

The Brennan Brothers: Bernie Brennan is Montgomery Ward & Company's chief executive. His older brother, Edward A. Brennan, is the chief executive of Sears, Roebuck and Company.

LIST OF TEN RICHEST PEOPLE IN THE CHICAGO AREA
(from *Forbes* magazine's 1990 list of 400 richest Americans)

1. Jay Arthur Pritzker, $2.5 billion, Chicago, financier.

2. Robert Alan Pritzker, $2.5 billion, Chicago, financier.

3. Lester Crown, $1.65 billion, Wilmette, inheritance.

4. Neil Gary Bluhm, $775 million, Winnetka, real estate.

5. Judd David Malkin, $775 million, Winnetka, real estate.

6. Marshall Field V, $540 million, Lake Forest, inheritance (media).

7. Robert William Galvin, $540 million, Barrington Hills, Motorola.

8. Samuel Zell, $450 million, Chicago, real estate.

9. John Jeffrey Louis Jr., $450 million, inheritance (Johnson Wax).

10. Bernard Brennan, $450 million, Winnetka, Montgomery Ward.

Jay Arthur Pritzker is ranked number one among the richest people in the Chicago area. Number two is another Pritzker, Robert Alan.

LIST OF TEN
BIGGEST EMPLOYERS IN ILLINOIS

1. State of Illinois, 127,755*
2. U.S. government, 57,119
3. U.S. Postal Service, 48,757
4. Chicago Board of Education, 45,399
5. Sears, Roebuck & Company, 42,500
6. City of Chicago, 41,525
7. Caterpillar, 30,539
8. Jewel Food Stores, 30,341
9. Cook County, 25,138
10. Illinois Bell, 21,318

*State of Illinois figure includes university and court systems.

LIST OF TEN
HIGHEST UNION MEMBERSHIPS
IN COOK COUNTY

1. International Brotherhood of Teamsters: 65,000.

2. Service Employees International Union: 50,000.

3. American Federation of State, County and Municipal Employees: 35,000 to 40,000.

4. American Federation of Teachers: 35,000.

5. United Food & Commercial Workers International Union: 30,000.

6. International Brotherhood of Electrical Workers: 30,000.

7. United Brotherhood of Carpenters and Joiners: 20,000.

8. United Steel Workers of America: 20,000.

9. Hotel Employees and Restaurant Employees International Union: 18,000 to 20,000.

10. Laborers International Union of North America: 15,000.

   Note: The figures above are estimates only, based on information from various local union leaders.

UNION INVOLVEMENT

The Chicago Federation of Labor claims about 500,000 workers—from 330 union locals—as members. For most of its twentieth century history, the CFL has been headed by just five men:

- John Fitzpatrick, a horseshoer (1904 and 1907-46)

- Charles Dold, a pianomaker (1905-06)

- William A. Lee, a bakery truck driver (1946-1984)
- Edward Brabeck, a plumber (1984-86)
- Robert Healy, a teacher (1987-)

Crewmen take a break at the Union Stockyards while waiting for the backup in the unloading pens to end. This 1946 scene was once the norm, but hard times forced the stockyards to close in 1971. *(Associated Press Photo)*

ILLINOIS MEMBERS OF THE FORTUNE 500

A ranking of industrial companies compiled by *Fortune* magazine on the basis of 1990 sales: (sales range from $28.277 billion to $592.3 million):

12.	Amoco, Chicago.	125.	Inland Steel Industries, Chicago.
38.	Sara Lee, Chicago.	126.	Navistar International, Chicago.
39.	Caterpillar, Peoria.	131.	FMC, Chicago.
42.	Motorola, Schaumburg.	139.	R.R. Donnelley & Sons, Chicago
59.	Baxter International, Deerfield.	163.	Premark International, Deerfield.
60.	Archer-Daniels-Midland, Decatur.	176.	Illinois Tool Works, Glenview.
62.	Deere, Moline.	183.	Brunswick, Skokie.
82.	Abbott Laboratories, Abbott Park.	186.	Great American Management, Chicago.
92.	Stone Container, Chicago.	192.	Tribune, Chicago.
93.	Quaker Oats, Chicago.	206.	USG, Chicago.
115.	Beatrice, Chicago.	214.	Dean Foods, Franklin Park.
117.	Whitman, Chicago.	245.	Square D, Palatine.

247. Sundstrand, Rockford.	363. CF Industries, Long Grove.
248. Morton Int'l., Chicago.	367. Amsted Industries, Chicago.
269. Imcera Group, Northbrook.	369. AM International, Chicago.
272. Fruit of the Loom, Chicago.	392. Interlake, Lisle.
275. Zenith Electronics, Glenview.	396. Alberto-Culver, Melrose Park.
293. Hartmarx, Chicago.	409. Helene Curtis Industries, Chicago.
301. Nalco Chemical, Naperville.	410. Commerce Clearing House, Riverwoods.
314. Outboard Marine, Waukegan.	418. Gaylord Container, Deerfield.
319. William Wrigley, Jr., Chicago.	440. Prairie Farms Dairy, Carlinville.
322. IMC Fertilizer Group, Nortbrook	456. Bell & Howell, Skokie.
335. Newell, Freeport.	468. Molex, Lisle.
352. Pittway, Northbrook.	474. Safety-Kleen, Elgin.

LIST OF TEN LARGEST BANKS IN ILLINOIS BY TOTAL ASSETS

Institution	City	Total Assets
1. First National Bank of Chicago	Chicago	$37.1 billion
2. Continental Bank	Chicago	$25.86 billion
3. Northern Trust Company	Chicago	$10.25 billion
4. Harris Trust and Savings Bank	Chicago	$10.02 billion
5. American National Bank and Trust Company	Chicago	$4.57 billion
6. Exchange National Bank*	Chicago	$3.34 billion
7. LaSalle National Bank*	Chicago	$1.5 billion
8. Cole Taylor Bank	Chicago	$1.17 billion
9. Magna Bank	Belleville	$929.2 million
10. First Midwest Bank	Waukegan	$923.1 million

*Exchange and LaSalle have merged

BACKGROUND ON CHICAGO'S FOUR TRADING EXCHANGES

CHICAGO BOARD OF TRADE: 141 W. JACKSON

Founded: April 1848. It trades agricultural and financial futures and options

Volume: In 1990, there were 154.2 million contracts traded by CBOT, an annual volume record. While difficult to estimate, the value of a year's worth of trades was estimated several years ago at $11 trillion by CBOT's economics department, using a figure of 143 million contracts.

Trading floor: 51,000 square feet.

Membership: 3,643 members, 1,402 of them full members.

Cost of a Seat: Most paid for a full seat was $550,000 in August 1987.

CHICAGO MERCANTILE EXCHANGE: 30 S. WACKER DR.

Founded: September 1919. It grew out of the Chicago Produce Exchange, which was founded on May 20, 1874, to provide a systematic market for butter, eggs, poultry and other farm products. Now it trades a broad array of futures, from currency contracts to frozen pork bellies.

Volume: In 1990, just under 103 million contracts were traded.

Trading Floor: Two trading floors totaling 70,000 square feet and thirty-four trading pits.

Membership: 3,100 either own or rent seats, but the exchange membership is 2,724 owners.

Cost of a Seat: Record seat prices CME division: $550,000, March 9, 1989; International Monetary Market division: $475,000, April 28, 1989; Index and Option Market division: $180,000, Sept. 21, 1987.

MIDWEST STOCK EXCHANGE: 440 S. LA SALLE ST.

Founded: May 15, 1882, as the Chicago Stock Exchange; through mergers the name was changed to Midwest Stock Exchange in 1949.

Volume: 2.44 billion shares.

Two board markers at the Midwest Stock Exchange in 1955. Though working as fast as possible, they were still 35 feet of teletype behind. *(Photo by Carmen Reporto)*

Trading Floor: 29,335 square feet.

Membership: 446 members.

Cost of a Seat: $30,000 as of March 1991; most paid: $105,000 in 1987.

Trades: 2,360 stocks are traded on the Midwest Stock Exchange.

CHICAGO BOARD OPTIONS EXCHANGE: LA SALLE AT VAN BUREN

Founded: April 26, 1973, to trade stock options and other options.

Volume: In 1990 there were 129,500,018 contracts.

Trading Floor: 45,000 square feet, with eight trading posts, six of which can have up to ten stations, and two of which are larger for the Standard & Poor's 100 Index Options (OEX) and Standard & Poor's 500 Index Options (SPX).

Membership: About 1,500 members.

Cost of a Seat: Highest price paid for a seat was $465,000 in 1987.

EXTREMES

■ The world's biggest cookie and cracker factory is at 7300 S. Kedzie, where Nabisco Biscuit Company made 2.4 billion Oreo cookies in 1990, among other baked goods.

■ The Chicago Board of Trade is the world's largest futures and options exchange, trading 154.2 million contracts in 1990. It is also the world's oldest futures and options exchange, having been founded in April 1848. The world's most actively traded contract, the treasury bond futures contract, is traded at CBOT.

■ Illinois produces more soybeans than any state in the United States.

■ Lyon & Healy in Chicago is the nation's oldest maker of standing string harps. It makes about 1,000 a year—concert grands start at about $8,000. Oh yeah, Harpo Marx played a Lyon & Healy Model 30.

■ Motorola's main cellular manufacturing plant in Arlington Heights makes 30 to 40 percent of the world's cellular phones.

■ The Chicago area is the number-one frozen pizza market in the nation. Chicagoans spend twice as much on frozen pizza as the average American consumer. Chicagoans buy more expensive pizzas and bigger pizzas—twenty to thirty ounces—than consumers nationwide. About 45 percent of the frozen pizzas sold here are covered with sausage. Chicago-area retailers make more room on their shelves for frozen pizzas than anywhere else in the country.

■ Oak-Brook-based McDonald's Corporation sells more hamburgers than any restaurant company in the world (more than 70 billion to date), and is the world's largest quick-service restaurant company. It has 11,800 restaurants in fifty-four countries (8,500 in the U.S.), and lays claim to being the largest owner of retail real estate in the world.

■ All the unsweetened and sugar-free Kool-Aid sold in the U.S. (most of the 2 billion quarts made each summer) is produced at the Kraft General Foods plant at 7400 S. Rockwell.

■ Chicago-based William Wrigley, Jr., Company is the world's largest manufacturer of gum, with more than 20 million packages sold daily. The company's mother plant is at Thirty-fifth and Ashland. Juicy Fruit and Wrigley's Spearmint were first sold in 1893.

■ Deerfield-based Walgreen Company is the nation's largest drugstore chain in terms of sales ($6.05 billion) and earnings ($174.6 million). It has 1,600 stores in twenty-nine states and Puerto Rico.

■ Oakbrook Terrace-based E.J. Brach Corporation lays claim to having the world's largest candy manufacturing plant, with its 2.2 million-square-foot plant at 4656 W. Kinzie. The company can produce more than 2 million pounds of candy per day. It is also the world's largest general-line candy manufacturer.

■ Oak Brook-based Waste Management is the world's largest garbage disposal company, the world's largest recycler and the world's largest environmental services company, according to the company.

■ PayDay Peanut Bar, made by Bannockburn-based Leaf, Inc., is the number one selling non-chocolate candy bar in the nation.

■ The world's largest coin-operated amusement game manufacturer is WMS Industries, parent company of Chicago-based Williams Electornics Games, Inc., and sister company of Midway Manufacturing Company (manufacturers of Bally/Midway Amusement games). They are also the world's only manufacturers of shuffle alleys or puck bowling games.

■ Oak Brook-based CBI Industries is the world's largest manufacturer of wind tunnels.

■ World Dryer, with a factory at 4546 W. Forty-seventh, has 2 million hand dryers in bathrooms around the globe, making it the nation's No. 1 hand-dryer company.

■ Skokie-based Klein Tools, which lays claim to being the first U.S. manufacturer of pliers (around 1857), makes 1 million pairs of pliers a year and is the largest manufacturer of pliers in U.S.

■ Chicago Board Options Exchange is the world's first and largest stock options exchange.

■ Illinois companies make more of the following than any other state, according to the most recent state figures (1987): explosives; prepared flour mixes for cakes and brownies; candy and confectionery products; some types of metal stampings; commercial printing gravure; cyclic crudes and intermediates (certain products refined out of petroleum); printing ink; certain chemical preparations; gaskets, packing and sealing devices; steel wire products; wire springs; farm machinery and equipment; construction machinery; power transmission equipment, such as that used by utility companies; certain office machines; automatic vending machines; measuring and dispensing pumps, such as those used at gas stations or chemical plants; service industry machines, such as those used for food processing or floor polishing; environmental controls; pollution controls.

■ Northern Bank Note Company in Countryside prints 40 percent of America's municipal bonds.

A CHICAGO STORY

Chicagoans have their own way of greeting local millionaires who move into their neighborhood. For Jesse Binga, it was bombs on his front porch.

Binga was unique to turn-of-the-century Chicago. He was a black millionaire, the first black to own a Chicago bank.

He came here for the 1893 World's Columbian Exposition as a bootblack with ten bucks in his pocket. Within two decades he was a millionaire. But money and success didn't solve everything.

When Binga moved into fancy South Side neighborhoods, his homes were bombed six times. Neighbors tried to buy his house to get him to move. He refused.

Here was a man who owned over 1,000 feet of frontage on South State Street, built the Binga State Bank, leased and operated real estate, and helped build a $500,000 community hall for Chicago blacks.

"Life is pretty much what you make it," he'd say, "and making it big means using every day of it."

In the 1920s he was a strong advocate of black self-help.

"Our group must learn to be self-sufficing, must own its own shops and banks, must make for the substantial businesses with a future in them, and not be trading upon nor fawning upon the good nature of the white man."

Nonetheless, his success, he said, was due in part to prejudice. "It was partly the disposition of the average white man to underestimate my knowledge of real estate values. They wouldn't believe that a colored man could take almost any old building and whip it into shape," he said in 1927.

But success didn't stay with Binga. In the Great Depression of the 1930s, many banks went under. Binga's was among them.

He lost his fortune and was convicted of embezzlement for which he spent three years in jail. Through it all, Binga maintained he was innocent and eventually received a full pardon. He ended his career as a janitor earning $15 a week dusting the altar and pews of a church to which he once donated $1,000.

"I have known Binga for thirty years, and he is a man of fine character," said Binga's attorney, Clarence Darrow. "He lost his fortune trying to keep his bank open."

When he died in 1950, the headline of his *Daily News* obituary read: "Jesse Binga Dies, Once a Millionaire."

Big Names Who Made It Big in Chicago: Marshall Field (1834-1906), department stores; Richard W. Sears (1863-1914), retailer; Aaron Montgomery Ward (1844-1913), retailer; George Mortimer Pullman (1831-1997), Pullman sleeping car; Philip D. Armour (1832-1901), meatpacker; Gustavus Swift (1839-1903), meatpacker; William Wrigley, Jr. (1861-1932), gum manufacturer.

OTHER THINGS MADE IN CHICAGO
(OR CHICAGO AREA)

Lamps: Lava Lites—2 million to 3 million made by Chicago-based Lava-Simplex Internationale since 1965; Stiffel Lamps, Chicago, makes more than 250,000 brass lamps a year.

Skeletons: Anatomical Chart Company, Skokie, claims to be the nation's biggest artificial skeleton company (a human skeleton goes for $2,000). The company makes a range of medical-related items, from medical charts to spandex suits that show your intestines.

Videotapes: With a huge Northbrook plant and another in California, Rank Video can copy up to 10 million videotapes a month, making it one of the biggest videotape duplicators in the nation.

Food and other stuff: Cracker Jack (19 tons a day at a plant in Northbrook); Tootsie Rolls and Tootsie Roll Pops (the plant at 7401 S. Cicero makes 20 million to 30 million pieces of candy a day); Cheerios; Vienna hot dogs (2501 N. Damen, Chicago, estimated to make 104 million hot dogs in 1991); NutraSweet; Health-O-Meter Scales; Murine, Blistex, Selsun Blue, Sparkle Glass Cleaner; Strombecker Corp.'s jump ropes, jacks, bubbles, paddles with red balls on elastic bands;

Ford Taurus, Mercury Sable; Hartmarx men's suit and topcoats; McGunn Safes; Fellowes Manufacturing Company's paper shredders; Chicago Roller Skate's roller skates.

Sources: *Chicago Sun-Times* reporters: P.J. Bednarski, Lisa Holton, Frederick H. Lowe, Patricia Moore, Nancy Millman, Susan Chandler, Delia O'Hara, Richard Roeper, Ray Long, Mark Brown; *Chicago Sun-Times* and *Daily News* clips; Illinois Secretary of State; listed exchanges above; Chicago Association of Commerce and Industry; office of Illinois Employment Security; *Fortune* and *Forbes* magazines; Sheshunoff & Co., Austin, Texas; Chicago Federation of Labor; Illinois Department of Commerce and Community Affairs; and various companies listed above.

WEATHER

"If you don't like Chicago's weather, wait a minute."

—Anonymous

SUNRISE, SUNSET

Earliest Sunrise: From June 9 through June 22, the sun rises in Chicago at 5:16 a.m., Daylight Savings Time.*

Latest Sunrise: From January 2 to January 6, the sun rises at 7:20 a.m.*

Earliest Sunset: From December 7 through December 12, the sun sets in Chicago at 4:20 p.m.*

Latest Sunset: From June 23 to July 3, the sun sets at 8:31 p.m., Daylight Savings Time.*

Longest day: June 21.

Shortest day: Dec. 21.

FIRSTS

The first local station of the National Weather Service predates the Chicago Fire, but was abandoned when the fire approached. All official records of the station were lost in the blaze. The weather service resumed observations on Oct. 16, 1871, from a rented room at what is now 427 W. Randolph St. In the 1930s, Rosenwald Hall, at Fifty-eighth Street and University Avenue, on the campus of the University of Chicago, was the National Weather Service's official observation site.

*Note: These are the precise times for 1991, and can vary from year to year by about one minute.

RECORD WARMEST AND COOLEST DAYS FOR EACH MONTH

Month	Warmest Temp.	Date	Coldest Temp.	Date
January	67	1-25-50	−27	1-20-85
February	75	2-27-76	−21	2-9-1899
March	88	3-29-86	−12	3-4-1873
April	91	4-22-80	7	4-7-82
May	98	5-31-34	27	5-9-83
June	104	6-20-88	35	6-4-45
July	105	7-24-34	45	7-7-83
August	102	8-5-18	42	8-28-86
September	101	9-2-53	29	9-30-84
October	94	10-6-63	14	10-25-1887
November	81	11-1-50	−2	11-24-50
December	71	12-2-82	−25	12-24-83

MONTHLY AVERAGES, TEMPERATURES AND SUNSHINE

Month	Normal Daily High	Normal Daily Low	Monthly Average Temp.	Chance of Sunshine Each Day
January	29.2	13.6	21.4	48%
February	33.9	18.1	26.0	46%
March	44.3	27.6	36.0	52%
April	58.8	38.8	48.8	52%
May	70.0	48.1	59.1	60%
June	79.4	57.7	68.6	70%
July	83.3	62.7	73.0	68%
August	82.1	61.7	71.9	66%
September	75.5	53.9	64.7	59%
October	64.1	42.9	53.5	53%
November	48.2	31.4	39.8	38%
December	35.0	20.3	27.7	44%
Full Year	58.7	39.7	49.2	55%

FIVE HOTTEST DAYS IN CHICAGO SINCE 1871

	Temp	Date
1)	105	7-24-34
2)	104	6-20-53
3)	104	6-20-88
4)	103	7-21-01

5) 102 on each of the following days: July 4, 1911, July 5, 1911, July 30, 1916, Aug. 5, 1918, June 1, 1934, July 10, 1936, July 3, 1949, July 7, 1980, and July 15, 1988.

TEN COLDEST DAYS
IN CHICAGO SINCE 1871

	Temp	Date		Temp	Date
1)	−27	1-20-85	6)	−21	2-9-1899
2)	−26	1-10-82	7)	−20	1-9-1875
3)	−25	12-24-83	8)	−20	1-25-1897
4)	−23	12-24-1872	9)	−19	2-9-33
5)	−22	1-21-84	10)	−19	1-16-77 and 1-15-79

Chicago winters are not something to take lightly. Armed with hat, gloves and a heavy coat, this man appears ready for a brisk walk along the Chicago River in December. *(Photo by Tom Cruze)*

MONTHLY EXTREMES
OF HOT AND COLD

Month	Average No. Days Zero or Below	Average No. Days 90 or Above
January	6.9	
February	2.5	
December	2.4	
May		1.0
June		4.9
July		7.8
August		5.0
September		2.0

Hottest Chicago summer on record: On forty-seven days in 1988, the daily high temperature was at least 90 degrees.

Coldest Chicago winter on record: On twenty-six days in the winter of 1874-75, the temperature dropped to zero or below.

Coldest Chicago calendar year on record: On thirty-three days in 1963, the temperature dropped to zero or below.

Freezing days in Spring and Fall: From 1873 to 1989, the temperature in Chicago has dropped below the freezing point—32 degrees—twenty-eight days in May and six days in September.

Average number of freezing days each year: Freezing or below is reached on an average of 123 days per year. There is a 50 percent likelihood that the temperature will fall to 32 degrees or lower by October 27, and that the last temperature of 32 degrees or lower in the spring will have occurred by April 22.

Daily average temperature range: The daily range in temperature varies considerably from day to day, but averages near 15 degrees in the cold season, November through March, and close to 20 degrees the rest of the year.

WIND

Month	Mean Wind Speed	Fastest Steady Wind	Fastest Wind Gust
January	11.6 (mph)	47	58
February	11.4	45	54
March	11.9	54	55
April	11.9	54	69
May	10.5	52	55
June	9.2	41	63
July	8.1	55	54
August	8.1	46	64
September	8.8	58	58
October	9.9	48	49
November	11.0	51	48
December	11.0	46	52
YEAR	10.3		

Fastest wind on record: 58 mph, set on a day in September 1959.

Fastest wind gust on record: 69 mph, set on April 29, 1984.

SNOW AND RAIN

Wettest month on record: August 1987, when 17.10 inches of rain fell.

Wettest 24 hours on record: Aug. 13-14, 1987, when 9.53 inches of rain fell.

Least rain in one month: .02 inches in September 1979.

Snowiest month on record: 35.3 inches of snow and ice in December 1978.

Snowiest 24 hours on record: 18.1 inches on January 26-27, 1967.

Earliest measurable snowfall: Oct. 18, 1972 (.02 inches fell).

Latest measurable snowfall: May 11, 1966 (.01 inches fell).

Only June snow: A trace of snow—too little to measure—fell on June 2, 1910.

Longest streak with measurable rain or snow: Nineteen days in December and January 1962.

Longest streak without measurable rain or snow: Twenty-nine days in December and January 1943.

Normal precipitation for one year: 33.34 inches.

TEN SNOWIEST SEASONS
(from 1871-1990)

	Season	Inches of Snow
1)	1978-79	89.7
2)	1977-78	82.3
3)	1969-70	77.0
4)	1966-67	68.4
5)	1951-52	66.4
6)	1917-18	64.1
7)	1964-65	59.5
8)	1903-04	59.5
9)	1981-82	59.3
10)	1961-62	58.9

BIGGEST SNOW JOBS

■ Chicago's single biggest snowstorm hit Jan. 26, 1967. It fell for twenty-nine hours and left 23 inches of snow (18.1 inches in the first twenty-four hours). It paralyzed the city, left strings of autos abandoned on the roads, and cost the city $5 million to plow.

■ The snowstorm of 1979, falling on Jan. 12-14, dropped 20.7 inches of snow on the Chicago area—on top of about 8 inches that had fallen less than two weeks before.

RAIN AND SNOW
MONTHLY NORMS AND RECORD HIGHS

(These records are for the years since 1959—the year the National Weather Service began taking measurements at O'Hare Airport).

Month	Normal Precipitation in inches of water	Maximum in 24 hours	Maximum Snow and ice pellets in one month	Maximum Snow and ice pellets in 24 hours
Jan.	1.6	2" in 1960	34.3 in 1979	18.1 in 1967
Feb.	1.31	1.9 in 1985	21.5 in 1967	9.7 in 1981
March	2.59	2.39 in 1985	24.7 in 1965	10.6 in 1970
April	3.66	2.78 in 1983	11.1 in 1975	10.9 in 1975
May	3.15	3.45 in 1981	1.6 in 1966	1.6 in 1966
June	4.08	3.09 in 1967	0	0
July	3.63	2.89 in 1962	0	0
Aug.	3.53	9.35 in 1987	trace in '89	trace in '89
Sept.	3.35	3.0 in 1978	trace in '67	trace in '67
Oct.	2.28	4.62 in 1969	6.6 in 1967	6.6 in 1967
Nov.	2.06	2.8 in 1985	10.4 in 1959	5.8 in 1975
Dec.	2.10	4.53 in 1982	35.3 in 1978	11 in 1969
TOTAL	33.34			

"LAKE EFFECT"

During a typical summer, cool breezes blow off the lake thirty to forty days, reducing lakefront temperatures by 4 or 5 degrees. When the wind is calm in summer, Downtown Chicago is as much as 5 degrees hotter than in rural areas because factories, air-conditioner exhausts and the like produce heat. In winter in Chicago, the lake creates a slight warming effect because the water is warmer than the air. Lake-effect snow in Chicago is more myth than reality. Because the winter wind usually blows from the northwest, it picks up moisture as it crosses the lake and dumps snow on the eastern shore—Michigan and Indiana. In a typical winter, the eastern shore gets 60 to 100 percent more snow than the western shore.

THE WINDY CITY

There's an ugly reason why Chicago is known as the "Windy City." It's called New York City.

When Chicago—hardly America's windiest city—was vying to become the site of the 1893 World's Columbian Exposition, its chief rival was New York. Newspapers in each city tried to present well-reasoned arguments touting their town for the fair.

In Chicago, for example, one newspaper said New York shouldn't get the fair because it's "the meanest city in America."

For its part, New York mostly treated Chicago like lint.

New York Sun editor Charles Dana, portraying Chicagoans as loud, self-promoting blowhards, told his readers to pay no attention to "the nonsensical claims of that windy city. It's people could not hold a world's fair, even if they won it."

Of course, Chicago did win it, held it and lived happily ever after, as did the name "Windy City."

PAST TENSE

Roads Clogged, Cars Abandoned
By Arthur Gorlick
(Chicago Daily News, Jan. 27, 1967)

Chicago's battered, windblown suburbs Friday presented a desolate scene of colossal snow drifts, abandoned cars and roads clogged so badly that many areas are virtually isolated.

Continuing snow and drifting augured little relief.

Thousands of people—mostly motorists and school children—remained trapped away from their homes.

Hundreds of them sought—and readily found—refuge, companionship and food in the homes of strangers.

Hospitals, schools, service stations, municipal buildings and police stations gave shelter to hundreds more.

A stranded motorist in Dolton suffered a heart attack and died after plodding through high snow in search of shelter.

There was drama in birth, too.

By telephone, Dr. Ulisse P. Cucco of Mount Prospect told Philip A. Anzelmo, 28, of Prospect Heights, how to deliver his wife's baby.

Sources: Paul W. Dailey, Richard Koeneman and Kevin Darmosal of the National Weather Service, Chicago bureau; Jim Ritter of the *Chicago Sun-Times.*

MEDIA

RADIO AND TV

FIRSTS

Chicago radio station: KYW, owned by the Westinghouse Corp., made its debut on Nov. 11, 1921. Mary Garden, an opera singer and manager of the Chicago Civic Opera Company, sang an aria from "Madame Butterfly." The broadcast originated from the Auditorium Theater.

Chicago TV station: Chicago's first commercial TV station, WBKB, started in 1939 as experimental W9XKB. It telecast fifteen minutes of news and short films each day. The rest of the time it transmitted a test pattern or a view of the Wrigley Building. In October 1943, W9XKB, having been awarded its commercial license, began broadcasting as WBKB. Three more stations started five years later—WGN (channel 9), WMAQ (on channel 5 and then called WNBQ) and WENR (channel 7). WGN's first show was a Golden Gloves boxing match; WMAQ opened from St. Louis with singer Jane Pickens and comic Al Kelly; and WENR served up a mystery show called "Standby for Crime," starring Mike Wallace. In 1953, CBS acquired WBKB for $6 million from Balaban & Katz, changed the call letters to WBBM-TV, and changed from channel 4 to channel 2.

TV commercial: For the Elgin Watch Company, on WBKB in 1943. The screen showed a large white clock while the announcer said something like, "It is 9 p.m., Elgin watch time, the time of the stars."

National radio soap opera: "Just Plain Bill," which began in 1932.

College on the radio: In 1956, WTTW-TV (channel 11) became the first station in the country to televise college courses for credit. Within five years, 15,000 students had enrolled. WTTW also claims to have produced the first movie review series in the country—"Sneak Previews"—and the nation's highest-rated cooking show—"The Frugal Gourmet."

First Unscripted Network Radio Program: The "University of Chicago Round Table," a radio talk show featuring U. of C. professors, premiered on WMAQ radio in February 1931, with a conversation about the Wickersham Commission report on prohibition. The show featured largely impromptu conversations—in a day when all other nationally broadcast shows were scripted. Among the guest hosts were John F. Kennedy, Ralph Bunche, Dean Rusk, Jawaharlal Nehru and Adlai Stevenson. The last show aired on June 12, 1955.

BACKGROUND

Illinois is home to 253 radio stations (108 AM and 145 FM) and 45 television stations. Of those, 100 radio stations (39 AM and 61 FM) and 13 TV stations are based in the Chicago area. Thirty-nine cable TV franchises and 18 college radio stations also serve the area. Four AM radio stations with 50,000-watt non-directional signals boast the greatest geographic reach—WBBM (780), WGN (720), WLS (890) and WMAQ (670).

Soaps R Us: In America's radio heyday, virtually all the big comedy and variety shows broadcast out of New York City. But for many years, beginning in 1932 with "Just Plain Bill," Chicago was America's radio soap opera capital. Several of the best old TV and radio soaps were created by Chicagoan Irma Phillip, including "The Road to Life," "The Guiding Light," and "As The World Turns."

EXTREMES

Top radio station: WGN has reigned as the king of Chicago radio since about 1968. That was the year WIND radio's wildly popular archconservative morning jock, Howard Miller, resigned, clearing the way for WGN's gentle Wally Phillips to climb atop the radio ratings. WGN, now led by morning man Bob Collins, continues to dominate the radio airwaves, almost always ranking No. 1 in the ratings.

Longest-running radio show: "Tenpin Tattler," a weekly WGN bowling program that debuted on Aug. 24, 1935, is the longest-running radio show in the world, according to the *Guinness Book of World Records*. The show's host, Sam Weinstein, is sometimes called "Mister Bowling." It is broadcast at 5:55 p.m., Saturdays.

Highest paid radio and TV personalities: Oprah Winfrey, at an estimated $44 million annually; and Paul Harvey, at about $7 million annually.

Oprah Winfrey, before she had her own nationally syndicated show, was the host of "A.M. Chicago" on WLS-TV.

Biondi's Dirty Joke: In May 1963, Dick Biondi, WLS-AM radio's original "Chicago Screamer" rock-and-roll deejay, was fired. Rumors spread throughout Chicago's high schools that he'd told a dirty knock-knock joke on the air. Thousands of teens swore they had heard him say it, although somehow their stories didn't agree. The truth, Biondi explained years later, is he never told the joke. He was fired, he said, for blowing up at his boss off the air.

Longest running local TV show: "City Desk" on WMAQ premiered in 1952.

FAMOUS CHICAGOANS

Steve Allen: From 1954 through 1957, this boy from Chicago's Hyde Park High School served as the first host of what would become a cultural institution—the "Tonight Show." He was followed by Jack Paar and Johnny Carson. Allen claimed to have discovered a great deal of talent while hosting the show, including Steve Lawrence and Eydie Gorme. ("I discovered Steve and Eydie—in the back seat of a car.")

Bozo: "Who's your favorite clown?" Bozo! "The Bozo Show," formerly called "Bozo's Circus," has been airing on WGN-TV since 1961, entertaining two generations of Chicago children. There are grown adults who admit they are still bugged that they blew it on bucket No. 6. More than 1 million Chicagoans have sat in Bozo's audience, most of them far-sighted folks who signed up for tickets five or ten years in advance. On March 17, 1990, when tickets went on sale again by phone after a ten-year freeze, 140,000 tickets were distributed in five hours and twenty minutes. WGN's original Bozo was Bob Bell. Today's Bozo is Joey D'Auria. The prize for nailing bucket No. 6 is $100 and a Schwinn bicycle.

Captain William C. Eddy: He was an electronics engineer who pioneered Chicago's first television station, WBKB. Eddy built the facilities for WBKB—the station owned by movie palace owner Barney Balaban—in 1939. He located his studio in the State-Lake Building. When the station started, it had eight employees and telecast fifteen minutes a day to an audience gathered around some fifty TV sets. Eddy also commanded a huge Navy radio and electronics school in Chicago—using the WBKB studios—graduating nearly 70,000 military electronics specialists during World War II. He died in 1989, at age eighty-seven.

Dave Garroway: His last word each day was "Peace." In 1949 in Chicago, Garroway started his "Garroway at Large" show, an NBC offering that epitomized the "Chicago School" of television—relaxed, wry and intimate. In 1952, Garroway moved to New York to serve as the original host of the "Today" show, for which he was paid $360,000 a year. But in 1961, one month after his wife, Pamela, died of a barbiturate overdose, he left the show to think and raise his children. He made a series of comeback attempts, but never achieved the same success. His last television appearance was on a thirty-year "Today" show retrospective in 1982. Later that year, on July 21, 1982, he killed himself by firing a shotgun into his head.

Don McNeill: His top-rated "Breakfast Club" was Chicago's unofficial alarm clock for thirty-five years. The "Breakfast Club," a cheerful combination of music, corny humor and patriotic and religious sentiment, was broadcast from Chicago on ABC from 1934 to 1969. More than 3 million fans sat in the studio audience, and thousands participated in the show itself. McNeill, born Dec. 23, 1907, got his first job in radio sweeping out a studio and filling in for announcers. His daily invocation was: "Each in his own words, each in his own way, for a world united in peace, let us bow our heads and pray."

Capt. William C. Eddy was the director of WBKB, Chicago's first commercial TV station.

Don McNeill was host of "Breakfast Club" from 1934 to 1969.

Disc Jockey Steve Dahl, from WLUP-AM, is known for his live remotes and colorful language on the air. *(Photo by Robert A. Davis)*

Dick Biondi was WLS-AM radio's original "Chicago Screamer" rock-and-roll deejay. *(Photo by Linda Schwartz Photography)*

> **D.J. on Cutting Edge:** Steve Dahl, a radio personality on WLUP-AM, underwent a vasectomy—live on the air—in March 1989, at the office of Dr. David Wilks, an Indiana urologist.

CHICAGO CONTRIBUTION

In the history of radio, many of the biggest adventure serials were made in Chicago. Among the Chicago classics were "Little Orphan Annie," "Captain Midnight," "First Nighter," "Ma Perkins," "Sky King," and "Jack Armstrong, the All-American Boy."

In the history of television, the "Chicago School" held sway in the nation for a few brief years. It was a low-budget style of programming noted for its creativity, simplicity and intimacy. Among America's most popular TV programs in the early 1950s were several that originated from Chicago: "Garroway At Large with Dave Garroway," "Kukla, Fran and Ollie," "The Jack Carter Show," "Marlin Perkins' Zoo Parade," "Studs' Place with Studs Terkel," "Cactus Jim," and "The Wayne King Show."

MADE IN CHICAGO
TELEVISION SHOWS AND TV MOVIES
(Since 1976)

1976: "Money to Burn," an NBC movie of the week and "Sparrow," a CBS pilot.

1977: "The Awakening Land," an NBC mini-series.

1978: "Huckleberry Finn," "One in a Million: The Ron LeFlore Story," "Dummy," "Flesh and Blood" and "The Duke"—all movies of the week. "The Chisholms," a mini-series.

1979: "Torn Between Two Lovers," a movie of the week; "Working Stiffs" and "Life on the Mississippi," both television pilots; "Miles to Go Before I Sleep," a documentary; "Bio-Ethics," a TV special.

1980: "Minnesota Strip" and "Welcome to Success: The Marva Collins Story," both movies of the week; "American Dream," "The Coach," "Concrete Cowboy" and "Chicago Story," all TV pilots; "Hill Street Blues," the opening scenes; "Come Along With Me," a TV special; "Skokie," a docu-drama; "American Dream No. 2 (Welcome to Wicker Park)," one episode of a six-part TV series.

1981: "Leave 'Em Laughing," "Will" and "Who Am I This Time," all movies; "Myths and Reality," "Isabel Buchanan" and "TV Inside &

Out," all documentaries; "Hill Street Blues," opening sequences; "Chicago Story," 13 episodes; "Any Friend of Nicholas" and "Soundstage with Doc Severinson," both TV specials; "Real Detectives—The Richard Speck Case," a docu-drama; "33 Prompton Place," a pilot; "Cities on the Great Lakes," an educational film.

1982: "The Prairie Years," "Story on Peoria, IL ZDF-TV," "Story on Yugoslavian Culture," "City Scapes," "A Walk Through the 20th Century," "Sandler and Young—The First 20 Years" and "Welcome to the U.S. Navy," all documentaries; "Hill Street Blues," opening scenes; "Travel America," a Japanese-made tourism film; "A Change of Heart," a movie; "Real People" and "Great American Bike Race," both TV specials; "It Takes Two," a series.

1983: "A Matter of Principle," "The Dollmaker," "Lost Honor of Kathryn Beck," "The Killing Floor," "Through Naked Eyes," "Gladiola Girls," "Hard Knox" and "The Roommate," all movies; "Through a Keyhole Darkly," a cable TV series; "Here's Chicago," a travel film; "The Mississippi," a series; "America the Beautiful," a documentary.

1984: "International Money Traders," "Fuji Television Special," "Elections '84," "Disney Agricultural Film," "Route 66," "The Nature of Things," "Portraits of America," "Pride of Place," "Chicago" and "Bauhaus Architecture," all documentaries; "Hawaiian Heat," a pilot; "Hill Street Blues," "Punky Brewster" and "Webster," TV series; "Toughest Man in the World," "First Steps," "The Imposter," "Myra Meets His Family" and "Two Fathers," all movies.

1985: "Lady Blue," "Knight Rider," series; "Welcome Home Bobby," "Final Jeopardy" and "Vital Signs," movies; "T.J. Hooker," one episode of the series; "America By Design," documentary; "Mary," opening scenes of series.

1986: "Jay Leno and the American Dream," TV special; "Jack and Mike" and "Crime Story," series; "Amerika," mini-series; "Night of Courage," movie; "Is Anybody Listening," cable special; "Home," pilot.

1987: "Jack and Mike," "Sable," "Moonlighting" and "Perfect Strangers," series; "Father Dowling," "Open Admissions," "The Father Clements Story" and "Conspiracy of Love," movies.

1988: "Some Kind of Woman," "Nightwatch," pilot; "Dreambreakers," movie.

1989: "America's Most Wanted," "West 57th Street," "Family Matters," "Inside Edition," "Anything But Love" and "Unsolved Mysteries," series; "Route 66," "American Writers" and "Making Sense of the 60's," documentary; "Generations" and "Santa Barbara," daytime dramas; "The David Letterman Show," several shows broadcast from Chicago; "Making a Case for Murder: The Howard Beach Story,"

Max Headroom, TV Pirate: On Nov. 22, 1987, a phony Max Headroom—the TV cartoon character—illegally invaded the TV airwaves to interrupt the programming on WGN-TV (channel 9) and WTTW-TV (channel 11). The first interruption, which lasted twenty-five seconds, occurred during the Channel 9 sports news. It showed the Headroom character rocking back and forth with his hands held in the air. The second interruption, for eighty-eight seconds during "Dr. Who" on Channel 11, showed Headroom with his pants down, being spanked with a fly swatter or spatula. The TV pirates were never caught.

"Sodacracker" and "The Road Not Taken: The Mary Thomas Story," movies.

1990: "The Kid Who Loved Christmas," "Good Night Sweet Wife" and "Johnny Ryan," movies; "Gabriel's Fire," pilot; "Women of Brewster Place," "Uncle Buck" and "America's Funniest People," series; "Richard Lewis Comedy Special," "Anything for Laughs," and "American Movie Classics," specials; "Janet Jackson Video," music video; "Generations," daytime drama.

Silent Nights in Radioland: In the 1920s, Monday night in Chicago was called "Silent Night" in radio jargon because all the stations signed off the air so that listeners could plug in their crystal set headphones and listen to out-of-town stations.

RADIO STATION CALL LETTERS
WHAT THEY STOOD FOR

- WGN—World's Greatest Newspaper (owned by the Chicago Tribune)
- WLS—World's Largest Store (owned by Sears, Roebuck & Co.)
- WIND—For INDiana, where the station first was licensed.
- WBBM—We Broadcast Better Music
- WBEZ—The B and E stand for Chicago Board of Education, which owns it.
- WMBI—Moody Bible Institute, which owns it.
- WVON—Voice of Negroes.
- WCRW—Clinton R. White, the original owner.
- WEDC—Emil Denemark Cadillac, a car dealership that owned the station.
- WSBC—World Storage and Battery Company, whose president, Joe Silverstein, owned the station.
- WTAQ—Western Towns Along the Q. (Quincy R.R.) It broadcasts from La Grange.

- WKKD—Kendall, Kane and Du Page Counties. It broadcasts from Aurora.
- WNIB—Northern Illinois Broadcasting Co.
- WJPC—Johnson Publishing Company, its owner.

WLS Stands Ready: If the big bomb hits, the president of the United States will be able to address Chicago-area residents immediately via one radio station—WLS-AM. WLS is one of thirty radio stations across the country participating in the federal government's Primary Entry Point program. In an emergency, the president can turn to his Trip Officer— an assistant who accompanies him everywhere—push a few buttons on a gadget carried in a suitcase, and gain immediate control of those thirty stations for an emergency announcement. Listeners will hear two tones, then a White House announcer telling them to "please stand by," and then the voice of the president. WMAQ-AM radio is assigned to pick up the WLS signal and relay it across the Midwest. WLS was selected for this program from among Chicago's 50,000-watt AM radio stations because its antenna in southwest suburban Tinley Park is the farthest from the expected target of an enemy attack—O'Hare Airport.

NEWSPAPERS AND MAGAZINES

FIRST

Newspapers: The *Chicago Democrat,* first published on Nov. 26, 1833, was Chicago's first newspaper. Published by a young printer, John Calhoun, the first issue reported that the town trustees had passed an ordinance making it illegal for a hog to run at large without a ring in its nose or a yoke about its neck. The fine for each offense was $2. During the Panic of 1837, Calhoun sold a half-interest in the newspaper to the flamboyant John Wentworth, the future mayor of Chicago.

Five daily newspapers publish in Cook County—the *Chicago Tribune,* the *Chicago Sun-Times,* the *Daily Herald* newspapers of the northwest suburbs, the *Southtown Economist* and the *Chicago Daily Defender.* In addition, thirty weekly publications are based in Chicago, and thirty are based in suburban Cook County. The biggest Chicago weekly is the *Chicago Reader,* distributed free. The biggest suburban weeklies are those of the north and west suburban Pioneer Press chain, owned by the *Sun-Times.*

Leading daily suburban newspapers, county by county: The *Naperville Sun* in Du Page; the *Aurora Beacon-News* in Kane; the *Waukegan News-Sun* in Lake; the Northwest Newspapers group in McHenry; and the *Joliet Herald News* in Will.

The *Chicago Sun-Times* has more reporters for whom city bridges are named than any other newspaper in town. On June 5, 1986, the Wabash Avenue Bridge over the Chicago River was renamed by the city for Irv Kupcinet, in honor of his fifty years as a journalist with the *Sun-Times* and one of its predecessors, the *Times*. "I never thought I'd be a bridge," Kup said. On April 19, 1991, the city named another bridge—the one spanning North Avenue at Goose Island—for *Sun-Times* Pulitzer Prize winner Art Petacque.

Magazines: Among the most prominent national magazines published in Chicago are *Advertising Age,* published by Crain Communications; *Ebony* and *Jet* magazines, published by Johnson Publishing Company; and *Playboy* magazine.

In 1977, Chicago newsman Will Leonard, sixty-four, keeled over in the city room of the *Chicago Tribune* after writing his "On the Town" column. As he was being transported, dying, to the hospital, he suddenly said, "I just realized. The lead is in the second graph."

FAMOUS CHICAGOANS

Col. Robert McCormick (1880-1955): He was the outspoken and politically conservative publisher and editor of the *Chicago Tribune* from 1910 to his death in 1955. The last of the old-fashioned American newspaper barons, McCormick used his paper to further his pet causes, railing each day against Communists, anarchists and FDR, and promoting American isolationism. McCormick's *Tribune* called itself the "World's Greatest Newspaper" and printed the American flag and a right-wing editorial cartoon on every front page. But the Trib was also, increasingly, a well-edited and well-managed newspaper, leading the country in standard-size newspaper circulation. Early in his career, the colonel—who earned his title in World War I—served in the Chicago City Council. He died at his Wheaton estate, Cantigny, on April 1, 1955.

Finley Peter Dunne (1868-1936): Chicago's tradition of impressive newspaper columnists began with Dunne, creator of the nationally famous Mr. Dooley. Martin Dooley, Dunne's literary alter-ego, was an Irish immigrant bartender on "Archy Road"—Archer Avenue—who expounded with an uncommon dose of common sense on the day's events. Mr. Dooley's musings, expressed in a rich and sometimes difficult brogue, were printed in newspapers across the United States beginning in the 1890s. Dunne wrote his first columns for the *Chicago Journal,* where he was editor. *Tribune* columnist Mike Royko, who has created a well-known alter-ego of his own—Slats Grobnik—acknowledges Dunne as a major influence.

Benjamin Franklin Taylor, of Wheaton, sometimes is called the "Ernie Pyle of the Civil War." He was internationally famous as a war correspondent for the Chicago Evening Journal, known for his touching and sensitive dispatches from Union camps.

CHICAGO CONTRIBUTIONS

The Front Page: The classic Chicago newspaper play, it was written by Chicago reporters Ben Hecht and Charlie McArthur. "The Front Page" is a send-up of newspaper life in Chicago in the 1920s, when reporters were notoriously loose and creative with the facts. The play's central character was modeled on the real-life newsman Hildy Johnson, whose paper once agreed to pay $200 to a killer for his Death Row memoirs. Johnson was assigned to deliver the money to the man in his cell on the day of his execution. A game of gin rummy was suggested, and Johnson left with the $200. As he was being strapped in the electric chair that night, the condemned man allegedly uttered these last words: "Don't play rummy with Hildy Johnson. I think he cheats."

Playboy magazine: This Chicago publication may not have started the sexual revolution, but it sure led the cheering. *Playboy* was the first legitimate and sophisticated monthly magazine to feature female nudity and sexually oriented material. It was founded in 1953 by Chicago native Hugh Hefner, who advocated in a seemingly endless series of "Playboy philosophy" essays that men should maintain complete freedom in all things, including sex. The first issue, which appeared on local newsstands in December 1953, featured a nude photograph of Marilyn Monroe as the "Sweetheart of the Month." In 1988, Hefner, having moved to Los Angeles, married a Miss January and retired as chairman and chief executive of Playboy Enterprises. His Phi Beta Kappa daughter, Christie Hefner, took over.

The Chicago Defender: When the great migration of Southern blacks to the North began, the *Chicago Defender* lead the way. The *Defender,* founded by Robert S. Abbott in 1905, urged black Americans to escape the South's Jim Crow oppression and move up to Chicago, where freedom was greater and jobs were waiting. Copies of the *Defender* were distributed throughout the South by porters on the Illinois Central R.R. Abbott was a Georgia printer and lawyer before founding the *Defender* in Chicago. In 1940, his nephew, John H. Sengstacke, took over.

In the days when Chicago newspapers were just a tad wilder, reporters penned some memorable lead sentences to their stories:

- When child murderer Richard Loeb was knifed to death in prison in a homosexual quarrel, Ed Lahey of the *Daily News* wrote: "Richard Loeb, who was a master of the English language, today ended a sentence with a proposition."

- When "Machine Gun" Jack McGurn, a golf enthusiast, was slain in cold blood near Eightieth Street, a reporter wrote, "Machine Gun Jack holed out last night. He died in the low eighties."

- And when reporter Robert J. Casey covered the 1938 trial of a woman accused of murdering several of her husbands, he wrote: "Anna Marie Hahn's 11 husbands came to court today—10 of them in glass jars and one in a blue serge suit."

GENEALOGY OF CHICAGO NEWSPAPERS FROM 1844:
(In alphabetical order)

AMERICAN: Founded July 4, 1900; merged with *Herald-Examiner* Aug. 26, 1939, to become *Herald-American.*

CHRONICLE: Founded 1895; discontinued 1908 with 50,000 circulation.

COURIER: Founded 1874, discontinued 1876.

DAILY NEWS: Founded Jan. 2, 1876; absorbed *Post & Mail,* August 1878; absorbed *Journal* Aug. 22, 1929; absorbed *Post,* Oct. 29, 1932; purchased 1959 by Marshall Field; discontinued March 4, 1978, last solely afternoon paper in city.

DAILY TELEGRAPH: Founded March 6, 1878, changed to *Morning Herald* May 10, 1881.

DAILY TIMES: Founded Sept. 3, 1929; absorbed by *Sun* in 1948 and became part of *Sun & Times;* then *Sun-Times* same year.

EVENING MAIL: Founded Aug. 18, 1870; merged in 1875 with *Evening Post* as *Post & Mail.*

EVENING POST: Founded Sept. 4, 1865; merged in 1875 with *Evening Mail* as *Post & Mail.*

EVENING PRESS & MAIL: Founded 1884, discontinued 1897 with 40,000 circulation.

EVENING RECORD: Founded 1861, discontinued 1870 with 1,280 circulation.

EXAMINER: Founded 1902, absorbed by *Herald* into *Herald & Examiner* May 2, 1918, with 157,338 circulation.

GLOBE: Founded 1887, discontinued 1895 with 16,800 circulation.

HERALD: Founded May, 1914, by merger of *Record Herald* and *Inter-Ocean.*

HERALD-AMERICAN: Founded Aug. 28, 1939, as merger of *Herald-Examiner* and *American;* acquired by *Tribune* in 1958; changed to *Chicago's American* and then in 1969 became *Today,* which was discontinued Sept. 13, 1974.

INTER-OCEAN: Founded March 25, 1872, as new name for *Republican;* absorbed by *Record-Herald,* May 1914, with 79,500 circulation.

JOURNAL: Founded 1844; absorbed by *Daily News* Aug. 22, 1929, with 80,161 circulation.

MORNING NEWS: Founded March 21, 1881, changed to *Morning Record,* March 13, 1893.

MORNING HERALD: Founded May 10, 1881; merged with *Times* as *Times-Herald,* March 4, 1895.

MORNING RECORD: Founded March 13, 1893; merged with *Times-Herald* as *Record-Herald,* March 21, 1901.

POST: Founded April 29, 1890; absorbed by *Daily News* Oct. 29, 1932, with 37,846 circulation.

POST & MAIL: Founded 1874 by merger of *Evening Post* and *Evening Mail.*

RECORD-HERALD: Founded March 28, 1901, by merger of *Morning Record* and *Times-Herald.*

REPUBLICAN: Founded Jan. 16, 1865; changed to *Inter-Ocean* March 25, 1872.

SUN: Founded Dec. 4, 1941; absorbed the *Times* and became *Sun & Times* in 1948; became *Sun-Times* in 1948.

SUN-TIMES: Founded 1948 from merger of *Sun* and *Times.*

TIMES: Founded June 1, 1861; merged with *Morning Herald* as *Times-Herald* March 4, 1895.

TIMES-HERALD: Founded March 4, 1895, as merger of *Times* and *Morning Herald;* merged with *Morning Record* to become *Record Herald* on March 21, 1901.

TODAY: Tabloid created 1969 from Chicago's American; discontinued Sept. 13, 1974.

TRIBUNE: Founded June 10, 1847; acquired *Herald-American* in 1958.

CLASSIC QUOTE

A Chicago attorney, Newton Minow, gave television its most disparaging label: "a vast wasteland." He introduced the phrase in a May 9, 1961, speech before the National Association of Broadcasters. Chal-

Newton Minow, a Chicago attorney and chairman of the FCC under President John F. Kennedy, labeled television "a vast wasteland" in 1961. *(Photo by Perry C. Riddle)*

lenging the TV executives to actually sit and watch the shows they aired, he said:

"You will see a procession of game shows, violence, audience participation shows, formula comedies about totally unbelievable families, blood and thunder, mayhem, violence, sadism, murder, Western badmen, Western good men, private eyes, gangsters, more violence, and cartoons. And, endlessly, commercials. . . . And most of all, boredom."

Sources: Robert Feder, TV/radio columnist, *Chicago Sun-Times;* Tom Tradup and Warren Shulz, WLS-AM radio; Chuck Schaden, Carla Wilson, WFLD-TV; Clare Denzler, WBBM-TV; Michael Malone, WGN-TV; Etta Gonzalez, WLS-TV; WMAQ-TV public relations; Bill Natale, WTTW-TV; Lorna Gladson, program director, WGN-AM radio; Joan Dry, Chicago Museum of Broadcast History; Dr. Joel Sternberg, television historian at St. Xavier College in Chicago; Dianne Bono, A.C. Nielsen Co.; Debbie Buckley, Arbitron Co.; Roy Bellavia, WSBC-AM; the *Broadcasting Yearbook,* a Times-Mirror Business Publication.

CRIME AND PUNISHMENT

FIRSTS

■ The first murder investigation in Chicago—before it became Chicago—was in the spring of 1812. At that time, John H. Kinzie lived on the north bank of the Chicago River, across from Fort Dearborn, and for whatever reason he was constantly being hassled by John Lalime, the fort's Indian interpreter, and maybe he was doing some hassling himself. At any rate, they didn't like each other. One day, when Kinzie was leaving the fort after a visit, Lalime came after him with a pistol. Kinzie wrestled it away, and Lalime was stabbed with his own knife and died. Kinzie, who was wounded, fled to Milwaukee with the help of Indians. Although Lalime was well-liked at the fort, the officers there eventually called it "justifiable homicide."

■ The first execution in Cook County came at 3:15 p.m., July 10, 1840. John Stone, who was convicted of murdering Mrs. Lucretia Thompson, was hanged near the lake about three miles south of what is now downtown Chicago. Until the end, he claimed his innocence.

■ What is probably the first execution of a woman in Illinois occurred Downstate in 1845 and drew about 4,000 spectators. Elizabeth Reed, who some local people thought was a witch, was convicted of murdering her husband by dropping arsenic in his tea. She came to her execution dressed in white, singing a song, and sitting on top of her coffin. A witness said, "She didn't seem nervous and mounted the scaffold without hesitation."

■ The first Chicago policemen were called constables, and the first "Police Constable" elected was apparently O. Morrison on Aug. 5, 1835. He was also the town collector. Before the constables, if an informer turned somebody in, he'd get half the fine.

■ The first time fingerprint evidence survived a test before the Illinois Supreme Court came in the case of Thomas Jennings, who was convicted of killing a Rock Island Line railroad man. Jennings' fingerprints were found at the dead man's home. Jennings was executed in 1912.

■ The first official police force was organized in 1855, with three precinct stations, a twenty-four-hour patrol service and authorization for eighty to ninety men. They wore leather badges attached to their hatbands.

■ Since the Chicago Fire of 1871 destroyed many city records, the identity of the first Chicago police officer killed in the line of duty is not a certainty. But he is believed to have been Casper Lauer, killed on Sept. 18, 1854. Lauer joined the force in 1849, and was stabbed by Patrick Cunningham during a struggle when Lauer tried to take him to the police station—details of the arrest are unclear. Lauer pulled his gun, and Cunningham said, "Don't shoot and I'll be safe." Lauer didn't fire. He kept Cunningham in custody, however, by knocking him down with his police "cane," until other officers came to help. Lauer died shortly thereafter, leaving a wife and three children. He was thirty-four.

■ The first Chicago policeman to have his star permanently retired and put in the Superintendent's Honored Star Case was Patrick O'Meara, who was killed in the line of duty on August 5, 1872.

EXTREMES

■ The most murders committed in Chicago in one year was 970 in 1974. About 69 percent of those murders were committed with firearms, most of which were handguns.

■ The most executions in one day in Cook County came on Feb. 16, 1912, when five were hanged: two brothers and two other men were hanged for robbing and killing a truck farmer at the intersection at Lincoln and Peterson. Thomas Jennings, whose conviction for killing a railroad man made history because his fingerprints were used as evidence, also was hanged that day.

■ John Wayne Gacy has been convicted of more murders (33) than anyone else in U.S. history.

■ Illinois had the fastest growing prison system in the nation in 1990. The number of prisoners increased that fiscal year by 20.9 percent.

■ Chicago's biggest cash crime occurred on Oct. 20, 1974, when $4.3 million was stolen from the Purolator warehouse, 127 W. Huron. Five men were convicted, including a former Purolator guard who lapsed into a coma shortly after he was arrested. All but $900,000 of the money was recovered.

John Wayne Gacy, about 1968,
has been convicted of more
murders than anyone else in U.S.
history.

■ What was called the "biggest almost crime in the country" took sixty-four minutes, involved about $70 million and was done with telephones and computers. In May of 1988, two $15,000-a-year bank clerks tried to defraud the First National Bank of Chicago of $70 million through a plan that involved transferring money by wire out of customer accounts into accounts at banks in Austria. The money was recovered and returned. Seven men were convicted in connection with the scheme. One of them, Gabriel Taylor, who had worked in the bank's international wire transfer room, said, "What I did was uncalled for, and I am sorry."

Ness Test: After putting Al Capone and plenty of his pals in prison, Eliot Ness still was required to take a government test to keep his job. Ness and ten of his men had to take the test in 1934 because of a law passed by Congress requiring the exam. At the time, Ness was the agent in charge of the Cleveland office of the alcohol tax unit of the Treasury Department.

NUMBER OF POLICE BY RACE AND GENDER

There were 12,100 sworn Chicago police officers as of late spring, 1991. Among male officers there were: 7,244 whites; 2,348 blacks; 700 Hispanics; 44 Orientals; and 15 Native Americans. Among female officers there were: 966 whites; 654 blacks; 117 Hispanics; 8 Orientals; and 4 Native Americans.

LIST OF TEN
LAST TEN YEARS OF MURDERS IN CHICAGO

Year	Total Murders	Murders committed with firearms	Murders committed with handguns
1981	877	546	374
1982	668	380	254
1983	729	429	290
1984	741	442	289
1985	666	378	261
1986	744	419	285
1987	691	374	260
1988	660	392	371
1989	742	433	417
1990	851	601	512

NUMBER OF MAJOR CRIMES IN CHICAGO BY YEAR

	1985	1986	1987	1988	1989	1990
Car Theft	44,892	48,400	39,693	45,012	45,898	48,626
Theft	121,264	121,455	119,072	128,584	130,153	130,000
Serious assault	29,096	33,409	34,194	35,988	37,615	41,114
Burglary	52,688	56,077	51,005	52,060	51,580	50,203
Sexual Assault	3,357	3,708	3,692	3,695	3,645	3,607
Murder	666	744	691	660	742	851
Robbery	26,892	30,678	29,879	28,975	31,588	37,156

STREET GANGS

Chicago police estimate there are 125 street gangs in Chicago, with more than 12,000 members ranging in age from eight to fifty-five years old. They identify themselves through earrings, colors and sweaters. Last year, street gangs were connected to at least 101 murders in Chicago, an increase of 40.3 percent from the 1989 total of 79.

ILLINOIS DEPARTMENT OF CORRECTIONS

Created in January 1970. More than 27,000 adults are in the system. The average annual cost to house and board an inmate is $16,000, the average annual cost to house and board a death row inmate ranges from $21,000 to $25,000. Budget: $496 million (1990). About 60 percent of the prison population comes from Cook County, and 15 to 20 percent from the collar counties. The average age of the prison population is thirty.

Prison Sales: Since 1904 Illinois prisons have produced both agricultural and industrial products. In 1990 the Correctional Industries sales were $28.9 million.

DEATH PENALTY IN ILLINOIS

The U.S. Supreme Court threw out the death penalty in 1972 and reinstated it in 1976. Illinois passed its present death penalty statute in 1977. The last person executed in Illinois was Charles Walker at 12:12 a.m., on Sept. 12, 1990. He short-circuited his appeals and asked to die. Before that, the last execution was the electrocution of James Duke, a convicted cop killer, in 1962. It's difficult to put an exact number on executions before Walker. Some facts, however, are known: 98 people, including one woman, have been electrocuted—67 in Cook County. And at least 102 people have been hanged in Cook County alone. At least two women have been executed.

LIST OF TEN
DEATH ROW'S LONGEST RESIDENTS

Name	Admitting Date	County	Race or Ethnic Group	Counts of Murder
John Szabo	12/3/79	Will	White	4
George Delvecchio	12/6/79	Cook	White	1
James P. Free, Jr.	12/11/79	Du Page	White	1
Kenneth Allen	1/17/80	Cook	Black	2
Hernando Williams	2/8/80	Cook	Black	3
John Wayne Gacy	3/14/80	Cook	White	33
Juan Caballero	3/28/80	Cook	Hispanic	3
Andre Jones	4/17/80	St. Clair	Black	3
Luis Ruiz	5/2/80	Cook	Hispanic	3
Durlynn Eddmonds	7/18/80	Cook	Black	1

LEOPOLD AND LOEB
SPARED FROM THE DEATH PENALTY

Late in the afternoon on May 21, 1924, Bobby Franks was casually walking home from school when Nathan Leopold and Richard Loeb rolled up in a rented touring sedan. Bobby knew them both. In fact, Loeb was a distant relative. So he took a ride. Leopold and Loeb were both in their late teens, both from wealthy families and both brilliant University of Chicago graduate students. They apparently had chosen Bobby to be the victim of a "perfect murder," an intellectual exercise.

The boy was killed and the body buried. A call was made to Bobby's parents claiming a kidnapping. The body, however, soon was found, along with Leopold's glasses. Eventually the two were arrested. At first they were cocky, but eventually they confessed. Defense lawyer Clarence Darrow was hired to save them from the death penalty. Darrow made a three-day final argument. "I am pleading for the future," he argued. "for a time when hatred and cruelty will not control the hearts of men, when we can learn...that all life is worth saving, and that mercy is the highest attribute of man." Darrow succeeded. Leopold and Loeb were given life.

Clarence Darrow is flanked by his two infamous clients, Nathan Leopold, Jr., (left) and Richard Loeb.

AVERAGE DAILY ILLINOIS PRISON POPULATION 1990

	Year Opened	Population	Capacity
Maximum Security			
Joliet	1860	1,344	761
Menard	1878	2,544	1,460
Pontiac		1,929	2,000
Stateville	1925	2,049	1,506
Medium Security			
Dwight	1930	715	470
Menard Psych.	1970	384	315
Centralia	1980	1,115	750
Danville	1985	1,118	896
Dixon (Coed)	1983	1,344	1,179
Graham	1980	1,122	750
Hill	1986	1,127	896
Illinois River	1989	809	750
Logan (Coed)	1977	1,146	1,204
Shawnee	1984	1,204	1,046
Sheridan	1941	1,005	624
Western Illinois	1989	829	728

	Year Opened	Population	Capacity
Minimum Security			
East Moline	1980	825	688
Jacksonville	1984	633	500
Lincoln	1984	697	558
Robinson	1991		600
Taylorville	1990		600
Vandalia	1921	953	599
Vienna	1965	992	835

COUNTY JAIL POPULATIONS 1990

	Capacity	Avg. Daily Population
Cook	6,139	6,790.8
Du Page	354	369.5
Lake	350	277.1
Kane	202	270.9
McHenry	104	41.7
Will	141	160.3

JUVENILE DETENTION CENTER POPULATIONS 1990

	Admitted		Average Daily Population	
	Male	Female	Male	Female
Cook	11,178	1,220	381	32
Du Page	488	103	24	6
Lake	404	30	12	1
Kane	373	56	17	2
McHenry and Will	N/A			

THE MOB

Chicago has a long tradition of gamblers, bootleggers, and general vice. There have always been mob bosses and they've often had political pals. And there's always been some guy somewhere trying to run things illegally. From the Civil War until his death in 1907, there was gambler Mike McDonald, according to Alson J. Smith's *Syndicate City*. And, of course, he had the Mike McDonald Democrats and the services of First Ward aldermen Michael "Hinky Dink" Kenna and Bathhouse John Coughlin. Then there was Mont Tennes, who was running gambling on the North Side when he started paying for a wire service that gave him horse racing results he could sell to Chicago bookies. Tennes also had some political clout—a West Side alderman who had his own gambling empire. Then there was Big Jim Colosimo, who was gunned down in 1920, which opened the way for Johnny Torrio, who was shot but not killed in 1925. After his brush with death, Torrio turned mob operations over to his protege, Al Capone.

BIG HITS

■ On May 11, 1920, mob boss Big Jim Colosimo was at his restaurant at Twenty-second and Wabash, where Big Jim O'Leary, the son of Mrs. O'Leary of Chicago Fire fame, had arranged a business meeting. While Colosimo was waiting for the meeting, somebody came out of the restaurant's cloakroom and gunned him down. His funeral was huge. The *Daily News* called it "the funeral of a man of power. Great politicians in silk hats moved Homerically about. Judges pushed their way through the jam. Banners floated in the air—banners of the First Ward Democratic club. . . ." The murder was never solved.

■ 1926 was the worst year for mobsters to go outside. There were a record seventy-five gangland slayings.

■ North Side gang boss Dion "Deanie" O'Banion used to be an altar boy at Holy Name Cathedral, 735 N. State. In November 1924, he was gunned down across the street from it. He owned part of a flower shop there, and that's where he was killed. The murder was never solved, and in October 1926, O'Bannion's buddy Hymie Weiss was gunned down on the other side of the street, right in front of the Cathedral.

■ On Feb. 14, 1929, four men, two dressed like cops, went into a garage at 2122 N. Clark, lined up seven men against a wall, pulled out machineguns and shotguns and killed them all. The St. Valentine's Day Massacre, believed to have been orchestrated by Al Capone against his rivals, gave Chicago an image that still lingers. (See Past Tense.)

■ Ken Eto was the highest-ranking Oriental in the Chicago mob in 1983. But that didn't stop hit men from shooting Eto three times in the head while in his car parked at the Montclare Theater, 7129 W. Grand. He didn't die. Five months later, two men suspected in the bungled hit were found in a car trunk at a Du Page County condominium complex. Eto went on to provide authorities with hundreds of pages of transcripts on the workings of the Chicago mob.

■ Anthony J. Spilotro and his brother Michael were found in a shallow grave in an Indiana cornfield in June 1966. They may have been slain because Tony resisted efforts to replace him as the Chicago mob's boss in Las Vegas. Although their heads and faces were beaten, the coroner said they died of asphyxiation. They may have been buried alive. As with many mob hits recorded by the Chicago Crime Commission, the Spilotro story ends with "Killer unknown."

Lady in Red: Moments after stepping out of the Biograph Theater at 2433 N. Lincoln, John Dillinger was gunned down by FBI agents in a nearby alley on July 22, 1934. Women dipped their skirts in his blood, and children sold bloodstained scraps of newspaper for a dime. But what happened to the two women he was with? Anna Sage, the "Lady in Red" who fingered Dillinger for the Feds, actually wore an orange dress that night. It just looked red under the marquee lights. She died in 1947 in Romania still complaining she was cheated out of $70,000 of reward money. After Dillinger died, authorities went through his pockets and found $7.80, a clip for a .38 and a watch with a picture of the other woman, Polly Hamilton. After the shooting, she changed her name. She insisted she knew Dillinger only as "Jimmy Lawrence," a clerk at the Board of Trade. She later married and never talked about Dillinger. Her relatives said she loved children, the Cubs and Christmas.

NUMBER OF CHICAGO GANGLAND KILLINGS BY YEAR

Year	#	Year	#	Year	#	Year	#
1919:	24	1937:	3	1955:	4	1973:	2
1920:	23	1938:	14	1956:	7	1974:	11
1921:	29	1939:	6	1957:	6	1975:	9
1922:	37	1940:	8	1958:	3	1976:	4
1923:	52	1941:	8	1959:	10	1977:	16
1924:	54	1942:	5	1960:	8	1978:	12
1925:	66	1943:	10	1961:	19	1979:	4
1926:	75	1944:	8	1962:	14	1980:	2
1927:	58	1945:	10	1963:	6	1981:	7
1928:	72	1946:	6	1964:	4	1982:	2
1929:	56	1947:	4	1965:	7	1983:	4
1930:	64	1948:	10	1966:	6	1984:	1
1931:	48	1949:	4	1967:	5	1985:	4
1932:	39	1950:	4	1968:	0	1986:	6
1933:	32	1951:	2	1969:	1	1987:	1
1934:	36	1952:	4	1970:	2	1988:	2
1935:	17	1953:	1	1971:	2	1989:	1
1936:	12	1954:	7	1972:	2	1990:	2

MURDERS, SHOOTINGS AND KIDNAPPINGS OF POLITICIANS

■ Carter Henry Harrison (1825-1893), who was elected to his final term as mayor in 1893 as the "World's Fair Mayor," was shot to death by a man who wanted to be a corporation counsel. The assassin had lobbied for the job with Harrison, but to no avail. After the shooting, the guy still didn't get the job.

■ William McSwiggin, known as "The Hanging Prosecutor" because of his ability to get the death penalty in murder trials, was machine-gunned to death on April 27, 1926, on a sidewalk outside a Cicero tavern. Killed with him were Thomas "Red" Duffy, a barber and a precinct captain, and James J. Doherty, a saloon-keeper. The papers screamed, "Who killed McSwiggin?" Was he with the mob or against it? The murder never was solved.

■ On April 19, 1928, Octavius C. Granady, a black candidate for Republican committeeman of the 20th Ward against Morris Eller, was murdered on election day. After leaving the polling place at 1222 S. Blue Island Avenue, Granady was chased in his car for a mile, curbed and shot to death. Several policemen were indicted, but the cases were dismissed. One witness said the killers' car had a "Vote for Eller" banner on it.

■ Chicago Mayor Anton Cermak (1873-1933) was shot by a bullet intended for President-elect Franklin D. Roosevelt while the two were making a public appearance in Miami on Feb. 15, 1933. The shots sounded like firecrackers, and one photographer joked to Cermak "Just like Chicago, eh mayor?" There was no answer from Cermak, who by then had a bullet in his lung. On March 6, Roosevelt was inaugurated. Cermak died two days later. Before he died, Cermak told Roosevelt, "I'm glad it was me instead of you."

■ A judge cleared Ald. Mathias "Paddy" Bauler of charges involved in the 1933 shooting of policeman John J. Ahearn, a former bodyguard of Mayor Cermak, outside Bauler's tavern. Bauler said that after he refused to let the policeman into the tavern, Ahearn called him a "big Dutch pig," hit him and shot at him. Bauler said he then pulled his own gun and shot into the ground. After the trial, Bauler said he was going to draft a new ordinance. "It's an outrage to let policemen flourish guns every time they get a few drinks," he said. "I'm going to see it stopped." He said he'd write an ordinance requiring police to leave their guns at work.

■ On Dec. 29, 1935, state Rep. Albert J. Prignano (D-Chicago), committeeman of the 20th Ward—known as the "Bloody 20th," was shot to death in front of his wife, mother and eight-year-old son on the doorstep of his home at 722 Bunker (Grenshaw). It was said that Frank Nitti had told him not to run for committeeman.

■ On July 9, 1936, state Rep. John H. Bolton was killed by a shotgun blast while riding in his car at about Harrison and Washtenaw. Some suggested he was killed because he was getting too interested in running gambling operations in his district without the approval of Frank Nitti, Al Capone's successor.

■ On Oct. 7, 1948, William John Granata, 27th Ward Republican committeeman, was found at 188 W. Randolph bleeding from knife and ax cuts on his neck. He died shortly thereafter. The murder remains unsolved.

■ On Feb. 6, 1952, Charles Gross, acting Republican committeeman of the 31st Ward, was walking down Kedzie Avenue near North Avenue when a black Ford rolled up. A spotlight focused on him. Gross was killed with seven blasts from a shotgun. He had been told not to run for committeeman.

■ State Rep. Clem Graver (R-Chicago), said to have been called by his first name by 10,000 people, was kidnapped from the garage of his house at 1013 W. Eighteenth Place on June 11, 1953. The disappearance remains a mystery.

■ Ald. Benjamin F. Lewis (24th), who liked big cars and expensive jewelry, was shot four times in the back of his head in his office at 3604 W. Roosevelt Rd. in February of 1963. Despite police checks into his debts (he owed $20,000), his various businesses and his possible romantic entanglements, and despite a $10,000 offer for information by Mayor Richard J. Daley, no one was ever charged.

■ In October 1979, south suburban Phoenix Mayor William Hawkins was gunned down outside his house after arriving home from his steel mill job in Riverdale.

■ In March 1979, Ald. Frank J. Brady (15th) was shot outside his Southwest Side home. He was wounded in the left shoulder in an apparent holdup attempt.

■ Proviso Township Democratic Committeeman Sal Pullia, thirty-three, a former tax extension chief for the Cook County clerk, disappeared on June 4, 1981. He was last seen leaving a restaurant near his home in Melrose Park. The night he disappeared, Pullia was said to have been slapped in the mouth by a well-known Democratic politician.

Closed for Hanging: For one hour on June 30, 1882—the very hour Charles Guiteau was hanged for assassinating President James A. Garfield—Chicago's City Hall was closed. The city council ordered the closing so that Guiteau's "terrible crime" would be "more fully impressed upon the minds of the people, and particularly the minds of evil doers."

■ Diane Masters, a trustee of Moraine Valley Community College, disappeared after a board meeting on March 19, 1982. Nine months later her decomposed body was found in the trunk of her car, which had been dumped into the Sanitary and Ship Canal in Willow Springs. Alan Masters, her lawyer husband, former sheriff's Lt. James Keating and former Willow Springs Police Chief Michael Corbitt were convicted for conspiring to murder her. The disappearance followed months of marital problems between the Masters.

MASS MURDERS AND SERIAL MURDERS

■ Richard Speck was convicted of killing eight Chicago student nurses at 2319 E. 100th on July 14, 1966. Speck was sentenced to death, but the death penalty was thrown out by the U.S. Supreme Court in 1972. Even though the death penalty is once again legal in Illinois, it can't be used against Speck. Without parole, Speck is scheduled to be released from prison in the year 2564. Each time Speck comes up for parole, relatives and friends of the victims argue against it. At a recent parole hearing, 21,768 people signed petitions to block his freedom.

■ John Wayne Gacy, who entertained children as "Pogo the Clown" and was a member of the Jaycees and a Democratic precinct captain, was convicted of luring thirty-three men and boys to his Norwood Park Township home and torturing, sodomizing and killing them— twenty-nine were found buried in the crawl space beneath his house. Gacy received twelve death sentences and twenty-one life terms and in 1980 was sent to Menard Correctional Center's Death Row. Gacy will turn fifty on St. Patrick's Day in 1992.

■ A three-story brick building with bay windows used to stand at the southwest corner of Sixty-third and Wallace. It was called Holmes murder castle. It was built by the handsome Herman Webster Mudget, also known as Henry H. Holmes, who came to Chicago shortly before the Columbian Exposition. On the ground floor Holmes ran a jewelry business and drugstore. He often hired pretty young women and advertised for boarders during the World's Fair. Upstairs and through the rest of the building was a maze of secret passages, trapdoors, enclosed staircases, hidden and soundproof rooms, an acid bath and a crematory. It was there he was said to have killed at least seven people, although he is suspected in more crimes across the country. Some reports have him murdering more than 150 people—mostly young women. Holmes was hanged in 1896 in Philadelphia after being convicted of killing a business associate. He told the hangman, "Don't bungle."

■ William Workman was sentenced to 100 to 300 years in prison for murdering seven people, including his mother, his father, his best friend, a pregnant woman and her twelve-year-old daughter, during a 1973 shooting rampage in Palos Hills. At the time of his arrest, police tear-gassed his house and Workman, a former mental patient who had been in and out of alcoholic treatment, came out holding a can of beer. He said "I am a child of God, and I will do whatever the ____ I want." He was found dead in his cell in 1981, apparently of natural causes.

HIGH-PUBLICITY UNSOLVED CRIMES

■ Northwest Side youths Robert Peterson, fourteen; John Schuessler, thirteen; and his brother Anton, Jr., eleven, disappeared on Sunday, Oct. 16, 1955. Two days later their naked bodies were found in a forest preserve on Lawrence Avenue near the Des Plaines River. All three were strangled. Flecks of a rare form of steel called "stainless austenitic" were found under the fingernails of one of the boys. But a search of metalworking hobbyists or shops that used that steel didn't produce the killer or killers. The Schuessler boys' father, who was said to have been worn out by grief and his own search for the killers, died of a heart attack a month after the three boys were buried.

■ The nude bodies of Barbara Grimes, fifteen, and her sister, Patricia, thirteen, were found in January 1957, beneath a steep embankment along German Church Road in southwest Cook County. The exact cause of death was never determined, but shock and exposure to cold were considered the secondary cause. The two South Side girls disappeared after leaving home to see a movie. Later a man with a slight Southern accent anonymously called the girls' mother and said he helped undress the girls and that the youngest girl's toes were crossed on both her feet. This was a fact the police had not made public.

■ North Sider Judith Mae Andersen was fifteen when she disappeared in August 1957, after leaving a friend's house and heading home. Her dismembered body later was found floating in oil drums in Montrose Harbor. She had been shot four times. While police felt they knew the identity of the murderer, no one was ever convicted.

■ On Sept. 18, 1966, the bludgeoned and stabbed body of Valerie Percy, twenty-one, daughter of Sen. Charles H. Percy (R-Ill.), was found in her bedroom at the family's Kenilworth mansion. It's believed she was killed by home invaders during a burglary.

■ Candy heiress Helen Brach, who lived in a Glenview mansion, disappeared on Feb. 17, 1977, or by one account Feb. 21. She was last seen shortly after leaving the Mayo Clinic in Rochester, Minn. Her handyman, John Matlick, reported her missing March 3, 1977. He said he last saw her on Feb. 21, when he drove her to O'Hare for a flight to Florida. Brach was declared legally dead in May 1984.

■ On June 6, 1980, the bodies of Bruce and Darlene Rouse were found stabbed and shotgunned in their thirteen-room Libertyville ranch house. The Rouse children—a daughter and two sons—told police they were in other parts of the house at the time of the killings. They also said they knew nothing of the murders until a co-worker of their father phoned to ask why he wasn't at work. In 1983, the daughter Robin, nineteen, died following a car accident in Racine, Wisconsin. There was no indication of foul play.

■ The so-called Tylenol killer took the first three victims on Sept. 29, 1982, when three people in one family died. Four more died in the next eighteen hours before police realized the deaths were related. The killer had slain seven people with Tylenol capsules laced with fifteen cents worth of cyanide. That was followed by hundreds of copycat poisonings nationwide and hundreds of false alarms. The capsules killed a store owner, a college student, a flight attendant, a postal worker, a housewife, a sales clerk and a twelve-year-old student. The victims lived in places ranging from the Gold Coast to DuPage County. The killer has never been found.

A CHICAGO STORY
THE UNTOUCHABLES

After a meeting of the so-called "secret six" in a Loop office, it was decided: Al Capone had to be stopped. The six were formally known as the Citizens Committee for the Prevention and Punishment of Crime, a committee of the Chicago Association of Commerce. The call for help went all the way to the White House. A young federal agent from Chicago named Eliot Ness (1903-1957) was chosen to lead the war against Capone by using the income tax division of the government and demolishing every brewery he could find. Ness handpicked a team of men to help him. Because they were said to be immune to Capone's bribes, they were called "The Untouchables."

Later described by a fellow Untouchable as "nervous and tense, sort of collegiate looking, ambitious, a nice guy doing a job," the tall, slender and handsome Ness started his government work in Chicago shortly after graduating from the University of Chicago in 1925. He was methodical and organized.

Using pins to mark the location of 2,700 illegal breweries and bars scheduled for raids throughout Cook County and beyond, Ness mapped out a war plan. He used such devices as a Mack truck with a

---

Capone Sues Untouchables: Acting as administrator of her brother's estate, the sister of Al Capone sued the producer, the sponsor and the network that carried the TV show "The Untouchables" for (among other things) appropriating "the name, likeness and personality" of Capone without seeking the permission of Capone's widow, Mae, or son, Albert. The lawsuit was filed in 1959 by Mrs. Mafalda Maritote, who lived on the West Side.

battering ram to level the garage doors of breweries. It was a plan of harassment, and the effort was felt.

In September 1932, the *Daily News* reported, "Hard times and constant molestation by prohibition agents have caused the Capone liquor syndicate to start delivering its beverages in small trucks rather than the huge trucks. . . ." Ness' crew was able to send Al Capone and sixty-eight others to federal prison.

Terrible Tommy: Hangings ended in the 1920s, but a gallows was kept for Terrible Tommy O'Connor until 1977. Convicted of murdering a policeman, he escaped from jail four days before he was to hang. The gallows was kept for fifty-six years, just in case O'Connor was found. He wasn't.

AL CAPONE

During a scrape in a whorehouse in New York in his younger days, Al Capone (1899-1947) was slashed with a razor from ear to lip on his left cheek, hence the nickname "Scarface." He was brought to Chicago to work for a mobster he had known in New York, and by 1925 he had started running a wildly profitable organized crime syndicate with illegal booze as its focus. With his wealth estimated at more than $100 million, Capone set up headquarters at the Metropole Hotel, 2300 S. Michigan, where he rented fifty rooms on two floors, complete with a recreation room, twenty-four-hour gambling and private elevators servicing his friends and associates. He was indicted in 1931, convicted of income tax evasion, sentenced to eleven years and did time in Atlanta and Alcatraz. He was released in 1939. Eight years later, with his nervous system racked by syphilis, Capone suffered a stroke and died on Jan. 25, 1947 in his twenty-five-room mansion in Miami.

Death on the Tracks: Only hours after being indicted in New York for the alleged extortion of movie industry executives, Frank "The Enforcer" Nitti, once a top Capone lieutenant, was found dead on a strip of railroad tracks at Harlem Avenue near Cermak Road. He allegedly shot himself. Nitti was dressed in shabby clothes and had a rosary in his pocket.

MOB NICKNAMES

● Paul *"The Waiter"* Ricca—supposedly he was once a waiter on Halsted Street and was in the restaurant business.

The most famous Chicago gangster: Al Capone.

- Charles *"Cherry nose"* Gioe—he had a big nose.
- Louis *"Little New York"* Campagna, also known as *"Lefty Louie"*—originally from New York.
- Claude Maddox a.k.a. *John Screwy Moore*—because he was a crazy guy.
- William *"Egan's Rats"* Heeney—member of Egan's Rats gang in East St. Louis.
- Murray *"The Camel"* Humphreys—liked camel hair coats.

- Sam *"Golfbag"* Hunt—carried a shotgun in a golf bag.
- Salvatore *"Mooney"* Giancana—used that name when he was arrested so he would appear to be Irish.
- Paul *"Needlenose"* Labriola—nicknamed by *Sun-Times* crime reporter Art Petacque because Labriola had a nose job that made it look pointed.
- Guy *"Lover boy"* Mendola—because he was a ladies man.
- Angelo *"The Hook"* LaPietra—because he was a tough guy.
- Joseph *"Joey O'Brien"* Aiuppa—imprisoned top mob boss used to fight professionally under name of Joey O'Brien.
- Joey *"The Clown"* Lombardo—had a penchant for clowning around with his friends and when he was arrested.
- Jacob M. *"The Senator"* Guzik, because he was the mob's fixer; and his brother Harry *"Greasy Thumb"* Guzik, because he would lick his thumb as he counted money to pay off cops.

The Wall: The white-washed brick wall against which seven men died at 2122 N. Clark Street in the St. Valentine's Day massacre was eventually dismantled and sold to a Canadian businessman. He used the bricks in a men's washroom in a singalong nightclub.

PAST TENSE

Here's how the *Chicago Daily News* covered the St. Valentine's Day massacre in its editions of Feb. 14, 1929:

Massacre 7 of Moran Gang

Victims Are Lined Against Wall; One Volley Kills All Assassins Pose as Policemen; Flee in "Squad Car" After Fusillade; Capone Revenge for Murder of Lombardo, Officers Believe.

Seven Moran-O'Banion gangsters were lined up against the wall of a beer-distributing point at 2122 North Clark street at 10:30 o'clock today. Four men, two of them in police uniforms, stood before them, armed with machine guns and sawed-off shotguns. The leader of the execution squad barked an or-

der and the seven fell, six dying at once, the seventh three hours later.

The execution, carried out with the precision of a Mexican firing squad, is charged by the police to the Capone-Lombardo interests. Greatest in point of numbers, it was also the most cold-blooded in the history of Chicago's gangland slaughters.

The dead as identified by police were:

GUSENBERG, PETER, notorious gunman for the O'Banion-Weiss-Drucci-Moran mob.

GUSENBERG, FRANK, brother of Peter. He died after the others, but refused to talk, though conscious.

WEINSHANK, AL, north side "alky" peddler.

MAY, JOHN, 1249 West Madison street, a $50-a-week mechanic, apparently killed to silence him.

CLARK, JOHN, brother-in-law of George "Bugs" Moran, leader of the gang.

DAVIS, ARTHUR, West Side racketeer.

FOSTER, FRANK, hoodlum.

A second theory, advanced by federal prohibition agents, was that the massacre was perpetrated by a band of rum runners from Detroit...

Killing Scene Too Gruesome for Onlookers

View of Carnage Proves a Strain on Their Nerves Is Like A Shambles

It's too much to tell. You go into the door marked "S-M-C Cartage company." You see a bunch of big men talking with restrained excitement in the cigarette smoke. You go through another door back of the front office. You go between two close-parked trucks in the garage.

Then you almost stumble over the head of the first man, with a clean gray felt hat still placed at the precise angle of gangster toughness.

The dull yellow light of a lamp in daytime shows dark rivulets of blood heading down to the drain that was meant for the water from washed cars. There are six of the red streams from six heads. The bodies—four of them well dressed in civilian clothes—two of them with their legs crossed as they whirled to fall.

It's too much...

CLASSIC QUOTES

In 1962, James Dukes, a convicted cop killer, was the last man to be executed in Cook County. At the time of his execution he left a copy of Plato's dialogues with Socrates' words underlined: "The hour of departure has arrived and we go our ways. I to die and you to live. Which is better, God only knows."

In 1927 Al Capone said, "I've been spending the best years of my life as a public benefactor. I've given people the light pleasures, shown them a good time. And all I get is abuse—the existence of a hunted man—I'm called a killer."

Sources: *Sun-Times* reporters Art Petacque; Jim Casey; Phillip J. O'Connor; Susan Chandler, *Chicago Sun-Times* and *Daily News*; *Syndicate City* by Alson J. Smith; Nic Howell, Illinois Department of Corrections; Chicago Crime Commission; Chicago Police Department; Dennis Bingham—*Chicago Police Star*; *History of Chicago Vol. I* by A.T. Andreas.

SPORTS

HOME-GROWN OLYMPIC CHAMPS

The U.S. Olympic committee lists eighty-seven Olympic medal winners who were born in the Chicago metropolitan area. Among them they have earned forty-seven gold medals, thirty-five silver medals and thirty-three bronze medals.

The Chicago area, of course, also boasts a number of Olympic heroes who were born elsewhere but called Chicago home. Among them are Atlanta-born runner Ralph Metcalf, who won an Olympic gold medal in track in 1936 and a silver and bronze in 1932; Alabama-born runner Jesse Owens, who infuriated Adolf Hitler by winning four gold medals in the 1936 games in Berlin; Tennessee-born runner Wilma Rudolph, who won three gold medals in 1960; and Romanian-born swimmer Johnny Weissmuller, who won three gold medals in 1924 and two in 1928.

The multiple-gold winners born in the Chicago area are:

Mark P. Arie, Chicago, two golds in trapshooting in 1920.

Bart Conner, Morton Grove, two golds in gymnastics in 1984.

William M. L. Fiske, Chicago, gold in the 5-man bobsled competition in 1928 and in the 4-man bobsled competition in 1932.

Clifford Barton Gray, Chicago, gold in the 5-man bobsled competition in 1928 and in the 4-man bobsled competition in 1932.

Barbara Pearl Jones, Chicago, gold in swimming in 1952 and in 1960.

Ethel Lackie, Chicago, two golds in swimming in 1924.

John Phillips Naber, Evanston, four golds in swimming in 1976.

Walter Steve Ris, Chicago, two golds in swimming in 1948.

Elizabeth (Betty) Robinson, Riverdale, gold in track and field in 1928 and again in 1936.

SUN-TIMES SPORTS STAFF'S
ALL-TIME HIGH SCHOOL TEAMS

FOOTBALL

Offense		Defense	
TE:	Rich Kreitling, Fenger, 1954	L:	Bill Fisher, Lane Tech, 1944
WR:	Pete Pihos, Austin, 1941	L:	Russell Maryland, Young, 1986
L:	George Connor, De La Salle, 1943	L:	Chris Zorich, Vocational, 1986
L:	Mike Kenn, Evanston, 1973	L:	Dave Butz, Maine South, 1969
L:	Dick Barwegan, Fenger, 1940	L:	Lou Rymkus, Tilden, 1936
L:	Dennis Lick, St. Rita, 1971	LB:	Dick Butkus, Vocational, 1960
L:	Chris Hinton, Phillips, 1978	LB:	Ray Nitschke, Proviso, 1953
QB:	Otto Graham, Waukegan, 1938	LB:	Clay Matthews, New Trier, 1973
RB:	Red Grange, Wheaton, 1921	DB:	Abe Woodson, Austin, 1952
RB:	Buddy Young, Phillips, 1943	DB:	Johnny Lattner, Fenwick, 1949
RB:	Bill DeCorrevont, Austin, 1937	DB:	Tim Foley, Loyola, 1975

Dick Butkus was a star in Chicago before he played with the Bears. The 1959 *Sun-Times* High School Player of the Year played for the Public High School Championship in Soldier Field as a member of Chicago Vocational.

BASKETBALL
Mark Aguirre, Westinghouse, 1978
Nick Anderson, Simeon, 1986
Nate Clifton, Du Sable, 1944
Terry Cummings, Carver, 1979
Dan Issel, Batavia, 1964
Hersey Hawkins, Westinghouse, 1984
Glenn Rivers, Proviso East, 1980
Cazzie Russell, Carver, 1962
Jack Sikma, St. Anne, 1972
Isiah Thomas, St. Joseph, 1979

	BASEBALL
1B:	Ted Kluszewski, Argo, 1941
2B:	Don Kolloway, Blue Island, 1936
3B:	Fred Lindstrom, Evanston, 1923
SS:	Lou Boudreau, Thornton, 1935
OF:	Kirby Puckett, Calumet, 1978
OF:	Dave Kingman, Prospect, 1967
OF:	Phil Cavarretta, Lane Tech, 1934
C:	Tom Haller, Lockport, 1953
P:	Denny McLain, Mt. Carmel, 1962
P:	Bill Gullickson, Joliet Cath., 1977
P:	Scott Sanderson, Glen. N., 1974
P:	Jim Clancy, St. Rita, 1972

BOXING

Raging Bull vs. Sugar Ray: It was a study in opposites, a blood bath, and one of the most memorable fights in Chicago Stadium history. Jake LaMotta—the Raging Bull—was the middleweight champ. Sugar Ray Robinson was the fleet-footed welterweight champ aiming for Jake's middleweight belt. It was Feb. 14, 1951. They battled toe to toe until 2:04 of round 13 when referee Frank Sikora stepped in and declared Robinson winner by TKO. LaMotta, blood flowing from his left eye, nose and mouth, was so enraged he tried to fight the ref.

The Long Count: Gene Tunney beat Jack Dempsey at Soldier Field to retain his heavyweight boxing title—but only thanks to an incredible second chance. Before 104,943 fans on Sept. 22, 1927, Dempsey floored Tunney with a left and a right to the jaw. The timekeeper started the count, but referee Dave Barry held it up until Dempsey—as required by the rules—stepped back from Tunney and moved to a neutral corner. The delay gave Tunney seven extra seconds to stagger to his feet. He rose on the count of nine, and went on to win.

Brown Bomber vs. Cinderella Man: When Joe Louis, the son of an Alabama cotton-picker, defeated Jim Braddock for the heavyweight crown at Comiskey Park on June 22, 1937, he became an instant hero to black America. Bleacher tickets were a modest $3.50—at Louis' insistence so that poor blacks could attend. The park was jammed with 55,000 fans. One headline read: "Chant for Blood Goes Up from Moonlit Arena and Blood Flows." As one sportswriter wrote: "With the impact, Louis—knowing he had made a perfect hit—stepped back to give his victim room to fall. He was so positive of the blow's effect he did not stand ready to charge in. He moved away, and when Jim Braddock poured to the floor, stood there and admired his handiwork."

Barney Ross (1909-1967): One of Chicago's two all-time greatest fighters (the other was Tony Zale), Ross became the first boxer in history to hold both the lightweight and welterweight crowns. He fought

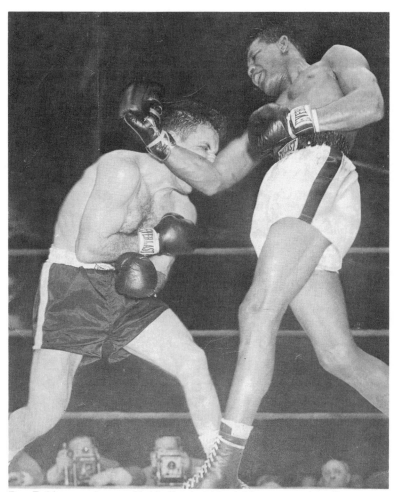

Ray Robinson misses with his fist, but his right arm smashes the nose of Jake LaMotta in the final round of the most memorable fight in Chicago Stadium history.

82 professional bouts and won 77 (24 by knockouts). He picked up the welterweight title on May 28, 1934, in a legendary 15-round split-decision in New York City against Ireland's Jimmy McLarnin. Four months later, in another bloodbath, Ross lost a rematch with McLarnin, but won the title back—and got his nose split open—in a third match the next spring. Ross retired from the ring in 1938, after losing the welterweight title to Henry Armstrong.

Tony Zale (born 1913): A Polish boy from Gary, Indiana, he was "The Man of Steel," revered for his punishing body blows. He fought 89 professional bouts and won 72 (46 by knockouts). He KOd Al Hostak for the title in 1940. After Navy duty, he successfully defended his middleweight title against Rocky Graziano in 1946, lost it to Graziano in 1947, and regained it from Graziano in 1948. He lost it for keeps to Marcel Cerdan in 1948. Graziano said: "There's only one way you can lick Zale. You got to kill him."

Other Great Chicago Fighters: Ernie Terrell (born 1939) was the best of the Chicago heavyweights, winning 47 of his 54 professional fights. Welterweight Jackie Fields, who began his professional career in 1924, won 77 of his 85 fights. Welterweight Johnny Bratton, beginning in 1944, won 65 of his 86 bouts.

THE CHICAGO WHITE SOX

OLD COMISKEY: 1910-1990

FIRSTS

Game: The Sox lost to St. Louis 2-0 on July 1, 1910.

Night game: Aug. 14, 1939, when the Sox beat St. Louis 5-2.

Home run: A grand slam by Lee Tannehill against Detroit on July 31, 1910.

EXTREMES

Capacity: 43,951.

Biggest one-game crowd: 54,215 against New York on June 19, 1953.

Biggest doubleheader: 55,555 against Minnesota on May 20, 1973.

Highest season attendance: 2,136,988 in 1984.

Lowest season attendance: 195,081 in 1918.

Roof shots: Babe Ruth hit the first roof shot homer at Old Comiskey on Aug. 16, 1927. Ron Kittle hit the last one on April 17, 1990.

Last day: Sept. 30, 1990. Sox beat Seattle 2-1.

NEW COMISKEY: 1991 TO PRESENT

Game: April 18, 1991; Sox lost to Detroit 16-0.

Capacity: 44,702.

Home is home: The playing field faces southeast (traditionally it's northeast). As in the old park, home plate is at Thirty-fifth and Shields, but now on the south side of Thirty-fifth Street.

WHITE SOX CURIOSITIES

Guilty of a punch in the nose: Robert E. Cantwell, Sr., president of the White Sox Rooters Association (1905-07), once punched an umpire in the nose, was found guilty by a jury and fined $75.

Pitcher wears glasses: White Sox pitcher Bill "Bullfrog" Dietrich became the first pitcher to wear eyeglasses and pitch a no-hitter, on June 1, 1937, as the Sox beat the St. Louis Browns 8-0.

Black Sox scandal: In 1920 White Sox owner Charles Comiskey kicked eight of his players off the team when they were accused of taking bribes to throw the 1919 World Series. They were cleared in court but banned from baseball for life.

Joe Jackson was one of eight Chicago White Sox players banned from baseball for his role in the Black Sox scandal.

All-Stars: Old Comiskey Park hosted the first Negro League All-Star Game and the first Major League All-Star Game (July 6, 1933). Babe Ruth slammed a homer and said, "This ain't the game of the century, it's the game of the cinchery."

Scary sirens: When the White Sox won the pennant in 1959, the city's air raid sirens were sounded. This scared and then angered Chicagoans. Explained Mayor Richard J. Daley: "The City Council passed a resolution decreeing that there be hilarity in the streets and shouting and celebration."

Veeck: After Bill Veeck took over the team in 1958 he did a few things differently. On one day, he brought a lady snake charmer to home plate, a juggler to first, clowns and dogs to second and a sword swallower to third. On another day, he gave away 15,000 beers. On a third day, he gave away 500 free tuxedo rentals. On other days he gave away 50,000 metal nuts and 22,000 fig bars.

First American League victims of a no-hitter: It happened May 9, 1901. The pitcher was Cleveland's Earl Moore. The Sox lost 4-2.

The linguist as catcher: For a short time in the 1920s, Moe Berg was a catcher and scholar for the White Sox. He graduated from Princeton and Columbia Law School (with honors), attended the Sorbonne in Paris, and was a founding member of the Linguistic Society of America. And he was a spy for the U.S. in World War II. Arthur Daley of the New York Times wrote of Berg, "He could speak a dozen languages and could hit in none of them." Lifetime—.243.

HALL OF FAMERS
(with five or more seasons)

Eddie Collins (Sox years 1915-26)   Red Faber (1914-33)
Ed Walsh (1904-16)   Luke Appling (1930-50)
Ted Lyons (1923-42;1946)   Harry Hooper (1921-25)
Ray Schalk (1912-28)   Early Wynn (1958-62)
Luis Aparicio (1956-62)   Hoyt Wilhem (1963-68)

WHITE SOX BATTING RECORDS
(as of end of 1990 season)

■ Luke Appling holds the career records for most runs batted in (1,116), most hits (2,749), most doubles (440) and most runs scored (1,319).

One of two Hall of Fame White Sox shortstops, Luke Appling holds numerous batting records for the team. *(Photo by Charles Gekler)*

■ Luke Appling holds the single-season batting average record with .388 in 1936 and the longest hitting streak, twenty-seven games also in 1936.

■ The single-season record for home runs is held by Carlton Fisk (37 in 1985) and Dick Allen (37 in 1972).

WHITE SOX HOME RUN LEADERS

1.	Carlton Fisk	192	7.	Greg Walker	113
2.	Harold Baines	186	8.	Pete Ward	97
3.	Bill Melton	154	9.	Dick Allen	85
4.	Ron Kittle	138		Carlos May	
5.	Minnie Minoso	135		Al Smith	
6.	Sherm Lollar	124			

ALL-TIME WHITE SOX BATTING AVERAGES

1.	Joe Jackson	.339	6.	Taffy Wright	.312
2.	Eddie Collins	.331	7.	Luke Appling	.310
3.	Carl Reynolds	.322		Rip Radcliff	
4.	Zeke Bonura	.317	8.	Earl Sheely	.305
5.	Bibb Falk	.315	9.	Minnie Minoso	.304

WHITE SOX PITCHING RECORDS

■ Ed Walsh holds White Sox records for most wins in a season (40 in 1908), most shutouts in a season (12 in 1908), lowest ERA (1.27 in 1910), most complete games (42 in 1908), most innings pitched (464 in 1908) and most strikeouts (269 in 1908).

■ Ted Lyons holds the White Sox career record for most wins (260), most losses (230), most innings pitched (4,161), most games started (484 tied with Red Faber) and most complete games (356).

■ Lowest career ERA: Ed Walsh (1.81).

■ Most career strikeouts: Billy Pierce, 1,796.

■ Total no-hitters: White Sox pitchers had thrown sixteen no-hitters as of the end of the 1990 season—including a game in which a Sox pitcher threw nine hitless innings but lost it in the tenth, and a game in which Melido Perez pitched a rain-shortened six-inning no-hitter in 1990 when the Sox beat the Yankees 8-0. Frank Smith pitched two no-hitters (1905 and 1908).

■ Most strikeouts in a game: Jack Harshman fanned 16 on July 25, 1954.

■ Cy Young Award Winners: Early Wynn (1959), LaMarr Hoyt (1983).

WHITE SOX TEAM RECORDS

■ Longest game: 25 innings (an American League record) over eight hours and six minutes (a Major League record).

■ Highest scoring game: The White Sox scored 29 runs to beat Kansas City on April 23, 1955—an American League record.

■ Longest winning streak: 19 (Aug. 2-23, 1906).

■ Longest losing streak: 13 (Aug. 9-26, 1924).

WHITE SOX YEAR-BY-YEAR RESULTS

Year	Pos.	W-L	Pct.	Manager
1901	1	83-53	.610	Clark Griffith
1902	4	74-60	.552	Clark Griffith
1903	7	60-77	.438	James L. Callahan
1904	3	89-65	.578	Callahan-Fielder Jones
1905	2	92-60	.605	Fielder Jones
1906	1	93-58	.616	Fielder Jones
1907	3	87-64	.576	Fielder Jones
1908	3	88-64	.579	Fielder Jones
1909	4	78-74	.513	William J. Sullivan
1910	6	68-85	.444	Hugh Duffy
1911	4	77-74	.510	Hugh Duffy
1912	4	78-76	.506	James J. Callahan
1913	5	78-74	.513	James J. Callahan
1914	6	70-81	.455	James J. Callahan
1915	3	93-61	.604	Clarence Rowland
1916	2	89-65	.578	Clarence Rowland
1917	1	100-54	.649	Clarence Rowland
1918	6	57-67	.460	Clarence Rowland
1919	1	88-52	.629	Kid Gleason
1920	2	96-58	.623	Kid Gleason
1921	7	62-92	.403	Kid Gleason
1922	5	77-77	.500	Kid Gleason
1923	7	69-85	.448	Kid Gleason
1924	8	66-87	.431	John Evers-Ed Walsh Eddie Collins-John Evers
1925	5	79-75	.513	Eddie Collins
1926	5	81-72	.529	Eddie Collins
1927	5	70-83	.458	Ray Schalk
1928	5	72-82	.468	Schalk-Russ Blackburne
1929	7	59-93	.366	Russ Blackburne

Year	Pos.	W-L	Pct.	Manager
1930	7	62-92	.403	Donie Bush
1931	8	56-97	.366	Donie Bush
1932	7	49-102	.325	Lew Fonseca
1933	6	67-83	.447	Lew Fonseca
1934	8	53-99	.349	Fonseca-Jimmy Dykes
1935	5	74-78	.487	Jimmy Dykes
1936	3	81-70	.536	Jimmy Dykes
1937	3	86-68	.588	Jimmy Dykes
1938	6	65-83	.439	Jimmy Dykes
1939	4	85-69	.552	Jimmy Dykes
1940	4	82-72	.532	Jimmy Dykes
1941	3	77-77	.500	Jimmy Dykes
1942	6	66-82	.466	Jimmy Dykes
1943	4	32-72	.532	Jimmy Dykes
1944	7	71-83	.461	Jimmy Dykes
1945	6	71-78	.477	Jimmy Dykes
1946	5	74-80	.481	Jimmy Dykes
				Ted Lyons
1947	6	70-84	.455	Ted Lyons
1948	8	51-101	.336	Ted Lyons
1949	6	63-91	.409	Jack Onslow
1950	6	60-94	.390	Onslow-Red Corriden
1951	4	81-73	.526	Paul Richards
1952	3	81-73	.526	Paul Richards
1953	3	89-65	.578	Paul Richards
1954	3	94-60	.610	Richards-Marty Marion
1955	3	91-63	.591	Marty Marion
1956	3	85-69	.552	Marty Marion
1957	2	90-64	.584	Al Lopez
1958	2	82-72	.532	Al Lopez
1959	1	94-60	.610	Al Lopez
1960	3	87-67	.565	Al Lopez
1961	4	86-76	.531	Al Lopez
1962	5	85-77	.525	Al Lopez
1963	2	94-68	.580	Al Lopez
1964	2	98-64	.605	Al Lopez
1965	2	95-67	.586	Al Lopez
1966	4	83-79	.512	Eddie Stanky
1967	4	89-73	.549	Eddie Stanky
1968	8T	67-95	.414	Stanky-Les Moss-Lopez
1969	5	68-94	.420	Lopez-Don Gutteridge
1970	6	56-106	.346	Gutteridge-Bill Adair
				Chuck Tanner
1971	3	79-83	.488	Chuck Tanner
1972	2	87-67	.565	Chuck Tanner
1973	5	77-85	.475	Chuck Tanner
1974	4	80-80	.500	Chuck Tanner
1975	5	75-86	.466	Chuck Tanner
1976	6	64-97	.398	Paul Richards
1977	3	90-72	.556	Bob Lemon
1978	5	71-90	.441	Lemon-Larry Doby
1979	5	73-87	.456	Don Kessinger-
				Tony LaRussa
1980	5	70-90	.438	Tony LaRussa
1981	5	54-52	.509	Tony LaRussa

Year	Pos.	W-L	Pct.	Manager
1982	3	87-75	.537	Tony LaRussa
1983	#1	99-63	.612	Tony LaRussa
1984	5T	74-88	.457	Tony LaRussa
1985	3	85-77	.525	Tony LaRussa
1986	5	72-90	.444	Tony LaRussa- Doug Rader- Jim Fregosi
1987	5	77-85	.475	Jim Fregosi
1988	5	71-90	.441	Jim Fregosi
1989	7	69-92	.429	Jeff Torborg
1990	2	94-68	.580	Jeff Torborg

#Won Western Division

POST-SEASON

The White Sox have been in four World Series:

1906: White Sox beat the Cubs, 4 games to 2.

1917: White Sox beat New York, 4 games to 2.

1919: In the so called "Black Sox" series, where eight players were later accused of throwing the series, the White Sox lost to Cincinnati, 5 games to 3.

1959: White Sox lost to Los Angeles, 4 games to 2.

In 1983, the White Sox lost the American League Championship Series to Baltimore, 3 games to 1.

CHICAGO CUBS

Grimm tacky tale: On Sept. 4, 1935, Cubs manager Charlie Grimm stepped on a tack after a Cubs victory. It was, he knew, an omen. The next day the Cubs won again and he stuck another tack in his shoes. And then again on the third day. In all, the Cubs won twenty-one games straight that month, clinching the pennant and forcing Grimm to hobble with twenty-one tacks in his shoes.

Hack hacked it: Hack Wilson, one of the greatest Cubs of all time, played equally hard in taverns all over town. Cubs manager Joe Mc-Carthy, hoping to convince Hack of the evils of drinking, once dropped a worm in a glass of whiskey and let Hack watch it die. Hack nodded and said, "Yeah, if you drink whiskey you won't get worms."

WRIGLEY FIELD HISTORIC MOMENTS

Babe Ruth's "called" shot: The Babe allegedly pointed to the center field bleachers just before hitting Charlie Root's next pitch there on Oct. 1, 1932, in the fifth inning of the third game of the World Series.

"The homer in the gloamin' ": Gabby Hartnett's home run shot in the gathering darkness at 5:37 p.m. broke a 5-5 tie in the ninth inning against the Pittsburgh Pirates on Sept. 28, 1938, propelling the Cubs to a pennant. On his way around the bases, Hartnett was mobbed by teammates, fans, vendors and ushers.

Ernie Banks' 500th home run: He walloped it on a cold and wet May 12, 1970, off Atlanta pitcher Pat Jarvis, and only 5,264 fans were there to see it. Said Banks after the game, "Let's play three today!"

Mr. Cub, Ernie Banks, waves to a packed Wrigley Field on Ernie Banks day in 1964.

Pete Rose ties Ty: Rose stroked his 4,191st career hit on Sept. 8, 1985, against Cub pitcher Reggie Patterson. It tied Rose with Ty Cobb for the most hits in baseball history. Rose went on to break the record.

First night game: August 8, 1988.

First National League game at Wrigley: A bear cub was brought to the first National League game at Wrigley—the Cubs vs. Cincinnati—on April 20, 1916.

Biggest one-game crowd: 51,556 fans on June 27, 1930, against Brooklyn. It was Ladies' Day, so 30,476 of the fans got in free.

Highest season attendance: 2,491,942 in 1989.

Lowest season attendance: 338,802 in 1918.

CUBS BATTING RECORDS
(as of end of 1990 season)

■ Heinie Zimmerman, who played third base for the Cubs, holds the club record for best batting average in a single season—.372 in 1912.

■ Bill Dahlen holds the record for the longest hitting streak—forty-two in 1894.

■ Cap Anson holds the Cubs' career records for runs batted in (1,715), hits (3,041), doubles (532) and runs scored (1,719).

■ Ryne Sandberg played 123 games in a row without making an error from June 21, 1989 to May 17, 1990.

■ In 1987, Andre Dawson became the first player from a sixth-place team to be voted the National League's Most Valuable Player. He hit 49 home runs.

■ Ernie Banks holds the club record for grand slam homers—12.

CURIOSITIES

■ On Aug. 22, 1982, Ernie Banks became the first Cub to have his uniform number—14—retired. On Aug. 13, 1987, Billy Williams' No. 26 was retired.

■ In 1958, Ernie Banks became the first member of a team with a losing record to be voted the National League's Most Valuable Player.

■ Only one Cub on the 1991 roster, catcher Erik Pappas, actually was born in the Chicago area, on April 25, 1966. He starred at Mount Carmel High School on the South Side, graduating in 1984.

■ Rick Sutcliffe in 1984 founded the Sutcliffe Foundation, which contributes to numerous charities in the Chicago area. He donates $100 to a local children's hospital every time he strikes out a batter.

■ Hack Wilson holds the Cubs and National League record for home runs hit by a Cub in a season—56 in 1930.

■ Most career strikeouts: 1,271, Ron Santo.

■ Most strikeouts in a season: 143, Byron Browne in 1966.

ALL-TIME CUBS HOME RUN LEADERS

1. Ernie Banks	512	6. Hank Sauer	198
2. Billy Williams	392	7. Ryne Sandberg	193
3. Ron Santo	337	8. Hack Wilson	190
4. Gabby Hartnett	231	9. Leon Durham	138
5. Bill Nicholson	205	10. Andre Dawson	136

ALL-TIME CUBS BATTING AVERAGES

1. Riggs Stephenson	.336	6. William L. Everett	.323
2. Bill Madlock	.336	7. Hack Wilson	.322
3. Cap Anson	.334	8. Mike Kelly	.316
4. Wm. Alexander Lange	.330	9. George Gore	.315
5. Kiki Cuyler	.325	10. Jim Ryan	.310

CUBS PITCHING RECORDS

■ Mordecai Brown holds Cub records for wins in a season (29 in 1908), shutouts in a season (10 in 1906), lowest ERA in a season (1.04 in 1906), lowest career ERA (1.8) and best win-loss record in a single season (29-9 in 1908).

■ Charlie Root holds the Cubs career record for most games pitched (605), most wins (201) most losses (156) and most walks (871).

■ Most games won in a row: 16, Rick Sutcliffe in 1984-85.

■ Most strikeouts in a game: 17, Jack Pfiester in 15 innings on May 30, 1906.

■ Most career strikeouts: 2,038, Ferguson Jenkins.

■ Cubs have pitched eight no-hit ballgames as of the end of the 1990 season, including two by Ken Holtzman—on Aug. 19, 1969, against the Atlanta Braves (at Wrigley) and on June 3, 1971, against the Reds (at Cincinnati).

■ No Cub has pitched a perfect game.

■ Cy Young Award winners: Fergie Jenkins in 1971, Bruce Sutter in 1979 and Rick Sutcliffe in 1984.

TEAM RECORDS

■ The Cubs' longest game was an 18-inning affair against Pittsburgh on Aug. 6, 1989, that lasted five hours and forty-two minutes. The Cubs lost 5-4.

■ The Cubs drove in 36 runs in a game against Louisville on June 29, 1897, a Major League record.

■ Longest winning streak: Twenty-one games in September 1935, to win the pennant.

CHICAGO CUBS YEAR-BY-YEAR RESULTS

Year	W-L	Pct.	Finish	Manager
1900	65-75	.464	5t	Loftus
1901	53-86	.381	6	Loftus
1902	68-69	.496	5	Selee
1903	82-56	.594	3	Selee
1904	93-60	.608	2	Selee
1905	92-61	.601	3	Selee-Chance
1906	*116-36	*.763	1	Chance
1907	107-45	.704	1	Chance
1908	99-55	.643	1	Chance
1909	104-49	.680	2	Chance
1910	104-50	.675	1	Chance
1911	92-62	.597	2	Chance
1912	91-59	.607	3	Chance
1913	88-65	.575	3	Evers
1914	78-76	.506	4	O'Day
1915	73-80	.477	4	Bresnahan
1916	67-86	.438	5	Tinker
1917	74-80	.481	5	Mitchell
1918	84-45	.651	1	Mitchell
1919	75-65	.536	3	Mitchell
1920	75-79	.487	5t	Mitchell
1921	64-89	.418	7	Evers/Killefer
1922	80-74	.519	5	Killefer
1923	83-71	.539	4	Killefer
1924	81-72	.529	5	Killefer
1925	68-86	.442	8	Killefer/Maranville-Gibson
1926	82-72	.532	4	McCarthy
1927	85-68	.556	4	McCarthy
1928	91-63	.591	3	McCarthy
1929	98-54	.645	1	McCarthy
1930	90-64	.584	2	McCarthy/Hornsby
1931	84-70	.545	3	Hornsby
1932	90-64	.584	1	Hornsby/Grimm
1933	86-68	.558	3	Grimm
1934	86-65	.570	3	Grimm
1935	100-54	.649	1	Grimm

Year	W-L	Pct.	Finish	Manager
1936	87-67	.565	2t	Grimm
1937	93-61	.604	2	Grimm
1938	89-63	.586	1	Grimm/Hartnett
1939	84-70	.545	4	Hartnett
1940	75-79	.487	5	Hartnett
1941	70-84	.455	6	Wilson
1942	68-86	.442	6	Wilson
1943	74-79	.484	5	Wilson
1944	75-79	.487	4	Wilson/Johnson/Grimm
1945	98-58	.636	1	Grimm
1946	82-71	.536	3	Grimm
1947	69-85	.448	6	Grimm
1948	64-90	.416	8	Grimm
1949	61-93	.396	8	Grimm/Frisch
1950	64-89	.418	7	Frisch
1951	62-92	.403	8	Frisch/Cavaretta
1952	77-77	.500	5	Cavaretta
1953	65-89	.422	7	Cavaretta
1954	64-90	.416	7	Hack
1955	72-81	.471	6	Hack
1956	60-94	.390	8	Hack
1957	62-92	.403	7t	Scheffing
1958	72-82	.468	5t	Scheffing
1959	74-80	.481	5t	Scheffing
1960	60-94	.390	7	Grimm/Boudreau
1961	64-90	.416	7	Himsl/Craft/Klein/Tappe
1962	59-104	.364	9	Tappe/Metro/Klein
1963	82-80	.506	7	Kennedy
1964	76-86	.469	8	Kennedy
1965	72-90	.444	8	Kennedy/Klein
1966	59-103	.364	10	Durocher
1967	87-74	.540	3	Durocher
1968	84-78	.519	3	Durocher
1969	92-70	.568	2	Durocher
1970	84-78	.519	2	Durocher
1971	83-79	.512	3t	Durocher
1972	85-70	.548	2	Durocher/Lockman
1973	77-84	.478	5	Lockman
1974	66-96	.407	6	Lockman/Marshall
1975	75-87	.463	5t	Marshall
1976	75-87	.463	4	Marshall
1977	81-81	.500	4	Franks
1978	79-83	.488	3	Franks
1979	80-82	.494	5	Franks/Amalfitano
1980	64-98	.395	6	Gomez/Amalfitano
1981	38-65	.369	6	Amalfitano
1982	73-89	.451	5	Elia
1983	71-91	.438	5	Elia/Fox
1984	96-65	.596	#1	Frey
1985	77-84	.478	4	Frey
1986	70-90	.438	5	Frey/Vukovich/Michael
1987	76-85	.472	6	Michael/Lucchesi
1988	77-85	.475	4	Zimmer
1989	93-69	.574	#1	Zimmer
1990	77-85	.475	4t	Zimmer

*Major League record
#Won Eastern Division

CUBS WORLD SERIES RESULTS

1906: White Sox beat Cubs, 4 games to 2.

1907: Cubs beat Detroit, 4 to 0.

1908: Cubs beat Detroit, 4 to 1.

1910: Philadelphia beats Cubs, 4 to 1.

1918: Boston beats Cubs, 4 to 2.

1929: Philadelphia beats Cubs, 4 to 1.

1932: New York beats Cubs, 4 to 0.

1935: Detroit beats Cubs, 4 to 2.

1938: New York beats Cubs, 4 to 0.

1945: Detroit beats Cubs, 4 to 3.

CUBS NATIONAL LEAGUE CHAMPIONSHIP SERIES RESULTS

1984: San Diego beats Cubs, 3 to 2.

1989: San Francisco beats Cubs, 4 to 1.

CUBS IN THE HALL OF FAME

Grover C. Alexander, 1938
Cap Anson, 1939
Ernie Banks, 1977
Roger Bresnahan, 1945
Lou Brock, 1985
Mordecai Brown, 1949
Lou Boudreau, 1970
Frank Chance, 1946
John Clarkson, 1963
Kiki Cuyler, 1968
Dizzy Dean, 1953
Hugh Duffy, 1945
Johnny Evers, 1946
Jimmie Foxx, 1951
Frankie Frisch, 1947
Clark C. Griffith, 1946
Burleigh Grimes, 1964
Gabby Hartnett, 1955

Billy Herman, 1975
Rogers Hornsby, 1942
Monte Irvin, 1973
Fergie Jenkins, 1991
George Kelly, 1973
King Kelly, 1945
Ralph Kiner, 1975
Chuck Klein, 1980
Fred Lindstrom, 1976
Rabbit Maranville, 1954
Joseph McCarthy, 1957
Robin Roberts, 1976
A.G. Spalding, 1939
Joe Tinker, 1946
Rube Waddell, 1946
Hoyt Wilhelm, 1985
Billy Williams, 1987
Hack Wilson, 1979

THE CHICAGO BEARS

SOLDIER FIELD

Opened: 1924. The Chicago Bears have played there for twenty years. Before that, the Bears played at Wrigley Field.

Largest Football Crowd: The all-time largest gathering of football fans in Chicago was at Soldier Field on Nov. 26, 1927, when 123,000 fans watched Notre Dame beat USC, 7-6.

Cheap Game: In 1920 you could buy an NFL franchise for $100.

EDDIE GOLD'S LIST OF TEN
MEANEST, TOUGHEST BEARS

1. **Ed Sprinkle**; Old necktie tackles
2. **Dick Butkus**; Close call for first
3. **Doug Atkins**; Biggest mean dude
4. **Bronko Nagurski**; Old pile-driver
5. **Bulldog Turner**; No pussycat
6. **Mike Ditka**; Ran with old stiff arm
7. **Doug Plank**; Loved tough contact
8. **Joe Fortunato**; Even looked fearful
9. **George Blanda**; Should've been a lineman
10. **Ed O'Bradovich**; He was no angel

BEARS INDIVIDUAL RECORDS

■ **Best passing season:** In 1965 Rudy Bukich completed 176 of 312 passes for 2,641 yards and 20 touchdowns. But in 1943 Sid Luckman completed 110 of 202 passes (54.5 percent) for 2,194 yards and 28 touchdowns for a rating of 107.8—the highest in Bear history.

■ **Highest QB rating:** Although Sid Luckman has more passing yards (14,686), Jim McMahon has the highest career rating (80.4) because he completed 874 of 1,513 passes (57.8 percent) for 11,203 yards and 67 touchdowns.

■ **Biggest passing game:** 468 yards by Johnny Lujack, who completed 24 of 39 passes on Dec. 11, 1949.

■ **Most career receiving yards:** Johnny Morris (1958-67), 5,059 yards on 356 catches.

Chicago loves a winner. An estimated 500,000 fans gathered at the Daley Center to honor the 1986 Chicago Bears—Super Bowl Champions. *(Photo by Tom Cruze)*

■ **Most career catches:** Walter Payton (1975-87) had 492 catches for 4,538 yards.

■ **Best career punting average (more than 75 punts):** George Gulyanics (1947-52) punted for an average of 44.5 yards per punt, 133 punts for 5,032 yards.

■ **Best career punt return (more than 25):** Ray "Scooter" McLean (1940-47) averaged 14.8 yards per return, 42 returns for 622 yards. (Gale Sayers is second with a 14.5 yard average).

■ **Payton cleans up:** Walter Payton (1975-87) holds twenty-seven Bears records and eight NFL records, including most yards rushing in an NFL career—16,726—and most yards gained in a single game: 275 yards on 40 carries against Minnesota on Nov. 20, 1977.

■ **Career scoring:** Walter Payton (1975-87) scored 750 points.

■ **Most career interceptions:** Gary Fencik (1976-87) had 38 interceptions for 483 yards, or an average of 12.7 yards per interception.

Running Blind: Elmer Angsman, a kid from Mount Carmel whom the *Daily News* described as a guy "who can't see his hand in front of his face without his contact lenses," ran ten times for 150 yards to carry the Chicago Cardinals to the NFL championship over Philadelphia on Dec. 28, 1947.

BEARS TEAM RECORDS

■ **Most points scored in a regular season game:** 61 against San Francisco (1965) and Green Bay (1980). The Bears scored 73 points to beat the Washington Redskins in the 1940 NFL championship.

■ **Most passing and rushing yards in a game:** 682 against New York on Nov. 14, 1943. Most passing yards: 488 yards (same game). Most rushing yards: 408 against the, yes, Brooklyn Dodgers on Oct. 20, 1935.

■ **Fewest passing and rushing yards in a game:** 24 against Detroit on Nov. 22, 1981. Fewest passing yards (net since 1952): minus 20 against Detroit (same game). Fewest rushing yards: 1 against Los Angeles on October 26, 1952.

■ **Most points allowed in a game:** 53 against the Chicago Cardinals on Nov. 27, 1955.

■ **Most rushing and passing yards allowed in a game:** 557 against Los Angeles on Oct. 24, 1954. Most passing yards allowed: 509 against Los Angeles on Dec. 26, 1982. Most rushing yards allowed: 393 against Detroit on Nov. 26, 1936.

■ **Fewest rushing and passing yards allowed in a game:** 12 against Detroit on Nov. 22, 1987. Fewest passing yards allowed (net since 1952): minus 22 against Atlanta on Nov. 24, 1985. Fewest rushing yards allowed: minus 36 against Philadelphia on Nov. 19, 1939.

Indoor Gridiron: On the day in 1932 the Bears were scheduled to play the Portsmouth (Ohio) Spartans (now the Detroit Lions) for the NFL championship, Chicago was covered in snow and below zero temperatures, making Wrigley Field unusable. So they played the game indoors at Chicago Stadium on an eighty-yard field. The Bears won 9-0.

CHICAGO BEARS YEAR-BY-YEAR RESULTS

Year	W-L	Coach	Playoffs
1920	10-1-2	George S. Halas	
1921	10-1-1	" "	
1922	9-3	" "	
1923	9-2-1	" "	
1924	6-1-4	" "	
1925	9-5-3	" "	
1926	12-1-3	" "	
1927	9-3-2	" "	
1928	7-5-1	" "	
1929	4-9-2	" "	
1930	9-4-1	Ralph Jones	
1931	8-5	" "	
1932	7-1-6	" "	
1933	10-2-1	George S. Halas	1-0
1934	13-0	" "	
1935	6-4-2	" "	
1936	9-3	" "	
1937	9-1-1	" "	
1938	6-5	" "	
1939	8-3	" "	
1940	8-3	" "	1-0
1941	10-1	" "	2-0
1942	11-0	" "	0-1
1943	8-1-1	Heartley "Hunk" Anderson	1-0
1944	6-3-1	" "	
1945	3-7	" "	
1946	8-2-1	George S. Halas	1-0
1947	8-4	" "	
1948	10-2	" "	
1949	9-3	" "	
1950	9-3	" "	0-1

Year	W-L	Coach	Playoffs
1951	7-5	" "	
1952	5-7	" "	
1953	3-8-1	" "	
1954	8-4	" "	
1955	8-4	" "	
1956	9-2-1	John L. Driscoll	0-1
1957	5-7	" "	
1958	8-4	George S. Halas	
1959	8-4	" "	
1960	5-6-1	" "	
1961	8-6	" "	
1962	9-5	" "	
1963	11-1-2	" "	
1964	5-9	" "	
1965	9-5	" "	
1966	5-7-2	" "	
1967	7-6-1	" "	
1968	7-7	Jim Dooley	
1969	1-13	" "	
1970	6-8	" "	
1971	6-8	" "	
1972	4-9-1	Abe Gibron	
1973	3-11	" "	
1974	4-10	" "	
1975	4-10	Jack Pardee	
1976	7-7	" "	
1977	9-5	" "	0-1
1978	7-9	Neill Armstrong	
1979	10-6	" "	0-1
1980	7-9	" "	
1981	6-10	" "	
1982	3-6	Mike Ditka	
1983	8-8	" "	
1984	10-6	" "	1-1
1985	15-1	" "	3-0 Super Bowl Champs
1986	14-2	" "	0-1
1987	11-4	" "	0-1
1988	12-4	" "	1-1
1989	6-10	" "	
1990	11-5	" "	1-1

Galloping Halas: In a game against the Oorang Indians in 1923, George Halas picked up a Jim Thorpe fumble and scored on a 98-yard run with Thorpe in pursuit.

BEARS FIRST-ROUND DRAFT PICKS 1979-1991

1979 Dan Hampton DT (Arkansas)/Al Harris DE (Arizona St.)

1980 Otis Wilson LB (Louisville)

1981 Keith Van Horne T (USC)

1982 Jim McMahon QB (BYU)

1983 Jim Covert T (Pittsburgh)/ Willie Gault WR (Tennessee)

1984 Wilber Marshall LB (Florida)

1985 William Perry DT (Clemson)

1986 Neal Anderson RB (Florida)

1987 Jim Harbaugh QB (Michigan)

1988 Brad Muster FB (Stanford)/ Wendell Davis WR (LSU)

1989 Donnell Woolford DB (Clemson)

1990 Mark Carrier, S (USC)

1991 Stan Thomas, OL (Texas)

CHICAGO BEARS IN THE HALL OF FAME
(Year admitted)

George Halas, 1963
George Blanda, 1981
George Connor, 1975
John (Paddy) Driscoll, 1965
Bill George, 1974
Ed Healy, 1964
Sid Luckman, 1965
George McAfee, 1966
Bronko Nagurski, 1963
Joe Stydahar, 1967
Clyde (Bulldog) Turner, 1966

Doug Atkins, 1982
Dick Butkus, 1979
Mike Ditka, 1988
Danny Fortmann, 1985
Harold (Red) Grange, 1963
Bill Hewitt, 1971
Roy (Link) Lyman, 1964
George Musso, 1982
Gale Sayers, 1977
George Trafton, 1964

Halas Handout: In his earliest days, George Halas couldn't get attention for his Chicago Bears. Things got so bad he was reduced to passing out handbills for the Bears at Stagg Field during University of Chicago games. The Bears finally grabbed the public's attention when Halas hired Red Grange.

Two Hall of Famers, George Halas (left) and Sid Luckman, plot their strategies for bringing the Bears another victory.

RETIRED NUMBERS

3—Bronco Nagurski RB-T
7—George Halas, E
34—Walter Payton, RB
42—Sid Luckman, QB
61—Bill George, LB
77—Red Grange, RB

5—George McAfee, RB
28—Willie Galimore, RB
41—Brian Piccolo, RB
56—Bill Hewitt, E
66—Clyde "Bulldog" Turner, C-LB

Breaking Bronko: Fullback-Tackle Bronko Nagurski was so feared that one NFL owner reportedly offered him $10,000 to retire.

CHICAGO BULLS

Where do they play? Chicago Stadium, 1800 W. Madison, opened in 1929. Capacity: 17,339. Biggest home crowd: 21,652 against Houston on April 8, 1977.

A flip of the coin: The first draft pick of 1979 was decided on a coin flip between the Bulls and Los Angeles Lakers. Bulls fans were surveyed and said they wanted Bulls General Manager Rod Thorn to call "heads." He did, but the $20 gold piece came up tails. Thorn then asked: "Two out of three?" The Lakers picked Magic Johnson—the Bulls picked David Greenwood. Bulls broadcaster Johnny Kerr, who coached the Phoenix Suns when that team lost a coin toss for the right to draft Kareem Abdul-Jabbar, said they too had listened to a fan poll, which goes to show: "If you start listening to the fans, you wind up sitting next to them."

First team: The starting five in the first game of the first season (1966) of the Chicago Bulls: Bob Boozer (F), Don Kojis (F), Len Chapell (C), Guy Rodgers (G), Jerry Sloan (G).

Stadium records: Most points scored: 68 by Philadelphia's Wilt Chamberlain, Dec. 16, 1967; most free throws made: 26 by Michael Jordan against New Jersey, Feb. 26, 1987; most rebounds: 37 by Tom Boerwinkle against Phoenix, Jan. 8, 1970; most three-pointers made: 7 by Michael Jordan against Golden State, Jan. 18, 1990; most points scored by a team: 152 by the Bulls against Phoenix, Jan. 8, 1970; most points scored by two teams: 285-Bulls (147) vs. Detroit (138) with two overtimes, Jan. 4, 1983.

CHICAGO BULLS RECORDS

■ **Most points scored in a game:** 69 Michael Jordan at Cleveland with one overtime, Mar. 28, 1990.

■ **Most free throws:** 26 by Michael Jordan against New Jersey in Chicago, Feb. 26, 1987.

■ **Most rebounds:** 37 by Tom Boerwinkle against Phoenix in Chicago, Jan. 8, 1970.

■ **Most three pointers:** 7 by Michael Jordan against Golden State in Chicago, Jan. 18, 1990.

■ **Most individual technical fouls:** 3—Dick Motta did it twice, against Boston in New York, Oct. 29, 1968, and against Seattle in Chicago, Feb. 2, 1971.

■ **Most team technical fouls:** 6 in Boston, Feb. 2, 1972.

■ **Most points scored:** 156 against Portland, March 16, 1984.

■ **Least points scored:** 65 against Phoenix, March 6, 1975.

■ **Most consecutive free throws:** 38 in two games against Detroit on Mar. 3 and Mar. 5, 1968.

■ **Most free throws made:** 55 against Phoenix, Jan. 8, 1970.

■ **Highest free throw percentage:** 1.000 (22 for 22) against Golden State in Chicago, Jan. 27, 1981.

■ **Highest team field goal percentage:** .705 (43 for 61) against Golden State, Dec. 2, 1981.

■ **Longest shot:** 84 feet by Norm Van Lier at San Antonio, Jan. 19, 1977.

■ **Most consecutive wins:** over all, 12 in 1973; at home, 15 in 1989-90; on the road, 8 in 1990.

■ **Longest overtime game:** 3:24, Chicago 156–Portland 155 with four overtimes on March 16, 1984.

■ **Longest game:** 2:40, Houston 116–Bulls 110 in Houston on Nov. 29, 1983.

■ **Shortest game:** 1:42, Bulls 105–Houston 91 in Chicago on Dec. 2, 1978.

■ **Most consecutive losses:** 13 in 1976.

NBA HONORS

Coach of the Year: Johnny Kerr, 1966-67; Dick Motta, 1970-71.

Most Valuable Player: Michael Jordan, 1987-88, 1990-91.

Rookie of the Year: Michael Jordan, 1984-85.

Executive of the Year: Jerry Krause, 1987-88.

Michael Jordan's Vital Stats: Birthdate: 2/17/63 in Brooklyn, New York; height, 6-6; first round draft pick in 1984 (3rd over all); first team All-America at North Carolina (1982-83 and 1983-84); co-captain of Gold Medal Olympic basketball team in 1984, averaging 17.1 points.

CHICAGO BULLS YEAR-BY-YEAR RESULTS

Season	Pos.	W-L	Playoffs	Top Draft Pick
1966-67	4th	33-48	0-3	Dave Schellhase (Purdue)
1967-68	4th	29-53	1-4	Clem Haskins (Western Kentucky)
1968-69	5th	32-49	—	Tom Boerwinkle (Tennessee)
1969-70	3rd	39-43	1-4	Larry Cannon (La Salle)
1970-71	2nd	51-31	3-4	Jimmy Collins (New Mexico State)
1971-72	2nd	57-25	0-4	Kennedy McIntosh (Eastern Michigan)
1972-73	2nd	51-31	3-4	Ralph Simpson (Michigan State)
1973-74	2nd	54-28	4-7	Kevin Kunnert (Iowa)
1974-75	1st	47-35	7-6	Maurice Lucas (Marquette)
1975-76	4th	24-58	—	Steve Green (Indiana)
1976-77	2nd	44-38	1-2	Scott May (Indiana)
1977-78	3rd	40-42	—	Tate Armstrong (Duke)
1978-79	5th	31-51	—	Reggie Theus (UNLV)

Season	Pos.	W-L	Playoffs	Top Draft Pick
1979-80	3rd	30-52	—	David Greenwood (UCLA)
1980-81	2nd	45-37	2-4	Ronnie Lester (Iowa)
1981-82	5th	34-48	—	Orlando Woolridge (Notre Dame)
1982-83	4th	28-54	—	Quintin Dailey (USF)
1983-84	5th	27-55	—	Sidney Green (UNLV)
1984-85	3rd	38-44	1-3	Michael Jordan (North Carolina)
1985-86	4th	30-52	0-3	Keith Lee (Memphis State)
1986-87	5th	40-42	0-3	Brad Sellers (Ohio State)
1987-88	2nd	50-32	4-6	Olden Polynice (Virginia)
1988-89	5th	47-35	9-8	Will Perdue (Vanderbilt)
1989-90	2nd	55-27	10-6	Stacey King (Oklahoma)
1990-91	1st	61-21	15-2	Toni Kukoc Yugoslavia

World Champions (1990-91): Beat Los Angeles Lakers 4 games to 1 in finals.

HARLEM GLOBETROTTERS

The Harlem Globetrotters, their name notwithstanding, are a Chicago phenomenon. The team, originally called the Savoy Big Five, was formed in 1927 by Chicagoan Abe Saperstein, with a starting lineup of five outstanding basketball players from Phillips High School. They traveled the country playing serious money games against white teams, and only started clowning in the 1950s. The Trotters were truly excellent. In one fierce game, they trounced the United States 1936 Olympic team—a team on which no black was allowed. They called themselves the Harlem Globetrotters because one charter player pointed out that all the great black jazz musicians and dancers came out of Harlem.

THE CHICAGO BLACKHAWKS

INDIVIDUAL RECORDS

■ Bobby Hull holds the records for goals in a season (58), games scoring three or more goals (28) and 30-goal-plus seasons (13).

■ Stan Mikita holds the records for assists in a season (926), seasons played (21), games (1,394) and 20-goal-plus seasons (14).

■ Fastest goal from the start of a game: :09 seconds, Gus Bodnar against the Rangers, Feb. 19, 1953.

■ Fastest two goals by one player in a game: :06 seconds apart, Jim Pappin against Philadelphia, Feb. 16, 1972.

■ Most saves in a game: 80, Sam LoPresti at Boston, March 4, 1941.

BLACKHAWK TEAM RECORDS (REGULAR SEASON)

- Most games won: 49 in 1970-71.
- Most games lost: 51 in 1953-54.
- Most games tied: 23 in 1973-74.
- Most goals scored: 351 in 1985-86.
- Most goals allowed: 363 in 1981-82.
- Most goals scored in a game: 12 at Philadelphia, Jan. 30, 1969.
- Most goals allowed in a game: 12 on seven occassions.
- Most games without a loss: 15, from Jan. 14 through Feb. 16, 1967.
- Most penalties in a game: 32 vs. Detroit on Dec. 23, 1988.

TOP GOAL SCORERS

1)	Bobby Hull	604
2)	Stan Mikita	541
3)	Denis Savard	351
4)	Steve Larmer	342
5)	Dennis Hull	298
6)	Bill Mosienko	258
7)	Ken Wharram	252
8)	Pit Martin	243
9)	Doug Wilson	225
10)	Doug Bentley	217

MOST ASSISTS

1)	Stan Mikita	926
2)	Denis Savard	662
3)	Doug Wilson	554
4)	Bobby Hull	549
5)	Steve Larmer	437
6)	Pierre Pilote	400
7)	Pit Martin	384
8)	Bob Murray	382
9)	Dennis Hull	342
10)	Doug Bentley	313

BLACKHAWKS YEAR-BY-YEAR RESULTS

Year	W	L	T	Year	W	L	T
1926-27	19	22	3	1943-44	22	23	5
1927-28	7	34	3	1944-45	13	30	7
1928-29	7	29	8	1945-46	23	20	7
1929-30	21	18	5	1946-47	19	37	4
1930-31	24	17	3	1947-48	20	34	6
1931-32	18	19	11	1948-49	21	31	8
1932-33	16	20	12	1949-50	22	38	10
1933-34	20	17	11	1950-51	13	47	10
1934-35	26	17	5	1951-52	17	44	9
1935-36	21	19	8	1952-53	27	28	15
1936-37	14	27	7	1953-54	12	51	7
1937-38	14	25	9	1954-55	13	40	17
1938-39	12	28	8	1955-56	19	39	12
1939-40	23	19	6	1956-57	16	39	15
1940-41	16	25	7	1957-58	24	39	7
1941-42	22	23	3	1958-59	28	29	13
1942-43	17	18	15	1959-60	28	29	13

Year	W	L	T
1960-61	29	24	17
1961-62	31	26	13
1962-63	32	21	17
1963-64	36	22	12
1964-65	34	28	8
1965-66	37	25	8
1966-67	41	17	12
1967-68	32	26	16
1968-69	34	33	9
1969-70	45	22	9
1070-71	49	20	9
1971-72	46	17	15
1972-73	42	27	9
1973-74	41	14	23
1974-75	37	35	8
1975-76	32	30	18

Year	W	L	T
1976-77	26	43	11
1977-78	32	29	19
1978-79	29	36	15
1979-80	34	27	19
1980-81	31	33	16
1981-82	30	38	12
1982-83	47	23	10
1983-84	30	42	8
1984-85	38	35	7
1985-86	39	33	8
1986-87	29	37	14
1987-88	30	41	9
1988-89	27	41	12
1989-90	41	33	6
1990-91	49	23	8

Stanley Cup: The Blackhawks won in 1933-34, 1937-38 and 1960-61.

BLACKHAWKS IN THE HALL OF FAME

Sid Abel	1952-53	Bobby Hull	1957-72
Doug Bentley	1939-52	Dick Irvin	1926-29
Max Bentley	1940-48	Gordon Keats	1928-29
George Boucher	1931-32	Hugh Lehman	1926-28
Frank Brimsek	1949-50	Ted Lindsay	1957-60
William Burch	1932-33	Harry Lumley	1951-52
Arthur Coulter	1931-36	Duncan MacKay	1926-28
Lionel Conacher	1933-34	Stan Mikita	1958-80
Cy Denneny	1927-28	Howie Morenz	1934-36
Cecil Dye	1926-27	Bill Mosienko	1941-55
Tony Esposito	1969-84	Bert Olmstead	1948-51
Phil Esposito	1963-67	Bobby Orr	1976-78
Bill Gadsby	1946-54	Pierre Pilote	1955-68
Charles Gardiner	1927-34	Earl Seibert	1936-44
Glenn Hall	1957-67	Allan Stanley	1954-56
George Hay	1926-27	John Stewart	1950-52

GOLF

Oldest course: The Chicago Golf Club near Wheaton is the oldest 18-hole golf course in the country. It was laid out in 1894 by Charles Blair MacDonald.

THE WESTERN OPEN

The Western Open has been played on courses from Dayton, Ohio, to Portland, Oregon. From 1974 to 1990, its permanent home was the

Butler National Golf Course in Oak Brook. But in September 1990, the Western Golf Association announced it would hold the 1991 tournament at Cog Hill's Dubsdread course in Lemont because Butler National did not comply with the PGA tour's policy concerning minority and female membership practices.

First champion: Willie Smith, at the Glenview Club, in 1899.

Five-time champion: Walter Hagen (1916, 1921, 1926, 1927, 1932).

Lowest score at Butler (on the regulation course): 275 by Wayne Levi in 1990 and Mark McCumber in 1989. D.A. Weibring shot 207 in 1987, but rain that year forced play to be held on nine holes at Butler and nine holes at the adjacent Oak Brook Village Golf Club.

WESTERN OPEN CHAMPIONS AT BUTLER NATIONAL

Year	Champion	Score	Year	Champion	Score
1974	Tom Watson	287	1983	Mark McCumber	284
1975	Hale Irwin	283	1984	Tom Watson	280
1976	Al Geiberger	288	1985	Scott Verplank	279
1977	Tom Watson	283	1986	Tom Kite	286
1978	Andy Bean	282	1987	D.A. Weibring	207
1979	Larry Nelson	286	1988	Jim Benepe	278
1980	Scott Simpson	281	1989	Mark McCumber	275
1981	Ed Fiori	277	1990	Wayne Levi	275
1982	Tom Weiskopf	276	1991	Ross Cochran (at Cog Hill)	275

CLASSIC QUOTE

"Most of the world's out makin' a living. The other 15 percent come out here. Let them get a job and find out what it's like."—**Cubs Manager Lee Elia on Cubs fans, April 29, 1983**

PAST TENSE

Sox Win World Title
(Daily News, Oct. 15, 1906)

The White Stockings are champions of the world and the American league is again on top.

Four times in six games the American leaguers defeated the National league's champions and the south siders thereby became champions of the world. Yesterday's game decided the fate of the world's flag and fortune gave it to the White Stockings.

Never was there a more jubilant crowd than the thousands of rooters who wedged themselves within the south side park yesterday to see the game. When the battle was over the White Stockings were actually the champions of the world. In an instant after the last out had been made the thousands who were standing in the field swarmed over it, cheering, howling, waving flags and jumping in the air in their delirium of joy.

Comiskey's men are now champions of everything in sight in the baseball world—champions of the world, champions of Chicago and champions of the American league. Where did any team ever, in the history of the sport, attain such glory?

On the showing of the last two games of the series the White Stockings had every right to win. The Cubs, worked to too high a pitch, became so nervous under the terrific strain that they finally broke down. Saturday it was seen they were not themselves. The pitchers had gone wrong and the fielding was not right. But yesterday was the climax. In the infield it was especially plain that the men had gone stale.

Sources: Eddie Gold, Taylor Bell, Ray Sons and Barry Cronin of the *Chicago Sun-Times*; *Sun-Times* and *Daily News* archives; media guides for the White Sox, Cubs, Bears, Bulls, Blackhawks; Eddie Gold of the *Chicago Sun-Times*; U.S Olympic Committee.

MOVIES

FIRSTS

■ The first movies shown in the Chicago area played at the Phoenix Opera House in Waukegan around 1898. The movies were made by Waukegan inventor Edward H. Amet and George K. Spoor. One showed two young women boxing—one of whom was Spoor's sister.

■ The first movie theater in Chicago opened with 300 seats in 1905 on State Street near Adams. The owner, Aaron Jones, used a Magniscope projector he bought from Waukegan inventor Edward H. Amet. Admission was a nickel.

> **Magic Mogul:** Chicago magician William N. Selig (1864-1948) was the first film producer to put a studio in Hollywood. Why? In 1907 he got fed up with the weather in Chicago—it was causing too many production delays. In 1896, Selig had established Selig Polyscope Company on the Near South Side and started making movies. As a partner in an animal show, he also made some of the first animal movies.

■ What is probably the first phony "newsreel" was shot in a tank of water in a Waukegan backyard in 1898. It was there that Edward H. Amet, the inventor of a moving pictures projector, made a "newsreel" of the Spanish-American War's naval battle of Santiago. After reading newspaper accounts of the battle, he made toy ships and floated them in a tank in his backyard. He used tiny explosives to simulate gunfire. It was apparently so realistic, the Spanish government used a set of the pictures in the court-martial of Admiral Pascual Cervera y Topete. He was cleared of charges that he was responsible for the destruction of the Spanish fleet.

■ The Central Park Theater, 3535 W. Roosevelt Rd., was the first air-conditioned movie theater in Chicago when it opened in 1917. Actually it was a pretty rustic form of air conditioning—ice-cooled refrigeration—but it helped. It was introduced by Chicago-based movie theater chain owners Barney Balaban and Sam Katz. Balaban

(1887-1971), who used to work for a Chicago cold storage company, became president of Paramount Pictures in 1936.

Movie Furrier: Chicago furrier Adolph Zukor (1873-1976) saw his first movie in Chicago and soon was a part of the industry. He started out by working with Marcus Loew and his chain of motion picture theaters. Eventually he became president of Paramount, which he built into one of Hollywood's major studios.

■ The first movie directory to appear in the *Chicago Daily News* on June 22, 1915, listed the offerings of ten movie theaters: Orchestra Hall, Fine Arts, Winchester, Hamlin, Bell, Elmo, Bijou, Alvin, Erie and Broadway.

Chicago Once Was Disneyland: Walt Disney was born in 1901 in a two-story wood house built by his carpenter father, Elias, at what is now 2156 N. Tripp. The family lived there until 1906, then moved to a farm in Marceline, Missouri. They later returned to Chicago and Disney attended McKinley High School in 1917, before heading off to France to drive a Red Cross ambulance in World War I. He died in 1966.

FILMS AND THE ECONOMY

In 1990, feature length films and television productions shot in Illinois brought about $65 million into the economy, and more than 14,000 local people were hired. About 50 percent of that money was generated in Chicago and the other 50 percent in the suburbs and nearby counties. An additional $17 million was brought in by the 400 to 500 commercials, industrial films, still photography projects, music videos, public service announcements, documentaries and educational films shot in Chicago.

Blue Island Model: Mrs. Jane Buckingham of Blue Island was the model for Miss Columbia—the statue that appeared with the Columbia logo at the beginning of all the old Columbia films.

NUMBER OF MOVIE SCREENS

There are 860 movie screens in the state of Illinois, 835 of them indoors. There are about 300 "first run" screens in the Chicago metropolitan area. Although it's difficult to be certain, there are about 1,400 video retailers in the Chicago area.

TOP GROSSING MOVIES IN CHICAGO AREA SINCE 1982
(Rounded to the nearest $100,000)

1982: *E.T.* $9.1 million
1983: *Return of the Jedi* $6.8
1984: *Ghostbusters* $6.2 million
1985: *Back to the Future* $5 million
1986: *The Color Purple* or *Top Gun* (amount unavail.)
1987: *Platoon* $4.1 million
1988: *Who Framed Roger Rabbit* $3.9 million
1989: *Batman* $7.9 million
1990: *Die Hard 2* $4 million

LIST OF TEN
TOP GROSSING MOVIES IN CHICAGO AREA FOR 1990

1. *Die Hard 2*
2. *Ghost*
3. *Pretty Woman*
4. *Teenage Mutant Ninja Turtles*
5. *Back to the Future 2*
6. *War of the Roses*
7. *Total Recall*
8. *Dick Tracy*
9. *Presumed Innocent*
10. *Home Alone*

MIGHTY HIGH STANDARDS

In 1959, Sgt. Vincent Nolen, then head of the police censorship board, explained his standard for judging a movie: It had to be suitable for his son, Little Willie. "Children should be allowed to see any movie that plays in Chicago," Nolen said. "If a picture is objectionable for a child, it is objectionable period."

It Started in Waukegan: Waukegan has often been called the birthplace of the motion picture industry because of what went on in the backyard of Edward H. Amet. In 1894 Amet went to Chicago to see Thomas A. Edison's moving picture machine. Amet thought it was too limited a device because only one person could view the moving pictures at a time. So Amet invented the Magniscope, a projection device for movies. In 1898, he asked two local women to come to his backyard. Once there he gave them boxing gloves and told them to swing away. They did, and Amet made a movie of it. Amet and the brother of one of the women, George Spoor, made a couple of such movies and showed them in the Waukegan Opera House. They grossed $400 in the first six days. Amet, however, didn't think there was much future to the business and sold his invention to a Philadelphia firm. By 1900, he was done with the movies.

THE ILLINOIS FILM OFFICE

Founded: It was created in 1975 as a division of the State of Illinois Department of Commerce and Community Affairs. Director: Suzy Kellett.

Employees: Eight.

Budget: $650,000 for fiscal 1990. It opened in 1976, when seven motion pictures or TV shows were shot wholly or in part in Illinois. In 1990, twenty-five were shot wholly or in part in Illinois.

Uncle Carl: The founder of Universal Studios started his movie career in Chicago. In 1906 Carl Laemmle (1867-1939) used $2,000 in savings to open the White Front Theater at Ashland and Milwaukee. Within two months he opened another nickelodeon and within three years he was producing motion pictures—*Hiawatha* was his first. In 1912, he formed Universal Film Manufacturing Company, and in 1915 he opened his 230-acre studio called Universal City in Hollywood. Known in Hollywoood as Uncle Carl, Laemmle had seventy relatives on the payroll.

THE CHICAGO FILM OFFICE

Created in 1975, the Chicago Film Office acts as liaison between movie production companies and the many different city offices and departments. It assists in bringing police and firemen to a film location or arranging for the necessary permits.

Censors Fall: On Jan. 29, 1968, the U.S. Supreme Court struck down Chicago's sixty-two-year-old censorship system of reviewing all films.

MOVIES SHOT IN CHICAGO AND ILLINOIS

When Chicago was home to some of the nation's early filmmakers in the early 1900s, the city and regional landscape was part of the scenery. The Chicago & North Western Railroad tracks in Ravenswood were used for filming Pearl White, the damsel in distress tied to the tracks, and many westerns were shot at Illinois Beach State Park near Waukegan. But when Hollywood became the nation's filmmaking capital, Chicago became less of a backdrop. Some shooting, however, was done in the area. For example, part of Alfred Hitchcock's *North by Northwest* (1959) was shot at the Ambassador East, and exterior scenes for Steve McQueen's *Bullitt* (1968) were shot around the city.

But there were problems with shooting in Chicago. Mayor Richard J. Daley, who held office from 1955 to 1976, didn't exactly encourage filmmaking in his city. At least not films that might malign the Chicago police, inconvenience the public or show crime in the city. Eventually that position weakened, and with the establishment of the Chicago Film Office and the Illinois Film Office, the movies have returned.

Favorite shooting locations include the elevated tracks, the intersection of Milwaukee, North and Damen avenues; lower Wacker Drive; the skyline, and the side streets and downtown areas of Wilmette and Winnetka.

Prior to 1976, when the Illinois Film Office starting keeping track of movies shot in Illinois, nobody kept tabs on what movies were filmed in the Chicago area. The following is the list since 1976:

1976: Silver Streak, Monkey Hustle, Whisper the Sounds, Rollercoaster, Looking for Mr. Goodbar.

1977: Damien-Omen II, The Fury, A Wedding, A Piece of the Action, Stony Island.

1978: Dreamer, Promises in the Dark.

1979: Roar, Somewhere in Time, My Bodyguard, The Blues Brothers, The Hunter, 1941, Ordinary People.

1980: The Music Box, Thief, The Perfect Circle, On the Right Track, Four Friends, Escape from New York City, Endless Love, Continental Divide.

1981: Pennies from Heaven, Isabel Buchanan (BBC documentary), They Call Me Bruce, Cities on the Great Lakes (TOEI Films-Tokyo—educational film)

Filming of the *Blues Brothers* movie in Chicago involved a car stunt where the Blues Brothers' car jumped over a Chicago police car.

1982: Things Are Tough All Over, Bad Boys, Story on Yugoslavian Cultural Activities (documentary), *Risky Business, Dr. Detroit, I Was a Mail Order Bride, National Lampoon's Vacation, The Apprentice, Class, Windy City, Sandler and Young—The First 20 Years* (documentary), *Welcome to the U.S. Navy* (documentary).

1983: Here's Chicago (Travel film), *Risky Business, Streets of Fire, Hambone and Hilly, Sixteen Candles, The Big Score, The Gardens Edge* (Short), *Come Around, America the Beautiful* (documentary), *Grandview U.S.A, The Naked Face, River Rats, Heartbreaker, The Ultimate Solution of Grace Quigley.*

1984: The Breakfast Club, World's Fair Film (documentary), *Touch & Go, Disney Agricultural Film* (documentary), *The Nature of Things* (Science/Educational), *Portraits of America* (documentary), *Pride of Place* (documentary), *Chicago* (documentary), *Untitled* (Educational Tapes), *Code of Silence, Weird Science, Bauhaus Architecture* (documentary).

1985: Death in California, Club Paradise, Just Another Saturday Night, Jo Jo Dancer, Lucas, Wildcats, Zoning, Nothing in Common, Ferris Bueller's Day Off, About Last Night, Manhunter, Raw Deal, Running Scared.

1986: No Mercy, Let's Get Harry, The Color of Money, Light of Day, Native Son, Personal Foul, End of the Line, The Untouchables, The Big Town, Big Shots, Jimmy Reardon, She's Having a Baby, Rent-A-Cop.

1987: Weeds, Adventures in Babysitting, Vice Versa, Planes, Trains and Automobiles, Poltergeist III, Above the Law, Switching Channels, Red Heat, Freak aka Geek, Betrayed, Midnight Run, Things Change.

1988: Child's Play, The Tender, Field of Dreams, Taxi Killers, Desire,

Men Don't Leave, Chains, Next of Kin, Major League, When Harry Met Sally.

1989: The Package, Uncle Buck, Music Box, Opportunity Knocks, Men Will Be Boys (short), *Miss Missouri, Victimless Crime, Flatliners, Father Jim, Shaking the Tree.*

1990: Home Alone, Child's Play II, Critical Action, Paradise Lost, Paradise Found, Where the Night Begins, Backdraft, Heaven is a Playground, Bix Beiderbecke, One Cup of Coffee, Only the Lonely, V.I. Warshawski, Curly Sue.

Reagan Was Here: Chicago has long been a center for industrial and public service films. By 1959, for example, Wilding Inc., then the world's largest producer of business motion pictures, was making 100 films a year in Chicago. Ronald Reagan, Alan Ladd, Jimmy Durante, Zasu Pitts and Gale Storm were among the actors who did such films in Chicago.

CHICAGO'S CONTRIBUTION

George K. Spoor teamed with Gilbert M. "Bronco Billy" Anderson (1882-1971), the world's first movie cowboy, to form Essanay Motion Picture Company in 1907, which established Chicago as an early major motion picture center. The "S" in Essanay, stands for Spoor and the "A" stands for Anderson.

Essanay productions featured such stars as Gloria Swanson, Wallace Beery, Charlie Chaplin, Ben Turpin and Francis X. Bushman. In fact, Swanson and Beery were married in 1916 on the Essanay lot at 1333-1345 W. Argyle. Bronco Billy himself made 385 movies including the pre-Essanay *The Great Train Robbery* (1903), one of the longest movies of its time and the first Western.

Spoor claimed to make Charlie Chaplin the first, or one of the first, $1,000-a-week film stars when he persuaded Chaplin to work for him for $1,250 a week. Many of the large homes on Castlewood Terrace on the North Side were built by film stars of the 1920s, most of whom worked for Spoor. Still, Spoor turned down Mary Pickford, Douglas Fairbanks and Fatty Arbuckle—they wanted too much.

At its peak, Essanay made several movies a week at about $1,000 a pop. In turn, the movies brought in about $20,000 apiece. Louella Parsons, who became a syndicated film columnist, was the head of Essanay's script-writing department. Ring Lardner also wrote for them.

Somewhere in each frame of each Essanay movie is the Essanay Indian Head trademark—appearing in such places as under a chair or on the wall. Essanay was not alone in doing this. The use of the symbol was to discourage print thieves from using their film. Essanay and several other companies formed the Motion Picture Patent Company to pool resources and keep out newcomers. This eventually led to an anti-trust suit involving a distributing agency formed by MPP, and MPP lost. With that, Essanay faded and by 1917 was pretty much finished.

Spoor went on to make money in the oil business, but he lost plenty investing in 3-D movies. He, along with P. John Berggren, produced a three-dimensional movie called *Danger Lights,* which was shown at the State-Lake Theater in 1930. Spoor died in 1953 at age eighty-one.

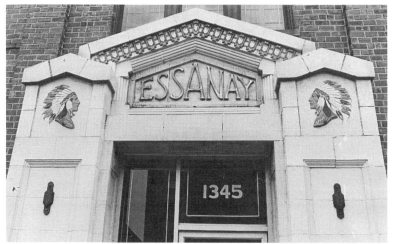

The entranceway to the Essanay Studio building at 1345 W. Argyle.

CLASSIC QUOTES

Late in his career, Chicago movie pioneer George K. Spoor was asked what he watches: "Movies? No, young fellow, I don't go to the movies much anymore. You see, there are only about thirty stories in the world, and by this time I guess I know them all by heart."

Italian movie director Ducio Tessari talking about Chicago while filming a Dino De Laurentiis production Two Tough Guys in Chicago (1973): "Chicago is like thirty-eight beautiful women. She is a flirt. She likes you to be nice to her. After you discover her, she is very proud."

Sources; *Chicago Sun-Times* and *Daily News* clips: *The Film Encyclopedia* by Ephraim Katz; National Association of Movie Theater Owners; Bruce Ingram; *Variety;* Illinois Film Office; Chicago Film Office.

LITERATURE

FIRSTS

The first book of poems published in Chicago, *Miscellaneous Poems,* was penned by a Du Page County resident, William Asbury Kenyon. They were printed by James Campbell & Company, in January 1845. One poem begins as follows: "Say: Did you hear of Black Hawk's War,/ When nature's own was struggled for?/ Terror struck all the country through,/ Raised by aggression's bugaboo."

Library in Chicago The Chicago Fire of 1871 destroyed much of the city, but not the public library because there was no public library. But, thanks to the fire, there soon would be. In the fire's aftermath, the people of Great Britain donated 17,355 books to Chicago. A makeshift library was established in 1873 to house the books and, one year later, relocated to a building at Lake and Dearborn streets. William Frederick Poole was appointed head librarian.

Best-Sellers: The Chicago Public Library owns more copies of two children's books by Dr. Seuss than any other book: *The Cat in the Hat* (1,173 copies) and *Green Eggs and Ham* (1,128 copies).

Big Little Magazine: *The Little Review,* an adventurous Chicago literary magazine edited by Margaret Anderson and Jane Heap during the 1920s, was the first American publisher of James Joyce's *Ulysses.*

EXTREME

Encyclopaedia Britannica, based in Chicago, lays claim to being the oldest continuously published reference work in the English language, first published by three Scotsmen in Edinburgh, Scotland, in 1768. *Britannica,* which changed hands several times over the decades, is owned today by the not-for-profit William Benton Foundation of Illinois, a supporting organization of the University of Chicago. Worldwide, the company has 8,300 employees and sales representatives.

Literary Mayor: Chicago's most literary mayor was Carter H. Harrison, the author of a book of travel sketches and a short work of fiction. Harrison traveled around the world in 1887 and 1888 and wrote a series of letters to the *Chicago Tribune.* In 1889, the letters became the basis of his first book, *A Race with the Sun.* Two years later he published *A Summer Outing and the Old Man's Story,* a collection of travel writing and fiction.

CHICAGO CONTRIBUTION

Harriet Monroe and Poetry magazine: Founded in 1912, Monroe's *Poetry* magazine provided a national forum for the developing free verse of modern poetry. It was among the first publications to carry the work of T.S. Eliot, Marianne Moore, William Carlos Williams, and Carl Sandburg. It's most famous poem is "Trees" by Joyce Kilmer. *Poetry* remains one of the most respected literary magazines in the United States, subscribed to by libraries around the world and read by publishers in search of new talent.

Harriet Monroe founded *Poetry* magazine in 1912.

The Jungle: Upton Sinclair's famous expose novel of the Chicago stockyards did little to stir American workers to revolt against capitalism—as he had hoped—but gave people indigestion. *The Jungle* (1906) created nationwide indignation over the quality of processed meat and helped bring about federal food inspection laws.

Upton Sinclair wrote of the
Chicago stockyards in *The
Jungle.*

FAMOUS CHICAGO WRITERS

Nelson Algren (1909-1981). He was called America's Dostoevsky, his subjects the lost souls and dispossessed of Chicago's soiled streets. Algren won the National Book Award for fiction in 1950 for his best selling novel, *The Man with the Golden Arm.* Among the best of his other works are the novel *A Walk on the Wild Side* (1958), the prose-poem *Chicago: City on the Make* (1951), and a collection of short stories, *The Neon Wilderness* (1947). Born in Detroit, Algren came to Chicago with his family at the age of three. Feeling unappreciated by Chicago, Algren picked up and left for good in 1975, resettling in New England.

Nelson Algren—America's
Dostoevsky.

George Ade (1866-1944). He was noted for his column for the *Chicago Record,* but his best work was *Fables in Slang* (1899), a collection of short sketches satirizing turn-of-the-century manners in a breezy vernacular language.

Sherwood Anderson (1876-1941). Best known for *Winesburg, Ohio* (1919), written in a small room in a Chicago boarding house. Anderson grew up in Clyde, Ohio, but moved to Chicago around 1900. Those were the days of the "Chicago Renaissance" in literature, and Anderson fell in with an ambitious crowd that included Carl Sandburg, Ben Hecht and Theodore Dreiser. His stories, largely autobiographical, explored what he called "the quiet desperation" of small-town life.

L. Frank Baum (1856-1919). Why the Land of Oz? "The time has now come," Baum wrote in his foreword to *The Wonderful Wizard of Oz,* "for a series of newer 'wonder tales' in which the stereotyped genie, dwarf and fairy are eliminated, together with the horrible and blood-curdling incidents devised by their authors to point a fearsome moral." Baum wrote thirteen Oz books. Born in Chittenango, New York, he ventured through the West as a farmer, journalist and businessman before moving to Chicago in 1891. He settled near Humboldt Park, where he wrote his first Oz books. In 1911, he moved to California.

Saul Bellow (born 1915). The business of writing, Bellow once said, is to reveal to readers, even at the risk of their displeasure, the secrets of their own heart. Bellow, whose writing combines a unique blend of side-of-the-mouth Chicagoese and heady intellectualism, generally is regarded to be Chicago's greatest living writer. He was awarded the Nobel Prize in 1976. Among his novels are *Dangling Man* (1944); *The Victim* (1947); *The Adventures of Augie March* (1953), winner of the National Book Award; *Herzog* (1961); *Seize the Day* (1964); *The Dean's December* (1982), and *More Die of Heartbreak* (1987).

Saul Bellow was awarded the
Nobel Prize in 1976.

Ray Bradbury (born 1920). Green Town, Illinois, the idealized small town of many of Bradbury's stories, was inspired by the town of his birth and early boyhood, Waukegan. *Dandelion Wine* (1957) is a gentle memoir of his boyhood there. Other books include *The Martian Chronicles* (1950), *Fahrenheit 451* (1953), *Something Wicked This Way Comes* (1962) and *R Is for Rocket* (1962).

Gwendolyn Brooks (born 1917). Poet laureate of Illinois, she was the first black woman to win a Pulitzer Prize, for *Annie Allen* (1949). Brooks, who grew up on the South Side, published more than seventy-five of her early poems in the *Chicago Defender* newspaper. Among her volumes of poems are *Bronzeville Boys & Girls* (1956), *The Bean Eaters* (1960), *Selected Poems* (1963) and *Family Pictures* (1970). She also wrote *Report from Part One: An Autobiography* (1972).

Gwendolyn Brooks was the first black woman to win a Pulitzer Prize (1949).

Edgar Rice Burroughs (1875-1950). He was born in Oak Park, worked in Chicago and never stepped foot in Africa. But he did stop by at the Lincoln Park Zoo once to check out its most famous ape, Bushman. Burroughs created Tarzan. In 1912, he was an office manager for Sears, Roebuck & Company when he sold his first book, *Tarzan of the Apes*, to the A.C. McClurg publishing firm for $700. It caught on. At the time of his death, he had earned at least $5 million in movie royalties and sold almost 40 million Tarzan books in fifty-seven languages. "I was not writing because of any particular urge to write or for any particular love of writing," he once said. "I was writing because I had a wife and two babies, a combination that does not work well without money." Soon after gaining fame, Burroughs moved to Los Angeles.

Cyrus Colter (born 1910). He published his first fiction at sixty, after a career as a Chicago attorney and member of the Illinois Commerce Commission. The collections of stories *The Beach Umbrella* (1970) and the novels *The River of Eros* (1972), *The Hippodrome* (1973) and *Night Studies* (1979) explore middle-class black life in Chicago.

Jack Conroy: (1899-1990). Best remembered for his 1933 proletarian novel *The Disinherited*, Conroy also edited several literary journals in the 1930s and 1940s that published the early work of Richard Wright and Nelson Algren. Conroy, a Chicagoan from 1938 to 1965, wrote *A World to Win* (1935) and *They Seek a City* (1944). In the 1930s, he was editor of the literary magazines the *Anvil* and the *New Anvil*. Algren was, for a time, his managing editor. He was born and died in Moberly, Missouri.

Theodore Dreiser (1871-1945). Before mass media wiped out regional literature, many of Chicago's writers shared a common voice of plain-speaking outrage. From Sherwood Anderson to James T. Farrell to Jack Conroy to Nelson Algren, they wrote with a Midwestern natural-ism about class exploitation, the dangers of worldly success and the falseness of the American Dream. Dreiser was a pioneer of this school of writing, his fervor compensating for often clumsy prose. Dreiser be-gan writing for the *Chicago Globe* in 1892. His first novel, *Sister Carrie* (1900), about a small-town girl who loses her virtue in the big city, evokes Chicago in photographic detail. It was judged obscene by some readers because Carrie is never punished for her transgressions. Among his other works are *An American Tragedy* (1925), *The Finan-cier* (1912) and *The Titan* (1914).

Theodore Dreiser's first novel, *Sister Carrie* (1900), was judged obscene by some readers.

James T. Farrell (1904-1979). He is best known for his realistic trilogy of novels concerning Studs Lonigan, a second-generation Irish-American growing up on the South Side. Farrell, who wrote more than fifty books, was praised and criticized for his style of naturalistic writing—plain and straightforward prose, largely devoid of symbolism and metaphor. His best novels explore a poverty of spirit common to the working-class friends of his youth.

Eugene Field (1850-1895). His most lasting works are two classic children's poems, "Wynken, Blynken and Nod" and "Little Boy Blue." But in his day, Field was praised for his pioneering "Sharps and Flats" column in the *Chicago Daily News*, a mixed bag of light verse, short stories and humor.

Henry Blake Fuller (1857-1929). He was a leader of the Chicago literary movement in the 1890s. *The Cliff-Dwellers* (1893), his best-known novel, tells the stories of the residents of a Chicago skyscraper. It is often called the first important American urban novel. Other works include *With the Procession* (1895) and *On the Stairs* (1918).

Ben Hecht (1894-1964). Chicago's "Front Page" era—the days when newspapers played loose with the facts and did just about anything for a scoop—are gone. But, thanks to Hecht, not forgotten. Hecht grew up in Racine, Wisconsin, and reported in Chicago—mostly for the *Chicago Daily News*. A central figure in Chicago's literary renaissance, he made his biggest splash when he wrote "The Front Page" (1928) with Charles MacArthur. (see Media).

Famous newspaperman from the "Front Page" era—Ben Hecht.

Ernest Hemingway (1899-1961). If, to his face, you had called Hemingway a Chicago writer, he might have slugged you. But Papa did grow up in Oak Park, and did graduate from Oak Park-River Forest High School and did live in Chicago for a time while struggling with his writing. Hemingway, widely recognized as one of the great authors of the twentieth century, produced six novels and more than fifty short stories, including *The Sun Also Rises* (1926), *A Farewell to Arms* (1929), *To Have and Have Not* (1937) and *For Whom the Bell Tolls* (1940). In 1954, he was awarded the Nobel Prize for literature.

Though not considered a Chicago writer, Ernest Hemingway did grow up in Oak Park.

Ring Lardner (1885-1933). He liked baseball, writing and plain English. So he put them all together and wrote some fine short stories, including the frequently anthologized "Haircut," "Champion," "Love Nest" and "Alibi Ike." Lardner's most popular novel, *You Know Me, Al: A Busher's Letters* (1916), consists of letters written by a fictional Chicago White Sox rookie, Jack Keefe, to a friend back home. Lardner was widely admired for his use of American vernacular.

Edgar Lee Masters (1869-1950). Chicago's claim on Masters, the author of *Spoon River Anthology* (1915), is tenuous. He was raised downstate near the Spoon River and seemed little touched by the dissenting voice of so many other Chicago Renaissance writers. But he wrote his best work in Chicago. Masters came to Chicago in 1892 and became a successful lawyer, knocking out plays, essays and poems in his free time. He wrote *Spoon River Anthology*, a book of free-verse epitaphs revealing the inner lives of people buried in a Spoon River cemetery, after reading a copy of *Epigrams from the Greek Anthology*.

Frank Norris (1870-1902). Norris and Theodore Dreiser are regarded among the first important naturalistic novelists in American literature. Together they inspired a generation of angry and pessimistic young writers, including James T. Farrell and Richard Wright. Norris was born in Chicago, but did not live in the city for long. He grew up in Oakland and San Francisco and returned to Chicago only to do research on his novel *The Pit* (1903), a fictional study of the Chicago Board of Trade's market manipulations.

Carl Sandburg (1878-1967). Like Field, Dreiser, Ben Hecht and Edna Ferber, Sandburg worked for the *Chicago Daily News*—for thirteen years. He covered the race riot of 1919—eventually writing a book about it. Sandburg, a poet of free-form verse heavily influenced by Walt Whitman, won a Pulitzer Prize for his biography of Abraham Lincoln. He wrote the poem that defined Chicago for the world— "Hog Butcher for the World, Tool Maker, Stacker of Wheat, Player with Railroads and the Nation's Freight Handler, Stormy, Husky, Brawling, City of the Big Shoulders."

Carl Sandburg penned the name "City of the Big Shoulders" for Chicago.

Studs Terkel (born 1912). He is an oral historian—America's best—an essayist, an actor, a radio host and a character—the guy in the red checked shirts and red socks. He is also an instinctive champion of the underdog and lost causes, a voice of grassroots Chicago. His interview books are *American Dreams: Lost & Found* (1980); *Division Street, America* (1967); *The Good War: An Oral History of World War Two* (1984), for which he won the Pulitzer Prize; *Working* (1974); *Hard Times: An Oral History of the Great Depression in America* (1970); and *The Great Divide: Second Thoughts on the American Dream* (1989). Terkel, who has hosted a daily radio talk show in Chicago since 1952, also has written an extended essay on the city, *Chicago* (1986).

Richard Wright (1908-1960). Born near Natchez, Mississippi, he came up from the South to Chicago in 1934 and found that racism and social injustice were no strangers to the North. In *Native Son* (1940), his best-known work, Wright tells the story of Bigger Thomas, a young South Side black man convicted of murder, but who is himself a victim of injustice. In *Black Boy* (1945), an autobiographical novel of his boyhood in the South, Wright achieved his greatest critical success. In Chicago, Wright worked as a postal clerk by day and wrote by night.

Richard Wright's greatest critical success came from *Black Boy.*

THE NEW CROP

Chicago can boast a list of notable working writers whose work has yet
to stand the test of time. Among them are: James Atlas, William
Brashler, Paul Carroll, Charles Dickinson, Stuart Dybek, Leon Forrest, Bill Granger, Larry Heineman, Bette Howland, Eugene Izzy, Stuart Kaminsky, Sarah Paretsky, Scott Spencer, Richard Stern and Scott
Turow.

WRITINGS ON CHICAGO

" 'It's a big town, dearest," Hurstwood answered. "It would be as
good as moving to another part of the country to move to the South
Side.' " *Sister Carrie* (1900), by Theodore Dreiser.

———————————

"Then there was the fabulous city in which Bigger lived, an indescrib-
able city, huge, roaring, dirty noisy, raw, stark, brutal; a city of extremes: torrid in summers and sub-zero winters, white people and
black people, the English language and strange tongues, foreign born
and native born, scabby poverty and gaudy luxury, high idealism and
hard cynicism!" *Native Son* (1945), from the preface by Richard
Wright.

———————————

"You feel stranded after dark. The air is penetrating. Particularly in
Hyde Park, with the ghosts of the old stockyards to the west, and to
the south—very much alive, a red glow from my windows—the inner
sanctums of the steel mills. Like the days after King's assassination—
the odor of smoke and cinders blowing over the city. The slums were
burning. The conditions I describe are only a dim reflection of the terror of that life." *Blue in Chicago* (1978), by Bette Howland.

———————————

"He had never been on the West Side, and he wondered about it. It
was probably like a city itself, and it had its gangs and bunches and
poolrooms all over, fellows just like their own bunch from Fifty-eighth
Street, fellows like himself, like Red and like Slug and Weary and all
the old boys." *The Studs Lonigan Story: Judgment Day* (1935), by
James T. Farrell.

"Like most Chicagoans, I'm insouciant about the ubiquitous payoffs which oil city life, proud as the next non-insider about the city's reputation: frauds, clout, Rat-a-tat-tat, Fast Eddies, Bathhouse Johns, Needlenose Labriolas, Don't-Make-No-Waves. Chicago's the country's real Disneyland, Oberammergau with real nails. For us, California's just Polynesia on wheels and the Sun Belt won't hold up anyone's pants. Since Mrs. O'Leary, our writers have been feeding this guff to the world, and to us." *The Position of the Body* (1986), by Richard Stern.

"But he enjoyed the city, all of it. Sometimes he crossed the ramparts that led out to a curving drive which edges the great and furious winter lake; he would stand there scanning its immensity, wondering what oceans there might really be in the world more vast. Then he would turn inland suddenly, in a way he had learned to do, and surprise his eyes with the great skyline, cut out and pasted against some mood of the sun." *All the Dark and Beautiful Warriors,* an unpublished novel by Lorraine Hansberry.

"This was different, the city softball league. Most of the guys were older, playing after work. The park was crowded with girlfriends, wives, and kids. They spread beach blankets behind the backstop, grilled hotdogs, set out potato salad, jugs of lemonade. Sometimes, in a tight game with runners on, digging in at short, ready to break with the ball, a peace I'd never felt before would paralyze the diamond. The moment of eternal stillness I felt as if I were cocked at the very heart of the Midwest." *Childhood and Other Neighborhoods* (1980), by Stuart Dybek.

"On Skid Row even the native-born no longer felt they had been born in America. They felt they had merely emerged from the wrong side of its billboards." *The Man With the Golden Arm* (1950), by Nelson Algren.

Streetless: Chicago had an Algren Street for a few weeks—named by Mayor Jane Byrne for Nelson Algren in 1982—but the enraged folks who lived there didn't want to change their personal stationery. The city backed off, and Algren Street, where the author had lived, is Evergreen Street evermore.

"Maureen, the waitress on the day shift at the Victoria Restaurant, was a real city girl. Hefty and double-chinned, she leaned against the counter smoking. Her white uniform was spotted, her skin pearly and coarse-pored. She had grown up on the South Side in an Italian neighborhood of bungalows with scalloped curtains and concrete stoops and flamingos in the yard. Her father worked in a Gary steel mill." *The Great Pretender* (1986), by James Atlas.

"He drove straight to Woodlawn Avenue—a dreary part of Hyde Park, but characteristically, his Chicago: massive, clumsy, amorphous, smelling of mud and decay, dog turds, sooty facades, slabs of structural nothing, senselessly ornamented triple porches with huge cement urns for flowers that contained only rotting cigarette butts and other stained filth." *Herzog* (1961), by Saul Bellow.

"He could tell himself otherwise, that La Salle Street was just another strip of Loop concrete. But he knew that the street named after the French explorer who was murdered by his own men was a sanctuary of capitalism, that vaunted economic system in which murder was one of the lesser crimes." *Traders* (1989), by William Brashler.

"Our double-vision, double-standard, double-value, and double-cross have been patent ever since—at least, ever since the earliest of our city fathers took the Pottawattomies for all they had." *Chicago* (1985), by Studs Terkel.

"Farther up Clark was the gigantic, blocks-long Sandburg complex, the world's greatest monument to urban paranoia. Even the children's playgrounds were surrounded by eight-foot-tall security fences. Fabe likened it to being in a luxurious federal joint...." *The Take* (1987), by Eugene Izzi.

Sources: Henry Kisor, book editor, *Chicago Sun-Times;* Roald Haffe, *Encyclopaedia Brittanica; World Book; Chicago,* a 1984 special issue of TriQuarterly magazine; *Chicago in Story,* by Clarence A. Andrews, Midwest Heritage Publishing Co., 1982; *Illinois Authors,* a publication of the Illinois State Library; *Du Page Roots,* by Richard A. Thompson, Du Page County Historical Society, 1985.

MUSIC

FIRSTS

The first performance of an opera in Chicago, Vincenzo Bellini's "La Sonnambula," went bust when the theater burned. The date was July 30, 1850. As the curtain rose for the second act at Rice's Theatre, the fire bell rang, the audience fled, and the theater, in one hour, was reduced to ashes. Eight years later, Carl Anshuts organized another orchestra and gave Chicago its first full season of classical music—beginning with "La Sonnambula."

The first piano in Chicago, owned by John B. Beaubien, was shipped to town in 1834.

The first musical organization in Chicago is said to have been the Chicago Harmonic Society, a choir group, which gave its first concert on Dec. 11, 1835, in the new Presbyterian church.

Stone Death. A former marine who was wounded in Vietnam fell to his death at the Rolling Stones' July 8, 1978, concert at Soldier Field. It remains the only death by other-than-natural causes at a major Chicago concert. The twenty-seven-year-old man plunged fifteen to twenty feet and landed on a concrete driveway. Police found no witnesses.

CHICAGO CONTRIBUTIONS

Muddy Waters and the Chicago Blues: When black Chicagoans from the Deep South crossed the old 12-bar country blues of the Mississippi Delta with the electric guitar and band style of the industrial North, they gave the world the Chicago blues. The blues, in turn, gave birth to rock and roll. Generally speaking, Chicago was fertile ground for this new urban sound because it was home to hundreds of thousands of blacks—creating a market for the music—a strong "race" record industry in the likes of Chess, Vee Jay and Cobra Records, and a huge number of recent arrivals from Mississippi. The Mississippi Delta's harsh, rhythmic and aggressive music was ideally suited for modern amplification. Chicago's most celebrated bluesman was Muddy Waters—born McKinley Morganfield in Rolling Fork, Mississippi— who died in 1983 at age sixty-eight. He became king of Chicago's bluesmen with such classics as "Hoochie Coochie Man," "Rollin' and Tumblin'" and "Got My Mojo Workin.'" He won six Grammy awards. Other blues artists who forged their art in Chicago include Jimmy Rogers, Homesick James, Tampa Red, Memphis Minnie, Sonny Boy Williamson, Little Walter, Sunnyland Slim, Big Walter Horton, Junior Wells, Willie Dixon, Howlin' Wolf, Jimmy Reed, Jo Jo Williams, Buddy Guy, Koko Taylor and Pinetop Perkins.

Thomas A. Dorsey and Gospel Music: He is called the "father of Gospel music." Born in 1899 outside Atlanta, Dorsey wrote more than 1,000 Gospel songs, including "Precious Lord," and is, in fact, credited with coining the music's very name—Gospel. Dorsey was among the first to cross the sound of raw blues with sacred church music to create the soulful foot-stomping sound that still fills many black churches. He started out, at the age of twelve, playing the blues on the piano in bordellos to support his family. He later composed his own blues and jazz tunes, playing professionally under the name "Georgia Tom." Eventually, he developed Gospel music as a way of reconciling an internal conflict between his religious upbringing and his love for the blues. Dorsey wrote his greatest hit—"Take My Hand, Precious Lord"—in 1931 while recovering from the loss of his wife and baby daughter in childbirth.

The father of Gospel music, Thomas A. Dorsey belts it out on his day. Mayor Harold Washington declared Aug. 7, 1983, Thomas A. Dorsey Day in Chicago.

The Austin High Gang and Chicago Jazz: Chicago was a hot center of jazz in the 1920s, with some of the new music's greatest talents—such as Louis Armstrong, Earl Hines, King Oliver, Jelly Roll Morton, and Bix Beiderbecke and the Wolverines—coming in from all over the

South and Midwest to jam. Many jazz critics today argue that jazz was, in fact, born in Chicago, spun out from the ragtime sounds of New Orleans. Among the best of Chicago's early homegrown jazzmen were the Austin High Gang, a group of teenage jazz fanatics from the West Side who pioneered the energetic Chicago style of jazz. The Austin High Gang included cornetist Jimmy McPartland, saxophonist Bud Freeman, banjo player Dick McPartland, bass tuba player Jim Lannigan, clarinetist Frank Teschemacher, pianist Dave North and drummer Dave Tough. Jimmy McPartland (1907-1991), like Benny Goodman, went on to play with Chicagoan Ben Pollack's band, generally credited with fusing elements of New Orleans and Chicago jazz into what then was called "swing." Freeman (1906-1991) went on to play with Eddie Condon, Tommy Dorsey and Benny Goodman. In a short story, John O'Hara wrote, "If I want to hear good saxophone, I'll find out where Bud Freeman's playing."

The Impressions and Chicago Soul: Chicago, much to the surprise of many, had a thriving soul music scene in the late 1950s and the 1960s. Among Chicago's soul masters were the Impressions, a group that included two of the true greats of soul music—Curtis Mayfield and Jerry "Iceman" Butler. Many music critics regard the Impressions' 1958 hit "For Your Precious Love" as Chicago's first soul record. Among Chicago's other great soul singers were the Shilites, and Pop Staples and the Staple Singers. Soul music in Chicago pretty much came to an end around 1984, when the last notable soul record label, Chi-Sound, closed its doors.

The Impressions as they looked in 1977.

House Music: Chicago's cutting-edge dance floor sound, house music is thumping, repetitive, bass-heavy and technically precise. The lyrics are simple, the beat primitive. It's an outgrowth of disco, but with a down-and-dirty groove. House was an underground Chicago phenomenon through the mid-1980s, with a few popular deejays pumping it out in local clubs such as the Warehouse—arguably the source of the music's name. In the late 1980s, house became the rage of New York and much of Western Europe. Madonna's "Vogue" is basically a house song.

FAMOUS CHICAGOANS

Benny Goodman: The "King of Swing" (1909-1986) was born to Russian Jewish immigrant parents, the eighth of eleven children, on Chicago's Near West Side. At age nine he begged to go along when his father took two older brothers to their synagogue, which was lending musical instruments for free. His brothers chose a tuba and a trumpet. He took what was left—a clarinet. Twenty years later, he became the first jazz artist to play Carnegie Hall. Goodman, who grew up in the Maxwell Street neighborhood, learned to play the clarinet in the Hull House settlement band. He got his first paying job with a five-man band in Humboldt Park when he was twelve. He dropped out of high school to join Ben Pollack's West Coast band when he was sixteen. Pollack also was from Chicago.

Mahalia Jackson: She was the queen of gospel music, singing with power and majesty for presidents, royalty and cleaning women. Jackson, who died in 1972 at age sixty, was the first performer to take traditional gospel singing to audiences beyond the black church. But while she sang all over the world, she never sang in a nightclub or any place that sold liquor. And she would not sing blues or jazz. Jackson is perhaps best remembered for her rendition of "Take My Hand, Precious Lord" at the 1963 March on Washington. Born in Louisiana, she came to Chicago as a teenager and found work as a beautician, then a factory hand, then a domestic. On Sundays, she sang in the Greater Salem Baptist Church on the South Side. In time, Jackson's fame grew and thousands of admirers packed baseball stadiums to hear her sing.

Pop Staples: Patriarch of the legendary Staple Singers, he wrote such hits as "Respect Yourself" and "I'll Take You There." Staples was born into a Mississippi farm family in 1925. The family would gather in the front yard after a day of picking cotton and sing from suppertime to bedtime. At age eighteen, Staples headed for Chicago. He sang in churches with his daughters—Cleotha, Mavis and Purvis. By the end of the 1940s, the Staples were the hit of the Midwest church circuit, performing in religious caravans.

Steve Goodman: He died young, but left behind several classic folk songs. For many years, Goodman (1948-1984) was at the very top of Chicago's modest folk music scene, the equal or better of such respected artists as Win Stracke, Bonnie Koloc, Bob Gibson, Hamilton Camp, John Prine, Jim Post, Bill Quateman, Michael Smith and Ed and Fred Holstein. Goodman wrote "The City of New Orleans," which Arlo Guthrie recorded for a hit; "Lincoln Park Pirates," about a particularly ruthless local towing company; "Go, Cubs, Go," which has become the ballclub's unofficial anthem; and—while succumbing to leukemia—the darkly humorous "A Dying Cub Fan's Last Request."

Steve Goodman wrote the unofficial anthem for the Chicago Cubs, "Go, Cubs, Go."

WORLD'S BEST
The Chicago Symphony Orchestra

Founded: 1891 by Theodore Thomas. When Thomas, a highly regarded New York musician, agreed to accept the Chicago position, he supposedly said, "I would go to Hell if they gave me a permanent orchestra."

First Concert: Oct. 16, 1891, in the Auditorium Theatre.

Former Musical Directors: Theodore Thomas (1891-1905), Frederick Stock (1905-42), Desire Defauw (1943-47), Artur Rodzinski (1947-48), Rafael Kubelik (1950-53), Fritz Reiner (1953-62), Jean Martinon (1963-68), Georg Solti (1969-91).

Current Musical Director: Daniel Barenboim. Born in Buenos Aires, Argentina, in 1942. First public piano performance in Buenos Aires at age seven. Studied in Salzburg, Paris and Israel. Made his piano debut in Vienna and Rome in 1952. Made his conducting debut in London in 1967 with the New Philharmonia Orchestra. Conducted the Chicago

Symphony Orchestra for the first time in 1970. From 1975 to 1989, he was music director of the Orchestre de Paris.

Greatest Musical Director: Georg Solti. He brought the orchestra to new heights of excellence—hiring more than two-thirds of its current musicians—and did a remarkable job of promotion through travel and recording. In 1971, Solti led the Chicago Symphony on a six-week tour of Western Europe that established its international reputation. In 1987, Chicago dedicated a bronze of his likeness in Lincoln Park.

The greatest musical director, Georg Solti, during rehearsal with the Chicago Symphony Orchestra.

The Musicians: 114 (37 violins, 12 violas, 10 cellos, 9 basses, 2 harps, 4 flutes, 1 piccolo, 4 oboes, 1 English horn, 4 clarinets, 1 E-flat clarinet, 1 bass clarinet, 4 bassoons, 1 contrabassoon, 1 saxophone, 6 horns, 4 trumpets, 4 trombones, 1 bass trombone, 1 tuba, 1 timpany, 4 percussion, 1 piano). Violinists Samuel Magad and Ruben Gonzalez are the co-concertmasters. Michael Morgan is assistant conductor.

Recordings: More than 90 for the London/Decca label.

Grammy Awards: 48, including 23 during Georg Solti's tenure.

Travels: 11 foreign tours (7 to Europe, 1 to the Soviet Union, 3 to the Far East and 1 to Australia), and dozens across the United States. Solti loved to travel. He adored the CSO, but never masked his indifference to Chicago.

Salaries: Base annual pay for a first-year CSO musician for the 1990-91 season was $59,280.

TEN FAMOUS CHICAGOANS
(Who made their musical mark elsewhere)

1. Ray Manzarek of the Doors
2. Roger McGuinn of the Birds
3. Jazz saxophonist Johnny Griffin
4. Singer/performance artist Laurie Anderson
5. Jazz singer Mel Torme
6. Drummer Buddy Miles
7. Jazz pianist Ramsey Lewis
8. Jazz singer Joe Williams
9. Singer Mandy Patinkin
10. Rock singer Warren Zevon

BIG CHICAGO BANDS

Aliotta, Haynes and Jeremiah ("Lake Shore Drive")

The American Breed ("Bend Me, Shake Me")

The Buckinghams ("Kind of a Drag")

Chicago ("If You Leave Me Now," "Hard to Say I'm Sorry")

Cryan' Shames ("Sugar and Spice," "Could Be We're in Love" and "Up on the Roof")

The Flock ("I Confess")

H.P. Lovecraft ("The White Ship")

Ides of March ("Vehicle")

Little Boy Blues ("I'm Losing You")

The Mauds ("Hold On")

The Mob ("Give It To Me")

New Colony Six ("Take Me Back")

REO Speedwagon ("Keep on Lovin' You," "Can't Fight This Feelin'")

Rotary Connection (with **Minnie Riperton**) ("Amen")

Rufus (with **Chaka Khan**) ('Tell Me Something Good")

Shadows of Knight ("Gloria")

Styx ("Babe")

Survivor ("Eye of the Tiger")

CTA Sues. The rock group Chicago once called itself the Chicago Transit Authority, but changed its name after the real CTA filed suit. Nevertheless, Chicago's 1969 debut album was titled Chicago Transit Authority, and it stayed on the charts for 148 weeks. Chicago, the first rock group to play Carnegie Hall, originally called itself the Missing Links, and then the Big Thing.

LIST OF TEN
BIGGEST ROCK CONCERTS

1. **Ted Nugent and Lynyrd Skynyrd**, Soldier Field, July 10, 1977 (85,000)

2. **Pink Floyd**, Soldier Field, June 19, 1977 (75,000)

3. **Rolling Stones**, Soldier Field, July 8, 1978 (75,000)

4. **Bruce Springsteen**, Soldier Field, Aug. 9, 1985 (70,000)

5. **Yes, Peter Frampton, Lynyrd Skynyrd**, Hawthorne Race Course, Aug. 16, 1976 (67,000)

6. **Emerson, Lake and Palmer**, Soldier Field, June 4, 1977 (65,000)

7. **Jeff Beck, Aerosmith, Jan Hammer Group**, Comiskey Park, July 10, 1976 (61,000)

8. **Journey and Santana**, Comiskey Park, Aug. 5, 1979 (60,000)

9. **The Beatles**, Comiskey Park, Aug. 20, 1965 (55,000)

10. **Paul McCartney**, Soldier Field, July 29, 1990 (53,000)

Note: All attendance figures were provided by local concert promoters and may, in some cases, be inflated. Michael Jackson failed to make the top 10, but the combined attendance for his three "Victory Tour" concerts at Comiskey Park, Oct. 13-15, 1984, topped 120,000.

CHICAGO'S SEMI-OFFICIAL SONG

"Chicago" ("That Toddling Town"), 1922, words and music by Fred Fisher. A chorus sang the song while Fred Astaire and Ginger Rogers danced in *The Story of Vernon and Irene Castle,* a 1939 film. The voice of Jane Froman, dubbed for Susan Hayward, sang it again in *With a Song in My Heart,* a 1952 film. "Chicago" is most closely identified with Frank Sinatra, but eighteen other performers include the song on recordings still commercially available—Count Basie, Tony Bennett, Eddie Condon, Jimmy Dorsey, Tommy Dorsey, Judy Garland, Benny Goodman, Stephane Grappelli, Jimmie Grier, Coleman Hawkins, Earl Hines, Al Hirt, Stan Mark, Billy May and his Orchestra, Memphis Slim, The Original Piano Trio, Django Reinhardt and Muggsy Spanier.

Chicago's second semi-official song is "My Kind of Town," 1964, words by Sammy Cahn, music by James Van Heusen. It was introduced by Frank Sinatra in *Robin and the 7 Hoods,* a 1964 film, and nominated for an Academy Award. Among those who have recorded the song are Sinatra, Jack Jones, Count Basie, Guy Lombardo and Mike Douglas.

Members of the rock group Chicago present Mayor Richard J. Daley with a T-shirt in 1976.

WLS SILVER DOLLAR SURVEY
Number-One Pop Song in Chicago Area
at Memorable Moments in History

■ **1958:** Nathan Leopold, child murderer, paroled on February 20. "Oh Julie" by the Crescendos.

■ **1959:** White Sox clinch American League pennant at Cleveland on September 22. "Mack the Knife" by Bobby Darrin.

■ **1960:** John F. Kennedy elected president by the closest popular vote in U.S. history on November 8. "Ruby Duby Du" by Tobin Mathews.

■ **1961:** Bay of Pigs invasion of Cuba in April. "Blue Moon" by the Marcels.

■ **1962:** Cuban Missile Crisis, October 16-28. "Monster Mash" by Bobby (Boris) Pickett and the Crypt Kickers.

■ **1963:** President Kennedy assassinated in Dallas on November 22. "Dominique" by the Singing Nun.

■ **1964:** The Beatles perform in Chicago, September 5. "This Time" by Troy Shondell.

■ **1965:** Lyndon Johnson inaugurated to full term as president, January 20. "Wonderland by Night" by Bert Kaempfert.

■ **1966:** Richard Speck murders eight student nurses in Chicago, July 14. "Wild Thing" by the Troggs.

■ **1967:** Great Chicago Snowstorm, January 26-27. "I'm a Believer/Steppin' Stone" by the Monkees.

■ **1968:** Robert F. Kennedy slain in Los Angeles, June 5. "This Guy's in Love with You" by Herb Alpert.

■ **1969:** First astronauts land on the moon, July 20. "In the Year 2525" by Zager and Evans.

■ **1970:** Kent State Shootings, May 4. "Vehicle" by the Ides of March.

■ **1971:** Excerpts from top-secret Pentagons Papers, detailing history of U.S. involvement in Indochina, published in *New York Times* on June 13. "Want Ads" by Honey Cone.

■ **1972:** Bobby Fischer becomes first American to win world chess title, September 1. "Brandy" by Looking Glass.

■ **1973:** An end to the military draft is announced, January 27. "Superstition" by Stevie Wonder.

■ **1974:** President Richard M. Nixon resigns, August 9. "The Night Chicago Died" by Paper Lace.

■ **1975:** Last Americans evacuate Vietnam in the fall of Saigon, April 29. "Philadelphia Freedom" by Elton John.

■ **1976:** Mayor Richard J. Daley dies, December 20. "Nadia's Theme" by DeVorzon & Botkin.

■ **1977:** Elvis Presley dies, August 16. "I Just Want to Be Your Everything" by Andy Gibb.

■ **1978:** *Chicago Daily News,* the last afternoon paper in Chicago, folds, March 4. "Stayin' Alive" by the Bee Gees.

■ **1979:** Second paralyzing snowstorm within two weeks hits Chicago, January 13. "Le Freak" by Chic.

■ **1980:** John Lennon slain in New York, December 8. "Lady" by Kenny Rogers.

■ **1981:** Americans held hostage in Iran return to U.S. on January 27. "(Just Like) Starting Over" by John Lennon.

■ **1982:** John Belushi dies from drug overdose, March 5. "Centerfold" by J. Geils Band.

■ **1983:** Harold Washington elected mayor, February 22. "Baby, Come to Me" by Patty Austin, with James Ingram.

■ **1984:** Chicago Cubs clinch National League East Division title, September 24. "What's Love Got to Do with It" by Tina Turner.

■ **1985:** Convicted rapist Gary Dotson paroled, May 12. "We Are the World" by USA for Africa.

■ **1986:** Chicago Bears win the Super Bowl, January 26. "Super Bowl Shuffle" by the Chicago Bears Shufflin' Crew.

■ **1987:** Dow Jones Average dives a record 508 points, October 19. "U Got the Look" by Prince.

■ **1988:** Dan Quayle, running for vice president, admits through a spokesman on August 18, that "calls may have been made" to get him into the National Guard, a move that shielded him from service in Vietnam. "Hands to Heaven" by Breathe.

■ **1989:** Berlin Wall falls on December 22. "Pump Up the Jam" by Technotronic.

(Note: These are the No. 1 songs as ranked by the WLS Silver Dollar Survey, which was begun in October 1960 and ended in 1987. Songs before 1960 are from WJJD's Forty Top Tunes survey. Songs for 1987 to 1989 are from a Z-95 WYTZ-FM survey).

Rock Jocks. Who were the original "Silver Dollar Survey" rock jocks on WLS-AM radio? Mort Crowley, Sam Holman, Gene Taylor, Dick Biondi, Ed Grennan, Jim Dunbar and Bob Hale.

LYRIC OPERA OF CHICAGO

Founded in 1954, the Lyric premiered with two sold-out performances of "Don Giovanni." Nicola Rossi-Lemeni starred in the title role. Eleanor Steber played the part of Donna Anna. The Lyric was organized and managed by opera manager Carol Fox, real estate businessman Lawrence Kelly and a young conductor on the rise, Nicola Rescigno. Star of the Lyric's first season was the diva Maria Callas, making her American debut. Fox resigned in 1981 for reasons of health, and Ardis Krainik succeeded her as general manager. The Lyric, as of the end of the 1990-91 season, has given 1,753 performances of 127 operas.

LIST OF TEN
OPERAS PERFORMED MOST BY THE LYRIC
(including 1990-91 season)

1. *Madama Butterfly* (68 performances, debut in 1955)

2. *La Boheme* (66, 1954)

3. *Tosca* (65, 1954)

4. *La Traviata* (52, 1954)

5. *Il Barbiere di Siviglia* (50, 1954)

6. *Carmen* (41, 1954)
   Rigoletto (41, 1955)
   Un Ballo in Maschera (41, 1955)

7. *Lucia di Lammermoor* (38, 1954)

8. *Don Giovanni* (35, 1954)

9. *Aida* (31, 1955)
   Le nozze di Figaro (31, 1957)

10. *L'Elisir d'Amore* (30, 1955)

Shilling Sherrill. Sherrill Milnes, an opera baritone from Downers Grove, sang the famous "When you're out of Schlitz, you're out of beer" advertising ditty.

RAVINIA

Best known as the summer home of the Chicago Symphony Orchestra, Thirty-six-acre Ravinia Park in Highland Park started out as a sort of super amusement park. When it opened on Aug. 15, 1904, it featured a dazzling electric fountain, a baseball field with grandstand, a merry-go-round, a theater with pipe organ and a dance hall. In its next ten years, it became recognized nationwide for its fine-arts performances. From 1913 to 1931, Ravinia offered opera every night of the week. Ravinia was closed for four years during the Depression, but was reopened in 1936 by the not-for-profit Ravinia Festival Association, a group of Highland Park businessmen. The big event that year was a concert by George Gershwin, attended by 7,831 people. Ravinia's current music director is James Levine.

PAST TENSE

The Day the Beatles Descended
By Leighton McLaughlin
(Chicago Sun-Times Sept. 6, 1964)

The Beatles made $1,000 a minute Saturday night in the International Amphitheatre during ritual bedlam.

More than bedlam. It was the loudest thing since Casey Jones hit that freight train.

Young lungs filled the huge hall with a sound that was wordless, wild, and to all appearances witless.

The four young Britons—John Lennon, Ringo Starr, Paul McCartney and George Harrison—were the last act in a two-hour rock 'n' roll show.

For their fans, they were the only act. The living gods of Beatlemania bounced onto the stage, and their faithful leaped into the air and began speaking in tongues.

The Beatles wore the vestments of their calling: pipe-stem pants, pointed shoes and one of the more curious haircuts in town.

They could not be heard over the roar. Standing 25 feet away from the stage, it was impossible to detect any more than an undercurrent of loud-tuned electric guitars.

A young fan took issue with this after the show. "It wasn't too bad," the girl said. "You could hear a little bit—sometimes."

If the energy expended by the fans were directed properly, the United States could have a man on the moon tomorrow.

In a sense, however, the energy has been captured. The Beatles made roughly $250 a man a minute.

That is $15,000 an hour, or $600,000 for a 40-hour week. With 52 weeks in a year and with paid vacation, that's $31,200,000 a year apiece. But, of course, they don't work full time.

Sources: Jeff Johnson and Laura Emerick *Chicago Sun-Times;* Don McLeese, former pop music critic *Chicago Sun-Times; History of Chicago,* by A.T. Andreas; *Chicago Soul,* by Robert Pruter, University of Illinois Press (1991); Susan Wade Dewey, Chicago Symphony Orchestra; Ravinia public relations staff; Danny Newman, Lyric Opera; Scott at Jam Productions; Dan Pankratz, Chicago Public Library's Music Information Center; Drew Hayes and Roe Conn, WLS-AM radio; Charles Guse, Chicago Federation of Musicians, Local 10-208.

ART

FIRST

■ The first Chicago artist was Samuel M. Brooks, who arrived around 1833. It didn't take him long to decide this wasn't for him and he left for California—maybe the light was better there.

Anti Nazi Art: The sculpture anchoring Heald Square on Wacker Drive was made in such a way as to protect it from Nazi vandals. The sculpture represents the last commission of Lorado Taft, who died before its completion. It depicts George Washington flanked by Robert Morris and Haym Salomon. Salomon, who was Jewish, died broke and largely forgotten after donating his entire fortune of $350,000 to help pay the bills of the Revolution. A Chicago lawyer, Barnet Hodes, pushed to make Salomon part of a city sculpture. While it was being created in the 1930s, however, there was a rash of anti-Semitism and Nazi bund activity in Chicago. Hodes thought the sculpture was in danger of being vandalized. "I went to Lorado Taft and induced him to interlock Washington's and Salomon's arms. In that way, any disfigurement of Salomon would also have injured Washington, and would have been a national disgrace," Hodes later recounted. The statue was erected in 1941.

EXTREMES

■ The record price for a painting sold at a Chicago auction was $1.3 million for Dutch artist Vincent Van Gogh's "Still Life with Flowers" in March 1991. For years it had hung in the living room of a suburban Milwaukee couple who didn't know it was an original. A commercial real estate agent and part-time art scout saw the painting at their home and began the investigation. The painting of a vase of flowers was authenticated as a work from the 1886-1887 period when Van Gogh was in Paris.

Vincent Van Gogh's "Still Life with Flowers" was sold for $1.3 million in March 1991.

■ The oldest Chicago Park District sculpture is "The Alarm," done in 1884 by John Boyle. It depicts a standing Indian man with a woman kneeling nearby with a child in her arms. The piece is now in Lincoln Park just north of the Gun Club.

> **Lincoln's Mask:** Life-masks of Lincoln's face done in 1860 by Chicago sculptor Leonard Volk provided the basis for a great deal of the later artwork done on Lincoln.

GALLERIES

River North is one of the most concentrated areas of art galleries in the city. Bounded by Chicago Avenue on the north, Erie Street on the south, Wells Street on the east and Orleans Street on the west, this disstrict has grown from sixteen to eighty galleries in the last decade.

Another cluster of major galleries is in the vicinity of the Museum of Contemporary Art, 237 E. Ontario.

A gallery district for cutting-edge exhibits is at Milwaukee Avenue, Ogden and Chicago. Located here are a handful of not-for-profit galleries that focus on exhibiting more than selling.

> **Air Mail Art:** A twenty-foot tall copper statue of Diana, which for half a century (until 1947) topped the Tower Building, 6 North Michigan, was used by Capt. Benjamin B. Lipsner in 1918 as a guide to land a plane in Grant Park. His flight helped begin air mail service between Chicago and New York.

Beardless: An Elmhurst portrait artist, George Healy, painted the only portrait of Abraham Lincoln without his beard.

THE SCHOOL OF THE ART INSTITUTE OF CHICAGO

Founded by thirty-five local artists in 1866, the School of the Art Institute of Chicago offers a range of degrees from Bachelor of Fine Arts to Master of Arts in art therapy. The school offers 350 courses each semester and has 314 full- and part-time faculty. Many of the faculty are practicing artists; there are school-run galleries; a studio-oriented environment; and the school's resources include the Art Institute of Chicago.

Enrollment: 1,675 degree students—1,381 undergraduate students; 294 graduate students; 60 certificate students.

Annual Tuition: $10,600

Alumni: Grant Wood (painter of "American Gothic"), Thomas Hart Benton, Georgia O'Keeffe, Ivan Albright, Claes Oldenburg (sculptor of the "Batcolumn"), Leon Golub, Nancy Spero, Robert Indiana, Ed Paschke, Elizabeth Murray, Jim Nutt, Karl Wirsum, Red Grooms, Richard Estes, Roger Brown, Walt Disney, Chuck Jones (illustrator and filmmaker who helped create Bugs Bunny and the Road Runner), Gahan Wilson (cartoonist), Vincente Minnelli (filmmaker), Victor Skrebneski (photographer), Lorado Taft (sculptor), Theordore Roszak (sculptor), Halston (fashion designer), Leroy Neiman, Margaret Burroughs (helped found DuSable Museum), Joe Sedelmaier (creator of such commercials as "Where's the beef?"), Herblock (Pulitzer Prize-winning cartoonist).

Controversy: In spring 1988, several aldermen accompanied by police marched down to the Art Institute and seized a student painting depicting the late Mayor Harold Washington in a brassiere and garter belt. About a year later the City Council denounced another student art exhibit that put the U.S. flag on the ground, so people could walk on it if they wanted.

THE HAIRY WHO

The 1960s saw six Art Institute graduates become a Chicago art movement. The six—Gladys Nilsson, James Falconer, Art Green, James

Nutt, Suellen Rocca and Karl Wirsum—became the Hairy Who. As described by *Daily News* art critic Franz Schulze in 1967, the Hairy Whoists "commit rather than withhold themselves. They do not preen. They couldn't care less whether their message is elegant or profound...They are charmed by anything which is ratty, cheap, ungainly or ludicrous in modern urban culture, but they do not strike any moralistic poses about it." When asked in 1967 why the Hairy Who, Karl Wirsum said "because we like the name Hairy Who." In an interview for *Chicago* magazine in 1988, Wirsum said the name came up when the group got together and some people were discussing somebody named Harry (who actually was a radio art critic) and what he had said. Wirsum asked "Harry Who?" and the name was born with a spin on the spelling. Their art has been described as tough stuff that assaulted the senses of the viewer. They had three Chicago shows in the late 1960s as the Hairy Who, and then moved on.

Meltdown: During World War II some thought was given to melting down all the monuments and memorials in Chicago's parks with an eye toward salvaging the copper. A study showed there was 135 tons of copper in the parks. To replace the sculpture and tablets after the war would have cost the city an estimated $500,000. The idea was stupid, and nothing was melted.

OUTDOOR ART

The Chicago Park District has about 100 sculptures. The city has an additional 50 to 55 sites, and corporations maintain countless works. Three government agencies help bring outdoor sculpture to public areas: the City of Chicago Public Art Program; the U.S. General Services Administration and the state Capital Development Board's Art in Architecture Program.

Statue Under Seige: In the early 1970s the Haymarket monument, a statue of an old-time policeman, was assigned twenty-four-hour police protection. The statue was then located on Randolph Street east of the Kennedy. It was later moved to police headquarters at Eleventh and State and now it's at the Chicago Police Academy, 1300 W. Jackson. The statue has seen rough times. In 1927 it was mowed down by a runaway street car and in October 1969 and October 1970 it was blown off its pedestal—the radical Weathermen took credit for the 1970 blast. Now, for its own safety, it has permanent police protection.

POPULAR OUTDOOR SCULPTURES

■ **Art Institute Lions,** bronzes made by sculptor Edward Kemys, who was considered the leading American sculptor of animals and was a favorite of Teddy Roosevelt. Mrs. Henry Field donated them. They've been there since May 10, 1894. Although most people may think the lions are the same, they stand in different poses.

■ **Ceres,** the Roman goddess, stands atop the Board of Trade building at 141 W. Jackson Boulevard at the foot of La Salle Street. It was put there in 1930. It's 30 feet high and stands 309 feet above the street. It's made of cast aluminum. Ceres was designed by John Storrs (1885-1956), an early modernist who was commissioned by the building's architects, Holabird and Root. Storrs was born in Chicago.

■ **Fountain of Time** by Chicago sculptor Lorado Taft is 110 feet long. It shows a wave of 100 figures passing by the figure of Time standing across a pool of water. It took fourteen years to build, it's made of steel reinforced concrete and was dedicated in 1922. It was built at Taft's studios, a couple of blocks away. It's at the end of the Midway Plaisance at Washington Park.

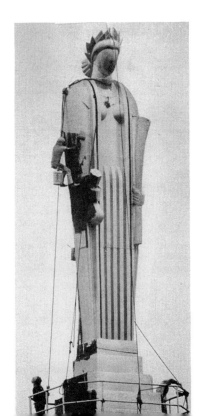

The statue of Ceres atop the Board of Trade Building receives much deserved renovation in 1971.

■ **Buckingham Fountain** is controlled by a computer 708 miles away in Atlanta. The computer regulates 1.5 million gallons of recirculating water shot as high as 140 feet and pushed through 133 jets at a rate of about 14,000 gallons a minute. The computer also controls 650 red, green, white and amber lights. Since its dedication in 1927, Buckingham Fountain has helped give Grant Park the look of a European park, which Chicago architect and planner Daniel Burnham envisioned. It's made of Georgia pink marble and patterned after a fountain at Louis XIV's palace at Versailles. The fountain was donated by Kate Sturges Buckingham in memory of her brother Clarence. It contains three circular pools layered on top of one another. The first level is the largest, with a diameter of 280 feet.

■ **The Bowman & the Spearman** were placed north and south of the Congress Expressway in Grant Park in 1928. Each of these bronze Indian warriors, poised for attack, weighs about 27,000 pounds and is 17 feet high. One is about to throw his spear, the other is about to shoot an arrow. They were created by Yugoslavian sculptor Ivan Mestrovic, who died in South Bend, Indiana, in 1962 as a member of the University of Notre Dame faculty. While visiting Chicago in 1926 for conferences about his sculptures, he called Chicago a city of dreams, "Not, mind you, of dreams fulfilled but dreams of fulfillment. A city of destiny—that is Chicago. Topographically the city has all those natural requisites that form the basis of conquest."

No Mountain Here: The statue of Gen. Philip Sheridan on his horse, near Belmont Avenue west of Lake Shore Drive in Lincoln Park, was done in 1923 by Gutzon Borglum, the same artist who did the great stone faces of Mount Rushmore.

TWENTIETH CENTURY ART

THE LOOP

Since Picasso's untitled work was erected at Daley Center Plaza in 1967, the Loop has become a magnet for contemporary art and internationally recognized artists. The Percent-for-Art Ordinance was enacted in 1978. It requires that a percentage of the cost of a new municipal building or the remodeling of an old one be used for artwork.

The Untitled Picasso

Unveiled: August 1967. **Weight:** 162 tons. **Height:** 50 feet. **Material:** Cor-Ten steel. **Location:** Daley Center Plaza. Some 50,000 people at-

The untitled Picasso was unveiled on August 17, 1967, in the Daley Center Plaza.

tended the dedication when Mayor Richard J. Daley pulled a white ribbon to let the covering fall. The Picasso is said to have laid the groundwork for what the city claims has made Chicago the international capital for outdoor twentieth century art.

Who talked Picasso into doing a sculpture for Chicago? A soft-spoken and modest Chicago architect, William E. Hartman, convinced Pablo Picasso to design a monumental sculpture for Chicago, even though Picasso had never been to the city. To help Picasso understand Chicago, Hartman, a senior partner in Skidmore, Owings & Merrill, gave him a photo album of famous Chicagoans (including Picasso's friend Ernest Hemingway), a fire chief's helmet, and Bears and White Sox uniforms. In turn, Picasso gave the design to Chicago for free. Some have said that's what it was worth.

What is it? At its unveiling, Chicagoans asked the question "What is it?" Some said it was an Afghan hound (Picasso owned one named Kabul) or a woman or a rusty bird, or a lion or nothing. One five-year-old said it looked like his brother. Picasso himself said, "People who try to explain pictures are usually barking up the wrong tree."

In September 1966, Mayor Daley was asked about it and said, "We had a discussion around our dinner table, and everyone had a different idea as to what it was. It was very amusing. They all laughed, and some said it has restored the art of conversation and it makes everyone a little humorous when they start to talk about it."

CALDER'S "FLAMINGO"

Dimensions: 53 feet high. **Location:** Federal Center. **Material:** Steel. Atop a bandwagon drawn by forty horses, Alexander Calder rode into the Loop with a circus parade to dedicate his "Flamingo" in October 1974. Calder and Mayor Daley used a five-foot pair of cardboard scissors to snip a rope and dedicate the sculpture with the release of hundreds of balloons.

CHAGALL'S "THE FOUR SEASONS"

Dimensions: 70 by 14 by 10 feet. **Location:** First National Plaza. **Material:** Mosaic. Its surface covers 3,000 square feet and weighs about 4,000 tons. Artist Marc Chagall said, "I chose the subject of the four seasons because I felt this represents the four seasons of all of life and of life itself." The mosaic is a colorful work of lovers, workers, mothers, trees, boats, animals and angels. The $1^1/2$-inch squares are held by cement suggested by Chicago architects because of its ability to handle the city winds. Chagall donated the design to the people of Chicago.

It was dedicated with the drop of a white curtain in September 1974. Chagall was there to signal the unveiling. He gave a kiss to a somewhat stunned Mayor Richard J. Daley. A day after the unveiling one Loop policeman said, "I like it better than the Picasso, but I don't like that much either."

Art by the Millions: More than 300 million copies of the "Love" graphic drawn by Robert Indiana, a graduate of The School of the Art Institute of Chicago, exist. The graphic was used for a postage stamp.

CLAES OLDENBURG "BATCOLUMN"

Dimensions: 100 feet tall. **Location:** Outside the Social Security Administration Center, 600 W. Madison. Claes Oldenburg's Batcolumn is a latticework sculpture of a baseball bat. It weighs 20 tons and is said to be able to withstand winds of 150 miles an hour. It cost $100,000 and was dedicated by Joan Mondale, the wife of Vice President Walter Mondale.

At the unveiling, a group of protesters, claiming to be surrealist artists, called the Batcolumn "a five-story nightstick...one more proof that capitalist culture is hopelessly played out." Oldenburg, who himself was clubbed by Chicago police during the 1968 Democratic Convention, said he found the protesters "rather playful."

MIRO'S CHICAGO

Dimensions: 39 feet tall. **Location:** Brunswick Plaza, 69 W. Washington. **Material:** Steel, wire-mesh, concrete, bronze and ceramic tile. At the 1981 dedication, Mayor Jane Byrne tried pulling the cord on the yellow drape to unveil the statue, and it got stuck on the nose, then on the arms of Spanish sculptor Joan Miro's woman. It took five workmen to yank it off. The upper third of the sculpture is bronze, the lower part is finished with a coating of tanned cement and other material. A couple weeks after the unveiling, a North Side machinist threw a quart of red paint at the sculpture. He said he didn't like it.

DUBUFFET'S MONUMENT WITH STANDING BEAST

Dimensions: 29-feet-tall. **Location:** In front of the State of Illinois Building, 100 West Randolph St. **Material:** Fiberglass. This 10-ton sculpture by French artist Jean Dubuffet was dedicated in 1989. At the ceremony, it took a healthy pull by Gov. James Thompson to drop 150 yards of blue nylon draping, to the applause of about 1,000 people. Thompson's daughter, Samantha, said if you stood in the middle of the sculpture you could see a "Snoopy" looking toward City Hall.

Who's on First: There's a statue of Lincoln in Grant Park and there's a statue of Grant in Lincoln Park.

CHICAGO AND NUDITY

■ One of the first exhibitions of art depicting nudity and prompting debate over the propriety of such a display was in 1850, when a picture titled "Greek Slave" was displayed at Tremont Hall.

■ "Universal Man," a charcoal print showing full frontal maleness, was the runner-up in the Museum of Science and Industry's Pan American art exhibit in 1975. Nonetheless, museum officials masked the genitals with tape. A couple days later, a young woman ripped the tape off. It remained that way.

Abe Times Two: Two sculptures of Abe Lincoln, both done by Irish-born sculptor Augustus Saint Gaudens (1848-1907), are considered world class: One is of a standing Lincoln in Lincoln Park and the other portrays a sitting Lincoln in Grant Park.

CLASSIC QUOTES

"Genius is but audacity, and the audacity of Chicago has chosen a star. It has looked upward to it, and knows nothing that it fears to attempt, and thus far has found nothing that it cannot accomplish."

—*Carter H. Harrison at the 1893 World's Columbian Exposition a few hours before he was assasinated.*

When artists James Nutt and his wife Gladys Nilsson, left Chicago in 1968, Nutt said, "I'd rather not make a big deal out of this...Chicago has an unfortunate attitude when someone leaves this city. You know, nobody called us when we moved to Evanston last year."

Source: *Chicago Sun-Times* and *Daily News*; Chicago Department of Cultural Affairs and its *Loop Sculpture Guide; Chicago's Public Sculpture* by Ira J. Bach and Mary Lackritz Gray; School of the Art Institute of Chicago; *History of Chicago* by A.T. Andreas; *Chicago* magazine.

ARCHITECTURE

FIRSTS

■ Chicago's first major architectural contribution was the "balloon frame," invented in 1833. Using it, a house was framed with two-by-four lumber, which was attached with machine-made nails, much like you see today. This made building cheaper and quicker. Before this, houses were built using shaped timber, posts, beams and braces, which was a slow, cumbersome process.

■ Chicago's first commercial building was probably the Eagle Exchange Tavern, built in 1829 by Mark Beaubien, an innkeeper, ferryman and entrepreneur. The frame building, on a corner of what is now Lake and Wacker, later was expanded and called the Sauganash Hotel.

■ Chicago's first brick building was built in 1837 at what is now 30 N. La Salle.

■ Chicago's first architect was John M. Van Osdel (1811-1891), who came here in 1837 to do a design job for the city's first mayor. His first commission was to draw the plans for the house of William B. Ogden. It was a square, two-story building with an observatory on top.

■ Real estate developer Arthur Rubloff coined the term "Magnificent Mile" in 1947 to refer to North Michigan Avenue.

EXTREMES

■ The oldest building in Chicago is a Greek revival-style house built in 1837 by Henry B. Clarke, a Chicago businessman, farmer and one-time city clerk (1846-48). Some believed it was modeled after the house of William B. Ogden, Chicago's first mayor. The two-story house, topped by an observatory, has survived two fires and two moves (1872 and 1977)—including a move over the L tracks. It is now at 1855 S. Indiana.

■ The world's tallest building is the 110-story Sears Tower, which rises 1,454 feet. On a windy day it can sway about six to ten inches, and in some offices at the top you can see the plants move.

■ The downtown building with the smallest windows is probably the one at 71 W. Van Buren, where some windows are only five inches wide. It is the William J. Campbell U.S. Courthouse Annex, also known as the Metropolitan Correctional Center. This modern jail, designed by Harry Weese & Associates, was built in 1975. There's an exercise yard on the roof—twenty-seven stories above the ground.

The Numbers: There are close to a half million buildings in Chicago.

■ Chicago architect Charles Atwood designed two buildings identified with the old and new of Chicago: the neo-classical Museum of Science and Industry, and the Reliance Building, 32 N. State, which some consider the first glass tower.

The Chicago Skyline is everchanging. Shown here are the AT&T Building (right) and 311 S. Wacker Building (left) under construction in 1989.

View from the East: Two wealthy, Harvard-educated brothers from Boston developed some of the most significant and highest-profile buildings in downtown Chicago. Yet, there's no evidence either of them ever saw the buildings or even visited the city. Peter Chardon Brooks and Sheperd Brooks were Boston developers who commissioned such Chicago buildings as the Montauk (1881), considered by many to be the city's first skyscraper; the Rookery; the north section of the Monadnock; and the Marquette Building, among others. The brothers preferred hanging out in Boston or at their New England family estate.

THE CHICAGO PLAN

Daniel Burnham (1846-1912), who some credit with saying "Make no little plans, they have no magic to stir men's blood...." was the chief of construction for the World's Columbian Exposition in 1893. Despite criticism from such big names as Louis Sullivan, the fair, with its White City and Beaux Arts style (neoclassical), had a huge impact on building across the country—neoclassical was in. Its influence, and Burnham's, would last well into the twentieth century. But after the fair, Burnham's focus on city planning intensified. In 1906, he was commissioned to create a plan for Chicago, and three years later his thick plan with inspirational illustrations was handed over to the Commercial Club of Chicago. The city has been talking about it ever since.

Daniel Burnham's idealistic "Chicago Plan" helped shape the city.

THE PLAN

1. **A green lush lakefront** with twenty-three miles of connected harbors, parks, and lagoons. This was to provide the breathing space for a city. While not fully realized, Chicago now has twenty-nine

miles of lakefront—twenty-four of those are public parks and beaches—although not all connected.

2. **A system of highways** to unite the city with the suburbs and beyond. While Burnham thought some of this plan could be accomplished with streets already in place, the spokes of the expressway system (Dan Ryan, Stevenson, Eisenhower, Kennedy and Edens) do seem to mesh with his vision.

3. **Improvement of rail terminals** into three areas and an organized system of loops for moving freight through the city. Basically, this didn't happen.

4. **A huge park system connected by tree-lined boulevards**—In the 1860s and 1870s, well before Burnham's plan, a ring of boulevards or an "emerald necklace" began to circle the city. They're still there, twenty-eight miles of them running from Garfield on the south to Diversey on the north. They link the city's major parks, including Jackson, Washington, McKinley, Douglas, Garfield, Humboldt and Lincoln. Farther out, the Cook County forest preserve system has 67,000 acres of greenery surrounding the city.

5. **A systematic arrangement of streets and avenues** to move traffic more efficiently. Through Burnham's influence, Ashland and Western were made through streets, and a two-level bridge was eventually put across the river at Michigan Avenue, in line with his plan. The two levels separated commercial and private traffic and virtually opened commerce on the North Side. Lower Wacker Drive on the south side of the river also was part of Burnham's plan, but he envisioned a lower level for the north side of the river, too.

6. **A cultural center** in the front yard of the city. This would be the harbor area at the lakefront that would act as a gate to the city. When Burnham conceived this plan, the Chicago Public Library (1891), the Art Institute (1893), and Orchestra Hall (1904) already were roughly packed into this gate area. Buckingham Fountain would later fit into the spirit of Burnham's opening to the city, but his massive civic center complex (a pentagonal plaza filled with federal, county, and city buildings at Halsted and Congress) was never realized.

A WALK DOWN DEARBORN: THE LESSONS OF TIME

Many believe Chicago is the birthplace of modern architecture, or at least was its midwife. Here they experimented in framing a building in riveted steel. Here the beauty of a building was in its efficiency. After the Chicago Fire, the modern architects of the city became the teachers and the students of the "Chicago School." And it's been said that if you walk down Dearborn, you can see the evolution of their work.

■ **Delaware Building (1872):** 36 W. Randolph (at Dearborn). Here is how the city looked after the Great Chicago Fire of 1871. After the downtown area was leveled by the fire, buildings were erected quickly. The Delaware was one of them. It's an old bearing-wall type building, typical of what went up after the fire. It originally had five stories— which made it one of the taller buildings when it was built. Two more stories were added in 1889. It is Italianate in style and built with brick, stone and some metal support.

■ **The Manhattan Building (1889-91):** 431 S. Dearborn. This sixteen-story building was the first in Chicago to be carried entirely on a metal skeletal frame. Since it was the first, it's not perfect. Still, it was the first pure use of such a frame—no party walls were used for support. It was designed by William LeBaron Jenney, the Chicago architect credited with being the pioneer of skeletal construction. The columns are cast iron. This so-called "Chicago construction" was first introduced by Jenney in the Home Insurance Building (135 S. La Salle, now the site of the Field Building). This was also one of the first buildings to make use of wind bracing.

■ **The Monadnock (1891, north part; 1893, south part):** 53 W. Jackson (the building runs south along Dearborn). This building represents the old and the new. It is part masonry bearing wall construction and part modern skyscraper with a skeleton of steel. It was designed as four separate buildings.

The north building, made of bearing wall construction, was designed by Burnham & Root for a client who insisted on simplicity: no ornamentation. That seemed okay by John Root. In 1890, referring to the modern office building, Root said, "To lavish upon them a profusion of delicate ornament is worse than useless. Rather should they by their mass and proportion convey in some large elemental sense an idea of the great stable conserving forces of modern civilization." Because it would be a high-rise with only masonry walls for support, the base walls of the Monadnock are six feet thick and taper as they rise the full 215 foot height of its sixteen stories. It's said to be the last skyscraper of solid masonry construction. It was originally designed as two buildings, the Monadnock and Kearsarge.

The south building was designed by Holabird and Roche. This was also to be two buildings, the Katahdin and the Wachusett (these and the other two names are mountains in New England—East Coast developers had some influence here). Unlike the north building, the south was built with a steel skeleton.

■ **Old Colony Building (1893-1894):** 407 S. Dearborn. This seventeen-story building with its rounded corners (designed by Holabird and Roche) was built with a massive steel skeleton and intricate wind bracing. The bracing worked so well that on Feb. 12, 1894, when winds were recorded at seventy to eighty miles an hour, the upper story moved only three-sixteenths of an inch. The three entrances of the building display carvings of the Plymouth Colony seal, i.e. Old Colony.

■ **Marquette Building (1894):** 140 S. Dearborn. Designed by Holabird & Roche, this seventeen-story building includes an attic story. It is considered one of the first steel frame buildings to "give direct, simple and forceful expression to its skeleton frame," according to the Landmarks Preservation Council of Illinois. It wasn't perfect, with its bulky corners not taking full advantage of a steel skeleton. Nonetheless, the exterior tells the viewer what's underneath. The design grid allows for expansive rectangular windows or so-called "Chicago windows." The lobby memorialized Pere Marquette, early explorer and missionary who came through Chicago in the late 1600s. Above each elevator there's a sculptured head of an explorer or Indian chief done by Edward Kemys, the same artist who did the two lions in front of the Art Institute. The mosaics were done by Tiffany Glass and Decorating Company of New York.

■ **Fisher Building (1895):** 343 S. Dearborn. This eighteen-story building is again a steel skeleton building, but it is considered a refinement of the art form of the skyscraper, a step beyond the Marquette Building. Designed by D.H. Burnham & Co., it is sheathed in expansive glass windows and decorative terra cotta. It was fireproofed—all steel work was protected with hollow fireclay tile.

■ **Federal Center:** Dirksen Building (30 stories), Kluczynski Building (45 stories) and Post Office (1 story). Located on Jackson, Dearborn, Adams and Clark streets, this cluster of federal buildings houses everything from courtrooms to IRS offices. It was designed by Ludwig Mies van der Rohe, who led architecture into a world of glass and steel skyscrapers and is considered the founder of the second "Chicago School" of architecture. The Federal Center is considered some of his best work. Each of the tall buildings is sleek, soaring curtains of dark glass and black steel.

TOP TEN
MUST-SEE CHICAGO BUILDINGS

1. **Auditorium:** (1889), designed by Dankmar Adler and Louis Sullivan, 17 stories. When this massive building at the northwest corner of Michigan Avenue and the Congress Expressway was finished, it was Chicago's tallest building. It was also the largest and heaviest in the city. It had 63,500 square feet and weighed well over 100,000 tons. It was also unique because it was a multi-use building with a hotel, offices, stores and a state-of-the-art theater with unobstructed

sightlines, a hydraulically operated stage, an early system of air conditioning and near perfect acoustics.

The packed Auditorium Theater in 1965 for a tribute to Adlai E. Stevenson.

2. **Carson, Pirie, Scott and Company Building:** (1889, 1903, 1906), 1 S. State St., 9 stories high with an addition. It was originally the Schlesinger and Mayer Store. This was the last large commercial building done by Louis Sullivan as his star in Chicago began to fade. The building has an iron and steel frame with wide bayed Chicago windows—well suited for a retailer who needs bright, open display areas. The ornamentation, particularly the metal swirls at the store's entrance, has been probably photographed as much as anything in Chicago.

3. **The Rookery:** (1885-1888), 209 S. La Salle. After the Chicago Fire of 1871, a water tank at the southeast corner of La Salle and Adams was converted into a temporary city hall and public library. The pigeons also liked it, so much so that the locals referred to that corner as the rookery (a breeding place for the gregarious rooks, a crow like bird). Even though one of the East Coast developers, Peter Brooks, offered twenty-two possible names for the eleven-story building, Rookery was so entrenched there was no turning back. In fact, rooks can be seen carved into the huge arched brown terra cotta entry on La Salle Street. The Rookery was designed by Burnham and Root and it's built as a hollow square with an interior courtyard designed to provide natural light for inner offices. Along this theme of light, the elevators have open cages and the lobby is topped with a cast iron skylight. A winding staircase also spirals up through the interior courtyard. This is also a transitional building in Chicago Architecture because the walls of the inner courtyard have iron frames, which was then a relatevely new building technique, yet the outer walls use the standard masonry system. In 1905, Frank Lloyd Wright remod-

eled the lobby, replacing much of the elaborate ornamentation with geometrically designed ironwork. He also added white marble mezzanine stairs and such details as rectangular planters.

4. **Chicago Board of Trade Building:** (1930), 141 W. Jackson Blvd. This was a new generation of Chicago buildings and was designed by the architectural firm Holabird & Root, which was founded by the sons of two big-name Chicago architects: William Holabird and John Wellborn Root. The Board of Trade is an important Chicago institution and its location reflects it—located at the foot of La Salle Street, its forty-five stories dominate this commercial canyon. It was built in a time when demand was drying up for buildings that looked like they were designed in ancient Greece. The new style was Art Deco or the so called Vertical Style—which emphasizes a vertical look with ornament bearing a geometrical style. The nine-story base is primarily for the Chicago Board of Trade, while the building is topped by a pyramidal roof. It has symmetrical setbacks on each side of the tower and a three-story Art Deco lobby. The artwork of the building carries the theme of commodity trading from the sheaves of wheat in the lobby's panels to the statue of Ceres, the Roman goddess of agriculture.

5. **Monadnock:** *See* A Walk Down Dearborn.

6. **State of Illinois Center:** (1985), Clark and Randolph. The seventeen-story building includes a breathtaking atrium running almost the full height. Its southern window exposures help heat the building in the winter. Designed by Helmut Jahn, this huge glass building cost $172.6 million and was afflicted with cost overruns and delays. Governor James Thompson was criticized for the building, some said it could have been more practical. When the building debuted, a ten-year-old, asked for his opinion, said, "I think they really messed up." Despite problems with roof leaks and air conditioning, and the mixed reviews from the man-on-the-street critics, step inside this glass coliseum and there's an incredi-

The southern window exposure and faulty air conditioning resulted in temperatures of up to 115 degrees in the State of Illinois Center in 1986, leading some employees to use beach umbrellas for shade.

ble view. You can even ride up its center on elevators walled with windows.

7. **333 W. Wacker Drive:** (1983), 333 W. Wacker. Designed by Kohn Pedersen Fox, the thirty-six story building sits on a triangular site. The 90 degree angle fits into the normal gridwork of downtown, while the hypotenuse curves with the river. That curving of 333 is done with green glass to reflect the river color and shape.

8. **The Reliance Building:** (1894), 32 N. State. This nearly century-old, sixteen-story building is one of the first glass tower skyscrapers. There's some confusion on who was the main architect, but John Root and Charles Atwood each worked on it, and Atwood probably did the bulk of it. The framing for the top ten floors was done in fifteen days, and pictures taken while it was going up could be confused with the skeleton of a modern skyscraper. It has been called a pure expression of skeletal frame construction, with its fully developed "Chicago windows" (large permanent windows with an openable window on each side). The upper floors were adorned with cream white, glazed terra cotta.

The Reliance building, 32 N. State, is considered by many to be the first glass tower.

9. **Wrigley Building:** (south building 1919-21, north Building 1923-24), 400 N. Michigan. The south building has sixteen stories plus a twelve-story tower. The north building duplicates that but with a smaller tower. It was designed by Graham, Anderson, Probst and White, who also did such buildings as the Shedd Aquarium, the Merchandise Mart and the Field Building. The Wrigley, with its spire modeled after a cathedral tower in Spain, has been floodlit at night since it was built. As a consequence, it's a dazzling white visual landmark for Downtown nighthawks. The building, from the ground up, is covered with six progressively whiter shades of

Ludwig Mies van der Rohe is considered the founder of the second "Chicago School" of architecture.

terra cotta. By doing this, the most light is reflected from the most ornamented part of the building.

10. **Sears Tower:** (1974) 233 S. Wacker. Designed by Skidmore, Owings and Merrill, this 110-story building—1,454 feet—was to be the largest headquarters for the largest retailer: Sears. It's still the tallest in the world. It's built with unique construction of bundled tubes, and the setbacks help to deflect the wind.

THE BIG GUYS

William LeBaron Jenney (1832-1907), sometimes referred to as the "father of the skyscraper," was a pioneer of skeleton construction with the Home Insurance Building.

Louis Sullivan (1856-1924) bridged the elegance of nineteenth century architecture with twentieth century innovations. His works include the Carson Pirie Scott & Company Building and the Getty Tomb in Graceland Cemetery.

John Wellborn Root (1850-1891) died while planning the World's Fair of 1893. He was Daniel Burnham's partner. Their work includes the Monadnock Building and The Rookery.

Ludwig Mies van der Rohe (1886-1969) brought the sleek, modern International School to America; Federal Center, IBM Building; 860-880 N. Lake Shore Drive.

Frank Lloyd Wright (1867-1959) was one of the originators of the Prairie School, a Midwestern-flavored building style with structures that hug the ground: Unity Temple, Oak Park; Robie House, 5757 S. Woodlawn.

Walter Burley Griffin (1876-1937) studied under Wright and spread Wright's Prairie School ideas. A string of Griffin-designed homes is in the Southwest Side's Beverly neighborhood. Griffin also designed Canberra, the capital of Australia.

HOUSES
The Commission on Chicago Landmarks' Chicago Houses-12 Popular Types

1. **Chicago Cottages:** Using balloon framing, these one- and one-and-a-half-story wooden cottages could be built in a couple of weeks. They started appearing in the 1830s. Example: south side of Menomonee between Orleans and Sedgwick.

2. **Frame Houses:** Often looking like farm houses, these were bigger than the cottages, often two or more stories, but built for the working-class family beginning in the 1850s. They often had a stoop, and the first floor was a bit above the street level in case the city decided to raise the grade, as it did a couple of times in the 1800s. Examples are in the Old Town Triangle neighborhood.

3. **Queen Anne:** Popular in the 1880s and 1890s, this is a style with many variations. Corner turrets and different colors, shapes and materials are often used on a Queen Anne house.

4. **Graystones:** Called such because they were generally built with gray limestone quarried in Joliet. Built mostly as single-family houses, typically between 1890 and 1915. Most graystones were built near parks and along boulevards and major streets. Example: south side of Addison Street, between Racine and Lakewood avenues, one block west of Wrigley Field.

5. **Stone Rows:** These are row houses built mostly in the 1880s and 1890s. They looked like graystones, but there was no space in between.

6. **Brick Rows:** Row houses were also built of brick around the late 1880s.

7. **Apartment Buildings:** There were no apartment buildings in Chicago until after the Great Fire of 1871. Before then, houses, hotels and boarding houses sheltered the city's population. By the mid-1880s apartment buildings were built all over the city.

8. **Two- and Three-Flats:** Many were built between 1910 and 1940, although they faded from style around the 1920s.

9. **Storefronts with Apartments:** Because commercial strip property was expensive, an owner got more bang for his buck by putting an apartment on top. These tended to be built after the 1900s, many with turrets and bay windows. Example: St. Benedict Flats, 40-52

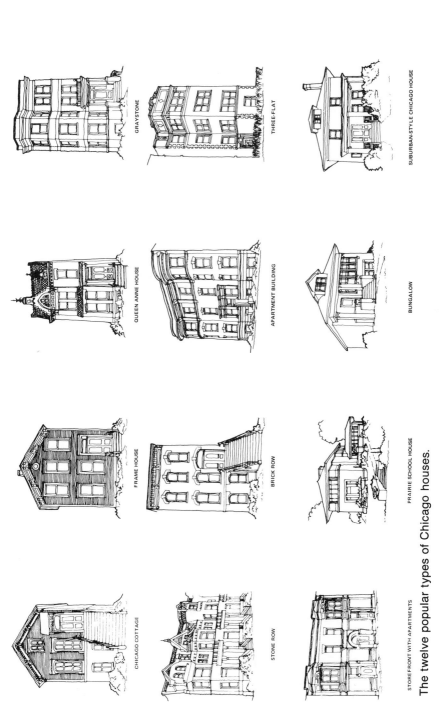

GRAYSTONE

THREE-FLAT

SUBURBAN-STYLE CHICAGO HOUSE

QUEEN ANNE HOUSE

APARTMENT BUILDING

BUNGALOW

FRAME HOUSE

BRICK ROW

PRAIRIE SCHOOL HOUSE

CHICAGO COTTAGE

STONE ROW

STOREFRONT WITH APARTMENTS

The twelve popular types of Chicago houses.

E. Chicago Avenue or Krause Music Store, 4611 N. Lincoln Avenue (with a Louis Sullivan-designed front).

10. **Prairie Schools:** Developed by Frank Lloyd Wright, the Prairie home looks modern and was designed for wide open areas. One classic is Robie House, 5757 S. Woodlawn Ave., built in 1908. One of the largest concentrations of Prairie-style homes is along Walter Burley Griffin Place (10432 South from 1600 West to 1756 West) in Beverly. Griffin worked in Wright's Oak Park studio.

11. **Bungalows:** These are those familiar one- and one-and-a-half-story rectangular houses often built of red brick. Some 100,000 of these workingman's specials were built during the 1920s. They originated in India and came to Chicago via California.

12. **Suburban-style Chicago Houses:** These are kind of like huge bungalows with a Prairie School flavor. They have big overhanging eaves and generally plenty of room.

SKYSCRAPERS

Before the Chicago Fire of 1871, the tallest buildings in Chicago were four to six stories high. Shortly after the fire, downtown buildings rose seven to eight stories. And then came the modern skyscraper. Chicago was hemmed in by the river and the lake, and it was only natural to build up. But masonry load-bearing walls could only go so high. Enter metal skeletal construction and the elevator. While nobody knows for sure where the first metal skeletal building was built, Chicago defin-

The oldest building in Chicago is moved over the L tracks at 44th and Calumet on its way to a new home.

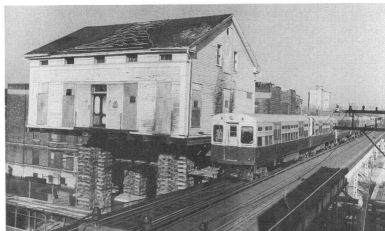

itely had a role, if not *the* role, in mastering the sky. The pioneer was William Le Baron Jenney. His Home Insurance Building (1884-85) was one of the first, if not the first, modern skyscrapers built with a metal skeleton—although part of it was built with party walls for support. The steel skeleton also helped provide bigger window space, hence the so called "Chicago window." The height of Chicago skyscrapers got higher quickly.

For example:

- 10 stories—Montauk Building (1882)

- 12 stories—Mallers Building (1884)

- 17 stories—Auditorium (1889)

- 21 stories—Masonic Temple (1892)

LIST OF TEN
CHICAGO'S TALLEST BUILDINGS

Some people look at Chicago as a chip-on-the-shoulder kind of city. They say it comes from being called names like "Second City" or "Hog Butcher for the World." This, of course, is baloney. Chicago is not obsessed with a "mine is bigger than yours attitude." That's New York's problem. New York City, for example, feels the need to have three of the world's five tallest buildings—the two World Trade Centers (north and south) and the Empire State Building. Chicago only has one, but it's THE BIG ONE. The Sears Tower, with its 110 stories of steel, has ruled the skies since 1974. Chicago also has ten of the 100 tallest buildings. But who's counting?

Chicago Rank	World Rank	Building	Yr. built	Stories	Height
1.	1	Sears Tower	1974	110	1,454 ft.
2.	7	Amoco	1973	80	1,136 ft.
3.	8	John Hancock	1968	100	1,127 ft.
4.	13	311 S. Wacker	1990	65	970 ft.
5.	22	Two Prudential Plaza	1990	64	912 ft.
6.	27	900 N. Michigan	1989	66	875 ft.
7.	28	AT & T Corp. Center	1988	64	875 ft.
8.	29	Water Tower Place	1976	74	859 ft.
9.	35	First National Bank	1969	60	850 ft.
10.	57	3 First National Plaza	1981	58	775 ft.

SUBURBAN HEIGHT

Some suburbs have height restrictions stopping building at 100 feet, or 150 in certain circumstances. Three of the tallest buildings in the suburbs are: Oak Brook Terrace Tower—31 stories, 425 feet high; 2 Pierce Plaza, Itasca—395 feet; State National Bank Building, Evanston—23 stories.

Shunned by Neighbors: John J. Glessner dropped a bundle of money for a fancy house designed by a fancy architect and built on a fancy street. When it was finished, his neighbors looked at it and shunned him and his house. Now the 1887 building is one of the city's architectural gems. Glessner, a manufacturer of farm machinery, commissioned Henry Hobson Richardson to design the Romanesque residence at 1800 S. Prairie—which was then the city's "Millionaires' Row." Its granite walls and massive curved archway over the front door give it the look of a fortress, which the neighbors found offensive. In fact, the focus of the design was never really meant for the neighbors, because the street side of the house was really the back side. It was designed to focus away from the street to a courtyard behind the house.

CLASSIC QUOTES

"Less is more."

Ludwig Mies van der Rohe

"Form follows function."

Louis Sullivan

Sources: *Wild Onion: A Brief Guide to Landmarks and Lesser-Known Structures in Chicago's Loop* by members of the Historic Resources Committee of the Chicago Chapter, American Institute of Architects. *Chicago Since the Sears Tower: A Guide to New Downtown Buildings* by Mary Alice Molloy. *Holabird & Roche Holabird & Root An Illustrated Catalog of Works;* Commission on Chicago Historical and Architectural Landmarks. *The Plan of Chicago: 1909-1979, An Exhibition of the Burnham Library of Architecture, The Art Institute of Chicago. Chicago 1930-70 and 1910-29 Building, Planning, and Urban Technology* by Carl W. Condit; Council on Tall Buildings and Urban Habitat, Lehigh University, Bethlehem, Pa.; *Dictionary of American Biography; The New Encyclopaedia Britannica.*

THEATER

FIRSTS

Professional Public Performance: On Feb. 24, 1834, a traveling show-man, noted for his fire-eating and ventriloquism skills, performed at the Dexter Graves' Mansion House on Lake Street. In an advertise-ment for the performance published in the *Chicago Democrat*, the showman, a "Mr. Bowers," promised he would "draw a red hot iron across his tongue, hands, etc., and...partake of a comfortable warm supper by eating fireballs, burning sealing wax, live coals of fire and melted lead." Admission was 50 cents for adults, 25 cents for children.

Theater: In October 1837, two theatrical entrepreneurs, Harry Isher-wood and Alexander McKenzie, paid $125 for a city permit to run a permanent theater in Chicago and, days or weeks later, staged their first production in the old Sauganash Hotel on Lake Street. The exact date of opening night and the name of the first play are in doubt, since the bill changed nightly. The room seated 300, and admission was 75 cents. The season lasted six weeks, after which the company went on tour. It returned to Chicago in the spring of 1838 and put on shows in the former Rialto auction house on Dearborn Street. Isherwood and McKenzie renamed the building "The Chicago Theater." In the fall of 1939, McKenzie and a new partner—the actor Joseph Jefferson—offered one more season of theater, including the city's first perform-ances of Shakespeare. The company then moved on, leaving Chicago little in the way of legitimate theater for the next five years.

Actor Fired in Chicago: His name is lost to history, but Harry Isher-wood recalled in a letter of memoirs that his original Chicago theater company employed a "young Irishman" who "became very unruly" and had to be fired. Isherwood said the young man, upon being told to leave, said, "Where can I go, with Lake Michigan roaring on one side and the bloody prairie wolves on the other?"

Circus: The first circus, headed by a trick-riding horseman, Oscar Stone, arrived in Chicago on Sept. 14, 1836, a Wednesday, and remained for several weeks. It pitched its tent on Lake Street. An eyewitness wrote: "The circus—I think it was called 'The Grand Equestrian Arena'—was not so extensive as Barnum's, nor did it have separate tents for horses or anything else. But the performance was wonderful." Admission was 25 cents.

Permanent Theater Building in Chicago: John Blake Rice (1809-1874), mayor of Chicago from 1865 to 1869 and a successful theatrical producer, built the first permanent theater in Chicago—Rice's Theater, on the south side of Randolph Street between State and Wabash. It opened on June 28, 1847, with a play called "The Four Sisters." It burned down in 1850, but Rice promptly built another one—of brick—at a cost of $11,000. Rice is regarded as one of the founders of drama in Chicago.

West Sider Spans the Globe: A Chicago West Sider led the struggle to give London another Globe Theater, identical to the one in which Shakespeare first performed his most famous plays. Sam Wanamaker, a Chicago native, battled with London officials for nineteen years to rebuild the 1,500-seat Globe almost on the very site of the original theater, along the Thames River. He struggled with financing, obtained an eviction order against gypsy squatters on the site, and broke ground for the new Globe Theater in 1988. It is scheduled for completion in 1992.

In 1984, the Chicago Theatre was a movie house. It was not until 1986 that live theater returned.

THE CHICAGO THEATRE

From 1921 through 1955, all of America's biggest stars, would-be stars and faded stars played the Chicago Theatre. Through a depression, a world war and a cold war, the theater's bookings precisely mirrored the changing tastes of American audiences. The Chicago, at State and Lake, opened on Oct. 26, 1921, with a film—*The Sign on the Door*—a fifty-piece orchestra, and Jesse Crawford at the "Mighty Wurlitzer." On Nov. 11, 1955, it discontinued stage shows during the screening of "Guys and Dolls." Live theater did not return to the Chicago until 1986 when, completely refurbished, it played host to Frank Sinatra.

TOP-GROSSING ACTS AT THE CHICAGO THEATRE
(From 1935 to 1955)

1. Dean Martin and Jerry Lewis, Aug. 2, 1951 ($62,201).
2. Milton Berle, Sept. 6, 1951 ($53,767).
3. Betty Grable, with Harry James & his Orchestra: Dec. 3, 1953 ($46,407).
4. Jackie Gleason and Company, July 17, 1952 ($29,708).
5. Frank Sinatra, with Skitch Henderson, May 23, 1946 ($26,250).
6. Danny Kay with Georgia Bibbs and Tip, Tap & Toe, Nov. 24, 1946 ($26,250).
7. Jack Benny, May 15, 1947 ($26,250).
8. Red Skelton & Show, Jan. 11, 1951 ($26,250).
9. Sid Caesar & Imogene Coca, June 14, 1951 ($26,250).
10. Danny Thomas, with Georgia Bibbs and Co., April 24, 1952 ($23,100).

THE REGAL THEATER

On the North Side stood the Chicago Theatre, where the the biggest white acts—and only occasionally black acts—played to largely white crowds. On the South Side stood the Regal, where the music was mostly black, and the audience black as well. The Regal, from 1928 to the late 1960s, was more than just a cultural landmark at Forty-seventh Street and King Drive. It was the musical and comedic soul of black Chicago. Duke Ellington, Louis Armstrong, Ella Fitzgerald, Tina Turner, Stevie Wonder, Gladys Knight, Sarah Vaughan, Cab Calloway, Jackie Wilson, Nat King Cole, Ray Charles, James Brown, Sammy

Davis, Jr., Aretha Franklin, Smokey Robinson, Moms Mabley, Miles Davis, The Impressions and dozens of other big acts played the Regal—Chicago's answer to Harlem's legendary Apollo Theater. The original Regal has been torn down, but the New Regal Theater, located in what was the Avalon Theater, 1645 E. Seventy-ninth, opened in 1986.

CHICAGO CONTRIBUTIONS

Steppenwolf: The nation's critics have called it "rock 'n' roll theater"— tough, physical and daring—performed by perhaps the best company of actors in the United States. The Steppenwolf Theatre Company has presented more than eighty productions since its debut in a Highland Park Unitarian church basement in 1974. It has traveled the world— from New York to London to Australia—won five Tony Awards and launched the careers of such nationally respected actors as John Malkovich, Terry Kinney, Laurie Metcalf, Joan Allen, Gary Cole, Glenne Headly, Tom Irwin, John Mahoney, Gary Sinise, Rondi Reed and Moira Harris. Steppenwolf was created when Sinise and several high school friends, including Jeff Perry and Terry Kinney, staged a production of Paul Zindel's "And Miss Reardon Drinks a Little." Productions of "Grease," "Rosencrantz and Guildenstern Are Dead" and "The Glass Menagerie" followed, and the group incorporated in 1975. The troupe moved out of the church basement and into a school basement, then to a 134-seat Broadway theater, and then, in 1982, to a 211-seat theater on North Halsted Street. Among the many celebrated productions that nailed down Steppenwolf's reputation were Lanford Wilson's "Balm in Gilead" (1980), Sam Shepard's "True West" (1982),

The Regal Theater was Chicago's answer to Harlem's legendary Apollo Theater. The original theater has been torn down, but the New Regal Theater (shown here) opened in 1986.

Lyle Kessler's "Orphans" (1985) and Frank Galati's adaptation of the John Steinbeck novel "The Grapes of Wrath" (1988). In April 1991, Steppenwolf moved into a new custom-made 500-seat home at 1650 N. Halsted.

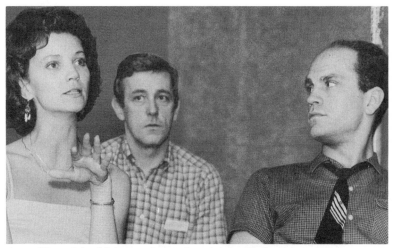

Joan Allen, John Mahoney (center) and John Malkovich were all members of the Steppenwolf Theater company in 1984.

Second City and Improvisational Theater: Second City is perhaps best known for the many outstanding comedians and actors who learned their craft there, but its great contribution to American theater is tightrope-walking live improvisation. Second City evolved from the Compass Players, founded in 1955 in Hyde Park and featuring—over the next several years—such talents as Shelley Berman, Alan Arkin, Jerry Stiller, Anne Meara, Mike Nichols, Elaine May, Ed Asner, Barbara Harris, Bernard Sahlins, Paul Sills and Sills' mother, improv guru Viola Spolin. On Dec. 16, 1959, Sills, Sahlins and former Composser Howard Alk opened Second City, taking the name from A.J. Liebling's 1951 *New Yorker* article, "Chicago, the Second City." In the course of the next thirty years, Second City significantly shaped the bounds and attitude of American humor. Television's "Saturday Night Live," with its lean sketches, live improvisation and macho veneer, borrows completely from Second City. Many of the show's biggest stars were Second City alums.

SECOND CITY ALUMNI WHO MADE IT BIG

Alan Alda	Dan Aykroyd	Peter Boyle
Jane Alexander	Jim Belushi	Hamilton Camp
Alan Arkin	John Belushi	John Candy
Ed Asner	Shelley Berman	Del Close

Brian Doyle-Murray	Elaine May	Harold Ramis
Aaron Freeman	Paul Mazursky	Joan Rivers
Mary Gross	Ann Meara	Avery Schreiber
Valerie Harper	Bill Murray	Martin Short
Barbara Harris	Michael Myers	David Steinberg
Tim Kazurinsky	Mike Nichols	Jerry Stiller
Robert Klein	Sheldon Patinkin	George Wendt
Shelley Long	Gilda Radner	

Avery Schreiber, Joan Rivers, Bill Alton and Del Close in a Second City production.

Jim Belushi rehearses for Second City's 25th anniversary show.

LIST OF FIFTEEN
A Sampling of Titles of Second City Revues

"Showdown at Credibility Gap"

"Premises, Premises"

"East of Edens"

"Sexual Perversity Among the Buffalo"

"I Remember Dada"

"Miro, Miro on the Mall"

"Glenna Loved It"

"Orwell That Ends Well"

"True Midwest"

"Kuwait Until Dark or Bright Lights Night Baseball"

"Flag Smoking Permitted in Lobby Only"

"Kukla, Fawn and Ollie"

"We Made A Mesopotamia, Now You Clean It Up"

"Rosebud Was the Sled"

"Turn Your Head and Kafka"

FAMOUS CHICAGOANS

David Mamet: Arguably America's greatest living playwright, he is also pure Chicago. Born Nov. 30, 1947, in Chicago, Mamet learned his craft writing plays during Chicago's theater boom of the early 1970s, and still peoples his plays with terse-talking Chicago street types. As Mamet once told *Sun-Times* entertainment writer Lloyd Sachs, "In Chicago, we know these guys. These are guys you go to buy an auto from on Western Avenue. These are guys like your Uncle Murray— nobody knows what he does. That's how society works here." In the 1970s, Mamet found success with his plays "Sexual Perversity in Chicago" (1973) and "American Buffalo" (1976). He won a Tony and Pulitzer for "Glengarry Glen Ross" (1984). Mamet also wrote the screenplays for *The Untouchables* (1987), *The Verdict* (1982), and the

Better known as a playwright, David Mamet also has acted, including this role as the Prince in "Snow White and the Seven Dwarfs."

remake of *The Postman Always Rings Twice* (1981). He wrote and directed *Things Change* (1988), and *House of Games* (1987). Intensely loyal, Mamet carried some of his old Chicago stage pals, such as actors Joe Mantegna and Mike Nussbaum, with him into the movies.

Jack Benny: He was the violin-playing tightwad from Waukegan. Benny (1904-1974) started in show business as a violin soloist, moved on to vaudeville, where he refined his vain fussbudget persona, and became one of the nation's most beloved radio and television funnymen. He was born Benny Kubelsky in Waukegan, the son of Russian Jewish immigrants who onced owned a saloon. He quit school in the ninth grade to take a job at $8 a week playing violin in the pit of Waukegan's Barrison Theater.

Recognize him? It is Jack Benny as he appeared in 1918.

Lorraine Hansberry: She died young, but left behind a classic play, "A Raisin in the Sun" (1959). Hansberry (1930-1965), who died of cancer in New York City, was the youngest of four children of a Chicago real estate broker. Her play is set on the South Side of Chicago where she spent her childhood, and explores a black family's struggle to escape

At age twenty-eight, Lorraine Hansberry had written her award-winning play, "A Raisin in the Sun."

the misery of the slums. Hansberry once said her intent was to "tell the truth about people, Negroes and life."

EXTREMES

Longest Running Play: "Sheer Madness," by Paul Portner, opened Sept. 22, 1982, in the Mayfair Theater of the Blackstone Hotel. Nine years later, it was still running strong. "Sheer Madness" is a comedy who-done-it, with audience participation and a different outcome each night. The Boston production of the play, which opened in 1980, is said to be the longest running non-musical play in U.S. history.

Most Lucrative Play: Andrew Lloyd Webber's "Phantom of the Opera" grossed $35 million during its run at the Auditorium Theatre, from May 24, 1990, to Feb. 16, 1991. Top ticket price was $55.

BACKGROUND

Theater Stats: The Chicago area is home to roughly 115 professional theater companies, with smaller companies coming and going each year. The industry employs more than 4,000 full- and part-time workers—a number that has held fairly steady since the middle 1980s—and has another 6,500 unpaid volunteers. In 1989, the most recent year for which figures are available, Chicago-area theaters earned a gross income of $66.5 million. Of the 700 to 1,000 productions mounted on local stages each year, four out of five are not-for-profit.

In the early 1960s, regional theater was almost invisible in Chicago. The city's theater scene was dominated by national touring companies that played big rooms such as the Arie Crown Theater, and a handful of safe middle-brow dinner theaters outside the Loop. But a theater boom hit the city in the late 1960s and 1970s, fueled by a growing baby-boomer audience and expanding funding sources. Among the more innovative and influential companies that popped up were the Body Politic (1966), the Organic (1969), the Piven Theatre Workshop (1972), Northlight (1974), Victory Gardens (1974), Wisdom Bridge (1974), Steppenwolf (1976), Pegasus Players (1978) and Remains (1979).

Audience Profile: During the 1988-89 season, the Chicago area's total theater attendance was 2,950,000. Audience surveys conducted annually by the League of Chicago Theaters show that, consistently, 49 percent are Chicagoans, 42 percent are suburbanites and the rest are tourists; 54 percent have at least one college degree; 49 percent earn at least $30,000 annually; 55 percent are female; and 48 percent are between 25 and 44 years old.

LIST OF TEN
OLDEST CHICAGO-AREA THEATERS

1. Northwestern University Theatre and Interpretation Center (1878)

2. Woodstock Opera House (1889)

3. Shubert Organization—operates Shubert and Blackstone theaters (1900)

4. Goodman Theatre—originally part of Goodman School of Drama (1925)

5. The Theatre School, DePaul U.—originally Goodman School of Drama (1925)

6. The Drama Group, Chicago Heights (1931)

7. Roosevelt University Theatre, Downtown (1945)

8. Des Plaines Theatre Guild (1946)

9. Court Theatre, Hyde Park (1954)

10. Theatre First, North Side (1957)

LIST OF FIVE
LARGEST THEATER FACILITIES

1. Arie Crown Theatre, McCormick Place (seating capacity—4,319)

2. Auditorium Theatre, 50 E. Congress Pkwy. (4,000)

3. Civic Center for the Performing Arts, 20 N. Wacker Dr. (3,531)

4. Chicago Theatre, 175 N. State St. (3,488)

5. Shubert Theatre, 22 W. Monroe St. (2,008)

JOSEPH JEFFERSON AWARD WINNERS

The Chicago theater community's equivalent of Broadway's Tony Award or Hollywood's Oscar is the Jeff Award, awarded since 1969 by the independent Joseph Jefferson Committee. Here are the winners:

BEST THEATRICAL PRODUCTION

1969—The Rose Tattoo—Ivanhoe

1970—Man of La Mancha—Candlelight

1971—Lady Audley's Secret—Goodman

1972—**The National Health**—Forum

1973—**One Flew Over the Cuckoo's Nest**—Arlington Park

1974—**Freedom of the City**—Goodman

1975—**The Philanthropist**—Goodman

1976—**Misalliance**—Academy Festival

1977—**Sizwe Banzi is Dead**—Goodman-Stage 2

1978—**You Can't Take It with You**—St. Nicholas

1979—**Morning's at Seven**—Academy Festival

1980—**Getting Out**—Wisdom Bridge

1981—**Balm in Gilead**—Steppenwolf

1982—**Kabuki Macbeth**—Wisdom Bridge

1983—**Moby Dick**—Remains

1984—**Glengarry Glen Ross**—Goodman

1985—**Hamlet**—Wisdom Bridge

      Orphans—Steppenwolf

1986—**Puntila and His Hired Man**—Remains

1987—**The Normal Heart**—Next & David Dillon

1988—**Passion Play**—Goodman

1989—**The Grapes of Wrath**—Steppenwolf

1990—**The Tale of Cymbeline**—Shakespeare Repertory

BEST ACTOR IN A PRINCIPAL ROLE

1969—Art Kassul—**The Subject Was Roses**

1970—Leonard Cimino—**The Man in the Glass Booth**

1971—Lee Pelty—**Fiddler on the Roof**

1972—William Munchow—**Child's Play**

1973—Dietrich Snelling—**Cabaret**

1974—Mark Medoff—**When You Comin' Back, Red Ryder?**

1975—Kenneth Welsh—**Resistible Rise of Arturo Ui**

1976—William J. Norris—**The Caretaker**

1977—Meshach Taylor—**Sizwe Banzi is Dead**

1978—Philip Kerr—**Otherwise Engaged**

1979—Byrne Piven—**The Man in 605**

1980—Frank Galati—**Travesties**

1981—Jack McLaughlin-Gray—**How I Got That Story**
1982—John Malkovich—**True West**
1983—Robert Drivas—**The Man Who Had Three Arms**
1984—William L. Petersen—**In the Belly of the Beast**
1985—Kevin Anderson—**Orphans**
1986—Denis Arndt—**Puntila and His Hired Man**
1987—Gary Cole—**Bang**
1988—Bill Cobbs—**Driving Miss Daisy**
1989—Robert Breuler—**A Walk in the Woods**
1990—Larry Yando—**Kiss of the Spider Woman**

BEST ACTRESS IN A PRINCIPAL ROLE

1969—No award
1970—Dolores Rothenberger—**Man of La Mancha**
1971—No award
1972—Melissa Hart—**Company**
1973—Marrian Walters—**Hot L Baltimore**
1974—Blaine Shore—**The Sea Horse**
1975—Barbara Gaines—**The Lesson**
1976—Carole Goldman—**View from the Bridge**
1977—Frances Hyland—**Long Day's Journey into Night**
1978—Carol Lockwood—**Ashes**
1979—Sonja Lanzener—**Porch**
　　　　Elizabeth Wilson—**Morning's at Seven**
1980—Roslyn Alexander—**Wings**
1981—Laurie Metcalf—**Balm in Gilead**
1982—Carmen Decker—**Clara's Play**
1983—Joan Allen—**And a Nightingale Sang**
1984—Barbara E. Robertson—**Kabuki Medea**
1985—Laurie Metcalf—**Coyote Ugly**
1986—Joan Allen—**A Lesson from Aloes**
1987—Laurie Metcalf—**Educating Rita**
1988—Geina Mhlope—**Have You Seen Zandile?**

1989—Linda Emond—**Pygmalion**

1990—Laura Esterman—**Marvin's Room**

EXTREME

The highest price for a dance ticket in Chicago—other than for a charity or fund-raising drive—is $77.50, which was charged for the best seats in the house when the Bolshoi Ballet played the Arie Crown Theatre in 1990.

DANCE

A Bear in Tights: Willie Gault, wide receiver for the Chicago Bears, danced one night in a Chicago ballet. For charity, Gault on Sept. 29, 1986, danced with ballerina Maria Terezia Balogh and the Chicago City Ballet in two segments from "Webern Pieces." Post-game analysis: He did not drop the Balogh.

Willie Gault rehearses with Maria Terezia Balogh for his performance with the Chicago City Ballet in 1986.

TWO CHICAGO DANCE GREATS

Ruth Page (1899-1991). She was Chicago's Grande Dame of Dance, the choreographer of some of America's most famous ballets and the founder in 1970 of the Chicago Repertory Dance Ensemble. Page was the first American woman to dance with the world famous Sergei Diaghilev Ballets Russes, the first American woman to dance with Anna Pavlova's company, the first American to commission a ballet with the famous Russian choreographer George Balanchine, and the first American to solo at New York's Metropolitan Opera House. In the late 1920s and 1930s, when America thought the only true ballet came out of Russia, Page began choreographing ballets with American themes, including "Frankie and Johnny." She also played a major role in the opera scene in Chicago, working at one time or another with every Chicago opera company, from the Lyric to the Chicago Grand Opera Company. Her Ruth Page Foundation School, founded in 1970 in a former Moose lodge at 1016 N. Dearborn, is considered one of the best ballet schools in the city. And Page's version of "The Nutcracker," which has played the Arie Crown Theatre every year since 1966, has become a Chicago Christmas tradition.

Maria Tallchief Paschen (born 1925). Her career as a prima ballerina began on an Osage Indian reservation in Oklahoma. Her career in Chicago, where she runs the School of Chicago Ballet, began in 1956 when she married builder Henry D. Paschen, Jr., a member of one of Chicago's wealthiest families. She previously was married to choreographer George Balanchine and was prima ballerina with the New York City Ballet from 1947 to 1960. Paschen founded the Chicago City Ballet in 1980, which collapsed in 1987. She now is artistic director of the Lyric Opera Ballet.

Maria Tallchief Paschen was dancing with the New York City Ballet Company in 1950. She now runs the School of Chicago Ballet.

CLASSIC QUOTE

Chicago censors in 1948 banned a production of Jean-Paul Sartre's play "The Respectful Prostitute." Mayor Martin H. Kennelly, invited to attend a private showing of the play, declined, saying, "I do not like the play. I do not like the title. The title alone would be enough to ban the show, as far as I'm concerned."

Sources: Hedy Weiss and Glenna Syse, *Chicago Sun-Times.* Larry Cose, former reporter for the *Sun-Times,* Second City; Barbara Corrigan, Auditorium Theatre; *The History of Chicago,* by A.T. Andreas; the League of Chicago Theatres; Marilyn Donaldson, *Stagebill.*

EDUCATION

FIRSTS

First Teacher: Eliza Chappel Porter (1807-1888) opened the first public school in Chicago in 1833, her salary paid from the Chicago School Fund. Classes were held in a one-room log cabin built as a store by early settler John S. Wright. It was furnished with benches, a small table, a globe, a world map, a United States map, a Bible and a few hymn books. Porter had twenty-five students. Two years later, she and her missionary husband, the Rev. Jeremiah Porter, left Chicago for Green Bay, Wisconsin.

First Chicago Public High School: Opened in 1856, at Halsted and Monroe streets. C.A. Dupree was the principal.

First College: St. Xavier College, now at 3700 W. 103rd St., was begun by five immigrant Irish nuns in 1846 in a building on Michigan Avenue between Madison and Monroe. The school moved to 49th Street and Cottage Grove Avenue after the Chicago Fire of 1871, and to 103rd Street in 1956.

First Teachers College: Chicago State University opened on Sept. 2, 1867, in a leaky freight car on a railroad siding in Blue Island. It was called the Cook County Normal School and had thirteen students.

First Catholic Lay Principal: Miss M. O'Riley, who in 1857 was head of the Immaculate Conception Elementary School in Waukegan.

First Catholic Elementary School in the Chicago Archdiocese: In 1837, school classes were taught on weekdays in St. James on the Sag Catholic Church, 107th Street and Archer Avenue in Lemont.

First Chicago Public School Music Teacher: Mr. Nelson Gilbert, appointed in December 1841 for $16 per month.

EXTREMES

Smallest College: Native American Educational Services College, established in 1974 for the study and service of Native American culture, had eighty-one full-time students in 1991, 95 percent of whom were Indians. NAES, at 2838 W. Peterson, offers extensive courses in Native American history, culture and language.

Biggest University: University of Illinois at Chicago, with an enrollment of 24,195 in 1991.

Biggest Private All-Girl School in America: Mother McAuley Liberal Arts High School, 3737 W. Ninety-ninth St., with 1,862 students. When founded in 1846, it was called the St. Francis Xavier Academy for Females and was located on Wabash, between Madison and Monroe.

Oldest Catholic College: The College of St. Mary, which became St. Mary of the Lake Seminary. Founded between 1844 and 1848.

Oldest Continuing Catholic High School: St. Patrick High School, 5900 W. Belmont, which previously was located at Adams and Desplaines streets. The school was started in 1857 by the Holy Cross Brothers and taken over in 1861 by the Christian Brothers.

BACKGROUND

Chicago Public Schools: Nation's third-largest public school system after New York and Los Angeles. Budget for 1990-91: $2.25 billion. Enrollment: 300,541 elementary school pupils, 100,789 high school students, and 7,112 students in other public school institutions. Of the total enrollment, 88 percent were minority (black, Hispanic, Asian and Native American) and 12 percent were white. Number of schools, as of May 1991: 502 elementary schools, 65 high schools and 36 other schools (such as one in Cook County Jail). Sources of revenue—47.9 percent local, 38.6 percent state, 13.4 percent federal.

In 1845, when Chicago erected its first two-story brick school building, at Dearborn and Madison streets, at a cost of $8,000, many people regarded it as an extravagance. The mayor recommended that the city change it into an insane asylum and confine the men who were responsible for its construction. But five years later Chicago had five more schools.

Chicago Roman Catholic Archdiocesan Schools: 189 elementary schools and 32 high schools within the city; 114 elementary and 17 high schools in suburban Cook County; 22 elementary and two high schools in Lake County. Enrollment in 1990-91—66,279 in Chicago elementary, and 22,402 in Chicago high schools; 38,542 in suburban Cook elementary and 13,711 in suburban Cook high schools; 7,214 in Lake County elementary and 1,400 in Lake County high schools. Total enrollment for entire archdiocese was 149,548 in the 1990-91 school year. Number of teachers: 4,593 in the elementary schools, and 1,852 in the high schools.

Other Private Schools in Chicago: 110 elementary schools, 17 high schools and 19 kindergarten-through-grade-12 schools (as of May 1990).

City Colleges of Chicago: Founded 1911. Now eight colleges, with an enrollment of 85,150 (as of May 1990). Budget in 1990-91: $284 million (including $92 million from local property taxes). Although established to provide students with the first two years of a four-year college education, a 1991 University of Chicago study revealed the city colleges instead have become training centers for adults who dropped out as teenagers from Chicago's public schools. Almost half the students in 1989 were enrolled in English as a Second Language classes, while fewer than 60 percent were enrolled in college-credit courses.

CHICAGO CONTRIBUTION

The Great Books of the Western World. This 60-volume, 37,000-page compilation, which includes 517 works by 130 authors, was created in 1952 by University of Chicago educators Mortimer Adler and Robert Hutchins. Published by the *Encyclopaedia Britannica* and revised only once—in 1990—it claims to contain within its covers all the timeless ideas and knowledge of the Western Hemisphere. Among its authors are Homer, Plato, Aristotle, Plutarch, Moliere, Dickens and Twain. One tiny school in the Chicago area—Shimer College in Waukegan—uses the "great books" approach to teaching, exploring these classics in seminar-sized classes.

FAMOUS CHICAGOANS

Julius Rosenwald (1862-1932). Belief in the importance of racial equality prompted Rosenwald, the man who ran Sears, Roebuck & Company from 1908 to 1924, to help finance construction of 4,500 schools for black children in the South, build YMCAs in twenty-five cities and give $2.7 million to build a model low-rent housing project at Forty-sixth Street and Michigan Avenue in Chicago. Rosenwald also established the Rosenwald Fund, with a $30 million endowment, and endowed the Museum of Science and Industry.

Irving Harris. Like a latter-day Rosenwald, Harris, born in 1910, is a multimillionaire philanthropist with a firm belief in the importance of good parents and good schools. Harris, president of the Standard Shares investment company, has given $7 million to the University of Chicago for a new Graduate School of Public Policy Studies, $4 million to the university for a medical school program in child psychiatry, and $5 million to Yale—his alma mater—to foster programs in child psychiatry, child development and social policy. He founded Evanston-based Family Focus in 1976, an organizaton that works with parents and young children, and the Erikson Institute for Early Child Development, a graduate program in child psychology at the University of Chicago. But Harris' most celebrated cause may be his Ounce of Prevention Fund, which works with inner-city schools to teach teenagers parenting skills and funds such controversial programs as a high school health clinic that dispenses birth control pills.

About 90 percent of Irving Harris' philanthropic efforts deal with early childhood development and the "close link between the cycle of poverty and very poor education."

ILLINOIS VS. CHICAGO COMPARISONS

	Illinois	Chicago
Public School Enrollment:	1,766,186	401,330
% White:	66.2	12.0
% Minority:	33.8	88.0
Average Daily Attendance:	93.5%	89.7%
ACT Average:	20.9	17.0
Graduation Rate:	78.4	47.4
Average 1st Grade Class Size:	22.6	25.2
Average H.S. Class Size:	19.0	21.8
Pupil/Teacher Ratio:	17.1	17.7
Average Teacher Salary:	$32,925	$36,359

	Illinois	Chicago
Spending Per Pupil:	$4,519	$5,265
8th Grade Reading Scores % in Nation's Top Quartile:	29.9	14.7
8th Grade Reading Scores % in Nation's Bottom Quartile:	22.0	35.7
8th Grade Math Scores % in Nation's Top Quartile:	34.3	14.2
8th Grade Math Scores % in Nation's Bottom Quartile:	23.5	44.3
% of Pupils With Limited English Proficiency:	4.1	11.0

Source: The Illinois Goal Assessment Program, November, 1990 Report

Chicago's public schools were formally segregated on March 23, 1863, when the City Council voted to create a separate school for black children on the South Side. The council was complying with a new state law that barred "negro and mulatto children" from white schools.

RACIAL MAKEUP
OF CHICAGO PUBLIC SCHOOLS
EMPLOYEE STAFF

	%Black	%White	%Hispanic	%Asian	%Amer.Indian
Teachers (23,684)	48.3	44.2	5.8	1.6	.1
Over-all Staff (42,048)	53.2	37.5	7.8	1.4	.1

Source: Chicago Board of Education reports for March, 1990

LIST OF TEN
Biggest Colleges and Universities*
(By Enrollment)

University of Illinois at Chicago: Founded 1965. One-hundred-and-seventy-acre campus on Chicago's Near West Side. Enrollment: 24,195. Tuition and fees for Illinois residents: $2,730. Faculty size: 2,037 (1,769 full-time and 268 part-time).

*(All figures are for 1990-91 school year).

DePaul University: Founded 1898. Roman Catholic. Thirty-acre campus at Fullerton and Seminary avenues on Chicago's North Side, plus facilities in the Loop at 243 S. Wabash. Enrollment: 15,387. Tuition and fees: $8,124. Faculty size: 734 (415 full-time and 319 part-time).

Loyola University: Founded 1870. Roman Catholic. Thirty-six-acre main campus at 6525 N. Sheridan Rd. Additional facilities in the Loop and Maywood. Enrollment: 14,343. Tuition and fees: $7,710. Faculty size: 746 (471 full-time and 275 part-time).

Northwestern University: Founded 1851. Sheridan Road campus in Evanston is 251 acres. Additional facilities in the Loop. Enrollment: 11,554 in 1991. Tuition and fees: $12,996. Faculty size: 870 (758 full-time and 112 part-time).

Northeastern Illinois University: Founded 1961. Sixty-seven acres at 5500 N. St. Louis Ave., Chicago. Enrollment: 10,293 in 1991. Tuition and fees: $1,909. Faculty size: 539 (371 full-time and 168 part-time).

University of Chicago: Founded 1891. One-hundred-and-seventy-five-acre campus in Hyde Park. Enrollment: 9,300 in 1991. Tuition and fees: $14,025. Faculty size: 598 (595 full-time and 3 part-time).

Columbia College: Founded 1890. Independent liberal arts commuter school. The campus consists of three downtown Chicago office buildings, at Congress and Michigan avenues. Enrollment: 6,498 in 1991. Tuition and fees: $5,480. Faculty size: 691 (142 full-time and 549 part-time).

Roosevelt University: Founded 1945. Downtown Chicago campus at 430 S. Michigan Ave. Enrollment: 6,374 in 1991. Tuition and fees: $6,822. Faculty size: 508 (151 full-time and 357 part-time).

Illinois Institute of Technology: Founded 1892. One-hundred-and-twenty-acre campus at 3300 S. Federal Ave. Enrollment: 6,300 in 1991. Tuition and fees: $11,760. Faculty size: 510 (284 full-time and 226 part-time).

Chicago State University: Founded in 1869, it is a state-run university with ten buildings on a 151-acre campus at Ninety-fifth Street and King Drive. Enrollment: 6,034 in 1991. Tuition and fees for Illinois residents: $1,772. Faculty size: 397 (280 full-time and 117 part-time).

Chicago's public school teachers were poorly paid in the old days—women more poorly than men. In 1842, the City Council voted to pay female teachers no more than $200 annually and male teachers no more than $400 annually. The schools were open forty-eight weeks a year.

Mortimer Adler helped create the sixty-volume *Great Books of the Western World.*

CLASSIC QUOTE

From Mortimer Adler, reknowned Chicago educator: "Try to have two hours every day to let the mind idle. An inactive two hours. Idling is very important. What comes out of it? Creativity."

Sources: Ann Tyskling, Independent Schools Assocation of Chicago; Roger Flaherty, Maribeth Vander Weele, Maureen O'Donnell and Bob Herguth, *Chicago Sun-Times*; *A History, Chicago State University, 1867-1979*, published by Chicago State University Foundation; Brother Don Houde, Archdiocese of Chicago; *Peterson's Guide to Four-Year Colleges, 1991*; Beverlee Markulin, Mother McAuley High School; "Chicago," a publication of the Chicago Public Schools and The King Company, 1951; the Chicago Municipal Reference Library.

RIOTS

MEMORABLE TOP TEN RIOTS
IN CHICAGO HISTORY

Beer Riots of 1855. A know-nothing mayor once shut down taverns on Sundays, triggering a riot by the Irish and the Germans. Mayor Levi D. Boone, a member of the Know-Nothing Native American Party, which opposed political and social rights for recent immigrants, tried to stem beer drinking among the newcomers by raising tavern license fees and enforcing the Sunday closing of taverns. But the new rules applied only to beer houses, not saloons selling only whiskey. The Germans rioted and were joined by the Irish. Leander Hunt, a Chicago police captain, lost his arm to a shotgun blast.

Haymarket Affair. It gave the world May Day. The date was May 4, 1886. The purpose was to protest police actions during a confrontation the day before between strikers and replacement workers at the McCormick Harvester Plant. The scene was the old Haymarket Square, 600 W. Randolph St. As the relatively small crowd—around 300 people—began to disband due to rain and indifference, the police moved in and ordered them to disperse. Somebody threw a bomb. A melee broke out. Eight policemen and two civilians were killed. Weeks later, in one of the most unjust trials in American history, eight anarchists were convicted of murder. One committed suicide. Four were hanged on Nov. 11, 1887. The remaining three were freed seven years later when Governor John Peter Altgeld, appalled by the verdict of the kangaroo court, pardoned all eight. But fearing another Haymarket affair, Chicago businessmen in the 1880s, including Marshall Field, donated North Shore land for the creation of Fort Sheridan and the Great Lakes Naval Training Center. In 1889 and 1892, international labor and socialist groups adopted May 1 as "May Day"—a time to honor labor and, specifically, the Haymarket "martyrs."

1919 Race Riots. Thirty-eight were killed. Another 537 were wounded. Hundreds were left homeless. For five days, from July 27 to July 31, blacks and whites rioted throughout Chicago, the violence beginning

A painting depicting the Haymarket affair.

on the South Side and spilling over into the West Side, North Side and the Loop. It began on a sweltering Sunday when a black teenager drowned in Lake Michigan after being stoned by white bathers. The boy, Eugene Williams, had inadvertently floated over from the black-patronized Twenty-fifth Street Beach to the white-patronized Twenty-ninth Street Beach. For the next five days blood poured as white gangs assaulted isolated blacks and black gangs assaulted whites. White gunmen drove through black neighborhoods, shooting randomly at pedestrians. Black snipers shot back. Finally, several regiments of National Guardsmen and a cooling rain quelled the violence.

Rent Strike Riot. On Aug. 3, 1931, 2,000 black Chicagoans on the South Side went on a rampage when a seventy-two-year-old widow was evicted from her home at 5016 S. Dearborn St. Three civilians were killed and three policemen injured. Many of those involved in the fracas were unemployed men who had been marching in a Depression-era "rent strike" parade to protest a rash of evictions. Colonel Robert Mc-Cormick's arch-conservative *Chicago Tribune*, however, ignored the obvious racial and economic causes of the riot, blaming it instead on "Red propaganda" and "2,000 communists, mainly colored."

Cicero Riot. Harvey E. Clark, Jr., a black man, was twenty-nine and a CTA bus driver when he moved into a modest Cicero apartment on West Nineteenth Street on June 7, 1951. Before the night was out, rioters had broken into the apartment and destroyed the family's possessions. Clark and his family fled. When the family attempted a second time to move into the apartment in July, rioting broke out for three days. The twenty-flat building was looted and trashed, the landlord went into hiding, and 400 National Guardsmen patrolled the streets.

An aerial view shows the burning 3200 block of West Madison on April 7, 1968.

More than 120 people were arrested. The Cicero riots made news around the world, and were cited frequently in anti-Western propaganda put out by communist countries. The Clarks moved back to Chicago, then to New York, and retired in Little Rock, Arkansas. The suburb's racial conflicts would continue for another thirty years.

West Side Riots. Riots broke out all over the Chicago area and across the nation in the spring and summer of 1968, in the days after the assassination of Dr. Martin Luther King, Jr. In Chicago, the biggest riots hit the West Side. Eleven people were killed. More than 500 were wounded or injured, many cut down by sniper fire. Almost 3,000 were arrested. Arson fires destroyed 162 buildings. Property losses were in excess of $10 million. The West Side riots began on Palm Sunday, April 7, 1968, three days after King's murder in Memphis, Tennessee. Young men charged down Madison Street and Roosevelt Road, smashing windows with their fists and looting stores. Seven thousand Illinois National Guard troops and 5,000 federal troops were called in. Eight days later, acres of the West Side reduced to rubble, the riots ended. Of the eleven dead, nine had been shot (two by police who said they had been fired on). One died of smoke inhalation in a looted store. One was found in a gutter where he had bled to death from a leg gash, possibly caused by broken glass in the window of a nearby store. All eleven were black males, aged sixteen to thirty-four.

Democratic Convention. The nation watched on TV as the Chicago police, during the 1968 Democratic National Convention, clubbed the sons and daughters of middle America. Many political analysts today contend those scenes marked the beginning of the end for Chicago's old-style Democratic Machine, giving birth to an independent political movement. In the summer of 1968, a time of nerve-fraying domestic tension, 10,000 anti-war protesters flocked to Grant Park and Lincoln Park to protest during the August 26-29 convention. On the convention's third night, the so-called "Battle of Chicago" broke out in Grant Park, sparked by protesters who taunted a tired and angry police force, calling them "pigs" and pelting them with garbage and human waste. The police had shown restraint. But now, for about twenty minutes outside the Conrad Hilton Hotel on Michigan Avenue, dozens of officers chanted "kill, kill, kill" and pummeled demonstrators savagely. One hundred and one demonstrators were hospitalized, and 192 police officers reported minor injuries. A national commission on violence headed by future governor Daniel Walker called it a "police riot."

Days of Rage. For about a week in October 1969, a radical group calling itself the Weathermen led thousands of angry young people in nightly rock-throwing sprees through the streets of Chicago's Loop and Gold Coast. They wore helmets and goggles, carried sticks and clubs and threw bottles. They were protesting the Vietnam War, police oppression and—as one speaker phrased it—"rich people." Scores of civilians and policemen were injured. Two civilians were shot. Windows were smashed in cars and businesses. And Richard J. Elrod, an assistant corporation counsel who later became Cook County sheriff,

The Weathermen led angry young people on a spree through the Gold Coast on Oct. 8, 1969.

was permanently paralyzed below the waist when he attempted a flying tackle on a running demonstrator. After a Weathermen bomb factory blew up in New York, the group's leaders, including Bernadine Dohrn and William Ayers, went into hiding. Ayers was the son of Thomas Ayers, the wealthy chief executive officer of Commonwealth Edison. In time, most of the leaders surrendered or were tracked down and arrested.

Sly and the Family Stone. When Sly and the Family Stone, a rock group, failed to show up on time for a concert in Grant Park on July 27, 1970, more than a few of the 50,000 fans flipped out. By the time their tantrum ended, 128 policemen and 33 civilians were injured, and 165 people were under arrest. The riot began with a show of impatience, as some in the audience trampled protective snow fences and mounted the stage, driving off the warm-up acts. Those on stage were pelted with bottles by the crowd, which had been told by announcers that Sly would not come on until the stage was cleared. And then the police moved in—four squad cars with four men in each. Almost immediately, the chant changed from "We want Sly" to "Off the pig."

Two different sides of the generation gap share the rear of a car at a Weatherman rally.

Bottles flew and cars burned. Gov. Richard Ogilvie later said that "every dropout, kickout and throwout in the city of Chicago was there."

Humboldt Park Riot. Three men were killed and more than 100 people were wounded on June 4 and 5, 1977, when Puerto Ricans rioted and fought police in Chicago's Humboldt Park after the annual Puerto Rican Day Parade. Two of those killed were shot by police officers in the confusion of the first day's rioting. The third man died in a building fire set by rioters. A federal panel later said the riot was triggered by the sense of "frustration and hopelessness, rage and violence" felt by many Puerto Ricans.

DISCO DEMOLITION

On July 12, 1979, all sorts of records were broken at Comiskey Park—mostly disco records. Disco Demolition started as a promotional gimmick, and ended up a fiasco. Thousands of young people swarmed onto the ballpark's playing field between games of a White Sox-Detroit Tigers twilight doubleheader and refused to leave, forcing postponement of the second game. Disco Demolition was the brainchild of Sox promotions executive Mike Veeck, son of team president Bill Veeck, and WLUP-FM disc jockey Steve Dahl. The gimmick called for 98-cent admission to anybody carrying a disco record. Dahl, wearing an army surplus helmet, proposed to blow up the records between games. But as he began to do just that, security broke down and thousands of people poured onto the field. One group dragged out the batting cage and destroyed it. Another group set fire to a pile of records in center field. Somebody else set fire to the base of the left field foul pole. "In their way of thinking," Bill Veeck said later, "I guess they were completely well-behaved."

RACE RIOTS HERE, THERE & EVERYWHERE

Between 1965 and 1969, race riots and smaller racial disturbances were virtually the order of the day in the Chicago area, as well as throughout the country. The city and many suburbs suffered through dozens of altercations, from school cafeteria brawls to shootouts.

In **Aurora,** the city council in 1967 refused to approve an open-housing ordinance, triggering four nights of rock-throwing and sniper shooting. In **Dixmoor,** 1,000 blacks rioted for two nights in 1964 when a white liquor-store owner roughed up a black woman he suspected of stealing a bottle of gin. In **Elgin,** seventy-five black youths in 1967 roamed the Wingate Park Shopping Center throwing firebombs. In **Evanston,** a band of about seventy young blacks ran through the central business district on Halloween, 1967, breaking sixty windows in stores, homes and cars. In **Harvey** in 1968, one young man in a mob of 200 blacks—angered by the police shooting of a teenager days before —fired a shotgun at the police, slightly injuring seven officers. In **Joliet,** rioters looted local stores and tried to set them afire in 1969. In **Maywood,** a mob of 300 people in 1968 stoned the village hall while the board met inside. In **Summit,** a fight between blacks and whites broke out during a high school student assembly. In **Waukegan,** bands of youths rioted for three nights in the city's black neighborhoods. In **Zion,** the police chief was hit with a baseball bat during a racially motivated fight in a local high school.

As Evanston Police Chief Bert Giddens said at the time, there was "a tremendous residue of hostility."

PAST TENSE

Says Lax Conditions Caused Race Riots
By Carl Sandburg
(Chicago Daily News, July 28, 1919)

Charges that colored officials have not properly protected their race and have permitted lax conditions which resulted in the race riots of today and yesterday were made today by Dr. George C. Hall, 3488 S. Park avenue, one of the best known colored men in the city.

Dr. Hall declared that an unwise police was at the bottom the cause of the outbreaks. He said that a serious political situation exists in the ward by reason of the fact that the two colored aldermen are responsible to white politicians, rather than to the voters who elected them.

"In the first place, the police had no business to undertake segregation of bathers with no ordinance or warrant of law or any form of consultation of the people concerned," said Dr. Hall. "The action of the police in this instance may be traced back to the same conditions that permit gambling to flourish at the present time to an extent never before known in recent years. The segregation line on the bathing beach was drawn by the police. Then when a boy got over the line and trouble arose, the police immediately spread their men out through the district. Wherever colored people were in the habit of congregating peacefully squads of policemen were placed. They drew the color line and followed a policy precisely as the authorities do in Georgia."

Shiny Bayonets and Rain Curb Rioters
(Chicago Daily News, July 31, 1919)

The bayonet, famed in the European war for its persuasive effect, was king in Chicago's race riot zone today. Bayonets wet with rain, not gore, gleamed at every street corner; they poked out under grocery store awnings and cottage porches; their glitter marked the outposts of Illinois militiamen from afar.

And every bayonet was the shiny tip of a loaded magazine rifle, while in support of thousands of infantry weapons were machine guns, belted for the fray, and several automatic rifles of the latest pattern, ready to speak their rapid chatter of death.

Rain, the great pacifier, was the right hand aid of five regiments of reserve militia and national guard which last night were posted in the disturbed districts by Adjt.-Gen. Dickson on Mayor Thompson's formal request.

The rain dripped and pattered on soldier and policeman, on the respectable and disorderly elements of the black and white races, cooling hot tempers and rusting mob enthusiasm.

CLASSIC QUOTE

"Shoot to kill." On April 15, 1968, the final day of the West Side riots, Mayor Richard J. Daley fumed that in any future outbreaks police would have orders "to shoot arsonists and looters—arsonists to kill and looters to maim or detain." Daley, under intense criticism, later moderated his order and his press secretary, Earl Bush, said reporters "should have printed what he meant, not what he said."

Sources: *Chicago Sun-Times* and *Chicago Daily News.*

COURTS

FIRSTS

■ **The first juvenile court** in the nation was started in Chicago in 1899, thanks to the efforts of pioneer social worker Julia Lathrop. The court's guiding principal was that children are much less responsible for their acts than adults and must be treated in a special way by the courts.

■ **The first court** in Illinois was French. The French were the first to settle Illinois. In 1699 the French established town commanders or judges for each of the Illinois settlements. The so-called Commandery answered to the governor of Louisiana. In 1722, a Provincial Council, with jurisdiction over civil and criminal matters, was established. This was the first court in Illinois—at least for which there's any record.

■ **The first Chicago courthouse** was built in 1835 at the southwest corner of Clark and Randolph. It had one story and a basement.

■ **The first Chicago lawyer** was Giles Spring, who started practicing about 1833. Spring's first case was against the second Chicago lawyer, John Dean Caton. It involved a $34 theft in a tavern in what Chicago historian A.T. Andreas calls the "first larceny case." Not that there weren't plenty of thieves in Chicago before 1833, but this apparently was the first time one of them was brought before a judge. When the prisoner was in front of the judge, the stolen money was founded wadded up in his sock.

■ **First Chicago divorce:** 1834—Angeline Vaughn petitioned for divorce from Daniel W. Vaughn, her husband of three years.

■ **Chicago's first official murder trial** was in 1834 and involved an Irishman accused of killing his wife. He was found not guilty. It was thought he was guilty of manslaughter and got off only because of a faulty jury instruction and a slick lawyer.

■ Charles E. Freeman became the **first black Illinois Supreme Court justice** when he took office on Dec. 3, 1990.

EXTREMES

■ **Illinois' largest jury verdict award for a personal injury case** was the $77,935,000 awarded Andrew Blake on Nov. 8, 1990, in Cook County Circuit Court. The medical malpractice and product liabilty case involved the blinding and brain damage of Blake as a three-month-old child. Legal pundits might quibble about the present cash value of the award because it is the total of periodic payments into the future. Probably the largest single present-value award was $39,255,340 awarded on March 20, 1986, in a product liability case in which George Chelos, a bartender, had to have his legs amputated because of a drug he was given during by-pass surgery in 1977.

■ **The longest jury trial** in U.S. history lasted three and a half years in Belleville, Illinois. It ended in late 1987. The case was brought against Monsanto Company by sixty-five Sturgeon, Missouri, residents who became ill after a railroad tanker spilled 19,000 gallons of chemicals containing dioxin in their town. The jury handed down an award of more than $16 million. There were 182 witnesses, 6,000 exhibits, 100,000 pages of transcripts, 600 days of court and eight weeks of deliberation.

■ Baker & McKenzie, founded in Chicago in 1949, is the **largest law firm** in the world, with 1,560 attorneys—as of March 31, 1991. Its Chicago office had 166 attorneys as of that date.

■ Cook County has the nation's **largest consolidated court system,** with about 6 million cases pending or filed in a year, according to the Cook County clerk's office.

LAWSUITS FILED BY COUNTY (1990)

	Felony Filings and Reinstatements	Traffic	Civil Filings
Cook	41,295	3,546,804 (and parking)	341,107
Du Page	3,519	94,720	94,072
Kane	1,658	77,532	25,343
Lake	3,186	143,156	34,887
McHenry	722	52,230	14,505
Will (Not available at time of printing)			

(Cook does not include felony preliminary hearings; all counties do not include juvenile and misdemeanor cases)

HOW MANY LAWYERS ARE THERE?

There are 57,589 lawyers registered to practice law in Illinois—in 1980 there were only 37,100. Here's how many lawyers there are by county:

Cook—32,374; Du Page—2,178; Kane—693; Lake—1,436; Will—464; McHenry—319.

Jacob I. Grossman, one of the prosecutors of Al Capone for income tax evasion in 1931, later joined U.S. District Court Judge James H. Wilkerson (the judge in the Capone trial) and William J. Froelich, another Capone prosecutor, in private practice.

HOW MUCH DO THEY MAKE?

Chicago-area lawyers working for law firms that mostly do commercial work average about $86,000 annually. Lawyers working for corporations make about $81,883 a year, according to David J. White & Associates, Inc., Wilmette. These figures, however, don't reflect smaller general practice law firms.

For 116 years, a law firm founded by Abraham Lincoln's son, Robert Todd Lincoln, thrived in Chicago. Founded in 1872, the firm of Isham, Lincoln and Beale closed its doors in 1988 after being buffeted by staff defections and a dwindling pool of high-paying clients.

FEDERAL COURT AND JUDGES

The U.S. District Court—Northern District of Illinois (Eastern Division)—has federal jurisdication for Cook, Du Page, Grundy,

---

Judge Kennesaw Mountain Landis (1866-1944), a federal judge in Chicago appointed by Theodore Roosevelt, became the first commissioner of baseball, serving from 1920 to 1944. It was said his courtroom was a place where "juries never went to sleep." He admitted "having sympathies to be taken advantage of," like with ex-soldiers, widows and people who stole out of necessity. And he wasn't timid with the powerful—in 1907 he leveled a $29 million fine against the Standard Oil Company of Indiana on a freight rebate case after he forced John D. Rockefeller, Sr., to come to Chicago and personally testify—the U.S. Supreme Court reversed the fine. As baseball commissioner, he barred eight Chicago White Sox players from baseball for life; even though they were acquitted in court—for taking bribes to throw the 1919 World Series. After he became baseball commissioner, he continued as a judge, despite criticism over his dual job status. Eventually he resigned his judgeship. As for his name, it comes from the Civil War battle of Kennesaw Mountain, where his father was wounded and lost a leg.

Judge Kennesaw Mountain Landis, the first commissioner of baseball, throws out the first ball at a White Sox-Tigers game in 1938.

Kane, Kendall, Lake, La Salle, and Will counties. McHenry County is in the Western Division. The Eastern Division had twenty active judges including Chief Judge James B. Moran; four senior judges; seven magistrates; and ten bankruptcy judges as of spring 1991.

What do federal judges make? A federal district court judge earns $125,100 annually; a court of appeals judge is paid $132,700.

Federal lawsuits filed in 1990: 7,550 civil lawsuits were filed in the Northern District, 694 criminal cases were assigned to federal district court judges and 107 criminal cases went to magistrates.

CIRCUIT COURT JUDGES: HOW DO YOU GET TO BE ONE?

■ Associate judges are appointed to a four-year term by a vote of the circuit judges.

■ Circuit judges are elected for a six-year term and then must be retained by the voters every six years.

A federal investigation of corruption in Cook County courts began in the late 1970s and involved three and a half years of undercover work and about ten years worth of investigation. It was dubbed "Greylord." At least eighty-six people have been convicted, including thirteen judges and forty-nine lawyers. Others convicted include clerks, policemen, Cook County sheriff's deputies, a state representative and a court-appointed receiver.

■ Illinois appellate judges are elected for ten-year terms from the state's five appellate districts.

■ Supreme Court justices are elected for ten-year terms from the appellate districts (three from Cook County, the other four from the rest of the state).

HOW MANY JUDGES ARE THERE?

There are 807 associate and full circuit court judges distributed among the twenty-two circuits of Illinois. The Chicago area is covered by five circuits. Here's how many judges each has:

12th—Will County: 20 associate and full circuit court judges.

16th—Kane, Kendall, DeKalb: 26

18th—Du Page: 36

19th—Lake, McHenry: 36

Cook—the only circuit without a number, it has 381 associate and full circuit court judges.

HOW MUCH DO THEY MAKE?

Associate judges are paid $75,113 (with cost of living raise in July 1991); Circuit Court judges are paid $80,599, as are chief judges; Illinois Appellate Court judges are paid $87,780; Illinois Supreme Court justices are paid $93,266. (A U.S. Supreme Court justice is paid $153,600 and the Chief Justice is paid $160,600.)

ILLINOIS SUPREME COURT JUSTICES

There are seven Illinois Supreme Court justices. They are elected for ten-year terms. After that they run for retention on a ballot voters mark "yes" or "no." There has never been an instance in Illinois history in which a state supreme court justice has not been retained. If a vacancy occurs on the court, the court itself fills the vacancy until the next election.

	Hometown	Birthdate	Date of Office
Benjamin K. Miller (Chief Justice)	Springfield	1/5/36	12/3/84
William G. Clark	Chicago	7/16/24	12/6/76
Thomas J. Moran	Lake Forest	7/17/20	12/6/76
Michael A. Bilandic	Chicago	2/13/23	12/3/90

	Hometown	Birthdate	Date of Office
James D. Heiple	Pekin	9/13/33	12/3/90
Charles E. Freeman	Chicago	12/12/33	12/3/90
Joseph F. Cunningham	Fairview Hts.	2/25/24	3/5/91

U.S. Supreme Court Justices Born in Illinois or Appointed from Illinois

Six U.S. Supreme Court justices have been appointed from Illinois, including one chief justice. They are:

Chief Justice Melville W. Fuller (born in Maine and appointed from Illinois) served from 1888 to 1910.

David Davis (born in Maryland and appointed from Illinois) served from 1862 to 1877.

John Marshall Harlan (second with that name to serve on the court) served from 1955 to 1971.

Arthur J. Goldberg served from 1962 to 1965.

Harry A. Blackmun has served from June 9, 1970, to present.

John Paul Stevens has served from Dec. 19, 1975, to present.

(Note: There have been 105 justices of the U.S. Supreme Court.)

FAMOUS CHICAGOAN

Clarence Darrow (1857-1938) was probably the most famous lawyer ever to come out of the Chicago corporation counsel's office. After leaving that job in the 1890s, Darrow went on to become a criminal defense attorney and activist. He defended union leaders like Eugene V. Debs, and he saved murderers Nathan Leopold and Richard Loeb from the death penalty. He defended John T. Scopes, a high school teacher who broke a Tennessee law by teaching evolution, and won an acquittal for a black family that fought to defend its home in an all-white neighborhood in Detroit.

CLASSIC QUOTES

Traveling in Palestine, Clarence Darrow asked a boatman the price of a trip over the area where it was said Jesus had walked on water. He was told it would be $15. "No wonder Jesus walked," Darrow replied.

Clarence Darrow on the death penalty: "The real reason why so many people tenaciously cling to the idea of capital punishment is because they take pleasure in inflicting pain on those they hate. Of course, they would not admit that this is the reason; at the same time the proof is very plain. All early punishments were mainly vindictive, but then, primitive people are more honest than civilized ones and are not so anxious to hide their motives. Civilized people think more of themselves."

Sources: *Chicago Sun-Times* and *Daily News;* Illinois Attorney Registration and Disciplinary Commission; Illinois State Bar Association; David J. White and Associates; American Bar Association; office of the Cook County clerk; Administrative Office of the Illinois Courts and its *A Short History of the Illinois Judicial Systems; History of Chicago*, by A.T. Andreas; Cook County Jury Verdict Reporter; the Federal Bureau of Investigation; office of the curator of the Supreme Court of the United States; *The New Encyclopaedia Britannica.*

RELIGION

FIRSTS

Jewish Congregation: Kehillath Anshe Mayriv, organized on Nov. 3, 1847. Its fifteen charter members, all German Jews, held services above the store of Jacob Rosenberg, at the corner of Lake and Wells. On June 13, 1851, the congregation dedicated its first synagogue. Today, the K.A.M.-Isaiah Israel Temple is located at 1100 E. Hyde Park Blvd.

Rabbi: Ignatz Kunreuther (1811-1884) came to Chicago to lead the K.A.M. congregation on Nov. 5, 1847. An Orthodox Jew born in Gelnhausen, Germany, he resigned in 1853 because he thought the congregation was leaning toward what he considered to be reform ideas.

Catholic: Jean Baptiste Point DuSable, who was also Chicago's first settler, was so devout he traveled 300 miles with his Indian bride to be married by a priest at Cahokia in the 1770s.

Catholic Priest: John Mary Iranaeus St. Cyr, dispatched to Chicago from St. Louis by Bishop Joseph Rosati, arrived in Chicago in April 1833. He said his first mass on May 5, 1833, in a log cabin at what is now Wacker Drive and Lake Street. He returned to St. Louis in 1837, leaving Chicago to an assistant.

Catholic Church: St. Mary's, a 36-by-24-foot frame church, was built in 1833 on a government-owned lot at the corner of State and Lake. Old St. Mary's now is located at Wabash and Van Buren streets.

Protestant to Preach a Sermon: On Oct. 9, 1825, the Reverend Isaac McCoy, a Baptist who ran a mission school near Niles, Michigan, preached a sermon at Fort Dearborn to a group of Native Americans.

Sunday School: The first Sunday school was held on Aug. 19, 1832, in a small frame building outside Fort Dearborn. It was taught by Luther Childs, Mrs. Seth Johnson, Mrs. Charles Taylor and the daughters of

Mark Noble and Philo Carpenter. At the time, the building did not have windows or a shingled roof.

Black Catholic Priest: Augustine Tolton, a former slave ordained a priest in downstate Quincy, came to Chicago in 1893 to run St. Monica Catholic Church, the city's first black parish. At the time he arrived, Chicago's small black Catholic population—no more than a few hundred people—worshipped in segregation on Sunday mornings, relegated to the basement of Old St. Mary's Catholic Church.

Catholic Bishop: William J. Quarter came to Chicago by boat in 1844, accompanied by his brother, the Reverend Walter Quarter. He built thirty churches, ordained twenty-nine priests and established Chicago's tradition of different churches for different ethnic groups.

Papal Visit: For thirty-seven hours in 1979, Pope John Paul II visited Chicago. He arrived at 7 p.m., on October 4, flying into O'Hare Airport on a 727 charter jet. He was greeted by Mayor Jane Byrne and Gov. James Thompson and serenaded at Holy Name Cathedral by operatic tenor Luciano Pavarotti. The next day, he presided over a morning mass at Five Holy Martyrs Catholic Church on the Southwest Side and then, at 4 p.m., over a much larger open-air mass in Grant Park. It featured a thirty-foot altar, 370 bishops, and 100,000 to 350,000 worshippers. "I am with you always," the pope said, "until the end of the world." At 9 p.m., he returned to Holy Name Cathedral to hear the Chicago Symphony Orchestra perform the last half of Anton Bruckner's Fifth Symphony. At 8 a.m., the next morning, he flew out of town. In truth, the pope had visited Chicago twice before—in 1969 and 1976—as Cardinal Karol Wojtyla. He was barely noticed.

BACKGROUND

Christians in Chicago area: 4.8 million.

Roman Catholics in Chicago-Area: 2,795,000 (2,350,000 in the Chicago archdiocese, plus 445,000 in the Joliet Diocese).

Protestants: 1,306,000, not including Episcopalians, who prefer to be listed as part of the worldwide Anglican Communion.

Eastern Orthodox Christians: 250,000.

Jews: 250,000.

Episcopalians (Anglicans): 50,000.

Bishops applaud as John Cardinal Cody (left) escorts Pope John Paul II during the pope's 1979 visit to Chicago.

Lutheran Church-Missouri Synod: 135,000.

Evangelical Lutheran Church in America: 135,000

Presbyterian Church (U.S.A.) (Cook, Lake, Du Page counties): 50,020.

Southern Baptist Convention: 35,000.

United Methodist Church (primarily Cook, Lake, Du Page): 44,664.

United Church of Christ (as of 1987): 70,000.

Baha'is: 1,500

Buddhists: 85,000 to 100,000.

Hindus: 70,000.

Muslims: 300,000.

Sikhs: 2,500.

Zoroastrians: 400 to 500.

Weeping Virgins: Chicago occassionally runs across a "weeping" icon or two. In April 1987, dozens of true believers filed into a second-floor flat on West Devon Avenue, rented by immigrant Iraqis, to kneel before a picture of the Virgin Mary that appeared marked by two faded tears. In December 1986, witnesses reported that an icon of the Virgin Mary at St. Nicholas Albanian Orthodox Church, 2701 N. Narragansett, had been weeping. Thousands of worshippers flocked to the church to witness the tears, which since have faded. And in 1984 a wooden statue of Mary in St. John of God Church, 1234 W. Fifty-second St., appeared to shed tears. Again, thousands called it a miracle, although an investigative team from the Roman Catholic Archdiocese of Chicago noted, "We are not able to eliminate the possibility that natural causes might explain the occurrence."

EXTREMES

Oldest Church Building: St. James on the Sag Catholic Church, at 107th and Archer in Lemont, was built by Irish immigrants in 1833 from Lemont limestone taken from the digging of the Illinois & Michigan Canal. The little church, which seats 300, is surrounded by the oldest cemetery in the Chicago area. Geographically isolated, it did not have a resident pastor until Rev. Joseph Bollman in 1882.

Oldest Catholic Church Building: Old St. Patrick Church, 140 S. Desplaines St., was constructed from 1852 to 1856, making it the oldest existing church building in the city and one of the few buildings to survive the Chicago Fire of 1871. Designated a historic city landmark in 1964, it is 64-by-24 feet. It is noted for its stained glass depictions of

---

Eucharistic Congress: Perhaps the greatest burst of pomp and circumstance for the Chicago area's Roman Catholic Church came from June 20-24, 1926, when Cardinal George Mundelein and the archdiocese hosted the Twenty-eighth International Eucharistic Congress, the first in the United States. As many as one million Catholics, including 12 cardinals, 64 archbishops, 309 bishops, 500 monsignors and 8,000 priests, came from all over the world to participate in the ceremonies and prayers at St. Mary of the Lake Seminary in Mundelein. A chorus of 62,000 school children sang at the opening ceremonies in Soldier Field. The Chicago Rapid Transit Company and the North Shore Line added 445 extra trains, totaling 2,785 cars, during the four days.

the great saints of Ireland: Patrick, Bridget, Finbar, Colman, Senan, Columban, Attracta, Columbkille, Carthage, Brendan and Gall.

Oldest Protestant Church: The Cathedral of St. James, 65 E. Huron, built of Joliet limestone, was dedicated in 1857, but gutted by the Chicago Fire of 1871. The church was rebuilt according to the original plans, and the original walls and bell tower were preserved. St. James parish was organized by the Rev. Isaac Hallam in 1834 at the request of one of Chicago's first families, the Kinzies.

Oldest Synagogue: Anshe Emet Synagogue, a Georgian-style structure at 3760 N. Pine Grove Ave., was dedicated in 1911. Anshe Emet, a Conservative Jewish congregation, bought the building from the congregation of Temple Sholom in 1928. The oldest former synagogue is now the Pilgrim Baptist Church, 3301 S. Indiana, which was dedicated as a temple by the K.A.M. congregation in 1891. It is an architectural gem designed by the firm of Adler and Sullivan. Dankmar Adler's father had been rabbi of the K.A.M. congregation from 1861 to 1883.

Oldest Black Protestant Church: Quinn Chapel A.M.E. Church houses the oldest black congregation in Chicago, tracing its origins back to 1844. It is named for William P. Quinn, an early bishop of the African Methodist Episcopal Church. Presidents William B. McKinley and William Howard Taft spoke in this church, McKinley in 1899 and Taft in 1911.

Oldest Black Catholic Parish: St. Elizabeth Parish, now at Forty-first and Michigan on the South Side, was founded by Irish Catholics in 1881. In 1924, St. Elizabeth's, having become a predominantly black parish, merged with St. Monica's.

LIST OF TEN
OLDEST CHURCH BUILDINGS
IN THE CHICAGO AREA

1. St. James on the Sag, Lemont (1833)

2. Old St. Patrick Catholic Church, 140 S. Desplaines St., Chicago (1856)

3. Cathedral of St. James, 65 E. Huron St., Chicago (1857)

4. Holy Family Church, 1080 W. Roosevelt, Chicago (1860)

5. St. Michael Catholic Church, 455 W. Eugenie St., Chicago (1869)

6. First Baptist Congregational Church, 60 N. Ashland Ave., Chicago (1871)

7. Second Presbyterian Church, 1939 S. Michigan Ave., Chicago (1874)

8. Trinity Episcopal Church, 125 E. Twenty-sixth St., Chicago (1874)

9. Holy Name Cathedral, 735 N. State St., Chicago (1875)

10. Olivet Baptist Church, 3101 S. Martin Luther King Dr., Chicago (1876)

A Church with Clout: Visit Holy Family Catholic Church at Roosevelt and May streets and you will see seven lights lit—day and night—before the image of Our Lady of Perpetual Help. The lights are an eternal reminder of how the church survived the Chicago Fire of 1871. As the story goes, the Reverend Arnold Damen, the founder of Holy Family, was in New York on the day the great fire struck. He heard the news, fell to his knees and prayed that, should God spare his church, he would keep a light burning within forever. The fire began within blocks of the church, but moved with the southwest winds away toward downtown.

CATHOLIC BISHOPS AND CARDINALS

1. William Quarter, appointed first bishop of Chicago in February 1844. Born in Killurine, Kings County, Ireland, on Jan. 24, 1806. Died April 10, 1848.

2. James O. Van De Velde, appointed Dec. 1, 1848. Born in Lebbeke, Belgium, on April 3, 1795. Died Nov. 13, 1855.

3. Anthony O'Regan, appointed July 25, 1854. Born in County Mayo, Ireland, 1809. Died Nov. 13, 1866.

4. James Duggan, appointed Jan. 21, 1859. Born in Maynooth, County Kildare, Ireland, on May 22, 1825. Died March 27, 1899.

5. Thomas Foley, appointed coadjutor bishop on Sept. 27, 1869. Born in Baltimore, Maryland, on March 6, 1822. Died Feb. 18, 1879.

6. Patrick A. Feehan, appointed first archbishop of Chicago on Sept. 10, 1880. Born in County Tipperary, Ireland, in 1829. Died July 12, 1902.

7. James E. Quigley, appointed archbishop of Chicago on Jan. 8, 1903. Died July 10, 1915.

8. George Mundelein, appointed archbishop of Chicago on Dec. 9, 1915. Created cardinal on March 24, 1924. Born in New York City on July 2, 1872. Died Oct. 2, 1939.

9. Samuel Stritch, appointed archbishop of Chicago on Dec. 27, 1939. Created cardinal on Feb. 18, 1946. Born in Nashville, Tennessee, on Aug. 17, 1887. Died May 27, 1958.

10. Albert Meyer, appointed archbishop on Sept. 19, 1958. Created cardinal on Dec. 14, 1959. Born in Milwaukee, Wisconsin, on March 9, 1903. Died April 9, 1965.

11. John Cody, appointed archbishop on June 16, 1965. Created cardinal on June 26, 1967. Born in St. Louis, Missouri, on Dec. 24, 1907. Died April 25, 1982.

12. Joseph Bernardin, appointed archbishop on July 10, 1982. Created cardinal on Feb. 2, 1983. Born in Columbia, South Carolina, on April 2, 1928.

Ripping Off the Pope: After Pope John Paul II visited Chicago in 1979, the city renamed a one-mile stretch of Forty-third Street in his honor. Within the first six months, twenty-three "Pope John Paul II Drive" signs were stolen.

A TIME LINE
CHICAGO'S CATHOLIC POPULATION

Year	Chicago archdiocese	Joliet archdiocese
1965	2,341,500	266,842
1970	2,424,591	310,820
1975	2,466,294	359,000
1980	2,406,728	411,000
1985	2,362,162	420,000
1990	2,350,000	445,000

FAMOUS CHICAGOAN

Joseph Cardinal Bernardin, archbishop of the Roman Catholic Archdiocese of Chicago.

April 2, 1928—Born in Columbia, South Carolina. Mother: Maria M. Simion Bernardin. Father: Joseph Bernardin.

April 26, 1952—Ordained a priest in his hometown after graduating St. Mary's Seminary, Baltimore, and Catholic University of America, Washington, D.C., where he earned a master's degree in education.

1952 to 1966—Served Diocese of Charleston, South Carolina, as parish priest, vicar general, diocesan consultor and administrator while diocese did not have a bishop. Named papal chamberlain in 1959 and domestic prelate in 1962 by Pope John XXIII.

March 9, 1966—Appointed auxiliary bishop of Atlanta by Pope Paul VI. Installed a month later at age thirty-seven, the youngest bishop in the United States.

April 10, 1968—Elected general secretary (chief executive officer) of National Conference of Catholic Bishops and United States Catholic Conference.

Nov. 21, 1972—Appointed archbishop of Cincinnati by Pope Paul VI, holding post nearly ten years.

July 10, 1982—Named by Pope Paul II as archbishop of Chicago after death of John Cardinal Cody. Installed August 25, and four months later was elevated to the Sacred College of Cardinals.

OTHER FAMOUS CHICAGOANS

St. Frances Xavier Cabrini (1850-1917), the "Saint of the Immigrants," died at Columbus Hospital, 2520 N. Lakeview St., on Dec. 22, 1917, the date now fixed as her feast day. In the days before her death, she was arranging for Christmas presents for poor children in Chicago. Mother Cabrini, born in Italy, came to the United States in 1889, where she divided her time between New York and Chicago while traveling frequently. Columbus is one of sixty-seven hospitals, schools and orphanages she established throughout the world. She was the first U.S. citizen to become a saint, canonized in 1946.

Minister Louis Farrakhan, a former calypso singer who played Rush Street nightclubs, leads the Nation of Islam—the Black Muslims. The Chicago temple of the Muslims was established in 1932 by Elijah Muhammad. It quickly became the nation's largest temple. When Muhammad died in 1975, his son, Warith Deen Muhammad, began leading the Muslims toward more orthodox Islam and allowed white members. Farrakhan split from the group, taking an estimated 10,000 of its members with him, and preached Muhammad's unadulterated teachings: blacks were the "original people" and whites were "artificial mutations" and "devils." Today, Warith Muhammad's group claims a membership of about 100,000, while Farrakhan's group is estimated to have 15,000 members. In 1984, Farrakhan enraged Jews and others by calling Adolf Hitler a "wickedly great" man and referring to Judaism as a "dirty religion." But he also has been praised for his emphasis on black self-reliance, the importance of strong families and moral rectitude.

Martin E. Marty (born 1928), a Lutheran theologian at the University of Chicago, is perhaps America's most renowned scholars of American religion. He is certainly the nation's best-known and most quoted theologian. Marty was born in West Point, Nebraska, earned his Ph.D. at the University of Chicago, joined its faculty in 1963, founded

Minister Louis Farrakhan is the leader of the Nation of Islam.

a Lutheran church in Elk Grove Village, has written forty books, and is senior editor of *Christian Century* magazine.

Selling Soles and Saving Souls: Religious revivalist Dwight L. Moody (1837-1899), who in 1864 founded the Near North Side church that bears his name, started out selling soles, not saving souls. He was a shoe salesman—a very good one—when he came to Chicago from Massachusetts in 1856. But he stopped selling footwear in 1860 to devote himself to preaching. He railed against alcohol, the theater, the teaching of evolution, stores doing business on the Sabbath and the Sunday papers. His evangelistic campaign at the Chicago World's Fair reportedly was attended by nearly 2 million. What made Moody stand out from other evangelists was his view that God was more benevolent than vengeful. In 1873, he returned to Massachusetts.

THE BIBLE BUTTON

If the South is America's Bible Belt, then west suburban Wheaton is metropolitan Chicago's Bible Button.

About three dozen nondenominational churches and publishing houses are based in Wheaton and neighboring Carol Stream, a concentration of religious headquarters unsurpassed in the United States.

The religious heart of Wheaton and Carol Stream is Wheaton College, started by Wesleyans as the Illinois Institute in 1853. Congregationalists took it over in 1859 and became famous for dispatching missionaries across the globe. The Billy Graham Center at Wheaton College is named for the college's most famous alumnus.

Among the evangelic groups based in Wheaton or Carol Stream are: (1) the National Association of Evangelicals, representing some 4 million members; (2) the Evangelical Alliance Mission, which fields more than 1,000 missionaries in twenty-seven countries; (3) Tindale Publishing House, which prints 60,000 religious books, periodicals and pamphlets a day (most notably the *Living Bible*); (4) Billy Graham's Christianity Today, Inc., which publishes *Christianity Today*, *Campus Life* and *Today's Christian Women* magazines; (5) MAP International, which distributes medical supplies and training materials for Christian health-care providers in underdeveloped countries; (6) the Slavic Gospel Association of Wheaton, which produces Bible instruction materials and shortwave religious radio programs in Slavic languages; (7) Bibles for the World, which supplies translations into numerous obscure tongues to churches for distribution; (8) the Chapel of the Air, which produces religious radio programming broadcast by more than 300 stations; and (9) Youth for Christ, which reaches an estimated 700,000 teenagers in 214 cities through clubs, camps and conferences.

Sources: Daniel J. Lehmann, religion writer, *Chicago Sun-Times;* Nancy Sandleback, an archivist for the Roman Catholic Archdiocese of Chicago; Kathy Ladien, Asher Library of the Spertus Museum of Judaica; *History of Chicago Jewry, 1911-1986,* published by Sentinel Publishing Co., Chicago, 1986; Stan Davis, National Conference of Christians and Jews; *History of Chicago,* by A.T. Andreas; *Chicago Daily News;* Chicago Metropolitan Association, United Church of Christ; Roman Catholic Church of Chicago's 1991 Directory; *Chicago Churches & Synagogues,* by George A. Lane, S.J. & Algimantas Kezys, Loyola University Press, Chicago, 1981.

TRANSPORTATION

FIRSTS

■ The first stagecoaches to run west of Chicago into what are now Du Page and Will counties were operated by Dr. John Taylor Temple beginning in 1834.

■ On Nov. 20, 1848, the Pioneer ran ten miles to the Des Plaines River on the strap-iron rails of Chicago's first railroad, the Galena and Chicago Union. It departed from Chicago's first railroad station, built on the west side of the Chicago River's North Branch at Kinzie Street. The railroad, which guaranteed the growth of Glen Ellyn, Wheaton, Winfield and West Chicago in Du Page County, was started by Chicago's first mayor, William Ogden. It was later renamed the Chicago and North Western. Strap-iron rails consisted of thin iron straps nailed to wooden rails.

■ The first horse-drawn rail streetcar went down State Street from Randolph to Twelfth Street on Feb. 14, 1859. Before that, all public transportation was on horse-drawn omnibuses, often over muddy streets.

■ The first Rapid Transit, or L, line began operating on June 6, 1892, from Congress to Thirty-ninth Street and was powered by coal-burning steam engines.

■ The first electric Ls ran in 1895 to Logan Square, Garfield Park and down Lake Street.

■ The first subway, the State Street subway, opened Oct. 17, 1943; the Dearborn Street subway opened Feb. 25, 1951.

ROADS

Chicago has 3,676 miles of streets, 193,968 street lights, and 2,575 traffic lights.

Illinois has 137,516 miles of roads, 7.2 million licensed drivers, and in 1989 about 81.6 billion miles were traveled by motor vehicles.

NUMBER OF MILES OF ROAD IN EACH COUNTY

	Rural	Municipal	Total
Cook	802	10,389	11,191
DuPage	672	2,163	2,835
Kane	1,055	969	2,024
Lake	893	1,816	2,709
McHenry	1,251	585	1,836
Will	1,823	966	2,789

EXPRESSWAYS

The major Chicago expressways often were completed in phases. The following list includes the dates the first section was completed and the last section was completed; the number of miles the expressway runs; and the highest average daily traffic and where it occurs.

Dan Ryan (includes parts of I-90/I-94): December 1961, December 1962; 13.4 miles long; 229,800 vehicles at Forty-third Street.

Kennedy (includes parts of I-90/I-94): December 1958, November 1960; 16.05 miles; 238,000 vehicles at Armitage.

Stevenson (I-55): August 1964, November 1966; 18.3 miles; 105,900 vehicles just west of the Dan Ryan.

Edens (I-94): December 1951, October 1959; 13.5 miles long; 155,200 vehicles north of East Lake Avenue.

Eisenhower (I-290): December 1954, December 1971; 20 miles long; 163,600 vehicles just west of the Kennedy and Ryan circle interchange.

I-57: December 1963, October 1970; 21.1 miles long; 83,500 vehicles just west of the Dan Ryan.

Kingery (includes parts of I-80/I-94): November 1950, July 1953; 3.26 miles long; 93,800 vehicles west of the Illinois-Indiana border.

I-290 (spur off the Eisenhower): All three sections were completed in December 1971; 10.71 miles; 108,200 vehicles at Woodfield Drive.

Calumet (includes parts of I-94, and Ill. 394): November 1950, December 1962; 11.45 miles; 107,400 at Martin Luther King Drive.

War Road: The army of General Winfield Scott, while in its westward march during the Black Hawk War, followed an Indian Trail leading to Beloit, Wisconsin. The tracks it left behind became a pioneer highway known as Army Trail Road, which still runs through Du Page County.

TOLLWAY

Founded: The State Tollway Commission was established in 1954, and the first toll roads opened in 1958. Illinois toll roads exist only in the six-county Chicago area.

Number of miles: 273.4 miles

Number of employees: about 2,000

Revenue: 1990—$241,078,000

Traffic: About 900,000 vehicles daily.

Toll plaza with the highest daily traffic: Deerfield Plaza on the Tri-State Tollway (I-294/94), which has 107,630 vehicles daily.

Biggest revenue toll plaza: Deerfield, which in 1990 brought in $20,250,594

Most toll booths: Cermak toll plaza on the Tri-State Tollway (I-294) has 23 lanes of manned and automatic booths.

Toll booth operators: Starting pay is $8.60/hour and goes up to $11.75/hour.

Accidents: In 1989, 1,748 people were killed on Illinois streets, or 2.1 deaths per 100 million vehicle miles traveled. That 2.1 rate was the lowest since 1920 (as far back as records are available) and was better than the national rate of 2.2.

EXTREMES

■ The most people killed on Illinois streets in one year was 2,600 in 1941, as of 1989.

■ The fewest people killed on Illinois streets in one year was 728 in 1920, but the record keeping at that time was not what you'd call reliable. In more recent times, the fewest killed came during World War II, when 1,328 were killed in 1943.

■ Western Avenue is the longest street in Chicago at 23.5 miles. The shortest street is Longmeadow, 31.6 feet.

■ O'Hare International Airport handles more than 60 million passengers a year—more than any other airport in the world.

LIST OF TEN WORST INTERSECTIONS FOR ACCIDENTS IN SIX-COUNTY CHICAGO AREA (1989)

Rank	Location	Accident number
1.	Illinois 50 and 127th St., Alsip	134
2.	Illinois 83 and Illinois 64 (North Ave.), Elmhurst	113
3.	Mannheim Rd. and Illinois 19 (Irving Park Rd.), around O'Hare	109
4.	Illinois 53 and Illinois 64 (North Ave.), Lombard/Addison	104
5.	Rand Rd. and Illinois 68 (Dundee Rd.) Palatine	100
6.	Ninety-fifth St. and Stony Island Ave., Chicago	93
7.	Illinois 58 (Golf Rd.) and Illinois 72 (Higgins Rd.), Hoffman Estates	91
8.	US 41 (Lake Shore Dr.) and Balbo Blvd., Chicago	90
9.	Illinois 72 (Higgins Rd.) and Illinois 83 (Busse Rd.), Elk Grove Village	84
10.	Illinois 72 (Higgins Rd.) and I-290 southbound ramps, Schaumburg	81

FAMOUS CHICAGOAN

After being convicted of embezzlement (later pardoned) in Philadelphia, Charles Tyson Yerkes (1837-1905) thought Chicago might be a place to make a buck. He came here in 1882, and soon had control of the Chicago street railway system. While doing such things as building

Early Chicago transit mogul Charles Tyson Yerkes was responsible for the building of the "Loop."

the Downtown Union Loop, known as the "Loop," he mastered the art of bribery and election fixing. He was said to have spent $1 million in bribes in order to get cheap use of city streets. In 1892, he donated the Yerkes Observatory at Lake Geneva, Wisconsin, to the University of Chicago. A womanizer and lover of priceless art, Yerkes was the basis of several Theodore Dreiser novels, including *The Titan* (1914). Eventually he was ostracized socially and politically in Chicago, so he left—with $15 million. He went to London, where he headed a syndicate to build the London subways.

THE SIX-COUNTY COMMUTER SYSTEM

RTA—Regional Transportation Authority
The RTA has jurisdiction over the six-county area. It provides funds to three local transportation operations as a supplement to their fare collections. The three include: the Chicago Transit Authority (CTA), which primarily runs the bus and rapid transit operations within Chicago; Metra, which oversees the commuter railroads; and Pace, which runs the suburban bus systems. State law requires the CTA, Metra and Pace to collectively recover 50 percent of operating costs from commuter fares and other revenues.

Private cars: Since the 1930s or maybe even earlier, private railroad cars have transported an elite crew of North Shore commuters. Two cars transport executives, stockbrokers and lawyers from such stops as Lake Forest and other points north, to and from their offices in downtown Chicago. Two clubs maintain the private cars on the Chicago & North Western Ry. The members travel in old passenger cars, refurbished by the clubs. The two cars are low-level and travel at the head of the train. But, says a Chicago & North Western spokesman, they're "definitely not deluxe." Each club has to assure it will buy sixty-five Metra tickets a month per car, and they also pay from $2,000 to $2,500 a month per car as rental. For this, they get a few bridge tables and their privacy.

CTA—CHICAGO TRANSIT AUTHORITY

Founded: The CTA was created by state legislation and began operating on Oct. 1, 1947.

Number of employees: 13,000.

Chicago Transit Board: The seven-member board consists of four members appointed by the mayor of Chicago (with the approval of the

City Council and the governor) and three appointed by the governor (with the approval of the state Senate and the mayor of Chicago).

Fleet: 2,200 buses; 1,217 rapid transit cars.

Bus stops: 12,900.

Rapid transit stations: 142.

Daily miles traveled: 232,000 by bus; 176,600 by rail.

Miles covered: CTA buses cover 2,142 route miles.

Area served: Chicago and 37 suburbs.

Ridership: 1.3 million trips are made on the buses on a weekday, and 420.6 million trips are taken annually. About 500,000 rail trips are made on a weekday and 147.3 million annually.

Loop: The "Loop" is almost synonymous with downtown Chicago. The definition of it is understood as coming from the boundaries created by the elevated tracks that run for two miles as a "loop" around the heart of Chicago's business district bordered by Lake on the north, Van Buren on the south, Wells on the west, and Wabash on the east. The system was built by transit magnate Charles Yerkes in the 1890s. The first Loop, however, was created for a cable car system on the east side of downtown by C. B. Holmes, president of the Chicago City Rail Way in 1880.

METRA

Founded: The first board meeting of Metra, or more formally the commuter rail service board of the Northeast Illinois Regional Commuter Railroad Company, was on June 8, 1984.

Number of employees: 2,200.

Fleet: 142 diesel and electric locomotives, of which 136 are used for commuter service; 684 diesel-hauled bi-level coaches; 206 self-propelled electric cars. Thirty additional locomotives are under construction, and Metra hopes to acquire 173 wheelchair-accessible cab cars by 1992.

Number of routes and number of miles: About a dozen routes covering 425.8 miles in Illinois and about 75 more miles counting the tracks to Kenosha, Wisconsin and the tracks to South Bend, Indiania.

Ridership: About 140,000 people travel on Metra during a typical rush hour, or 277,000 passenger trips a day.

Busiest single route: Metra/Burlington Northern service from west suburban Aurora to Chicago. It has 51,300 passenger trips a day, or about 26,000 people.

What's in a name: Metra is not a company. It's just a service mark used for marketing the commuter rail services of the Northeast Illinois Regional Commuter Railroad Company.

PACE

Founded: Mid-1984.

Number of employees: 1,300.

Fleet: 700 buses and 145 lift-equipped vehicles.

Ridership: 40.3 million passengers in 1990, which beat the previous record of 38.3 million in 1985.

Busiest route: Route 352 Halsted, which runs from the Dan Ryan rapid transit station at Ninety-fifth Street to Chicago Heights. Its average weekday ridership is 6,000.

THE AIR

CHICAGO MIDWAY AIRPORT

Founded: In 1923, a single cinder runway existed at what would become Midway Airport, located at 5700 S. Cicero. By the end of 1927, five runways were in use. On Dec. 12, 1927, Mayor William Hale Thompson dedicated it as the Chicago Municipal Airport.

Work force: 3,500 people, including airline and other airport jobs.

Number of passengers: In 1990 there were 320,247 arrivals and departures carrying 8,794,256 passengers.

Busiest year (since 1950): In 1959 there were 431,400 arrivals and departures carrying 10,040,353 passengers.

O'HARE INTERNATIONAL AIRPORT

Founded: Formerly a military airport facility named Orchard Place, O'Hare was officially named in 1949. O'Hare was opened to domestic commercial traffic in October 1955.

Size: 7,700 acres.

Work force: 45,000 people work for the airlines and in other airport jobs.

ORD: O'Hare Airport sits on what used to be farmland and the site of an aircraft assembly plant. The airport's first name was Orchard Place—the ORD on the baggage checks is a contraction of Orchard.

Number of passengers: 165,000 travelers pass through O'Hare every day.

Busiest year: In 1990, there were 810,865 arrivals and departures carrying 60,010,234 passengers.

Namesake: O'Hare Airport was named for Medal of Honor recipient Navy Lt. Edward "Butch" O'Hare, whose millionaire father was murdered gangland style in 1939.

Naval Academy graduate O'Hare was the son of Edward J. O'Hare, who was once the president of Sportsman's Park. The father controlled the patents on the electrical rabbits chased by racing dogs, and was a director of the old Hawthorne Kennel Club, which was a dog track until dog racing was outlawed in Illinois.

O'Hare's father was rumored to be a front man for Al Capone, who was believed to own a portion of Hawthorne. Edward J. O'Hare was shot to death in the middle of the day on Nov. 8, 1939, while riding in his car at Ogden and Rockwell. The murderers were never found.

O'Hare's parents were divorced, and he attended Western Military Academy at Alton, Illinois, where his roommate and close friend was Paul Tibbets, who later piloted the Enola Gay, the B-29 bomber that dropped the atomic bomb on Hiroshima on Aug. 6, 1945.

O'Hare was awarded the Medal of Honor for saving the aircraft carrier Lexington. He flew alone between the ship and an advancing formation of nine Japanese bombers. He shot down five and severely damaged a sixth, while the rest fled. President Franklin D. Roosevelt called it "one of the most daring, if not *the* most daring single action in the history of combat aviation."

O'Hare survived that fight but was lost in action Nov. 23, 1943, while flying a Hellcat fighter off the Marshall Islands in the Pacific.

MERRILL C. MEIGS FIELD

Founded: December 1948 at Fifteenth Street and the lakefront.

Number of passengers: In 1990 there were 61,066 arrivals and departures carrying 232,596 passengers.

Busiest year (since 1950): In 1980 there were 87,610 arrivals and departures carrying 468,933 passengers.

THE WATER

ILLINOIS INTERNATIONAL PORT DISTRICT

Founded: June 1955. In 1909 the city planned to have its port activity at the mouth of the Chicago River. But in 1921, the Lake Calumet Harbor Act was passed allowing Chicago to build a deepwater harbor at Lake Calumet. A massive construction project began in the 1950s and was completed in 1958, in time for the 1959 opening of the St. Lawrence Seaway.

Revenue: $3,044,858 in fiscal year 1990—this was the highest annual income in Port District history and only the second time it surpassed the $3 million mark.

Government: Run by a nine-member board of directors—four appointed by the governor and five by the mayor.

Amount of cargo shipped: Steel (936,177 tons) and grain (289,155 tons) dominate shipping, which also includes salt, cement, stone and processed ore. Total shipments for 1989 were 2,161,128 tons, down from 2,479,944 tons in 1988.

Annual number of ships calling at Port District facilities: 175.

Annual number of barges calling at Port District facilities: 813.

CLASSIC QUOTE

Early Chicago transit mogul Charles Tyson Yerkes said his secret of success was "buy old junk, fix it up a little, and unload it upon other fellows."

Sources: *Chicago Sun-Times* and *Chicago Daily News* clips; Chicago Transit Authority; George Krambles, retired executive director of the CTA; Du Page County Guide 1831-1939; Illinois State Tollway Authority; Illinois Department of Transportation; IDOT's Accident Records Section of the Division of Traffic Safety; National Highway Traffic Safety Administration; *Dictionary of American Biography;* Metra; Pace; Illinois International Port District; Chicago Department of Aviation.

MUSEUMS

FIRSTS

■ The Museum of Contemporary Art was the first museum (and only museum as of spring 1991) to be wrapped by Christo (1969), and the first museum to be cut open with a chain saw (by artist Gordon Matta-Clark, 1978, who cut into the brownstone that now houses the annex galleries).

■ The Adler Planetarium, which opened in 1930, was the nation's first planetarium and, for that matter, the first planetarium in the Western Hemisphere. The sky projector was invented in 1923, by a German firm.

EXTREMES

■ With 115,000 members, the Art Institute has the largest regional membership of any art museum in the country.

■ The John G. Shedd Aquarium is the world's largest indoor aquarium. Its Oceanarium also is the world's largest indoor marine mammal habitat.

Big Donors: The Field Museum, the Art Institute, the Shedd Aquarium, the Museum of Science and Industry, and the Adler Planetarium were made possible largely by the donations of department store executives connected with Sears and Marshall Field's.

■ The biggest crowd for an exhibit at the Field Museum was the 1,348,111 people who came to see the Treasures of Tutankhamun from April 15 through Aug. 15, 1977.

THE MUSEUMS

THE MUSEUM OF SCIENCE AND INDUSTRY

Location: Fifty-seventh Street and Lake Shore Drive, Chicago, IL 60637; phone: (312) 684-1414.

Traffic Stops for Sub's Way: The U-505 German submarine that sits next to the Museum of Science and Industry was captured off the coast of Africa on June 4, 1944. The thousand-ton, 252-foot-long sub was eventually towed 3,000 miles from Portsmouth, New Hampshire. A 352-foot channel, 9 feet below Lake Michigan's water line, was dredged east of the the museum for a floating dry dock to help move the sub onto land. The sub arrived here on June 26, 1954, and weeks later, 15,000 people watched it come ashore. Thousands more were on hand to watch it move on steel rollers and rails across Lake Shore Drive. Traffic was stopped at 7 p.m., Friday, September 3, and the sub didn't clear the highway until 4:15 a.m., the next morning.

Founded: 1933, but the building was originally built as the Palace of Fine Arts in 1893 for the World's Columbian Exposition. Sears executive Julius Rosenwald modeled the museum on the Deutsches Museum in Munich, Germany, which he visited in 1911. The MSI opened in time for the 1933 Century of Progress Exposition.

Attendance: 3,790,646 million (1990).

Admission: The museum started charging for admission in June 1991: adults–$5, seniors–$4, children–$2 and under five years old–free.

Exhibits: The museum emphasizes science education. Among some of the popular exhibits are the "Coal Mine," a reproduction of a Southern Illinois coal mine, which has been at the museum since 1933—in 1990, 357,930 visitors went through it; the U-505 submarine; a sixteen-foot-tall walk-through replica of the human heart; one of the world's largest model train displays; the Omnimax Theater five-story-high, seventy-six-foot-wide domed screen; the Apollo 8 spacecraft, the first to circle the moon (on loan from the National Air and Space Museum, Smithsonian Institution, since 1971).

Through the Roof: In 1971, the 9,260-pound Apollo 8 capsule, the first manned spacecraft to orbit the moon, couldn't fit through the doors of the Museum of Science and Industry. So it was lowered into the museum through a fifteen-foot hole chopped in the roof.

The founder: Julius Rosenwald (1862-1932) was born almost across the street from Abe Lincoln's house in Springfield, and was selling house-wares door-to-door when he was ten. By 1895, he owned a small Chicago clothing factory, and one of his customers, Richard Sears, came to him looking for an investor. Rosenwald became part owner of Sears, Roebuck & Co. Sears retired in 1908, and Rosenwald took charge. He also became incredibly wealthy—at one point he was said to be worth $150 million. With that wealth he donated millions toward the building of schools for blacks throughout the South and the building of YMCAs for blacks in 25 cities. He also founded the Museum of Science and Industry, donating about $5 million at the outset and more through his estate. During his life he was said to have given away more than $62 million.

Julius Rosenwald founded the Museum of Science and Industry.

FIELD MUSEUM OF NATURAL HISTORY

Location: Lake Shore Drive at Roosevelt Road, Chicago, IL 60605; phone: (312) 922-9410

Deep Fill: The Field Museum was built on more than thirty feet of land-fill. By 1975, it had settled almost two feet (21 inches), cracking concrete and forcing repairs.

Founded: A state charter was granted on Sept. 16, 1893, six weeks before the World's Columbian Exposition was to end. The point here was to make the "Columbian Museum of Chicago" the place to put the many collections assembled for the exposition. The name was changed to the Field Museum of Natural History after Marshall Field was persuaded to donate $1 million. The museum opened to the public on June 2, 1894, in its original building in Jackson Park. The present building was finished in June 1920, and the museum moved to this site in 1921.

Attendance: 1,465,938 (1990)

Admission: Adults–$3, seniors and children–$2, maximum for a family is $10, Thursday is free.

Building: The museum orignally was housed in what is now the Museum of Science and Industry building in Jackson Park. Marshall Field, a major benefactor, liked the neoclassical style of the Fine Arts Building and wanted something similar for a new building. A new place was needed, since the old one literally was falling apart—mortar was falling on visitors and the building was becoming unsafe and overcrowded. Daniel Burnham signed the original plans for the building in 1906, but construction didn't begin until 1915. It cost more than $7 million and was opened to the public in 1921. Burnham, who virtually worshipped cleanliness and order, liked a white stone look so dirt would show up easily and the staff would be forced to keep things clean.

Exhibits: Called a "three-tier exhibit plan," the museum has three types of exhibits: 1. Introductory Exhibits (designed for all ages, these present information in easy to understand ways and include exhibits such as Sizes, which shows the broad range of sizes of living things). 2. Major Thematic Exhibits (comprehensive looks at subjects like geology, biology and cultures, such as Inside Ancient Egypt and Traveling the Pacific). 3. Resource Centers (visitors can get further details or answer questions raised by the major thematic exhibits, by using the quiet areas with books, videotapes, audiotapes, maps, photographs and other materials, with educators and volunteers helping guide the curious).

Lost in the Basement: In 1962, a priceless collection of Greek, Roman and Etruscan treasures was found in the basement of the Field Museum of Natural History. It had been there, untouched, since 1901. The discovery of the dusty chests containing sculptures, jewelry and important writings led the discoverer, a thirty-two-year-old scientist, to quote a former professor: "We do not need more excavations. We need to excavate the storerooms of museums."

Who is Field? Marshall Field (1834-1906) founded Marshall Field & Company. Field came from Massachusetts to Chicago in 1856, and worked as a clerk in a dry goods firm. Field gave $1 million to help establish a museum of natural history and bequeathed millions more for the present building. Other members of Field's family contributed time and money to the museum. One of them, Stanley Field, was museum president and chairman of the board for more than fifty years.

> **The Name Game:** From 1903 until 1943, the Field Museum of Natural History was called just that. Then it was called the Chicago Natural History Museum until 1966, when it was once again called the Field Museum.

ADLER PLANETARIUM

Location: 1300 S. Lake Shore Drive, Chicago, IL 60605; phone: (312) 322-0300.

Founded: Opened to the public in May 1930.

Attendance: 654,466 (1990)

Admission: Adults–$3, children (6-17)–$1.50, Sky Shows are limited to adults and children age 6 and over (those under 6 can go with their family to the Children's Sky Show for $1.50 per person).

Exhibits: The big deal here is the Sky Show. Visitors start with a multi-media presentation in the 430-seat Kroc Universe Theater. After the presentation, the projection screen and wall panel rise to reveal a 77-foot long escalator where a ride to the Sky Show includes music and special effects, including blinking points of light created by 25,000 feet of optic cable. Then it's into the 68-foot Sky Theater dome, which uses a planetarium projector supported by 150 special effects projectors, a helium/neon and argon laser projector and a video projection system. Every year four Sky Shows and Children's Sky Shows are created by some six astronomers, two artists and four technicians. There are also three floors of exhibits, including the "Hall of Telescopes," which houses telescopes dating back to Galileo.

Who is Max Adler? Adler (1866-1952) was a vice president and director of Sears, Roebuck & Co. who gave $1 million toward the building of the planetarium. His wife was the sister of Julius Rosenwald, the Sears executive who helped found the Museum of Science and Industry. In the 1890s, Adler gave up a career as a concert violinist—he studied at the Royal Academy in Berlin—and went to work for Sears. After his retirement, thirty years later, he continued to play, using one of his two Stradivarius violins.

JOHN G. SHEDD AQUARIUM

Location: 1200 S. Lake Shore Drive, Chicago, IL 60605; phone: (312) 939-2438.

Founded: The Aquarium opened to the public in 1929 without any fish in the tanks. It officially opened May 30, 1930. It cost $3.25 million. The recently added Oceanarium cost $45 million.

Attendance: 1 million annually, but with the addition of the Oceanarium, attendance is expected to grow to 1.5 million. The first year the aquarium opened, more than 4 million people visited.

Admission: Admission to both the Oceanarium and the aquarium is $7 for adults and $5 for children. If you just visit the aquarium: Adults–$3, children–$2.

Size: The original building has 225,000 square feet. The Oceanarium adds 170,000 square feet.

Admission: Admission to both the Oceanarium and the aquarium is $7 for adults and $5 for children. If you just visit the aquarium: Adults–$3, children–$2. You cannot buy admission just to the oceanarium. From March through October the aquarium is open from 9 a.m. to 5 p.m.; November through February from 10 a.m. to 5 p.m. The Oceanarium's hours are 9 a.m. to 6 p.m. year round. Closed Christmas and New Year's Day.

Size: The original building has 225,000 square feet. The Oceanarium adds 170,000 square feet.

Exhibits: There are 203 exhibit tanks of fresh or salt water maintained at three different temperatures—tropical, temperate and cold—and 75 miles of pipe. The largest tank is the Oceanarium's 2 million gallon Whale Harbor tank. Excluding the Oceanarium, the largest tank is the Coral Reef exhibit tank, which holds 90,000 gallons. There are 120 reserve tanks and reservoirs holding 2 million gallons. The Oceanarium holds 3 million gallons of water, which is completely filtered every one and a half hours.

Specimens: 6,000 specimens represent more than 600 species of fish, invertebrates, reptiles, amphibians and mammals.

Who's John G. Shedd? John Graves Shedd (1850-1926) went from growing up in a New Hamsphire farmhouse to living in a twenty-four-room Gothic mansion at 4515 S. Drexel as a rising executive of Marshall Field & Company. He became president when Marshall Field died in 1906, and held that position until 1922. Shedd gave $3 million to the creation of the Shedd Aquarium, most of it after his death. He left an estate of close to $20 million.

Extremes: The Beluga whales are the largest creatures at the Shedd Aquarium. They were born in the Arctic Ocean or in Hudson Bay. Each weighs about 980 pounds and is 9 to 10 feet long.

Boxcar Water: It took 160 railroad cars to bring the first million gallons of salt water to the Shedd Aquarium in 1930. The water came from Key West, Florida. It cost $50,000 to get it here.

ART INSTITUTE OF CHICAGO

Location: Michigan Avenue at Adams Street, Chicago, IL 60603; phone: (312) 443-3600.

Founded: May 24, 1879, as the Chicago Academy of Fine Arts. Named the Art Institute of Chicago on Dec. 23, 1882.

Attendance: 1,410,951 people for fiscal year 1989.

Admission: Suggested donation adults–$6, seniors or children–$3 (must give something), servicemen free. Tuesday is free.

Collection: More than 300,000 works of art; European Painting—950 works from Middle Ages to 1900 with a strength in 19th century French painting; 20th century Painting and Sculpture—1,500 paintings and sculptures representing the major movements in Europe and America from 1900 to present; American Arts—7,500 objects ranging from decorative arts to paintings and sculpture from the Colonial period through 1900; European Decorative Arts and Sculpture and Classical Art—30,000 objects including glass, silver, ceramics, miniature rooms and paperweights; 6,000 classical objects ranging from Greek and Roman stone sculpture to Egyptian scarabs and Syrian mosaics; Textiles—14,000 textiles and 66,000 sample swatches from 100 A.D. to the present representing many countries, with a strength in 16th century and 17th century English needlework; Prints and Drawings—8,500 drawings and 60,000 prints ranging from French 19th century prints and 18th and 19th century drawings to works on paper by Durer, Rembrandt and Goya; Architecture—archive of 80,000 drawings concentrating on Chicago architects and Chicago buildings; it includes architectural models and the reconstruction of the Adler and Sullivan trading room from the old Chicago Stock Exchange (1893-94); Photography—first exhibition was in 1900, but a collection was not begun until Georgia O'Keefe donated a large part of the Alfred Stieglitz collection in 1949; Asian Art—35,000 objects, including objects of archaeological and artistic significance; Africa, Oceania, and the Americas—2,000 objects, with strength in ceramics from major ancient civilizations of Southwest, Meso-America, and Andean South America.

LIST OF TEN MOST POPULAR ART INSTITUTE EXHIBITIONS BY ATTENDANCE

"The Vatican Collection," 1983	685,544
"Pompeii A.D. 79," 1978	489,118
"Monet in the '90s," 1990	456,217
"The Art of Paul Gauguin," 1988	374,477
"A Day in the Country (Impressionists)," 1985	369,766
"Paintings by Renoir," 1973	352,987
"The Search for Alexander (the Great)," 1981	319,892
"Georgia O'Keefe," 1988	314,398
"Toulouse-Lautrec: Paintings," 1979	282,112
"John Singer Sargent," 1987	217,084

The Big Collection: The collection of an eccentric Chicago candy manufacturer who maintained a museum above his Loop candy store in the late 1800s became the biggest single source of artifacts for the Chicago Historical Society's collection. In 1889, Charles Frederick Gunther (1837-1920), who was also an alderman and an unsuccessful candidate for governor, bought Richmond, Virginia's, Libby Prison and rebuilt it on South Wabash Avenue. Among his artifacts was Lincoln's deathbed. Gunther paid $1,500 for it and other pieces from the room in which the sixteenth president died. The Historical Society bought the Gunther collection in 1920 for $150,000. But some of the pieces were not kept. Fragments of bones, said to have belonged to the 12 apostles, and a collection of shoes, including the patent leather ones worn by President McKinley the day he was assassinated, were auctioned off.

THE CHICAGO HISTORICAL SOCIETY

Location: 1601 N. Clark, Chicago, IL 60614; phone: (312) 642-4600.

Founded: 1856, it acts as the historian of Chicago.

Attendance: 225,000 a year (1990).

Admission: Suggested admission (voluntary) adults–$3; seniors and students between 17 and 22 with school ID–$2; children (6-17) and members–$1 and children under 6 are free. Mondays free.

Collection: 20 million objects, images and documents. The society has an internationally recognized costume collection; nearly 1 million photographs; and oddities and rarities like Abraham Lincoln's deathbed, the wooden gun used by John Dillinger to escape from Lake

County Jail, the Pioneer (Chicago's first locomotive) and the 1900 evening gown of Mrs. Potter Palmer, a queen of Chicago society.

Exhibits: Permanent exhibits include Chicago Dioramas; Chicago History Galleries; Fort Dearborn Exhibit; Illinois Pioneer Life Gallery; We the People: Creating a New Nation, 1765-1820.

The Oldest: Founded in 1856, the Chicago Historical Society is the city's oldest cultural institution.

THE CHICAGO ACADEMY OF SCIENCES

Location: 2001 N. Clark, Chicago, IL 60614; phone: (312) 871-2668.

Founded: 1857, by Dr. Edmund Andrews and natural history buffs, including the Academy's first director, Robert Kennicott (1835-1866). Andrews also founded the Chicago Medical College.

Attendance: 91,726 actually went through the museum in 1990. But a total of 655,546 people participated in museum programs, including the Academy's Dinamation exhibits of automated prehistoric creatures.

Admission: adults–$1, seniors and children (6-17)–50 cents. Mondays are free and members get in free—there are about 1,800 members.

Exhibits: The big draw is the "Dino-Rama" exhibit with gargantuan robotic dinosaurs; Children's Gallery designed for touching and exploring; life-size dioramas of such scenes as Chicago's wilderness in the early 1900s and Great Lakes wilderness areas—the Academy houses more than 326,000 specimens of flora and fauna gathered in the eighteen century throughout the Great Lakes (many of the specimens are now extinct or endangered); and many walk-through exhibits such as a prehistoric coal forest or an Illinois cave.

Yukon Death: Robert Kennicott, director and curator of the Chicago Academy of Sciences, was appointed head naturalist for an expedition surveying a telegraph route through Alaska to Europe. Kennicott, who had a heart condition, died in 1866, at the age of thirty, along the banks of the Yukon River during the expedition. His compass and some drawings were lying next to him. Some say he had been weakened by saving a Russian explorer from drowning. William Stimpson, a leading authority in marine invertebrates, took over at the academy. But the Chicago Fire of 1871 destroyed the academy and all it collections. It also destroyed two decades worth of Stimpson's work—his manuscripts and collections. In six months, Stimpson too was dead.

The Philanthropist: Matthew Laflin (1803-1897) came to Chicago in 1837 and bought 140 acres for $300. For Laflin, that was just the beginning. He made millions in real estate. In 1892, Laflin donated $75,000 to construct a new museum building for the Chicago Academy of Sciences.

ORIENTAL INSTITUTE MUSEUM

Location: 1155 E. Fifty-eighth Street, Chicago, IL 60637; phone: (312) 702-9521.

Founded: 1919, by James Henry Breasted (1865-1935), professor of Egyptology at the University of Chicago, with financial assistance from John D. Rockefeller, Jr.

Admission: Free.

Galleries: Five galleries devoted to Egypt, Assyria, Mesopotamia, Persia, and Palestine.

Collection: 70,000 officially registered objects. Some of the more popular items include a forty-ton Assyrian sculpture of light-colored stone depicting a man's face, bull's body and eagle's wings; Egyptian mummies; a seventeen-foot-tall statue of King Tut (1325 B.C.).

MUSEUM OF CONTEMPORARY ART

Location: 237 East Ontario St., Chicago, IL 60611; phone (312) 280-5161.

Founded: 1967. In the spring of 1995, the musuem is scheduled to move to 234 E. Chicago Ave.

Christo wrapped the Museum of Contemporary Art in 1969.

Admission: Adults–$4, seniors and students–$2.

Collection: The only Chicago museum dedicated solely to contemporary art. It organized the first major museum shows for Claes Oldenberg, Christo and Jeff Koons among others.

THE DUSABLE MUSEUM OF AFRICAN AMERICAN HISTORY:

Location: 740 E. Fifty-sixth Place, Chicago, IL; phone (312) 947-0600.

Founded: Chartered in February 1961, and opened on Oct. 21, 1961. Margaret Burroughs, an art teacher at DuSable High School and an activist involved with the arts and history, founded the museum. It was established to "preserve and interpret" African American history.

Attendance: The museum's attendance started with 2,500 visitors and is up to 82,000 a year.

Admission: Adults–$2, children (14-18)–$1, children under 13–50 cents.

Building: Housed in a former Chicago Park District administration building in Washington Park.

Collection: Has 10,000 African-American pieces ranging from art work to historical memorabilia.

Black History: Called the "Father of Negro History," Dr. Carter G. Woodson (1875-1950), a University of Chicago graduate with a Harvard doctorate, helped launch a black history movement in 1915 when he convened a conference in Chicago that resulted in the establishment of the Association for the Study of Negro Life and History.

CLASSIC QUOTE

William Rosenwald, son of Julius Rosenwald, quoted his father as once saying, "Shall we devote the few precious days of our existence only to buying and selling...only to shuffling our feet in the dance-....Surely there is something finer and better, something that dignifies it and stamps it with a touch of the divine. It is unselfish effort, helpfulness to others that enobles lives and not because of what it does for others but more because of what it does for ourselves."

Sources: *Chicago Sun-Times* and *Daily News*; all the museums listed above; Low & Clift Encyclopedia of Black America.

PARKS, ZOOS AND FOREST PRESERVES

FIRST

Chicago Park: Dearborn Park, which no longer exists, is considered Chicago's first park. It was established in 1839 on a portion of what had been Fort Dearborn, at Wacker and Michigan. The land was reluctantly donated to the city by the United States government. Most other parks established before 1869—such as Union and Washington Square parks—were donated piecemeal to the city by real estate developers who figured a nice park would improve property values.

EXTREME

■ Lincoln Park Zoo is the oldest public zoo in America, founded in 1868 with a gift of a pair of swans from New York's Central Park.

FAMOUS CHICAGOAN

Bushman: He was more than a gorilla. He was a cult figure. Bushman, a lowlands gorilla from the French Cameroons, was king of Lincoln Park Zoo almost from the day he arrived, on Aug. 15, 1930, to the day he died, New Year's Day, 1951. When Knute Rockne, the legendary Notre Dame football coach, heard Bushman liked to play football, he sent him an autographed ball. When a member of France's prestigious Alexander Dumas Gourmand Club saw Bushman devour twenty-two pounds of food in one setting, he instantly made Bushman a member. "And then to see him insist on guavas for dessert, certainly the choice of a gourmet, we knew he qualified," the Frenchman said. The Lincoln Park monkey house today is named Bushman Hall. And Bushman, stuffed for good, is on permanent display at the Field Museum.

CHICAGO CONTRIBUTION

Sixteen-inch softball: Outside Chicago, almost nobody plays it. Inside Chicago, it's king. By one account, 16-inch softball evolved from an indoor version of baseball; by another, it was invented at Chicago's Farragut Boat Club in 1887 when a Yale man tossed a bound-up boxing glove at a Harvard man and the Harvard man whacked it with a broomstick. The final score was 43-42, although historians failed to note which team won. In 1933, the first national tournament was held, in conjunction with Chicago's Century of Progress world's fair, before 70,000 fans in Soldier Field. One year later, Harry Hannin formed the Windy City Softball League, making bare-handed 16-inch softball—the ball has a fat 16-inch circumference—a Chicago institution. Throughout the rest of the country, and even in some suburbs, 12-inch softball, in which players wear fielder's gloves, is the norm.

CHICAGO PARK DISTRICT

Founded in 1934, from the consolidation of 22 smaller park commissions. Number of parks: 562. Total acreage: 6,785.9. Baseball and softball diamonds: 828. Basketball backboards: 1,164. Bathing beaches: 32. Beach houses: 13. Bicycle paths: 19. Bowling greens: 4. Bridle paths: 4. Croquet courts: 1. Football/soccer fields: 222. Golf courses: 6. Gymnasiums: 183. Handball courts: 30. Boat docks, moorings, slips and storage spaces: 7,005. Horseshoe pits: 229. Lagoons: 15. Sandboxes: 315. Senior citizen centers: 82. Shuffleboard courts: 77. Swimming pools: 58. Tennis courts: 708. Oval running tracks: 25. Volleyball courts: 355.

Chicago is celebrated for its twenty-two miles of scenic lakefront and city parks, many of them linked by tree-lined boulevards. They make up Chicago's "Emerald Necklace," justify the city slogan "Urbs In Horto"—City in a Garden—and make it obvious that Chicago is not Cleveland. It happened, more or less, according to plan. In the two decades after the Great Chicago Fire of 1871, most of Chicago's major parks were developed and maintained by visionary commissioners of three early park districts—the South Park Commission, the West Park Commission and the Lincoln Park Commission. They plotted out the big parks and twenty-eight miles of linking boulevards—from Garfield on the south to Diversey on the north—and hired exceptional men to design them. The three great landscape architects in Chicago history were Frederick Law Olmsted, William LeBaron Jenney and Jens Jensen. Led by Jensen, they developed a Prairie School of Landscape.

Lincoln Park: Acreage: 1,200. Originally called Cemetery Park, Lincoln Park was a chunk of sand dunes and swamps adjacent to a city cemetery at Clark Street and the lakefront. In 1885, it was renamed in honor of the assassinated president. From Diversey Avenue north to Ardmore, Lincoln Park is entirely manmade, consisting of landfill. Between North Avenue and Diversey Avenue, it is built on the only remaining natural lakeshore land in Chicago.

Grant Park: Acreage: 319. On the 1836 subdivision plat for the town of Chicago, a small plot of muddy shoreland was designated as "public ground, forever to remain vacant of building." Lake Park, as it was called beginning in 1844, was expanded for the first time in the days after the Chicago Fire of 1871, when tons of debris from the fire were dumped there between a railroad track and an offshore breakwater. Over the years, the park would be expanded regularly, always with landfill. At the turn of the century, it was renamed Grant Park in honor of Gen. Ulysses S. Grant. Today it is frequently called Chicago's "front yard," free and clear of buildings thanks to court battles waged by A. Montgomery Ward, the mail-order pioneer, and the landscaping plans of architect Daniel Burnham.

Jackson Park: Acreage: 542. At Sixty-third Street and Stony Island Avenue. Founded 1869. Named Jackson Park, in honor of the president, in 1881. Laid out by Olmsted, designer of suburban Riverside and New York's Central Park, it remained undeveloped until chosen to be the site of the Columbian Exposition of 1893. Olmsted turned the sand dunes and marshes into lagoons and wooded islands for the fair. According to Olmsted's original plan, a canal was to run the entire length of Midway Plaisance between Jackson and Washington parks, but it was never built.

Humboldt Park: Acreage: 206. 1400 N. Sacramento. Opened 1871. Named for the German naturalist and scientist, Baron Alexander von Humboldt. The park's design was begun by Jenney and completed by Jensen, a Danish-American landscape architect who served as superintendent of the West Park Commission in 1894.

Garfield Park: Acreage: 184. 100 N. Central Park Ave. Opened 1874. Originally called Central Park—hence Central Park Avenue—it was renamed for President James A. Garfield a few days after he was assassinated in 1881. The park was designed by Jenney with one side having a simple rural manner, while the other half has a formal terrace and a Byzantine-style conservatory.

Douglas Park: Acreage: 174. Fourteenth Street and Albany Avenue. Opened 1878. Named for U.S. Sen. Stephen A. Douglas. It was designed by Jenney, who included a man-made lake, with a music stand on an island, and a greenhouse.

Columbus Park: Acreage: 134. 500 S. Central Ave. Opened 1922. Designed between 1913 and 1922, it is the masterpiece of Jensen's native American landscape style. Like the architect Frank Lloyd Wright, Jensen tried to use local forms and materials and tried to create a park that looked as much as possible like the prairies and forests of the Midwest. In Columbus Park, he wrote, "The playgrounds represent a natural meadow, with pools and woodlands bringing to the city child a bit of Illinois that otherwise would remain hidden."

Washington Park: Acreage: 366. 5531 S. King Dr. Opened 1874. Washington Park was designed by Olmsted at the same time he designed Jackson Park. His original plans for both parks were destroyed in the Chicago Fire of 1871, but the work was completed—on a more limited scale.

Alice's White Deer: White deer wander near Argonne National Laboratories in Du Page County, descendants of white deer brought to the area in the 1930s by Erwin Freund, a Chicago businessman who owned a patent on a sausage casing. Freund was so fascinated by Lewis Carroll's "Alice in Wonderland" stories that he named his estate Tulgey Woods, after a forest mentioned in the stories. The estate later was absorbed by Argonne.

COUNTY FOREST PRESERVES AND PARKS

Cook County Forest Preserve: Acreage: 67,152 (including 3,630 in Chicago); founded 1915. The district maintains 137 major woods (including 2,200 picnic groves), 36 lakes and ponds, 5 nature centers, 8 bicycle trails (67.9 miles), 187 miles of horseriding trails, 124 baseball fields, 14 golf courses and driving ranges, 7 boat ramps, 5 toboggan slides, 3 swimming pools, the Brookfield Zoo, the Chicago Botanic Garden and the Chicago Portage National Historic Site. In an average summer, more than 1.4 million people visit the nature centers, and more than 1.5 million picnic in the groves. The Cook County forest preserves are renowned for its residential bird life, especially in the Palos area. More than 290 species of birds have been reported in the preserves.

Birthing the A-Bomb: The birthplace of the atomic bomb is in Cook County's forest preserves near Palos Hills. The World War II Manhattan Project, which paved the way for development of the atomic bomb, was transplanted from the University of Chicago to the forest preserve, near Archer Avenue and 107th Street, after the world's first nuclear chain reaction was induced at the university. Radioactive remains from testing are buried there, in Red Gate Woods, on a 200-acre site. The site today features two markers. One proclaims that "the world's first nuclear reactor" was rebuilt and buried on the site. The second warns, "Caution, do not dig. Buried in this area is radioactive material."

Du Page County Forest Preserve: Acreage: 23,000; founded 1915. The district maintains 43 preserves, including 60 miles of rivers and streams, 600 acres of lake water, and 120 miles of trails.

The largest preserve is Waterfall Glen (2,470 acres), which surrounds Argonne National Laboratory. The county's only artesian well is located in Waterfall Glen, as well as the county's "leaning forest"— a stand of pine trees that have been growing sideways ever since they were blown over but not killed by a tornado in 1976. Other special features are the Danada Equestrian Center in Wheaton, which has a nineteen-room estate house and a twenty-three-stall Kentucky Derby-style stable, and the restored Old Graue Mill at Fullersburg Woods, where milling demonstrations are offered.

Waterfall Glen: Du Page County's largest nature preserve, it was named for an early president of the forest preserve district, Seymour "Bud" Waterfall—and not for its manmade waterfall.

Lake County Forest Preserve: Acreage: 18,000; founded 1958. The district maintains 13 woods, groves and river trails, 10 major lakes, 49 miles of trails, 2 golf courses, and the Lake County Museum (with 16,000 historical artifacts) in the Lakewood Forest Preserve near Wauconda.

Kane County Forest Preserve: Acreage: 3,421; founded 1925. The district maintains 25 preserves, plus 21 acres of Fox River shoreline and a 6.2-mile Fox River pathway. The largest is the Burnidge preserve (484 acres) on Coombs Road west of Randall Road. Among the district's highlights is the Nelson Lake Marsh Nature Preserve (201 acres), a 10,000-year-old virgin marsh near Batavia, and the Fabyan Forest Preserve (245 acres), near Illinois 25 and 31, which features a sixty-eight-foot turn-of-the-century Dutch windmill pictured in 1980 on a U.S. postage stamp.

The Early Moose Gets the Permit: Jim "Moose" Murphy, of Chicago Ridge, is the king of picnic permits in the Chicago area. Every New Year's Day from 1983 to 1991, Murphy has camped out in the County Building beginning at 5:30 a.m. or so to buy the first forest preserve picnic permit of the year. His survival kit usually includes a television set, a lawn chair and a slow cooker, sometimes filled with a venison rump roast.

McHenry County Conservation District: Acreage: 6,919; founded 1970; Visitors—488,000 in 1990. The district maintains 28 parks, woods and wetland areas, of which 13 are open to the public. The largest is Glacial Park (2,540 acres), south of Richmond at Harts Road and Illinois 31. A boardwalk there allows visitors an up-close view of an ancient bog.

Will County Forest Preserve: 15 woods and nature preserves, 2 educational facilities—the Plum Creek Nature Center in the Goodenow Grove Forest Preserve near Crete and Isle a la Cache Museum, located on an 80-acre island, in Romeoville. Lake Renwick is called the largest protected heron rookery in Illinois, with more than 250 breeding pairs.

Morton Arboretum: 1,500 acres; founded 1922 by Joy Morton, founder of the Morton Salt Company. The arboretum's mission is to teach the public about ornamental trees, shrubs and vines. It has 500 acres of native woodlands, 100 acres of wetlands and 75 acres of restored savanna and meadows—more than 45,000 plants in all. Among the more popular attractions are 100 formal hedges, a rose garden, a wildflower garden, and a garden of fragrance flowers. The arboretum is located along the East-West Tollway near Lisle in Du Page County.

Chicago Botanic Garden: 300 acres, 20 separate gardens, more than 800,000 trees, shrubs and flowers, 10 greenhouses. The garden, opened in 1972, is managed by the Chicago Horticultural Society and is funded 75 percent by the Cook County Forest Preserve District. It is located in unincorporated Cook County on Lake-Cook Road, a half mile east of the Edens Expressway.

The idea of a Botanic Garden in Chicago was conceived as early as 1853, when John Wright and Dr. John Kennicott, editors of an early horticultural journal, *Prairie Farmer,* recommended that Chicago acquire 300 acres on the outskirts of town for parks and a garden. In 1963, the county and the horticultural society finally established the site. The garden was designed by landscape architect John O. Simonds, using as his models the garden islands of Suchow and Yuan Ming Yuan near Beijing.

Lincoln Park Zoo: 35 acres, 1,900 animals, 29 endangered species, 4 million annual visitors—more than any other zoo in the United States—and one of the last free zoos in the country. At 2200 N. Cannon Dr., the zoo is owned by the Chicago Park District. *Biggest animal:* Suti, the African elephant, 6,740 pounds—and growing. "Suti" is short for *Sun-Times,* which sponsored a contest to name her. *Biggest bird:* the Cinereous Vulture, with a 9-foot wingspan. *Smallest animal:* the Poison Dart Frog, about the size of a dime, in the Reptile House.

Lincoln Park zoo boasts America's largest polar bear pool—266,000 gallons, and America's largest captive lowland gorilla collection, with thirty-two born since 1970. In 1990, the zoo achieved a significant world's "first" when it sent a female Asian elephant, Bozie, to Dickerson Park Zoo in Springfield, Missouri, to breed, and then brought her back to Chicago to give birth. It was considered a major breakthrough for captive breeding when baby Shanti was born in October 1990.

The King of Lincoln Park Zoo: Bushman plays with his new toy, a tire from Adolf Hitler's car.

FIVE BIGGEST STARS OF LINCOLN PARK ZOO

1. Shanti, the 840-pound baby elephant.

2. Koundu, a male silverback gorilla, who weighs close to 500 pounds. Hams it up in the old Bushman tradition.

3. Dinkum and Cobber, two female koalas; and R.J., a male koala.

4. Denise and Erika, Bengal tigers.

5. Thor and Chuchki, polar bears.

Howling: When Chicago's air-raid sirens sound at 10:30 a.m., on Tuesdays, the wolves at Lincoln Park Zoo howl.

Brookfield Zoo: 204 acres, 70 buildings, 2,300 animals, 1.9 million annual visitors. Owned by the Cook County Forest Preserve District, the zoo, near First Avenue and Thirty-first Street in the western suburbs, opened on June 30, 1934. *Largest animal*—Affie the elephant, whose trunk has more than 40,000 muscles and tendons. *Biggest bird*—Pat the Ostrich, weighing almost 300 pounds. *Smallest animal*—a Poison Arrow Frog, about the size of dime. *Most popular exhibit*—Seven Seas Panorama, where 10,000 visitors daily view the dolphin show.

Brookfield Zoo was started after Edith Rockefeller McCormick donated 83.13 acres of undeveloped land to the Cook County Forest Preserve District for use as a zoological park. The zoo's first president was John T. McCutcheon, cartoonist for the *Chicago Tribune*. Its most celebrated acquisition was Su-lin, a giant panda from China purchased for $8,750 in April 1936. On Sunday, Aug. 22, 1936, when Su-lin was first put on exhibit, the zoo was packed with 53,524 visitors—the largest attendance in its history, except for the 58,304 on opening day.

FIVE BIGGEST STARS OF BROOKFIELD ZOO

1. Basilla and Bulka; walruses

2. Nemo, Stormy, Windy and Tapeko; dolphins

3. Zhivago, the Siberian tiger

4. Inka, Dinka and Doo; Kodiak bears

5. Cookie the Cockatoo (at age 58, the zoo's oldest resident)

Animal Stage Names: Popular zoo animals, like Hollywood stars seeking privacy, sometimes go by stage names. The animal's public name is the stage name—the one called out by the public so often that the animal ignores it. The animal's real name—the one to which it will respond—is known only to its keepers.

FIVE OUTSTANDING PLAYGROUNDS

1. **Pirates' Cove,** Leicaster and Biesterfield roads in Elk Grove Village, features a wooden replica of a buccaneer's frigate, with portholes, a dungeon, twin twenty-five-foot masts and cannons.

Speakers pipe in the sloshing sounds of a boat at sea. Another treat is the jungle cruise, in which children in small boats wind their ways through tunnels of "jungle," complete with foliage and mechanized animals.

2. **Bynum Adventure Playground,** 600 E. Fifty-ninth St., Chicago, offers kids a large six-track undulating slide, a high observation tower with a thatched roof, and a teepee-shaped net for children to scale. Bynum, one of the Chicago Park District's most popular attractions, sits beside a pretty lagoon.

3. **Sunset Park,** 1801 Sunset Rd., Highland Park, is exceptional because of its setting—a towering and beautiful woods. It's also got some great play stuff for children—a Cinderella's coach, lots of climbing equipment and more.

4. **Larry M. Fink Park,** 1377 Deer Creek Pkwy., Highland Park, named for a victim of the 1979 DC-10 crash at O'Hare, offers a circular track for tricycles, complete with stop signs and railroad crossing signs; plus a redwood tree house.

5. **Pioneer Village,** on the northwest corner of Merchants' Park, at 18350 Harwood Ave., Homewood, offers a wood-frame fort, a split-rail fence, a covered wagon made of metal piping, three brightly colored teepees and eight-foot-high metal climbing trees.

CLASSIC QUOTE

In James T. Farrell's *Studs Lonigan* trilogy, Studs is sitting one day in Chicago's Washington Park, daydreaming. He "listened to the sounds of the park, and it seemed as if they were all, somehow, part of himself."

Sources: Illinois Department of Conservation; Homewood Park District; Erma Tranter, Friends of the Park; John Lynch and Bob Willoughby, Chicago Park District's Planning Department; Ron Losew, Cook County Forest Preserves; Sandy Rodman, Du Page County Forest Preserve District; Andy Kimmel, Lake County Forest Preserve District; Carol Liefer, Lincoln Park Zoo; Linda Rucins, Brookfield Zoo; Stan Zoller, Chicago Botanic Garden; Joe Larkin, Morton Arboretum.

THE PEOPLE

CHICAGO'S FIRST SETTLER

Jean Baptiste Point Du Sable (1745-1818), a black man of Haitian and French descent, who came to Chicago around 1780 as a fur trader and built his house on the north bank of the Chicago River, just east of what is now Michigan Avenue. He lived there, trading with the Indians, until 1796. Du Sable and his wife Catherine, who was a Potawatomi, and their children left Chicago for Peoria. They later moved to St. Charles, Missouri, where Du Sable died at the home of his daughter.

SOME OF THE THINGS WE DO THE MOST

Adults in the Chicago area are 184 percent more likely to eat liver sausage and 107 percent more likely to eat canned hams than adults in the country's other major cities. They're 28 percent more likely to smoke cigars, 38 percent more likely to buy cat treats and dog biscuits and 148 percent more likely to go to the horse races. And they're 112 percent more likely to have used a home decorating service, 71 percent more likely to own roller skates, 64 percent more likely to have bought golf clubs and 63 percent more likely to have bought a bowling ball in the last twelve months. They're also 32 percent more likely to own a luxury car, 177 percent more likely to own a snowblower and 160 percent more likely to have bought ceramic wall tile in the last year.

A CENTURY OF POPULATION INFORMATION BY COUNTY

Year	Cook	Du Page	Kane	Lake	McHenry	Will
1890	1,191,922	22,551	65,061	24,235	26,114	62,007
1900	1,838,735	28,106	78,792	34,504	29,759	74,764
1910	2,405,233	33,432	91,862	55,058	32,509	84,371
1920	3,053,017	42,120	99,499	74,285	33,164	92,911
1930	3,982,123	91,998	25,327	104,387	35,079	110,732

Year	Cook	Du Page	Kane	Lake	McHenry	Will
1940	4,063,342	103,480	130,206	121,094	37,311	114,210
1950	4,508,792	154,599	150,388	179,097	50,656	134,336
1960	5,129,725	313,459	208,246	293,656	84,310	91,617
1970	5,493,766	487,966	251,005	382,638	111,555	247,825
1980	5,253,655	658,835	278,405	440,372	147,897	324,460
1990	5,105,067	781,666	317,471	516,418	183,241	357,313

COUNTIES

Cook

	1980	Percent	1990	Percent	% Change
Total Population	5,253,190		5,105,067		− 2.8
Black	1,346,464	25.6	1,317,147	25.8	− 2.2
Hispanic	499,319	9.5	694,194	13.6	+ 39.0
Asian, Pacific Islander	111,594	2.1	188,565	3.7	+ 69.0
White, Other	3,795,132	72.2	3,599,355	70.5	− 5.2
Median Home Value			$102,100		

Du Page

	1980	Percent	1990	Percent	% Change
Total Population	658,177		781,666		+ 18.8
Black	7,809	1.2	15,462	2.0	+ 98.0
Hispanic	17,293	2.6	34,567	4.4	+ 99.9
Asian, Pacific Islander	18,665	2.8	39,634	5.1	+ 112.3
White, Other	631,703	96.0	726,570	93.0	+ 15.0
Median Home Value			$137,100		

Kane

	1980	Percent	1990	Percent	% Change
Total Population	278,405		317,471		+ 14.0
Black	13,724	4.9	19,006	6.0	+ 38.5
Hispanic	26,118	9.4	43,535	13.7	+ 66.7
Asian, Pacific Islander	1,694	.6	4,474	1.4	+ 164.1
White, Other	262,987	94.5	293,991	92.6	+ 11.8
Median Home Value			$102,500		

Lake

	1980	Percent	1990	Percent	% Change
Total Population	440,372		516,418		+ 17.3
Black	28,241	6.4	34,771	6.7	+ 23.1
Hispanic	21,064	4.8	38,570	7.5	+ 83.1
Asian, Pacific Islander	6,020	1.4	12,588	2.4	+ 109.1
White, Other	406,111	92.2	469,059	90.8	+ 15.5
Median Home Value			$136,700		

McHenry

	1980	Percent	1990	Percent	% Change
Total Population	147,724		183,241		+ 24.0
Black	108	.1	310	.2	+ 187.0
Hispanic	3,020	2.0	6,066	3.3	+ 100.9
Asian, Pacific Islander	550	.4	1,293	.7	+ 135.1
White, Other	147,066	99.6	181,638	99.1	+ 23.5
Median Home Value			$111,000		

Will

	1980	Percent	1990	Percent	% Change
Total Population	324,460		357,313		+ 10.1
Black	31,481	9.7	38,361	10.7	+ 21.9
Hispanic	13,778	4.2	19,973	5.6	+ 45.0
Asian, Pacific Islander	2,816	.9	4,774	1.3	+ 69.5
White, Other	290,163	89.4	314,178	87.9	+ 8.3
Median Home Value			$89,900		

CHICAGO SINCE THE BEGINNING

Year	Population	Year	Population
1840	4,470	1920	2,701,705
1850	29,963	1930	3,376,438
1860	112,172	1940	3,396,808
1870	298,977	1950	3,620,962
1880	503,185	1960	3,550,404
1890	1,099,850	1970	3,366,957
1900	1,698,575	1980	3,005,072
1910	2,185,283	1990	2,783,726

CITY OF CHICAGO

1 ROGERS PARK

	1980	Percent	1990	Percent	% Change
Total Population	55,525		60,378		+ 8.7
Black	5,225	9.4	16,580	27.5	+ 217.3
Hispanic[1]	6,621	11.9	12,005	19.9	+ 81.3
Pacific Islander[2]	3,797	6.8	5,319	8.8	+ 40.1
White, Other[3]	46,503	83.8	38,479	63.7	− 17.3

Named for former New Yorker Philip Rogers (1812-1856), who built a cabin at what is now the intersection of Ridge and Lunt avenues. His son-in-law, Patrick L. Touhy, was one of the pioneer developers of the Rogers Park area.

2 WEST RIDGE

	1980	Percent	1990	Percent	% Change
Total Population	61,129		65,374		+ 6.9
Black	442	.7	2,142	3.3	+ 384.6
Hispanic	2,266	3.7	5,398	8.3	+ 138.2

---

[1]Hispanic is an ethnic category, but Hispanics are included in the above race categories. The number of Hispanics should not be added with the race categories to compute total population.

[2]Category includes Asians.

[3]"Other" includes Native Americans and people who do not identify themselves as one of the specified races, except in Chicago listing (pp. 341–342), where further breakdowns have been supplied.

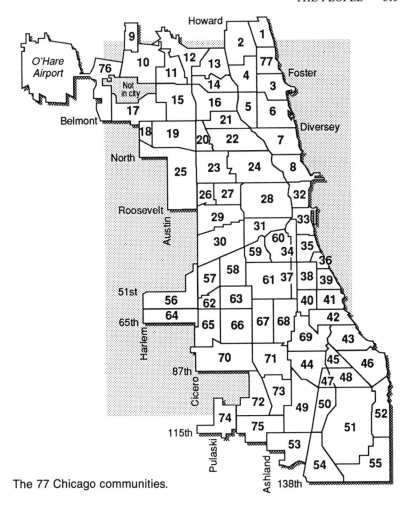

The 77 Chicago communities.

	1980	Percent	1990	Percent	% Change
Pacific Islander	4,492	7.3	10,824	16.6	+ 141.0
White, Other	56,195	91.9	52,408	80.2	− 6.7

Settled in the 1830s and 1840s by farmers, this area is west of the Rogers Park ridge.

3 UPTOWN

	1980	Percent	1990	Percent	% Change
Total Population	64,414		63,839		− .9
Black	9,703	15.1	15,735	24.6	+ 62.2
Hispanic	14,984	23.3	14,398	22.6	− 3.9
Pacific Islander	6,890	10.7	9,263	14.5	+ 34.4
White, Other	47,821	74.2	38,841	60.8	− 18.8

So named because it's located up shore from Chicago.

4 LINCOLN SQUARE

	1980	Percent	1990	Percent	% Change
Total Population	43,954		44,891		+ 2.1
Black	236	.5	1,211	2.7	+ 413.1
Hispanic	4,973	11.3	10,353	23.1	+ 108.2
Pacific Islander	3,685	8.4	6,252	13.9	+ 69.7
White, Other	40,033	91.1	37,428	83.4	− 6.5

Lincoln Avenue runs through the heart of this neighborhood.

5 NORTH CENTER

	1980	Percent	1990	Percent	% Change
Total Population	35,161		33,010		− 6.1
Black	412	1.2	1,076	.3	+ 161.2
Hispanic	6,684	19.0	9,048	27.4	+ 35.4
Pacific Islander	1,468	4.2	1,794	5.4	+ 22.2
White, Other	33,281	94.7	30,140	91.3	− 9.4

Located in the approximate center of the North Side.

6 LAKE VIEW

	1980	Percent	1990	Percent	% Change
Total Population	97,519		91,031		− 6.7
Black	6,757	6.9	5,820	6.4	− 13.9
Hispanic	18,333	18.8	12,932	14.2	− 29.5
Pacific Islander	5,163	5.3	4,083	4.5	− 20.9
White, Other	85,599	87.8	81,128	89.1	− 5.2

Named for the city of Lake View (incorporated in 1887; annexed to Chicago in 1889), of which this was a part. Settled in 1836; a hotel called Lake View House was built there in 1836 with, yes, a lake view.

7 LINCOLN PARK

	1980	Percent	1990	Percent	% Change
Total Population	57,146		61,092		+ 6.9
Black	4,909	8.6	3,715	6.1	− 24.3
Hispanic	5,991	10.5	3,981	6.5	− 33.6
Pacific Islander	1,702	3.0	1,469	2.4	− 13.7
White, Other	50,535	88.4	55,908	91.5	+ 10.6

So named because it is adjacent to the lakefront Lincoln Park, which was named for the president in 1865.

8 NEAR NORTH

	1980	Percent	1990	Percent	% Change
Total Population	67,167		62,842		− 6.4
Black	22,000	32.8	14,666	23.3	− 33.3
Hispanic	1,944	2.9	1,856	3.0	− 4.5
Pacific Islander	988	1.5	1,774	2.8	+ 79.6
White, Other	44,179	65.8	46,402	73.8	+ 5.0

Bordered by the Chicago River and the lake, this is one of Chicago's oldest communities, included in the incorporation in 1837. Because lands south of the river were developed first and reliable bridges came later, this fashionable area was not particularly desirable real estate for decades.

9 EDISON PARK

	1980	Percent	1990	Percent	% Change
Total Population	12,457		11,426		– 8.3
Black	0	0.0	3	0.0	+ 0.0
Hispanic	120	1.0	217	1.9	+ 80.8
Pacific Islander	71	.6	151	1.3	+ 112.7
White, Other	12,386	99.4	11,272	98.7	– 9.0

Originally a separate town, it was dubbed "The Electric Suburb" after six electric streetlights were installed. In 1881, it was named in honor of Thomas A. Edison.

10 NORWOOD PARK

	1980	Percent	1990	Percent	% Change
Total Population	40,585		37,719		– 7.1
Black	7	.0	21	.1	+ 200.0
Hispanic	390	1.0	1,005	2.7	+ 157.7
Pacific Islander	369	.9	739	2.0	+ 100.3
White, Other	40,209	99.1	36,959	98.0	– 8.1

This community was developed by the Norwood Land and Building Association, formed in 1868. An 1867 novel by Henry Ward Beecher, *Norwood: or Village Life in New England,* apparently inspired the name.

11 JEFFERSON PARK

	1980	Percent	1990	Percent	% Change
Total Population	24,583		23,649		– 3.8
Black	5	.0	16	.1	+ 220.0
Hispanic	395	1.6	1,041	4.4	+ 163.5
Pacific Islander	302	1.2	801	3.4	+ 165.2
White, Other	24,276	98.8	22,832	96.5	– 5.9

In 1845, folks here wanted to name the community in honor of President James Monroe. But another town already had the name, so they settled for Jefferson.

12 FOREST GLEN

	1980	Percent	1990	Percent	% Change
Total Population	18,991		17,655		– 7.0
Black	11	.1	9	.1	– 18.2
Hispanic	295	1.6	583	3.3	+ 97.6
Pacific Islander	475	2.5	1,068	6.0	+ 124.8
White, Other	18,505	97.4	16,578	93.9	– 10.4

It is, as the name implies, a heavily wooded area.

13 NORTH PARK

	1980	Percent	1990	Percent	% Change
Total Population	15,273		16,236		+ 6.3
Black	143	.9	140	.9	− 2.1
Hispanic	846	5.5	1,481	9.1	+ 75.1
Pacific Islander	1,533	10.0	3,361	20.7	+ 119.2
White, Other	13,597	89.0	12,735	78.4	− 6.3

So named because it was north of Chicago's central business district and pastoral in appearance.

14 ALBANY PARK

	1980	Percent	1990	Percent	% Change
Total Population	46,075		49,501		+ 7.4
Black	279	.6	1,681	3.4	+ 502.5
Hispanic	9,074	19.7	15,738	31.8	+ 73.4
Pacific Islander	6,502	14.1	11,939	24.1	+ 83.6
White, Other	39,294	85.3	35,881	72.5	− 8.7

Named for Albany, New York, the hometown of a real estate developer in the 1800s, De Lancey Lauderbach.

15 PORTAGE PARK

	1980	Percent	1990	Percent	% Change
Total Population	57,349		56,513		− 1.5
Black	51	.1	166	.3	+ 225.5
Hispanic	1,486	2.6	4,419	7.8	+ 197.4
Pacific Islander	758	1.3	1,637	2.9	+ 116.0
White, Other	56,540	98.6	54,710	96.8	− 3.2

A trail that would become Irving Park Road and two ridges in this community were portage routes for Indians and explorers moving between the Chicago River and the Des Plaines River.

16 IRVING PARK

	1980	Percent	1990	Percent	% Change
Total Population	49,489		50,159		+ 1.4
Black	63	.1	479	1.0	+ 660.3
Hispanic	4,267	8.6	12,222	24.4	+ 186.4
Pacific Islander	2,525	5.1	4,289	8.6	+ 69.9
White, Other	46,901	94.8	45,391	90.5	− 3.2

The original town name was Irvington, in honor of American author Washington Irving (1783-1859).

17 DUNNING

	1980	Percent	1990	Percent	% Change
Total Population	37,860		36,957		− 2.4
Black	183	.5	160	.4	− 12.6
Hispanic	613	1.6	1,882	5.1	+ 207.0

	1980	Percent	1990	Percent	% Change
Pacific Islander	248	.7	882	2.4	+ 255.6
White, Other	37,429	98.9	35,915	97.2	− 4.0

Named for Andrew Dunning, a Union officer turned farmer turned land developer, who came to the area in the mid-1860s.

18 MONTCLARE

	1980	Percent	1990	Percent	% Change
Total Population	10,793		10,573		− 2.0
Black	0	0.0	36	.3	+ 0.0
Hispanic	179	1.7	1,199	11.3	+ 569.8
Pacific Islander	37	.3	238	2.3	+ 543.2
White, Other	10,756	99.7	10,299	97.4	− 4.2

The origin of the name Montclare is uncertain, but the Milwaukee Road had a Mont Clare train station near Harlem and Fullerton that may have been named for Montclair, New Jersey.

19 BELMONT CRAGIN

	1980	Percent	1990	Percent	% Change
Total Population	53,371		56,787		+ 6.4
Black	43	.1	718	1.3	+ 1569.8
Hispanic	3,072	5.8	17,066	30.1	+ 455.5
Pacific Islander	674	1.3	1,981	3.5	+ 193.9
White, Other	52,654	98.7	54,088	95.2	+ 2.7

In the late 1800s the Cragin Manufacturing Company set up business in this community, which is bordered on the north by Belmont Avenue.

20 HERMOSA

	1980	Percent	1990	Percent	% Change
Total Population	19,547		23,131		+ 18.3
Black	74	.4	464	2.0	+ 527.0
Hispanic	6,101	31.2	15,923	68.8	+ 161.0
Pacific Islander	509	2.6	647	2.8	+ 27.1
White, Other	18,964	97.0	22,020	95.2	+ 16.1

Named Hermosa by the city when annexed to Chicago in 1889.

21 AVONDALE

	1980	Percent	1990	Percent	% Change
Total Population	33,527		35,579		+ 6.1
Black	60	.2	451	1.3	+ 651.7
Hispanic	6,863	20.5	13,359	37.5	+ 94.7
Pacific Islander	982	2.9	1,229	3.5	+ 25.2
White, Other	32,485	96.9	33,899	95.3	+ 4.4

Named for Avondale, Pennsylvania, by Uptown developer John L. Cochran.

22 LOGAN SQUARE

	1980	Percent	1990	Percent	% Change
Total Population	84,768		82,605		− 2.6
Black	2,236	2.6	5,600	6.8	+ 150.4
Hispanic	43,829	51.7	54,740	66.3	+ 24.9
Pacific Islander	1,224	1.4	1,256	1.5	+ 2.6
White, Other	81,308	95.9	75,749	91.7	− 6.8

Named for Union General John Alexander Logan (1826-1886), who was also a congressman and senator from Illinois.

23 HUMBOLDT PARK

	1980	Percent	1990	Percent	% Change
Total Population	70,879		67,573		− 4.7
Black	25,215	35.6	34,150	50.5	+ 35.4
Hispanic	28,872	40.7	29,735	44.0	+ 3.0
Pacific Islander	1,341	1.9	635	.9	− 52.6
White, Other	44,323	62.5	32,788	48.5	− 26.0

Named for the bordering city park. The park was named for German scientist Alexander Von Humboldt (1769-1859).

24 WEST TOWN

	1980	Percent	1990	Percent	% Change
Total Population	96,428		87,703		− 9.0
Black	8,671	9.0	9,306	10.6	+ 7.3
Hispanic	54,691	56.7	54,361	62.0	− .6
Pacific Islander	1,212	1.3	1,050	1.2	− 13.4
White, Other	86,545	89.8	77,347	88.2	− 10.6

Named for its location north and west of the Loop.

25 AUSTIN

	1980	Percent	1990	Percent	% Change
Total Population	138,026		114,079		− 17.3
Black	101,831	73.8	99,172	86.9	− 2.6
Hispanic	8,148	5.9	4,154	3.6	− 49.0
Pacific Islander	2,509	1.8	1,009	.9	− 59.8
White, Other	33,686	24.4	13,898	12.2	− 58.7

Originally the village of Austinville, it was named for developer Henry W. Austin, who bought 280 acres there in 1865.

26 WEST GARFIELD PARK

	1980	Percent	1990	Percent	% Change
Total Population	33,865		24,095		− 28.8
Black	33,475	98.8	23,895	99.2	− 28.6
Hispanic	278	.8	133	.6	− 52.2
Pacific Islander	46	.1	18	.1	− 60.9
White, Other	344	1.0	182	.8	− 47.1

This community lies west of Garfield Park, named for the president four years after his assassination in 1881.

27 EAST GARFIELD PARK

	1980	Percent	1990	Percent	% Change
Total Population	31,580		24,030		− 23.9
Black	31,263	99.0	23,769	98.9	− 24.0
Hispanic	263	.8	151	.6	− 42.6
Pacific Islander	14	.0	17	.1	+ 21.4
White, Other	303	1.0	244	1.0	− 19.5

This community includes Garfield Park, named for the president.

28 NEAR WEST SIDE

	1980	Percent	1990	Percent	% Change
Total Population	57,305		46,197		− 19.4
Black	42,810	74.7	30,956	67.0	− 27.7
Hispanic	5,705	10.0	4,416	9.6	− 22.6
Pacific Islander	1,326	2.3	2,412	5.2	+ 81.9
White, Other	13,169	23.0	12,829	27.8	− 2.6

This old neighborhood, in which waves of immigrants settled, lies immediately west of the Loop.

29 NORTH LAWNDALE

	1980	Percent	1990	Percent	% Change
Total Population	61,534		47,296		− 23.1
Black	59,370	96.5	45,574	96.4	− 23.2
Hispanic	1,653	2.7	1,471	3.1	− 11.0
Pacific Islander	92	.1	65	.1	− 29.3
White, Other	2,072	3.4	1,657	3.5	− 20.0

So named by a real estate firm in 1870.

30 SOUTH LAWNDALE

	1980	Percent	1990	Percent	% Change
Total Population	75,204		81,155		+ 7.9
Black	6,476	8.6	7,254	8.9	+ 12.0
Hispanic	55,700	74.1	69,131	85.2	+ 24.1
Pacific Islander	258	.3	230	.3	− 10.9
White, Other	68,470	91.0	73,671	90.8	+ 7.6

See North Lawndale.

31 LOWER WEST SIDE

	1980	Percent	1990	Percent	% Change
Total Population	44,951		45,654		+ 1.6
Black	477	1.1	508	1.1	+ 6.5
Hispanic	34,867	77.6	40,227	88.1	+ 15.4
Pacific Islander	129	.3	146	.3	+ 13.2
White, Other	44,345	98.7	45,000	98.6	+ 1.5

Named for its location. It used to be called the Southwest Side.

32 LOOP

	1980	Percent	1990	Percent	% Change
Total Population	6,462		11,954		+ 85.0
Black	1,231	19.0	2,429	20.3	+ 97.3
Hispanic	222	3.4	679	5.7	+ 205.9
Pacific Islander	232	3.6	452	3.8	+ 94.8
White, Other	4,999	77.4	9,073	75.9	+ 81.5

Named for the two miles of CTA elevated track that loop the business district.

33 NEAR SOUTH SIDE

	1980	Percent	1990	Percent	% Change
Total Population	7,243		6,828		− 5.7
Black	6,819	94.1	6,387	93.5	− 6.3
Hispanic	108	1.5	108	1.6	+ 0.0
Pacific Islander	87	1.2	51	.7	− 41.4
White, Other	337	4.7	390	5.7	+ 15.7

Named for its location.

34 ARMOUR SQUARE

	1980	Percent	1990	Percent	% Change
Total Population	12,475		10,801		− 13.4
Black	3,162	25.3	2,398	22.2	− 24.2
Hispanic	603	4.8	471	4.4	− 21.9
Pacific Islander	4,990	40.0	5,647	52.3	+ 13.2
White, Other	4,323	34.7	2,756	25.5	− 36.2

Named for Armour Square Park, which was developed as part of the nearby Illinois Institute of Technology, then called the Armour Institute of Technology. The school was funded by the meatpacking family in the late 1800s.

35 DOUGLAS

	1980	Percent	1990	Percent	% Change
Total Population	35,700		30,652		− 14.1
Black	30,906	86.6	28,064	91.6	− 9.2
Hispanic	313	.9	253	.8	− 19.2
Pacific Islander	928	2.6	807	2.6	− 13.0
White, Other	3,866	10.8	1,781	5.8	− 53.9

Named for U.S. Sen. Stephen A. Douglas, who lived and is buried there—at the east end of Thirty-fifth Street. Douglas helped develop the area in the 1850s.

36 OAKLAND

	1980	Percent	1990	Percent	% Change
Total Population	16,748		8,197		− 51.1
Black	16,647	99.4	8,145	99.4	− 51.1
Hispanic	97	.6	34	.4	− 64.9

	1980	Percent	1990	Percent	% Change
Pacific Islander	8	.0	8	.1	+ 0.0
White, Other	93	.6	44	.5	− 52.7

In the mid-1800s, Oakland was called Cleaverville in honor of its founder, industrialist Charles Cleaver. He named one street Oakland Crescent because it was lined with oak trees.

37 FULLER PARK

	1980	Percent	1990	Percent	% Change
Total Population	5,832		4,364		− 25.2
Black	5,758	98.7	4,303	98.6	− 25.3
Hispanic	71	1.2	41	.9	− 42.3
Pacific Islander	2	.0	2	.0	+ 0.0
White, Other	72	1.2	59	1.4	− 18.1

Named for the park district's Fuller Park.

38 GRAND BOULEVARD

	1980	Percent	1990	Percent	% Change
Total Population	53,741		35,897		− 33.2
Black	53,427	99.4	35,693	99.4	− 33.2
Hispanic	350	.7	146	.4	− 58.3
Pacific Islander	46	.1	29	.1	− 37.0
White, Other	268	.5	175	.5	− 34.7

Named for the wide thoroughfare, first called Grand Boulevard, that runs through the neighborhood. The boulevard's name later was changed to South Parkway and then Dr. Martin Luther King, Jr., Drive.

39 KENWOOD

	1980	Percent	1990	Percent	% Change
Total Population	21,974		18,178		− 17.3
Black	17,024	77.5	13,945	76.7	− 18.1
Hispanic	241	1.1	241	1.3	+ 0.0
Pacific Islander	331	1.5	462	2.5	+ 39.6
White, Other	4,619	21.0	3,771	20.7	− 18.4

Early settler Dr. John A. Kennicott built an estate here in the 1850s and called it Kenwood to honor his mother's Scottish birthplace.

40 WASHINGTON PARK

	1980	Percent	1990	Percent	% Change
Total Population	31,935		19,425		− 39.2
Black	31,726	99.3	19,303	99.4	− 39.2
Hispanic	205	.6	48	.2	− 76.6
Pacific Islander	21	.1	13	.1	− 38.1
White, Other	188	.6	109	.6	− 42.0

Named for park district's Washington Park.

41 HYDE PARK

	1980	Percent	1990	Percent	% Change
Total Population	31,198		28,630		− 8.2
Black	11,610	37.2	10,875	38.0	− 6.3
Hispanic	721	2.3	895	3.1	+ 24.1
Pacific Islander	1,510	4.8	2,481	8.7	+ 64.3
White, Other	18,078	57.9	15,274	53.3	− 15.5

Attorney Paul Cornell (1822-1904) founded this community in the 1850s and named it Hyde Park after the like-named fashionable areas of London and New York.

42 WOODLAWN

	1980	Percent	1990	Percent	% Change
Total Population	36,323		27,473		− 24.4
Black	34,759	95.7	26,365	96.0	− 24.1
Hispanic	285	.8	178	.6	− 37.5
Pacific Islander	123	.3	169	.6	+ 37.4
White, Other	1,441	4.0	939	3.4	− 34.8

Settled in the 1850s by Dutch truck farmers, it was annexed in 1889.

43 SOUTH SHORE

	1980	Percent	1990	Percent	% Change
Total Population	77,743		61,517		− 20.9
Black	73,929	95.1	59,956	97.5	− 18.9
Hispanic	917	1.2	497	.8	− 45.8
Pacific Islander	217	.3	98	.2	− 54.8
White, Other	3,597	4.6	1,463	2.4	− 59.3

Named for its location.

44 CHATHAM

	1980	Percent	1990	Percent	% Change
Total Population	40,725		36,779		− 9.7
Black	40,113	98.5	36,456	99.1	− 9.1
Hispanic	271	.7	198	.5	− 26.9
Pacific Islander	50	.1	42	.1	− 16.0
White, Other	562	1.4	281	.8	− 50.0

45 AVALON PARK

	1980	Percent	1990	Percent	% Change
Total Population	13,792		11,711		− 15.1
Black	13,258	96.1	11,482	98.0	− 13.4
Hispanic	109	.8	81	.7	− 25.7
Pacific Islander	45	.3	35	.3	− 22.2
White, Other	489	3.5	194	1.7	− 60.3

The Isle of Avalon, this neighborhood's namesake, is called the burial place of the legendary King Arthur.

46 SOUTH CHICAGO

	1980	Percent	1990	Percent	% Change
Total Population	46,422		40,776		− 12.2
Black	22,186	47.8	25,331	62.1	+ 14.2
Hispanic	18,229	39.3	13,644	33.5	− 25.2
Pacific Islander	40	.1	94	.2	+ 135.0
White, Other	24,196	52.1	15,351	37.6	− 36.6

Named for a railroad station there called South Chicago in the 1870s.

47 BURNSIDE

	1980	Percent	1990	Percent	% Change
Total Population	3,942		3,314		− 15.9
Black	3,491	88.6	3,205	96.7	− 8.2
Hispanic	100	2.5	16	.5	− 84.0
Pacific Islander	4	.1	2	.1	− 50.0
White, Other	447	11.3	107	3.2	− 76.1

Subdivider Col. W.W. Jacobs in the 1880s named this community for Civil War Gen. Ambrose E. Burnside.

48 CALUMET HEIGHTS

	1980	Percent	1990	Percent	% Change
Total Population	20,505		17,453		− 14.9
Black	17,795	86.8	16,128	92.4	− 9.4
Hispanic	1,481	7.2	920	5.3	− 37.9
Pacific Islander	118	.6	93	.5	− 21.2
White, Other	2,592	12.6	1,232	7.1	− 52.5

Calumet is an Indian word that roughly means "peace pipe."

49 ROSELAND

	1980	Percent	1990	Percent	% Change
Total Population	64,372		56,493		− 12.2
Black	62,749	97.5	55,825	98.8	− 11.0
Hispanic	550	.9	283	.5	− 48.5
Pacific Islander	130	.2	60	.1	− 53.8
White, Other	1,493	2.3	608	1.1	− 59.3

Named for the roses residents grew outside their homes in the 1870s.

50 PULLMAN

	1980	Percent	1990	Percent	% Change
Total Population	10,341		9,344		− 9.6
Black	7,896	76.4	7,370	78.9	− 6.7
Hispanic	642	6.2	780	8.3	+ 21.5
Pacific Islander	22	.2	21	.2	− 4.5
White, Other	2,423	23.4	1,953	20.9	− 19.4

Named for railroad car manufacturer George Pullman, who built a company town there in 1880.

51 SOUTH DEERING

	1980	Percent	1990	Percent	% Change
Total Population	19,400		17,755		− 8.5
Black	10,630	54.8	10,493	59.1	− 1.3
Hispanic	4,763	24.6	5,038	28.4	+ 5.8
Pacific Islander	31	.2	29	.2	− 6.5
White, Other	8,739	45.0	7,233	40.7	− 17.2

Named for the Deering Harvester Company, which later merged into International Harvester.

52 EAST SIDE

	1980	Percent	1990	Percent	% Change
Total Population	21,331		20,450		− 4.1
Black	25	.1	13	.1	− 48.0
Hispanic	2,678	12.6	8,177	40.0	+ 205.3
Pacific Islander	30	.1	62	.3	+ 106.7
White, Other	21,276	99.7	20,375	99.6	− 4.2

Hegewisch and the East Side are Chicago's two easternmost neighborhoods.

53 WEST PULLMAN

	1980	Percent	1990	Percent	% Change
Total Population	44,904		39,846		− 11.3
Black	40,701	90.6	37,452	94.0	− 8.0
Hispanic	2,309	5.1	1,771	4.4	− 23.3
Pacific Islander	50	.1	41	.1	− 18.0
White, Other	4,153	9.2	2,353	5.9	− 43.3

Located west—and south—of Pullman.

54 RIVERDALE

	1980	Percent	1990	Percent	% Change
Total Population	13,539		10,821		− 20.1
Black	13,089	96.7	10,592	97.9	− 19.1
Hispanic	176	1.3	150	1.4	− 14.8
Pacific Islander	4	.0	4	.0	+ 0.0
White, Other	446	3.3	225	2.1	− 49.6

The Little Calumet River flows through this community, which adopted the name around 1873.

55 HEGEWISCH

	1980	Percent	1990	Percent	% Change
Total Population	11,572		10,136		− 12.4
Black	29	.3	66	.7	+ 127.6
Hispanic	718	6.2	1,290	12.7	+ 79.7
Pacific Islander	42	.4	56	.6	+ 33.3
White, Other	11,501	99.4	10,014	98.8	− 12.9

Named for Adolph Hegewisch, president of United States Rolling Stock Company, developer of this neighborhood in 1883.

56 GARFIELD RIDGE

	1980	Percent	1990	Percent	% Change
Total Population	37,935		33,948		− 10.5
Black	5,116	13.5	4,361	12.8	− 14.8
Hispanic	1,566	4.1	2,509	7.4	+ 60.2
Pacific Islander	347	.9	409	1.2	+ 17.9
White, Other	32,472	85.6	29,178	85.9	− 10.1

Named for Garfield Boulevard—honorng the president—and a glacial ridge which runs through this community.

57 ARCHER HEIGHTS

	1980	Percent	1990	Percent	% Change
Total Population	9,708		9,227		− 5.0
Black	8	.1	2	.0	− 75.0
Hispanic	354	3.6	779	8.4	+ 120.1
Pacific Islander	21	.2	50	.5	+ 138.1
White, Other	9,679	99.7	9,175	99.4	− 5.2

Named for Archer Avenue, which in turn was named for Col. William B. Archer, construction supervisor of the Illinois and Michigan Canal beginning in the late 1830s. But there are no heights in Archer Heights.

58 BRIGHTON PARK

	1980	Percent	1990	Percent	% Change
Total Population	30,770		32,207		+ 4.7
Black	34	.1	38	.1	+ 11.8
Hispanic	4,539	14.8	12,044	37.4	+ 165.3
Pacific Islander	333	1.1	652	2.0	+ 95.8
White, Other	30,403	98.8	31,517	97.9	+ 3.7

In the 1850s, Chicago Mayor John Wentworth built a nearby race track here called Brighton Park.

59 McKINLEY PARK

	1980	Percent	1990	Percent	% Change
Total Population	13,248		13,297		+ .4
Black	5	.0	20	.2	+ 300.0
Hispanic	2,129	16.1	5,255	39.5	+ 146.8
Pacific Islander	71	.5	372	2.8	+ 423.9
White, Other	13,172	99.4	12,905	97.1	− 2.0

Named for the park district's McKinley Park, which was named for the president.

60 BRIDGEPORT

	1980	Percent	1990	Percent	% Change
Total Population	30,923		29,877		− 3.4
Black	39	.1	43	.1	+ 10.3
Hispanic	6,584	21.3	7,796	26.1	+ 18.4

	1980	Percent	1990	Percent	% Change
Pacific Islander	546	1.8	5,071	17.0	+828.8
White, Other	30,338	98.1	24,763	82.9	−18.4

Barges going down the Chicago had to stop at a low bridge at Ashland Avenue and unload, making this area a port.

61 NEW CITY

	1980	Percent	1990	Percent	% Change
Total Population	55,860		53,226		−4.7
Black	12,239	21.9	21,998	41.3	+79.7
Hispanic	19,945	35.7	20,906	39.3	+4.8
Pacific Islander	174	.3	185	.3	+6.3
White, Other	43,447	77.8	31,043	58.3	−28.5

The name originally referred to a more affluent section of the old town of Lake.

62 WEST ELSDON

	1980	Percent	1990	Percent	% Change
Total Population	12,797	12,266	−4.1		
Black	7	.1	4	.0	−42.9
Hispanic	297	2.3	1,135	9.3	+282.2
Pacific Islander	32	.3	74	.6	+131.3
White, Other	12,758	99.7	12,188	99.4	−4.5

So named because it was west of a railroad town called Elsdon.

63 GAGE PARK

	1980	Percent	1990	Percent	% Change
Total Population	24,445		26,957		+10.3
Black	163	.7	1,368	5.1	+739.3
Hispanic	2,701	11.0	10,574	39.2	+291.5
Pacific Islander	139	.6	228	.8	+64.0
White, Other	24,143	98.8	25,361	94.1	+5.0

Named for George W. Cage, whose family owned land in the area. He was a charter member of the South Park Commission.

64 CLEARING

	1980	Percent	1990	Percent	% Change
Total Population	22,584		21,490		−4.8
Black	5	.0	9	.0	+80.0
Hispanic	916	4.1	1,615	7.5	+76.3
Pacific Islander	37	.2	132	.6	+256.8
White, Other	22,542	99.8	21,349	99.3	−5.3

This area was first developed as a railroad freight clearing yard.

65 WEST LAWN

	1980	Percent	1990	Percent	% Change
Total Population	24,748		23,402		− 5.4
Black	52	.2	61	.3	+ 17.3
Hispanic	599	2.4	2,519	10.8	+ 320.5
Pacific Islander	64	.3	191	.8	+ 198.4
White, Other	24,632	99.5	23,150	98.9	− 6.0

Part of the old Chicago Lawn community jutted a few blocks west of Central Park Avenue and, consequently, became known as West Lawn.

66 CHICAGO LAWN

	1980	Percent	1990	Percent	% Change
Total Population	46,568		51,243		+ 10.0
Black	4,782	10.3	13,603	26.5	+ 184.5
Hispanic	4,940	10.6	14,549	28.4	+ 194.5
Pacific Islander	510	1.1	926	1.8	+ 81.6
White, Other	41,276	88.6	36,714	71.6	− 11.1

A model community at Sixty-third and Central Park was named Chicago Lawn in 1876 by land developers.

67 WEST ENGLEWOOD

	1980	Percent	1990	Percent	% Change
Total Population	62,069		52,772		− 15.0
Black	60,882	98.1	51,949	98.4	− 14.7
Hispanic	686	1.1	331	.6	− 51.7
Pacific Islander	55	.1	48	.1	− 12.7
White, Other	1,132	1.8	775	1.5	− 31.5

Named for its location—west of Englewood.

68 ENGLEWOOD

	1980	Percent	1990	Percent	% Change
Total Population	59,075		48,434		− 18.0
Black	58,395	98.8	48,027	99.2	− 17.8
Hispanic	497	.8	231	.5	− 53.5
Pacific Islander	56	.1	69	.1	+ 23.2
White, Other	624	1.1	338	.7	− 45.8

Named by early settlers from Englewood, New Jersey.

69 GREATER GRAND CROSSING

	1980	Percent	1990	Percent	% Change
Population	45,218		38,644		− 14.5
Black	44,660	98.8	38,352	99.2	− 14.1
Hispanic	266	.6	189	.5	− 28.9
Pacific Islander	51	.1	23	.1	− 54.9
White, Other	507	1.1	269	.7	− 46.9

Because two train lines both claimed the right of way, an 1853 train accident killed eighteen people at Seventy-fifth and South Chicago Avenue.

70 ASHBURN

	1980	Percent	1990	Percent	% Change
Total Population	40,477		37,092		− 8.4
Black	1,084	2.7	3,720	10.0	+ 243.2
Hispanic	905	2.2	2,331	6.3	+ 157.6
Pacific Islander	219	.5	393	1.1	+ 79.5
White, Other	39,174	96.8	32,979	88.9	− 15.8

Renamed Ashburn in 1908 because there was already a downstate town called Clarkville—the neighborhood original name.

71 AUBURN GRESHAM

	1980	Percent	1990	Percent	% Change
Total Population	65,132		59,808		− 8.2
Black	64,094	98.4	59,299	99.1	− 7.5
Hispanic	463	.7	204	.3	− 55.9
Pacific Islander	57	.1	29	.0	− 49.1
White, Other	981	1.5	480	.8	− 51.1

The former communities in this area were called Auburn (platted in 1872) and Gresham (platted as South Englewood in the 1870s).

72 BEVERLY

	1980	Percent	1990	Percent	% Change
Total Population	23,360		22,385		− 4.2
Black	3,178	13.6	5,416	24.2	+ 70.4
Hispanic	308	1.3	393	1.8	+ 27.6
Pacific Islander	94	.4	115	.5	+ 22.3
White, Other	20,088	86.0	16,854	75.3	− 16.1

Said to be named for Beverly, Massachusetts, the home of an early settler.

73 WASHINGTON HEIGHTS

	1980	Percent	1990	Percent	% Change
Total Population	36,453		32,114		− 11.9
Black	35,778	98.1	31,732	98.8	− 11.3
Hispanic	177	.5	140	.4	− 20.9
Pacific Islander	34	.1	20	.1	− 41.2
White, Other	641	1.8	362	1.1	− 43.5

The "Washington" refers to the president. The "heights" refers to its elevation. The community once included a chunk of neighboring Beverly, which boasts the highest elevation in Chicago.

74 MOUNT GREENWOOD

	1980	Percent	1990	Percent	% Change
Total Population	20,084		19,179		− 4.5
Black	93	.5	249	1.3	+ 167.7
Hispanic	154	.8	362	1.9	+ 135.1
Pacific Islander	36	.2	71	.4	+ 97.2
White, Other	19,955	99.4	18,859	98.3	− 5.5

When a cemetery developer, George Waite, came to the area in 1877, he was struck by its heavily forested prehistoric ridge, so he called his cemetery Mount Greenwood. The neighborhood took its name from the cemetery.

75 MORGAN PARK

	1980	Percent	1990	Percent	% Change
Total Population	29,315		26,740		− 8.8
Black	18,320	62.5	17,305	64.7	− 5.5
Hispanic	280	1.0	340	1.3	+ 21.4
Pacific Islander	72	.2	88	.3	+ 22.2
White, Other	10,923	37.3	9,347	35.0	− 14.4

Named for an early developer, Thomas Morgan, who bought up land there in 1844.

76 O'HARE

	1980	Percent	1990	Percent	% Change
Total Population	11,068		11,192		+ 1.1
Black	165	1.5	319	2.9	+ 93.3
Hispanic	288	2.6	519	4.6	+ 80.2
Pacific Islander	196	1.8	315	2.8	+ 60.7
White, Other	10,707	96.7	10,558	94.3	− 1.4

Named for the nearby and noisy airport. The airport, in turn, was named for World War II Navy pilot Edward H. "Butch" O'Hare.

77 EDGEWATER

	1980	Percent	1990	Percent	% Change
Total Population	58,561		60,703		+ 3.7
Black	6,514	11.1	12,087	19.9	+ 85.6
Hispanic	7,805	13.3	10,567	17.4	+ 35.4
Pacific Islander	5,665	9.7	7,321	12.1	+ 29.2
White, Other	46,382	79.2	41,295	68.0	− 11.0

Named for its location by its developer, John Lewis Cochran.

TWENTY WEALTHIEST SUBURBS*

(ranked by median home values)

Bannockburn	$500,000 plus
Barrington Hills	$500,000 plus

Kenilworth	$500,000 plus
Mettawa	$500,000 plus
South Barrington	$500,000 plus
Lake Forest	$493,700
Winnetka	$483,500
Oak Brook	$477,000
Long Grove	$430,200
Glencoe	$426,700
Riverwoods	$407,900
Golf	$395,900
Burr Ridge	$384,600
Inverness	$365,200
Lincolnshire	$343,900
Deer Park	$318,200
North Barrington	$307,000
Hawthorn Woods	$305,700
Wayne	$300,800
Northfield	$296,700

*According to 1990 census

MUNICIPALITIES

ADDISON

	1980	Percent	1990	Percent	% Change
Total Population	29,759		32,058		+ 7.7
Black	246	.8	541	1.7	+ 119.9
Hispanic	1,732	5.8	4,287	13.4	+ 147.5
Asian, Pacific Islander	811	2.7	1,905	5.9	+ 134.9
White, Other	28,702	96.4	29,612	92.4	+ 3.2

Village; President Anthony Russotto, about $2,400.* Incorporated: 1884. Motto: "Village of Friendship." Origin of Name: While there are a couple of different versions, the most popular is that the early New England settlers saw the landscape and terrain and were reminded of Addison, New York. MHV**: $126,000.

ALGONQUIN

	1980	Percent	1990	Percent	% Change
Total Population	5,834		11,663		+ 99.9
Black	2	.0	20	.2	+ 900.0
Hispanic	67	1.1	202	1.7	+ 201.5
Asian, Pacific Islander	22	.4	150	1.3	+ 581.8
White, Other	5,810	99.6	11,493	98.5	+ 97.8

Village; President Donald R. Brewer, $9,000. The first settlers came in 1834. It was incorporated in 1890. First called Cornish's Ferry, in honor of Dr. Andrew B. Cornish, who settled there in 1835. Then called Osceola, until someone discovered an Illinois town already us-

---

*Each mayor's or president's annual salary is listed after his or her name.
**MHV stands for median home value—as determined by the 1990 U.S. Census.

ing that name. Finally, in March 1844, Samuel Edwards named it Algonquin, based on a boat named the Algonquin, which in turn was named for a confederation of Indian tribes. MHV: $133,300.

ALSIP

	1980	Percent	1990	Percent	% Change
Total Population	17,134		18,227		+ 6.4
Black	101	.6	885	4.9	+ 776.2
Hispanic	441	2.6	730	4.0	+ 65.5
Asian, Pacific Islander	148	.9	296	1.6	+ 100.0
White, Other	16,885	98.5	17,046	93.5	+ 1.0

Village; Mayor Arnold A. Andrews, $46,508. First settled in the 1830s, incorporated in 1927. Alsip was settled by Hanna and Joseph Lane, who had a blacksmith business, but the village got its name from the Alsip Brickyard, which used to be in the area. The brickyard was established in about 1885 by Frank Alsip, who never lived in Alsip. MHV: $94,600.

ANTIOCH

	1980	Percent	1990	Percent	% Change
Total Population	4,419		6,105		+ 38.2
Black	1	.0	9	.1	+ 800.0
Hispanic	34	.8	120	2.0	+ 252.9
Asian, Pacific Islander	26	.6	54	.9	+ 107.7
White, Other	4,392	99.4	6,042	99.0	+ 37.6

Village; Mayor Robert C. Wilton, $5,500. Incorporated: 1892. Antioch is a biblical name. It was first used to refer to the town when it was settled in 1839. MHV: $104,400.

ARLINGTON HEIGHTS

	1980	Percent	1990	Percent	% Change
Total Population	66,116		75,460		+ 14.1
Black	288	.4	479	.6	+ 66.3
Hispanic	1,149	1.7	2,046	2.7	+ 78.1
Asian, Pacific Islander	1,255	1.9	2,797	3.7	+ 122.9
White, Other	64,573	97.7	72,184	95.7	+ 11.8

Village; Mayor William Maki, $4,800. Incorporated: 1887). Motto: "City of Good Neighbors." The village was settled in 1836 by Asa Dunton, a stonecutter from New York. It was originally called Dunton. In 1874, real estate developers, looking to spice up the name, convinced voters that "Arlington" was the way to go. But there was already an Arlington in Illinois, so they added Heights, explaining that the village was 704 feet above sea level and 104 feet above Chicago. MHV: $169,100.

AURORA

	1980	Percent	1990	Percent	% Change
Total Population	81,293		99,581		+ 22.5
Black	8,459	10.4	11,814	11.9	+ 39.7
Hispanic	14,482	17.8	22,864	23.0	+ 57.9

	1980	Percent	1990	Percent	% Change
Asian, Pacific Islander	473	.6	1,314	1.3	+ 177.8
White, Other	72,361	89.0	86,453	86.8	+ 19.5

City; Mayor David L. Pierce, $57,300. Incorporated: 1857. Motto: "City of Lights"—one of the first cities in 1881 to use electric street lights. Some early settlers came from the area of Aurora, New York. MHV: $81,900.

BANNOCKBURN

	1980	Percent	1990	Percent	% Change
Total Population	1,316		1,388		+ 5.5
Black	35	2.7	95	6.8	+ 171.4
Hispanic	25	1.9	15	1.1	− 40.0
Asian, Pacific Islander	53	4.0	155	11.2	+ 192.5
White, Other	1,228	93.3	1,138	82.0	− 7.3

Village; President William Trukenbord, no salary. Incorporated: 1924. Named for Bannockburn, Scotland. MHV: $500,000 plus.

BARRINGTON

	1980	Percent	1990	Percent	% Change
Total Population	9,029		9,504		+ 5.3
Black	10	.1	16	.2	+ 60.0
Hispanic	111	1.2	157	1.7	+ 41.4
Asian, Pacific Islander	66	.7	119	1.3	+ 80.3
White, Other	8,953	99.2	9,369	98.6	+ 4.6

Village; President Theodore J. Forsberg, $1,200. First permanent settlers arrived in 1834, south of the village proper, but by 1846 there was a school building in what is now downtown Barrington. The town was laid out in 1854 and incorporated in 1873. It was known as Barrington Center because many of the settlers hailed from Great Barrington in Berkshire County, Massachusetts. MHV: $218,100.

BARRINGTON HILLS

	1980	Percent	1990	Percent	% Change
Total Population	3,631		4,202		+ 15.7
Black	2	.1	7	.2	+ 250.0
Hispanic	23	.6	55	1.3	+ 139.1
Asian, Pacific Islander	35	1.0	116	2.8	+ 231.4
White, Other	3,594	99.0	4,079	97.1	+ 13.5

Village; President James A. Kempe, no salary. Incorporated: 1957. Origin of name: see Barrington. MHV: $500,000 plus.

BARTLETT

	1980	Percent	1990	Percent	% Change
Total Population	13,254		19,373		+ 46.2
Black	30	1.0	303	1.6	+ 133.1
Hispanic	346	2.6	654	3.4	+ 89.0
Asian, Pacific Islander	550	4.1	669	3.5	+ 21.6
White, Other	12,574	94.9	18,401	95.0	+ 46.3

Village; President John Stark, $3,700. Settled in 1843 and incorporated in 1891. Motto: "Progress with Pride." Named in honor of first two settlers, Luther and Lyman Bartlett. MHV: $132,600.

BATAVIA

	1980	Percent	1990	Percent	% Change
Total Population	12,574		17,076		+ 35.8
Black	584	4.6	423	2.5	– 27.6
Hispanic	397	3.2	506	3.0	+ 27.5
Asian, Pacific Islander	90	.7	214	1.3	+ 137.8
White, Other	11,900	94.6	16,439	96.3	+ 38.1

City; Mayor Jeffery Schielke, $15,000. Incorporated: 1833 as a village, and 1891 as a city. Motto: "City of Energy" because the early business in the area was the manufacture of windmills and because Fermilab is on the border. First settler was Christopher Columbus Payne, who was born in Pennsylvania. Batavia is Dutch for "fair meadows." MHV: $136,900.

BEACH PARK

	1980	Percent	1990	Percent	% Change
Total Population	8,468		9,513		+ 12.3
Black	0	0.0	312	3.3	
Hispanic	0	0.0	559	5.9	
Asian, Pacific Islander	0	0.0	117	1.2	
White, Other	8,468	100.0	9,084	95.5	+ 7.3

Village; President H. James Solomon, no salary. Incorporated: 1989. Named for its location west of Illinois Beach State Park. MHV: $93,400.

BEDFORD PARK

	1980	Percent	1990	Percent	% Change
Total Population	988		566		– 42.7
Black	0	0.0	0	0.0	+ 0.0
Hispanic	30	3.0	13	2.3	– 56.7
Asian, Pacific Islander	4	.4	0	0.0	– 100.0
White, Other	984	99.6	566	100.0	– 42.5

Village; President Charles F. Ploszek, $9,000. Incorporated: 1940. E.T. Bedford (1849-1931) founded the village. He was president and founder of Corn Products, now CPC International, still headquartered in Bedford Park. MHV: $87,300.

BEECHER

	1980	Percent	1990	Percent	% Change
Total Population	2,024		2,032		+ .4
Black	0	0.0	0	0.0	+ 0.0
Hispanic	16	.8	13	.6	– 18.8
Asian, Pacific Islander	4	.2	3	.1	– 25.0
White, Other	2,020	99.8	2,029	99.9	+ .4

Village; Mayor Landis Wehling, $900. Laid out in 1870 and incorporated in 1883. Motto: "A Proud Past and a Promising Future." T.L.

Miller, an English cattleman who raised Angus cattle in the Beecher area, was a big fan of Henry Ward Beecher (1813-1887), the nationally popular preacher. Miller suggested the village name. MHV: $88,100.

BELLWOOD

	1980	Percent	1990	Percent	% Change
Total Population	19,811		20,241		+ 2.2
Black	6,956	35.1	14,352	70.9	+ 106.3
Hispanic	1,105	5.6	1,197	5.9	+ 8.3
Asian, Pacific Islander	291	1.5	330	1.6	+ 13.4
White, Other	12,564	63.4	5,559	27.5	− 55.8

Village; Mayor Sigel C. Davis, $57,000. Incorporated: 1900. Motto: "Bellwood, the Heart of Proviso Township:" Originally called Lovedale, which lasted about a year. The present name stems from Chicagoans taking the train into the area around the turn-of-the-century for picnics in the woods. Pretty young women or "belles" would come out in their crinoline gowns and stroll through the woods. It came to be known as the woods of the belles and eventually Bellwood, without the "e." MHV: $74,100.

BENSENVILLE

	1980	Percent	1990	Percent	% Change
Total Population	16,124		17,767		+ 10.2
Black	44	.3	171	1.0	+ 288.6
Hispanic	1,353	8.4	3,333	18.8	+ 146.3
Asian, Pacific Islander	432	2.7	1,115	6.3	+ 158.1
White, Other	15,648	97.0	16,481	92.8	+ 5.3

Village; President John C. Geils, $6,000. Incorporated: 1884. Motto: "Reflection on Our Heritage." Originally a German settlement, no one is sure if it was named for somebody named Bensen or a place in Germany. MHV: $106,800.

BERKELEY

	1980	Percent	1990	Percent	% Change
Total Population	5,467		5,137		− 6.0
Black	0	0.0	231	4.5	+ 0.0
Hispanic	88	1.6	304	5.9	+ 245.5
Asian, Pacific Islander	61	1.1	221	4.3	+ 262.3
White, Other	5,406	98.9	4,685	91.2	− 13.3

Village; President Karl J. Ermisch, $6,000. Incorporated: 1924. On May 1, 1915, the village's name was selected after four residents petitioned the townspeople to accept the name of Berkeley, apparently because somebody had liked the name Berkeley, California. It wasn't formalized, however, until incorporation in 1924. MHV: $95,900.

BERWYN

	1980	Percent	1990	Percent	% Change
Total Population	46,849		45,426		− 3.0
Black	13	.0	54	.1	+ 315.4
Hispanic	1,128	2.4	3,573	7.9	+ 216.8

	1980	Percent	1990	Percent	% Change
Asian, Pacific Islander	319	.7	790	1.7	+ 147.6
White, Other	46,517	99.3	44,582	98.1	− 4.2

City; Mayor Joseph Lanzillotti, $25,000. Incorporated: 1908. Motto: "City of Homes." Berwyn, a Welsh word, is named after the Philadelphia suburb of Berwyn. The subdivision was named in 1890 after its developers saw the name on a railroad timetable. MHV: $90,200.

BLOOMINGDALE

	1980	Percent	1990	Percent	% Change
Total Population	12,659		16,614		+ 31.2
Black	213	1.7	275	1.7	+ 29.1
Hispanic	267	2.1	452	2.7	+ 69.3
Asian, Pacific Islander	355	2.8	845	5.1	+ 138.0
White, Other	12,091	95.5	15,494	93.3	+ 28.1

Village; President Samuel J. Tenuto, $4,800. Motto: "Growth with Pride." The first settler was Lyman Meacham, in the spring of 1833. The village incorporated in the late 1800s with Roselle within its border. But friction with Roselle caused a dissolution in 1922 and the smaller village of Bloomingdale incorporated in 1923. Origin of the name is uncertain, but in 1837 there was a Bloomingdale post office. MHV: $147,200.

BLUE ISLAND

	1980	Percent	1990	Percent	% Change
Total Population	21,855		21,203		− 3.0
Black	1,077	4.9	2,978	14.0	+ 176.5
Hispanic	3,469	15.9	5,280	24.9	+ 52.2
Asian, Pacific Islander	108	.5	73	.3	− 32.4
White, Other	20,670	94.6	18,152	85.6	− 12.2

City; Mayor Donald E. Peloquin, $14,000. Incorporated: 1835. Motto: "City on the Hill" and "Pride in Our Past, Confidence in Our Future." *The Chicago Democrat* newspaper in 1834 described Blue Island as a table of land rising out of an immense plain. The sides and slopes were covered with herbage, which when viewed from a distance appeared to stand in an "azure mist of vapor." Another possiblity is offered by H.B. Robinson, a member of a pioneering Blue Island family, who said the town was so named because a tribe of Indians living on the ridge painted their faces blue. MHV: $64,300.

BOLINGBROOK

	1980	Percent	1990	Percent	% Change
Total Population	37,261		40,843		+ 9.6
Black	2,539	6.8	6,384	15.6	+ 151.4
Hispanic	1,689	4.5	2,391	5.9	+ 41.6
Asian, Pacific Islander	1,546	4.1	2,046	5.0	+ 32.3
White, Other	33,176	89.0	32,413	79.4	− 2.3

Village; President Roger C. Claar, $20,000. Incorporated: 1965. Motto: "A Place to Grow." Bolingbrook is named after its sister city, Bolingbroke, England. MHV: $94,300.

BRAIDWOOD

	1980	Percent	1990	Percent	% Change
Total Population	3,429		3,584		+ 4.5
Black	15	.4	21	.6	+ 40.0
Hispanic	50	1.5	56	1.6	+ 12.0
Asian, Pacific Islander	5	.1	8	.2	+ 60.0
White, Other	3,409	99.4	3,555	99.2	+ 4.3

City; Mayor Robert J. Peterson, $720. Incorporated: 1873. James Braidwood (1831-1879) was a civil engineer and coal mine operator who helped direct the building of mines near the city. MHV: $58,000.

BRIDGEVIEW

	1980	Percent	1990	Percent	% Change
Total Population	14,155		14,402		+ 1.7
Black	44	.3	24	.2	− 45.5
Hispanic	488	3.4	674	4.7	+ 38.1
Asian, Pacific Islander	94	.7	170	1.2	+ 80.9
White, Other	14,017	99.0	14,208	98.7	+ 1.4

Village; President John Oremus, $15,000. Incorporated: 1947. Motto: "A Well Balanced Community." The name was inspired by the view from the Harlem Avenue Bridge, which is north of the village. MHV: $92,900.

BROADVIEW

	1980	Percent	1990	Percent	% Change
Total Population	8,618		8,713		+ 1.1
Black	2,625	30.5	4,667	53.6	+ 77.8
Hispanic	196	2.3	187	2.1	− 4.6
Asian, Pacific Islander	169	2.0	167	1.9	− 1.2
White, Other	5,824	67.6	3,879	44.5	− 33.4

Village; President Emil Parkes, $43,000. Incorporated: 1914. Motto: "A Balanced Community." Named after an early Illinois Central Railroad station. MHV: $83,400.

BROOKFIELD

	1980	Percent	1990	Percent	% Change
Total Population	19,395		18,876		− 2.7
Black	11	.1	33	.2	+ 200.0
Hispanic	351	1.8	583	3.1	+ 66.1
Asian, Pacific Islander	178	.9	178	.9	+ 0.0
White, Other	19,206	99.0	18,665	98.9	− 2.8

Village; President Kevin Close, $2,700. Incorporated: 1893. Motto: "The World's Most Visited Village" (because of the Brookfield Zoo). Samuel Gross, a land speculator and developer, founded the town as Grossdale. Some townspeople, however, didn't like Gross or his business dealings and in 1900 voted to change the name. "Brookfield" was chosen in a contest. MHV: $105,100.

BUFFALO GROVE

	1980	Percent	1990	Percent	% Change
Total Population	22,230		36,427		+ 63.9
Black	142	.6	373	1.0	+ 162.7
Hispanic	345	1.6	711	2.0	+ 106.1
Asian, Pacific Islander	487	2.2	1,595	4.4	+ 227.5
White, Other	21,601	97.2	34,459	94.6	+ 59.5

Village; President Sidney Mathias, $5,000. Incorporated: 1958. In the days of the Potawatomies, there were plenty of buffalo grazing from Wheeling Woods to Long Grove. A buffalo skeleton was found in a creek, so it was called Buffalo Creek. The town took its name from the creek. MHV: $163,600.

BULL VALLEY

	1980	Percent	1990	Percent	% Change
Total Population	509		574		+ 12.8
Black	3	.6	4	.7	+ 33.3
Hispanic	4	.8	10	1.7	+ 150.0
Asian, Pacific Islander	5	1.0	4	.7	− 20.0
White, Other	501	98.4	566	98.6	+ 13.0

Village; President Ronald Parrish, no salary. Incorporated: 1977. The area has been called Bull Valley for years, possibly because farmers used to keep their bulls in the valley. MHV: $262,900.

BURBANK

	1980	Percent	1990	Percent	% Change
Total Population	28,462		27,600		− 3.0
Black	5	.0	11	.0	+ 120.0
Hispanic	887	3.1	1,305	4.7	+ 47.1
Asian, Pacific Islander	182	.6	312	1.1	+ 71.4
White, Other	28,275	99.3	27,277	98.8	− 3.5

Village; Mayor Harry J. Klein, $39,100. Incorporated: 1970. Motto: "Beauty, Loyalty, Honor and Pride." But the city has also used "City of Champions" because of the success of its Little League and high school wrestling and football teams. The village name was taken from the Burbank Manor Fire District and Burbank School, already in existence. MHV: $89,600.

BURLINGTON

	1980	Percent	1990	Percent	% Change
Total Population	442		400		− 9.5
Black	0	0.0	0	0.0	+ 0.0
Hispanic	3	.7	3	.8	+ 0.0
Asian, Pacific Islander	1	.2	0	0.0	− 100.0
White, Other	441	99.8	400	100.0	− 9.3

Village; President Everett Andersen, $3,000. Incorporated: 1906. Many of the early settlers hailed from Burlington Massachusetts. MHV: $85,900.

BURNHAM

	1980	Percent	1990	Percent	% Change
Total Population	4,030		3,916		− 2.8
Black	35	.9	636	16.2	+ 1717.1
Hispanic	362	9.0	557	14.2	+ 53.9
Asian, Pacific Islander	20	.5	31	.8	+ 55.0
White, Other	3,975	98.6	3,249	83.0	− 18.3

Village; President Eldreth "Rocky" Rundlett, $4,400. Incorporated: 1907. Name decided by a coin toss. The residents wanted to name the town for either of two prominent real estate brokers, both of whom helped establish the area. Finally one resident tossed a coin. Samuel Burnham won. MHV: $63,800.

BURR RIDGE

	1980	Percent	1990	Percent	% Change
Total Population	3,833		7,669		+ 100.1
Black	8	.2	55	.7	+ 587.5
Hispanic	41	1.1	148	1.9	+ 261.0
Asian, Pacific Islander	170	4.4	649	8.5	+ 281.8
White, Other	3,655	95.4	6,965	90.8	+ 90.6

Village; President William T. Zucek, $480. Incorporated: 1956. Motto: "It's a Very Special Place." Named for the Burr Oaks on a ridge in the area. MHV: $384,600.

CALUMET CITY

	1980	Percent	1990	Percent	% Change
Total Population	39,697		37,840		− 4.7
Black	2,360	5.9	8,962	23.7	+ 279.7
Hispanic	1,521	3.8	2,426	6.4	+ 59.5
Asian, Pacific Islande	179	.5	212	.6	+ 18.4
White, Other	37,158	93.6	28,666	75.8	− 22.9

City; Mayor Robert C. Stefaniak, $29,040. Incorporated: 1923. Motto: "City of Homes." Chalumet is a Norman-French word for a shepherd's pipe. When French explorers traded with Indians, calumet came to mean "pipe of peace." MHV: $64,300.

CALUMET PARK

	1980	Percent	1990	Percent	% Change
Total Population	8,788		8,418		− 4.2
Black	2,636	30.0	6,061	72.0	+ 129.9
Hispanic	1,016	11.6	715	8.5	− 29.6
Asian, Pacific Islander	27	.3	9	.1	− 66.7
White, Other	6,125	69.7	2,348	27.9	− 61.7

Village; Mayor Ronald Romanowski, $4,800. Incorporated: 1925. See Calumet City for origin of the name. MHV: $63,500.

CAROL STREAM

	1980	Percent	1990	Percent	% Change
Total Population	15,472		31,716		+ 105.0
Black	618	4.0	1,081	3.4	+ 74.9
Hispanic	618	4.0	1,801	5.7	+ 191.4
Asian, Pacific Islander	446	2.9	1,853	5.8	+ 315.5
White, Other	14,408	93.1	28,782	90.7	+ 99.8

Village; President Ross Ferraro, $760. Incorporated: 1959. The village's founder, Jay Stream, wanted to cheer up his young daughter Carol while she was recovering from a car accident, so he named the village in her honor. MHV: $128,700.

CARPENTERSVILLE

	1980	Percent	1990	Percent	% Change
Total Population	23,272		23,049		− 1.0
Black	224	1.0	1,009	4.4	+ 350.4
Hispanic	2,141	9.2	3,840	16.7	+ 79.4
Asian, Pacific Islander	170	.7	294	1.3	+ 72.9
White, Other	22,878	98.3	21,746	94.3	− 4.9

Village; President John V. Skillman, $6,600. Incorporated: 1887. Named for Charles V. Carpenter, who settled the area in 1837, and his son Angelo, who helped bring industry in the 1850s. MHV: $78,900.

CARY

	1980	Percent	1990	Percent	% Change
Total Population	6,640		10,043		+ 51.2
Black	2	.0	26	.3	+ 1200.0
Hispanic	117	1.8	219	2.2	+ 87.2
Asian, Pacific Islander	18	.3	48	.5	+ 166.7
White, Other	6,620	99.7	9,969	99.3	+ 50.6

Village; President George Kraus, $4,000. Incorporated: 1893. William B. Cary settled the area in the 1860s. MHV: $125,300.

CHANNAHON

	1980	Percent	1990	Percent	% Change
Total Population	3,734		4,266		+ 14.2
Black	7	.2	18	.4	+ 157.1
Hispanic	50	1.3	95	2.2	+ 90.0
Asian, Pacific Islander	11	.3	8	.2	− 27.3
White, Other	3,716	99.5	4,240	99.4	+ 14.1

Village; President Michael Rittof, $17,280, plus $40 per meeting. Once the site of a Potawatomie village, the first white settlers came in 1832. The town incorporated in 1961. It was apparently named by the Potawatomie, who used the area to play and fish. MHV: $84,900.

CHICAGO

	1980	Percent	1990	Percent	% Change
Total Population	3,005,072		2,783,726		− 7.4
Black	1,197,000	39.8	1,087,711	39.1	− 9.1
Asian	69,191	2.3	104,118	3.7	+ 50.5
White	1,490,216	49.6	1,263,524	45.4	− 15.2

	1980	Percent	1990	Percent	% Change
American Indian	6,072	.2	7,064	.3	+ 16.3
Other	242,593	8.1	321,309	11.5	+ 32.4
Hispanic	422,061	14.0	545,852	19.6	+ 29.3

City; Mayor Richard M. Daley, $115,000. Aldermen are paid $55,000. Incorporated as a village in 1833, as a city in 1837. Motto: "Urbs in Horto," meaning city in a garden. Chicago is an Indian name for something powerful or big—or maybe something overwhelmingly stinky, such as a wild onion. MHV: $78,700.

CHICAGO HEIGHTS

	1980	Percent	1990	Percent	% Change
Total Population	37,026		33,072		− 10.7
Black	10,651	28.8	11,607	35.1	+ 9.0
Hispanic	4,205	11.4	4,976	15.0	+ 18.3
Asian, Pacific Islander	92	.2	99	.3	+ 7.6
White, Other	26,283	71.0	21,366	64.6	− 18.7

City; Mayor Douglas M. Troiani, $20,000. Incorporated as a village in 1892, as a city in 1901. Motto: "Crossroads of the Nation" because it has the intersection of Lincoln and Dixie highways. Named for its proximity, located eight miles south, to Chicago. MHV: $62,500.

CHICAGO RIDGE

	1980	Percent	1990	Percent	% Change
Total Population	13,473		13,643		+ 1.3
Black	17	.1	41	.3	+ 141.2
Hispanic	263	2.0	502	3.7	+ 90.9
Asian, Pacific Islander	63	.5	106	.8	+ 68.3
White, Other	13,393	99.4	13,496	98.9	+ .8

Village; Mayor Eugene L. Siegel, $21,500. Incorporated: 1914. Motto: "Village of Patriotism." When Chicago hosted the 1893 Columbian Exposition, it needed extra dirt for construction and landscaping at Jackson Park. Railroad cars were dispatched to what is now Chicago Ridge and filled with dirt for the fair. The removal of so much dirt left valleys and ridges, so the area became known as "the Ridge." MHV: $90,500.

CICERO

	1980	Percent	1990	Percent	% Change
Total Population	61,232		67,436		+ 10.1
Black	74	.1	141	.2	+ 90.5
Hispanic	5,271	8.6	24,931	37.0	+ 373.0
Asian, Pacific Islander	356	.6	1,092	1.6	+ 206.7
White, Other	60,802	99.3	66,203	98.2	+ 8.9

Town; President Henry Klosak, $57,100. Incorporated: 1867. Motto: "An Enterprising Town Building for the Future." Augustus Porter, a founder of Cicero, suggested the name of his hometown, Cicero, New York. MHV: $73,200.

CLARENDON HILLS

	1980	Percent	1990	Percent	% Change
Total Population	6,870		6,994		+ 1.8
Black	29	.4	41	.6	+ 41.4
Hispanic	85	1.2	132	1.9	+ 55.3
Asian, Pacific Islander	70	1.0	161	2.3	+ 130.0
White, Other	6,771	98.6	6,792	97.1	− .3

Village; President John D. Purdy, Jr., no salary. Incorporated: 1924. Motto: "The Volunteer Community." Robert Harris, a former president of the Chicago Burlington and Quincy Railroad and a real estate investor, is credited with naming the village. He named it either for Clarendon Hills, England, or the Clarendon District of Boston. MHV: $166,700.

COUNTRY CLUB HILLS

	1980	Percent	1990	Percent	% Change
Total Population	14,676		15,431		+ 5.1
Black	1,750	11.9	8,871	57.5	+ 406.9
Hispanic	353	2.4	388	2.5	+ 9.9
Asian, Pacific Islander	429	2.9	338	2.2	− 21.2
White, Other	12,497	85.2	6,222	40.3	− 50.2

City; Mayor Dwight W. Welch, $5,600. A German farm community in the 1870s, it incorporated as a city in 1958. Its motto was "The City with Country Charm." Now the unofficial motto is "Catch the Spirit." Name was chosen by the developer J.E. Merrion, who envisioned a community with a rural and country club flavor. MHV: $73,000.

COUNTRYSIDE

	1980	Percent	1990	Percent	% Change
Total Population	6,538		5,716		− 12.6
Black	10	.2	57	1.0	+ 470.0
Hispanic	132	2.0	195	3.4	+ 47.7
Asian, Pacific Islander	44	.7	60	1.0	+ 36.4
White, Other	6,484	99.2	5,599	98.0	− 13.6

City; Mayor Carl W. LeGant, $8,400. Incorporated: 1960. Motto: "Business Oriented, Citizen Friendly." Named for the country-like landscape. MHV: $131,700.

CREST HILL

	1980	Percent	1990	Percent	% Change
Total Population	9,252		10,643		+ 15.0
Black	1,005	10.9	1,979	18.6	+ 96.9
Hispanic	314	3.4	635	6.0	+ 102.2
Asian, Pacific Islander	99	1.1	66	.6	− 33.3
White, Other	8,148	88.1	8,598	80.8	+ 5.5

City; Mayor Donald Randich, $6,000. Incorporated: 1960. The name is a twist on the name of a local shopping center, the Hillcrest Shopping Center, at Plainfield Road and North Larkin Avenue. The city couldn't call itself Hillcrest because there already was another Illinois town by that name. MHV: $64,300.

CRESTWOOD

	1980	Percent	1990	Percent	% Change
Total Population	10,852		10,823		− .3
Black	316	2.9	436	4.0	+ 38.0
Hispanic	205	1.9	291	2.7	+ 42.0
Asian, Pacific Islander	73	.7	92	.9	+ 26.0
White, Other	10,463	96.4	10,295	95.1	− 1.6

Village; Mayor Chester Stranczek, $6,000. Incorporated: 1928. Mottos: "Great Today, Greater Tomorrow" and "Village on the Move." When the village incorporated, suggested names were submitted and two were voted on: Crestwood and Allenwood. Crestwood won. MHV: $93,100.

CRETE

	1980	Percent	1990	Percent	% Change
Total Population	5,417		6,773		+ 25.0
Black	53	1.0	303	4.5	+ 471.7
Hispanic	39	.7	151	2.2	+ 287.2
Asian, Pacific Islander	6	.1	45	.7	+ 650.0
White, Other	5,358	98.9	6,425	94.9	+ 19.9

Village; President Michael Einhorn, $6,000. Settled in 1836, incorporated in 1880. Willard Wood, who settled in the area in 1836, opened his Bible to the New Testament, and the first name he saw was Crete— in St. Paul's journey as a prisoner to Rome. MHV: $106,900.

CRYSTAL LAKE

	1980	Percent	1990	Percent	% Change
Total Population	18,590		24,512		+ 31.9
Black	15	.1	49	.2	+ 226.7
Hispanic	242	1.3	610	2.5	+ 152.1
Asian, Pacific Islander	116	.6	287	1.2	+ 147.4
White, Other	18,459	99.3	24,176	98.6	+ 31.0

City; Mayor George Wells, $4,800. Incorporated: 1914. Motto: "A Good Place to Live." Named for its locaton on Crystal Lake. MHV: $119,600.

DARIEN

	1980	Percent	1990	Percent	% Change
Total Population	14,536		18,341		+ 26.2
Black	66	.5	204	1.1	+ 209.1
Hispanic	258	1.8	380	2.1	+ 47.3
Asian, Pacific Islander	1,019	7.0	1,657	9.0	+ 62.6
White, Other	13,451	92.5	16,480	89.9	+ 22.5

City; Mayor Carmen D. Soldato, $4,500. Incorporated: 1969. Motto: "A Nice Place to Live." Sam Kelley, one of the original aldermen, had grown up back East and was familiar with the wealthy community of Darien, Connecticut, so he suggested the name. MHV: $159,000.

DEER PARK

	1980	Percent	1990	Percent	% Change
Total Population	1,368		2,887		+ 111.0
Black	4	.3	38	1.3	+ 850.0
Hispanic	53	3.9	25	.9	− 52.8
Asian, Pacific Islander	17	1.2	74	2.6	+ 335.3
White, Other	1,347	98.5	2,775	96.1	+ 106.0

Village; President James M. Peterson, $3,600. Incorporated: 1957. There's a forest nearby called Deer Grove, full of deer. MHV: $318,200.

DEERFIELD

	1980	Percent	1990	Percent	% Change
Total Population	17,430		17,327		− .6
Black	44	.3	91	.5	+ 106.8
Hispanic	223	1.3	246	1.4	+ 10.3
Asian, Pacific Islander	194	1.1	379	2.2	+ 95.4
White, Other	17,192	98.6	16,857	97.3	− 1.9

Village; President Bernard Forrest, no salary. Settled in 1835 and incorporated in 1903. Motto: "Progress through Service." Named after Deerfield, Massachusetts. MHV: $232,200.

DES PLAINES

	1980	Percent	1990	Percent	% Change
Total Population	53,568		53,223		− .6
Black	160	.3	325	.6	+ 103.1
Hispanic	2,139	4.0	3,520	6.6	+ 64.6
Asian, Pacific Islander	1,473	2.7	2,504	4.7	+ 70.0
White, Other	51,935	97.0	50,394	94.7	− 3.0

City; Mayor D. Michael Albrecht, $6,000. Founded in 1835, but not incorporated until 1925. Motto: "City of Destiny." Named for its location along the Des Plaines River. Des Plaines is French for "the plains." MHV: $130,000.

DIAMOND

	1980	Percent	1990	Percent	% Change
Total Population	1,170		1,077		− 7.9
Black	0	0.0	0	0.0	+ 0.0
Hispanic	26	2.2	17	1.6	− 34.6
Asian, Pacific Islander	2	.2	0	0.0	− 100.0
White, Other	1,168	99.8	1,077	100.0	− 7.8

Village; Mayor David Wilcox, $360. Incorporated: 1895. On Feb. 16, 1883, during a thaw, the area's diamond mine flooded, trapping seventy-eight miners inside. The bodies were never recovered, and the mine never reopened. When the village incorporated twelve years later, it was named after the coal mine. MHV: $75,500.

DIXMOOR

	1980	Percent	1990	Percent	% Change
Total Population	4,175		3,647		− 12.6
Black	2,765	66.2	2,106	57.7	− 23.8

	1980	Percent	1990	Percent	% Change
Hispanic	83	2.0	258	7.1	+210.8
Asian, Pacific Islander	4	.1	2	.1	−50.0
White, Other	1,406	33.7	1,539	42.2	+9.5

Village; President Kenneth L. Steinhagen, $3,200. Incorporated: 1922. First named Specialville for onetime Mayor Charles Special. The name was changed in 1929 to Dixmoor, the origin of which is uncertain. MHV: $46,700.

DOLTON

	1980	Percent	1990	Percent	% Change
Total Population	24,766		23,930		−3.4
Black	487	2.0	9,127	38.1	+1774.1
Hispanic	731	3.0	1,085	4.5	+48.4
Asian, Pacific Islander	222	.9	279	1.2	+25.7
White, Other	24,057	97.1	14,524	60.7	−39.6

Village; Mayor J. Michael Peck, $9,500. Incorporated: 1892. Named in honor of the first settler, George Dolton, who arrived with his family in 1837, settling at about 134th and Indiana. MHV: $65,100.

DOWNERS GROVE

	1980	Percent	1990	Percent	% Change
Total Population	45,572		46,858		+2.8
Black	471	1.0	809	1.7	+71.8
Hispanic	585	1.3	1,140	2.4	+94.9
Asian, Pacific Islander	1,239	2.7	1,975	4.2	+59.4
White, Other	43,862	96.2	44,074	94.1	+.5

Village; Mayor Betty Cheever, $1,200. The first settlers arrived in 1832. The city incorporated in 1873. Named in honor of a first settler in 1832, Pierce Downer, who hailed from New York. MHV: $143,900.

EAST DUNDEE

	1980	Percent	1990	Percent	% Change
Total Population	2,618		2,721		+3.9
Black	1	.0	11	.4	+1000.0
Hispanic	42	1.6	85	3.1	+102.4
Asian, Pacific Islander	13	.5	15	.6	+15.4
White, Other	2,604	99.5	2,695	99.0	+3.5

Village; President Kenneth Swanson, about $1,680 ($70 per meeting). Incorporated: 1887. It used to be part of Dundee, but with development the Fox River split the town into east and west. An early settler, Alexander Gardiner, suggested the name in honor of his hometown of Dundee, Scotland. MHV: $111,900.

EAST HAZEL CREST

	1980	Percent	1990	Percent	% Change
Total Population	1,362		1,570		+15.3
Black	17	1.2	382	24.3	+2147.1
Hispanic	117	8.6	91	5.8	−22.2
Asian, Pacific Islander	3	.2	5	.3	+66.7
White, Other	1,342	98.5	1,183	75.4	−11.8

Village; President Thomas A. Brown, $2,400. Incorporated: 1918. Named for its location east of Hazel Crest. MHV: $68,600.

ELBURN

	1980	Percent	1990	Percent	% Change
Total Population	1,224		1,275		+ 4.2
Black	2	.2	0	0.0	− 100.0
Hispanic	4	.3	7	.5	+ 75.0
Asian, Pacific Islander	8	.7	1	.1	− 87.5
White, Other	1,214	99.2	1,274	99.9	+ 4.9

Village; Mayor John Hicks, $1,500. Incorporated: 1885. The first settlers wanted to call the town Melbourne, but that name was already in use downstate; so they dropped the"M," simplified the spelling and called it Elburn. A second explanation is that Elburn is Scottish for "Great Stream"—it was said in winter you could skate from Elburn to Kaneville. MHV: $106,100.

ELGIN

	1980	Percent	1990	Percent	% Change
Total Population	63,798		77,010		+ 20.7
Black	4,206	6.6	5,630	7.3	+ 33.9
Hispanic	6,529	10.2	14,576	18.9	+ 123.3
Asian, Pacific Islander	646	1.0	2,670	3.5	+ 313.3
White, Other	58,946	92.4	68,710	89.2	+ 16.6

City; Mayor George VanDeVoorde, $1,800. Founded in 1835. Organized as a village in 1846. Incorporated as a city in 1854. Motto: "Urbs fluminis," which means "City by the River (Fox River)." Elgin took its name from a Congregationalist hymn tune. Many of these tunes, like Elgin, were named after Scottish towns. The Elgin tune was the favorite of James T. Gifford, a Congregationalist who founded Elgin in 1835. MHV: $96,800.

ELK GROVE VILLAGE

	1980	Percent	1990	Percent	% Change
Total Population	28,907		33,429		+ 15.6
Black	226	.8	263	.8	+ 16.4
Hispanic	741	2.6	1,192	3.6	+ 60.9
Asian, Pacific Islander	1,440	5.0	2,287	6.8	+ 58.8
White, Other	27,241	94.2	30,879	92.4	+ 13.4

Village; President Charles J. Zettek, $6,100. Incorporated: 1956. Motto: "On This Land We Build with Dignity." Named by the developer, the Centex Corporation, for the elk in nearby Ned Brown Forest Preserve. MHV: $137,900.

ELMHURST

	1980	Percent	1990	Percent	% Change
Total Population	44,276		42,029		− 5.1
Black	186	.4	186	.4	+ 0.0
Hispanic	945	2.1	1,148	2.7	+ 21.5
Asian, Pacific Islander	1,024	2.3	1,278	3.0	+ 24.8
White, Other	43,066	97.3	40,565	96.5	− 5.8

City; Mayor Charles H. Garrigues, $6,250. Incorporated as a village in 1882, as a city in 1910. Unofficial motto: "Tree Town." The name, dating to about 1869, was inspired by the towering elms on Cottage Hill in central Elmhurst. MHV: $135,600.

ELMWOOD PARK

	1980	Percent	1990	Percent	% Change
Total Population	24,016		23,206		– 3.4
Black	8	.0	21	.1	+ 162.5
Hispanic	405	1.7	1,001	4.3	+ 147.2
Asian, Pacific Islander	122	.5	239	1.0	+ 95.9
White, Other	23,886	99.5	22,946	98.9	– 3.9

Village; President Peter N. Silvestri, $18,360. Incorporated: 1914. Motto: "The Village with Pride." Named for the many elm trees once in the village. MHV: $116,300.

ELWOOD

	1980	Percent	1990	Percent	% Change
Total Population	814		951		+ 16.8
Black	0	0.0	0	0.0	+ 0.0
Hispanic	12	1.5	29	3.0	+ 141.7
Asian, Pacific Islander	0	0.0	3	.3	+ 0.0
White, Other	814	100.0	948	99.7	+ 16.5

Village; President Dale Archer, $3,450. Incorporated: 1869. MHV: $65,700.

EVANSTON

	1980	Percent	1990	Percent	% Change
Total Population	73,706		73,233		– .6
Black	15,801	21.4	16,749	22.9	+ 6.0
Hispanic	1,715	2.3	2,689	3.7	+ 56.8
Asian, Pacific Islander	2,004	2.7	3,535	4.8	+ 76.4
White, Other	55,901	75.8	52,949	72.3	– 5.3

City; Mayor Joan Barr, $10,565. Evanston incorporated as a town in 1863, as a city in 1892. It was named for John Evans, a founder of Northwestern University. MHV: $184,800.

EVERGREEN PARK

	1980	Percent	1990	Percent	% Change
Total Population	22,260		20,874		– 6.2
Black	53	.2	85	.4	+ 60.4
Hispanic	229	1.0	432	2.1	+ 88.6
Asian, Pacific Islander	161	.7	205	1.0	+ 27.3
White, Other	22,046	99.0	20,584	98.6	– 6.6

Village; Mayor Anthony Vacco, $39,075. Incorporated: 1893. Motto: "Village of Churches." There were many old and large evergreens in the area when it was settled. MHV: $88,800.

FLOSSMOOR

	1980	Percent	1990	Percent	% Change
Total Population	8,423		8,651		+ 2.7
Black	297	3.5	910	10.5	+ 206.4
Hispanic	114	1.4	97	1.1	− 14.9
Asian, Pacific Islander	262	3.1	446	5.2	+ 70.2
White, Other	7,864	93.4	7,295	84.3	− 7.2

Village; Mayor Frank Maher, Jr., no salary now, but it will be $4,800 after the next local election. Incorporated: 1924. The Illinois Central Railroad purchased 160 acres to get the landfill needed to raise its track grade in preparation for the World's Fair of 1893. But when it found Flossmoors dirt unsuitable as fill, it decided to develop the area. In the 1890s, a contest was held to name it, and the U.S. Post Office selected the winner: Floss-moor—Scottish for dew on the flowers or gently rolling countryside. MHV: $170,400.

FORD HEIGHTS

	1980	Percent	1990	Percent	% Change
Total Population	5,347		4,259		− 20.3
Black	5,252	98.2	4,208	98.8	− 19.9
Hispanic	91	1.7	43	1.0	− 52.7
Asian, Pacific Islander	2	.0	2	.0	+ 0.0
White, Other	93	1.7	49	1.2	− 47.3

Village; President Gloria D. Bryant, $6,000. Incorporated: 1949. In 1987, the city, thinking its name of East Chicago Heights was more a direction than a name, changed it to Ford Heights because it's located near the Ford Motor stamping plant. MHV: $38,200.

FOREST PARK

	1980	Percent	1990	Percent	% Change
Total Population	15,177		14,918		− 1.7
Black	636	4.2	1,942	13.0	+ 205.3
Hispanic	447	2.9	734	4.9	+ 64.2
Asian, Pacific Islander	861	5.7	1,260	8.4	+ 46.3
White, Other	13,680	90.1	11,716	78.5	− 14.4

Village; Mayor Lorraine Popelka, $8,000. Incorporated in 1884 as the village of Harlem. The name was changed in 1907 to Forest Park, probably because of its parklike environment at the time. MHV: $93,000.

FOREST VIEW

	1980	Percent	1990	Percent	% Change
Total Population	764		743		− 2.7
Black	0	0.0	1	.1	+ 0.0
Hispanic	12	1.6	18	2.4	+ 50.0
Asian, Pacific Islander	2	.3	1	.1	− 50.0
White, Other	762	99.7	741	99.7	− 2.8

Village; President Richard Grenvich, $5,000. Incorporated: 1924. Named for the view of the forest preserves across Harlem Avenue. MHV: $100,000.

FOX LAKE

	1980	Percent	1990	Percent	% Change
Total Population	6,831		7,478		+ 9.5
Black	8	.1	26	.3	+ 225.0
Hispanic	83	1.2	230	3.1	+ 177.1
Asian, Pacific Islander	26	.4	30	.4	+ 15.4
White, Other	6,797	99.5	7,422	99.3	+ 9.2

Village; President Francis Meier, $7,000. Incorporated: 1907. Motto: "The Heart of the Chain O'Lakes." It was first called Nippersink Point, but later renamed to highlight it's location on Fox Lake. The Indians are said to have named the lake. MHV: $84,400.

FOX RIVER GROVE

	1980	Percent	1990	Percent	% Change
Total Population	2,515		3,551		+ 41.2
Black	0	0.0	10	.3	+ 0.0
Hispanic	50	2.0	99	2.8	+ 98.0
Asian, Pacific Islander	11	.4	30	.8	+ 172.7
White, Other	2,504	99.6	3,511	98.9	+ 40.2

Village; President Daniel Shea, $3,000. Incorporated: 1919. Named for its location on the Fox River. MHV: $121,200.

FOX RIVER VALLEY GARDENS

	1980	Percent	1990	Percent	% Change
Total Population	520		665		+ 27.9
Black	2	.4	0	0.0	− 100.0
Hispanic	2	.4	12	1.8	+ 500.0
Asian, Pacific Islander	2	.4	2	.3	+ 0.0
White, Other	516	99.2	663	99.7	+ 28.5

Village was incorporated in 1969. MHV: $105,700.

FRANKFORT

	1980	Percent	1990	Percent	% Change
Total Population	4,357		7,180		+ 64.8
Black	4	.1	10	.1	+ 150.0
Hispanic	33	.8	89	1.2	+ 169.7
Asian, Pacific Islander	16	.4	122	1.7	+ 662.5
White, Other	4,337	99.5	7,048	98.2	+ 62.5

Village; President Kenneth R. Biel, $5,400. Incorporated: 1855. Unofficial motto: "1890s Charm." First called Chelsea, then Frankfort Station—for Frankfurt, Germany. First settlers were German. MHV: $164,100.

FRANKLIN PARK

	1980	Percent	1990	Percent	% Change
Total Population	17,507		18,485		+ 5.6
Black	15	.1	30	.2	+ 100.0
Hispanic	1,543	8.8	3,849	20.8	+ 149.4
Asian, Pacific Islander	159	.9	242	1.3	+ 52.2
White, Other	17,333	99.0	18,213	98.5	+ 5.1

Village; President Jack B. Williams, $25,000. Incorporated: 1892. Named for Lesser Franklin, who in 1890 planned a modern residential and industrial community in this area. Many of the streets are named for his family: his wife Sarah, and their children, Dora, Pearl, Gustav, Rose and Edgington. There also are streets named Lesser and Franklin. MHV: $99,200.

GENEVA

	1980	Percent	1990	Percent	% Change
Total Population	9,881		12,617		+ 27.7
Black	37	.4	13	.1	− 64.9
Hispanic	135	1.4	177	1.4	+ 31.1
Asian, Pacific Islander	54	.5	146	1.2	+ 170.4
White, Other	9,790	99.1	12,458	98.7	+ 27.3

City; Mayor William Ottilie, $12,000. Founded in 1835, incorporated in 1858. Unofficial motto: "Moving Ahead with a Sense of History." Some early settlers were from Geneva, New York. MHV: $147,900.

GILBERTS

	1980	Percent	1990	Percent	% Change
Total Population	405		987		+ 143.7
Black	0	0.0	0	0.0	+ 0.0
Hispanic	0	0.0	20	2.0	+ 0.0
Asian, Pacific Islander	1	.2	5	.5	+ 400.0
White, Other	404	99.8	982	99.5	+ 143.1

Village; President Ronald P. Lammers, $5,040. Platted in 1855, incorporated in 1890. Unofficial motto: "A Growing Community." MHV: $151,500.

GLEN ELLYN

	1980	Percent	1990	Percent	% Change
Total Population	23,649		24,944		+ 5.5
Black	245	1.0	497	2.0	+ 102.9
Hispanic	272	1.2	659	2.6	+ 142.3
Asian, Pacific Islander	431	1.8	780	3.1	+ 81.0
White, Other	22,973	97.1	23,667	94.9	+ 3.0

Village; President Arthur W. Angrist, $600. Settled in 1834, incorporated as Glen Ellyn in 1892. The suburb has had many names, such as Stacy's Corner, Newton's Station, Danby, and Prospect Park. Its current name dates from the late 1800s. A prominent resident, Thomas E. Hill, purchased land in a glen with a manmade lake that he named for his wife Ellen. It was called Lake Glen Ellyn (which is the Welsh spelling of Ellen). Hill is also a main street in town. MHV: $162,500.

GLENCOE

	1980	Percent	1990	Percent	% Change
Total Population	9,200		8,499		− 7.6
Black	379	4.1	275	3.2	− 27.4

	1980	Percent	1990	Percent	% Change
Hispanic	143	1.6	129	1.5	– 9.8
Asian, Pacific Islander	77	.8	198	2.3	+ 157.1
White, Other	8,744	95.0	8,026	94.4	– 8.2

Village; President Elizabeth Warren, no salary. Incorporated: 1869. One of the first settlers was the farmer Matthew D. Coe. In 1853, he sold his farm to Walter Gurnee, a former Chicago mayor, who named it Coe's Glen. MHV: $426,700.

GLENDALE HEIGHTS

	1980	Percent	1990	Percent	% Change
Total Population	23,163		27,973		+ 20.8
Black	377	1.6	776	2.8	+ 105.8
Hispanic	850	3.7	1,725	6.2	+ 102.9
Asian, Pacific Islander	2,040	8.8	3,718	13.3	+ 82.3
White, Other	20,746	89.6	23,479	83.9	+ 13.2

Village; President Michael Camera, $5,000. Incorporated: 1959. Motto: "Proud and Progressive." The village's developer, Harold Reskin, wanted to call the village Glendale because it sat between Glen Ellyn and Bloomingdale. But a town in southern Illinois already had that name. As the story goes, he offered to paint that town's water tower and police cars with a new name if they'd change it. They told him to pound sand. So he added Heights to the name. MHV: $105,500.

GLENVIEW

	1980	Percent	1990	Percent	% Change
Total Population	32,060		37,093		+ 15.7
Black	279	.9	285	.8	+ 2.2
Hispanic	453	1.4	898	2.4	+ 98.2
Asian, Pacific Islander	1,011	3.2	2,752	7.4	+ 172.2
White, Other	30,770	96.0	34,056	91.8	+ 10.7

Village; President James Smirles, $1,200. Incorporated: 1899. Glenview has had several names, such as South Northfield and Glen Oak. In 1895, Hugh Burnham, who lived at Shermer and Glenview, suggested the name Glenview because there was a good view of a glen from the upstairs of his house. MHV: $235,600.

GLENWOOD

	1980	Percent	1990	Percent	% Change
Total Population	10,538		9,289		– 11.9
Black	1,009	9.6	2,330	25.1	+ 130.9
Hispanic	221	2.1	293	3.2	+ 32.6
Asian, Pacific Islander	69	.7	70	.8	+ 1.4
White, Other	9,460	89.8	6,889	74.2	– 27.2

Village; Mayor Fred W. Delaney, $12,000. First settled in 1840s, incorporated in 1903. Originally named Hickory Bend when it was surveyed in 1871. Early settler O.P. Axtell suggested changing the name to Glenwood because of the large number of wooded glens in the area. MHV: $86,000.

GODLEY

	1980	Percent	1990	Percent	% Change
Total Population	373		322		− 13.7
Black	1	.3	0	0.0	− 100.0
Hispanic	0	0.0	5	1.6	+ 0.0
Asian, Pacific Islander	1	.3	0	0.0	− 100.0
White, Other	371	99.5	322	100.0	− 13.2

Village; President Robert A. Willis, $480. Incorporated: 1888. The origin of the name is uncertain. MHV: $46,700.

GOLF

	1980	Percent	1990	Percent	% Change
Total Population	482		454		− 5.8
Black	0	0.0	0	0.0	+ 0.0
Hispanic	11	2.3	21	4.6	+ 90.9
Asian, Pacific Islander	9	1.9	11	2.4	+ 22.2
White, Other	473	98.1	443	97.6	− 6.3

Village; President Leo Cronin, $1. Incorporated: 1928. In the late 1800s, Milwaukee Road president Albert J. Earling started playing golf at the Glenview Club, so he had a rail siding built nearby for his private car. That siding became the Golf Station. MHV: $395,900.

GRAYSLAKE

	1980	Percent	1990	Percent	% Change
Total Population	5,260		7,388		+ 40.5
Black	1	.0	59	.8	+ 5800.0
Hispanic	67	1.3	204	2.8	+ 204.5
Asian, Pacific Islander	50	1.0	70	.9	+ 40.0
White, Other	5,209	99.0	7,259	98.3	+ 39.4

Village; Mayor Marvin E. Smith, $3,000. Incorporated: 1895. William Gray was one of the first residents. MHV: $111,600.

GREEN OAKS

	1980	Percent	1990	Percent	% Change
Total Population	1,415		2,101		+ 48.5
Black	0	0.0	12	.6	+ 0.0
Hispanic	7	.5	11	.5	+ 57.1
Asian, Pacific Islander	5	.4	64	3.0	+ 1180.0
White, Other	1,410	99.6	2,025	96.4	+ 43.6

Village; President Elaine Palmer, $2,000. Incorporated: 1960. Motto: "Community of Country Living." Named for, yes, all the green oaks. MHV: $256,700.

GURNEE

	1980	Percent	1990	Percent	% Change
Total Population	7,179		13,701		+ 90.8
Black	99	1.4	432	3.2	+ 336.4
Hispanic	109	1.5	426	3.1	+ 290.8
Asian, Pacific Islander	121	1.7	529	3.9	+ 337.2
White, Other	6,959	96.9	12,740	93.0	+ 83.1

Village; Mayor Richard A. Welton, $7,000. Settled in about 1835, incorporated in 1928. Motto: "Rural Community of the Future." When the Chicago, Milwaukee and St. Paul Railroad laid tracks through the area in 1873, the town was named for Walter Gurnee, a former Chicago mayor and member of the railroad's board of directors. MHV: $131,600.

HAINESVILLE

	1980	Percent	1990	Percent	% Change
Total Population	187		134		– 28.3
Black	0	0.0	0	0.0	+ 0.0
Hispanic	27	14.4	14	10.4	– 48.1
Asian, Pacific Islander	1	.5	0	0.0	– 100.0
White, Other	186	99.5	134	100.0	– 28.0

Village; Mayor George Benjamin, $6,120. Incorporated: 1846. Named for early founder Elijah Haines, an attorney and friend of Abe Lincoln. Haines' brother was Chicago Mayor John Charles Haines (1858-59). MHV: $83,300.

HAMPSHIRE

	1980	Percent	1990	Percent	% Change
Total Population	1,735		1,843		+ 6.2
Black	1	.1	1	.1	+ 0.0
Hispanic	39	2.2	36	2.0	– 7.7
Asian, Pacific Islander	4	.2	1	.1	– 75.0
White, Other	1,730	99.7	1,841	99.9	+ 6.4

Village; Mayor William Schmidt, $5,000. First settler, in 1836, was Zenas Allen (said to be a relative of Ethan Allen). Incorporated: 1876. Motto: "Where Farm and City Meet." Originally developed at U.S. 20 and Big Timber Road as a crossroads for pioneers. It was called Henpeck, either because there were so many hens eating grain that had fallen from the wagons or (residents say tongue in cheek) because there was a henpecked husband who left his wife and founded Harmony, a town nearby. Hampshire Township was settled mostly by people from New Hampshire. MHV: $92,300.

HANOVER PARK

	1980	Percent	1990	Percent	% Change
Total Population	28,850		32,895		+ 14.0
Black	390	1.4	1,188	3.6	+ 204.6
Hispanic	1,748	6.1	3,616	11.0	+ 106.9
Asian, Pacific Islander	1,089	3.8	2,435	7.4	+ 123.6
White, Other	27,371	94.9	29,272	89.0	+ 6.9

Village; President Sonya Crawshaw, $2,400. Incorporated: 1958. Named for Hanover Township. MHV: $101,900.

HARVARD

	1980	Percent	1990	Percent	% Change
Total Population	5,126		5,975		+ 16.6
Black	0	0.0	20	.3	+ 0.0

	1980	Percent	1990	Percent	% Change
Hispanic	228	4.4	847	14.2	+271.5
Asian, Pacific Islander	5	.1	16	.3	+220.0
White, Other	5,121	99.9	5,939	99.4	+16.0

City; Mayor Robert Iftner, $13,000. Founded in 1856, incorporated in 1891. Motto: "Home of Milk Day," an annual three-day festival with farm tours, cattle shows and a parade. The city was laid out in 1856 by three railroad men, one of whom was E.G. Ayer, who named it for Harvard in Massachusetts. MHV: $75,400.

HARVEY

	1980	Percent	1990	Percent	% Change
Total Population	35,810		29,771		−16.9
Black	23,491	65.6	23,813	80.0	+1.4
Hispanic	1,643	4.6	1,932	6.5	+17.6
Asian, Pacific Islander	65	.2	81	.3	+24.6
White, Other	12,254	34.2	5,877	19.7	−52.0

City; Mayor David Johnson. Settled in 1874, incorporated in 1891. Turlington W. Harvey was an early land owner in the area in 1890 and Harvey L. Hopkins founded the town's first industry. Turlington Harvey wanted the town to be named Turlington, but the postmaster suggested Harvey as a compromise for both men. MHV: $49,900.

HARWOOD HEIGHTS

	1980	Percent	1990	Percent	% Change
Total Population	8,228		7,680		−6.7
Black	3	.0	5	.1	+66.7
Hispanic	138	1.7	264	3.4	+91.3
Asian, Pacific Islander	92	1.1	209	2.7	+127.2
White, Other	8,133	98.8	7,466	97.2	−8.2

Village; Mayor Ray Willas, $25,000. Incorporated: 1948. Motto: "Serving People with Pride." The name is a combination of Harlem Avenue, which runs through the village, and Norwood Park Township, of which the village is a part. MHV: $126,300.

HAWTHORN WOODS

	1980	Percent	1990	Percent	% Change
Total Population	1,658		4,423		+166.8
Black	6	.4	51	1.2	+750.0
Hispanic	12	.7	29	.7	+141.7
Asian, Pacific Islander	2	.1	96	2.2	+4700.0
White, Other	1,650	99.5	4,276	96.7	+159.2

Incorporated: 1958. MHV: $305,700.

HAZEL CREST

	1980	Percent	1990	Percent	% Change
Total Population	13,973		13,334		−4.6
Black	1,662	11.9	6,869	51.5	+313.3
Hispanic	329	2.4	401	3.0	+21.9
Asian, Pacific Islander	228	1.6	158	1.2	−30.7
White, Other	12,083	86.5	6,307	47.3	−47.8

Village; President Martin J. Kauchak, $6,000. Settled in 1870, incorporated in 1912. Motto: "A Proud Past...A Promising Future." Named for the many hazelnut bushes in the area. MHV: $68,200.

HEBRON

	1980	Percent	1990	Percent	% Change
Total Population	786		809		+ 2.9
Black	2	.3	4	.5	+ 100.0
Hispanic	6	.8	19	2.3	+ 216.7
Asian, Pacific Islander	0	0.0	0	0.0	+ 0.0
White, Other	784	99.7	805	99.5	+ 2.7

Village; President William Sergeant, $2,400. Incorporated: 1895. Motto: "Green Giants" because in 1952 this tiny town took the state high school basketball championship. The team was the Hebron-Alden Green Giants. Early settler Bella H. Tryon, who settled here around 1836, used to invite other families to her home to sing. She chose Hebron as the village name because it was one of her favorite songs. MHV: $76,700.

HICKORY HILLS

	1980	Percent	1990	Percent	% Change
Total Population	13,778		13,021		− 5.5
Black	4	.0	41	.3	+ 925.0
Hispanic	275	2.0	532	4.1	+ 93.5
Asian, Pacific Islander	109	.8	204	1.6	+ 87.2
White, Other	13,665	99.2	12,776	98.1	− 6.5

City; Mayor Daniel Riley, $10,800. Incorporated: 1951. The city rests on rolling hills, and an oak and hickory forest once covered the area. MHV: $113,700.

HIGHLAND PARK

	1980	Percent	1990	Percent	% Change
Total Population	30,611		30,575		− .1
Black	547	1.8	787	2.6	+ 43.9
Hispanic	837	2.7	1,438	4.7	+ 71.8
Asian, Pacific Islander	391	1.3	723	2.4	+ 84.9
White, Other	29,673	96.9	29,065	95.1	− 2.0

City; Mayor Daniel M. Pierce, $9,500. Incorporated: 1869. Motto: "The Salvation of the Community Is Watchfulness of the Citizen." Named for the city's developers, the Highland Park Land Company. MHV: $257,000.

HIGHWOOD

	1980	Percent	1990	Percent	% Change
Total Population	5,452		5,331		− 2.2
Black	277	5.1	223	4.2	− 19.5
Hispanic	640	11.7	1,272	23.9	+ 98.8
Asian, Pacific Islander	99	1.8	89	1.7	− 10.1
White, Other	5,076	93.1	5,019	94.1	− 1.1

City; Mayor Fidel Ghini, no salary. Incorporated: 1887. Unofficial motto often used by the mayor: "Highwood First, America Second." Name describes the town's setting. MHV: $134,400.

HILLSIDE

	1980	Percent	1990	Percent	% Change
Total Population	8,279		7,672		− 7.3
Black	27	.3	482	6.3	+ 1685.2
Hispanic	186	2.2	440	5.7	+ 136.6
Asian, Pacific Islander	123	1.5	374	4.9	+ 204.1
White, Other	8,129	98.2	6,816	88.8	− 16.2

Village; President Joseph T. Tamburino, $5,000. Incorporated: 1905. Motto: "Hub of the Western Suburbs." The Illinois Central Railroad dubbed the area Hillside because its station was at the top of a hill. MHV: $94,200.

HINSDALE

	1980	Percent	1990	Percent	% Change
Total Population	16,726		16,029		− 4.2
Black	72	.4	128	.8	+ 77.8
Hispanic	197	1.2	245	1.5	+ 24.4
Asian, Pacific Islander	387	2.3	605	3.8	+ 56.3
White, Other	16,267	97.3	15,296	95.4	− 6.0

Village; President Martin Gross, no salary. Incorporated: 1873. Unofficial motto: "Rooted in the Past, Reaching for the Future." While the origin isn't certain, it may have been named for a man who never lived in Hinsdale. The village was said to have been named for H. W. Hinsdale, who came to Chicago in the 1840s, by his friend Charles G. Hammond, general superintendent of the Burlington Railroad. Hammond may have named the Hinsdale station for his pal. There are other theories, like it being named for Hinsdale, New York, the hometown of Isaac S. Bush, an early postmaster. MHV: $284,300.

HODGKINS

	1980	Percent	1990	Percent	% Change
Total Population	2,005		1,963		− 2.1
Black	0	0.0	3	.2	+ 0.0
Hispanic	299	14.9	595	30.3	+ 99.0
Asian, Pacific Islander	7	.3	14	.7	+ 100.0
White, Other	1,998	99.7	1,946	99.1	− 2.6

Village; President Noel Cummings, $8,400. Incorporated: 1896. Named for Jefferson Hodgkins, president of Kimball and Cobb Stone Company, which bought land in the Hodgkins area in 1888 and operated a quarry in the village. MHV: $78,800.

HOFFMAN ESTATES

	1980	Percent	1990	Percent	% Change
Total Population	37,272		46,561		+ 24.9
Black	503	1.3	1,334	2.9	+ 165.2

	1980	Percent	1990	Percent	% Change
Hispanic	1,203	3.2	2,543	5.5	+ 111.4
Asian, Pacific Islander	1,481	4.0	3,727	8.0	+ 151.7
White, Other	35,288	94.7	41,500	89.1	+ 17.6

Village; President Michael J. O'Malley, $9,000. Incorporated: 1959. Motto: "Growing to Greatness." In 1954, a local farmer sold 160 acres to Sam and Jack Hoffman, owner of Father and Son Construction Company. They built the first subdivision in what would become Hoffman Estates. The first homes in 1955 sold for about $14,500, with down payments as small as $700 and interest rates of 4 percent. MHV: $133,800.

HOLIDAY HILLS

	1980	Percent	1990	Percent	% Change
Total Population	802		807		+ .6
Black	0	0.0	1	.1	+ 0.0
Hispanic	15	1.9	24	3.0	+ 60.0
Asian, Pacific Islander	0	0.0	3	.4	+ 0.0
White, Other	802	100.0	803	99.5	+ .1

Village; Incorporated: 1976. MHV: $92,800.

HOMETOWN

	1980	Percent	1990	Percent	% Change
Total Population	5,324		4,769		− 10.4
Black	1	.0	2	.0	+ 100.0
Hispanic	50	.9	85	1.8	+ 70.0
Asian, Pacific Islander	6	.1	20	.4	+ 233.3
White, Other	5,317	99.9	4,747	99.5	− 10.7

City; Mayor Raymond Forsyth, $3,600. Incorporated: 1953. Motto: "Where a House Is a Home." In the late 1940s developer Joseph Merrion wanted this area to be a place with a "hometown" atmosphere for returning servicemen. MHV: $66,900.

HOMEWOOD

	1980	Percent	1990	Percent	% Change
Total Population	19,724		19,278		− 2.3
Black	424	2.1	1,233	6.4	+ 190.8
Hispanic	132	.7	280	1.5	+ 112.1
Asian, Pacific Islander	155	.8	344	1.8	+ 121.9
White, Other	19,145	97.1	17,701	91.8	− 7.5

Village; President John T. Doody, Jr., $3,700. Settlers arrived in 1830; first subdivision platted in 1853; incorporated in 1893. Motto: "Friendly Living." Delayed by a railroad accident around what is now Homewood, Jabez Howe walked around the area, liked it and eventually brought his family there. In 1869, the name of the settlement was changed to Homewood, at the suggestion of Howe, who said it was like a home in the woods. MHV: $99,900.

HUNTLEY

	1980	Percent	1990	Percent	% Change
Total Population	1,646		2,453		+ 49.0
Black	1	.1	0	0.0	− 100.0
Hispanic	50	3.0	44	1.8	− 12.0
Asian, Pacific Islander	4	.2	10	.4	+ 150.0
White, Other	1,641	99.7	2,443	99.6	+ 48.9

Village; President James Dhamer, $2,575. Incorporated: 1851. Motto: "The Friendly Village with Country Charm." Thomas Huntley was a settler in the 1840s. MHV: $104,000.

INDIAN CREEK

	1980	Percent	1990	Percent	% Change
Total Population	236		247		+ 4.7
Black	1	.4	0	0.0	− 100.0
Hispanic	1	.4	1	.4	+ 0.0
Asian, Pacific Islander	0	0.0	4	1.6	+ 0.0
White, Other	235	99.6	243	98.4	+ 3.4

Village. Incorporated: 1958. MHV: $167,000.

INDIAN HEAD PARK

	1980	Percent	1990	Percent	% Change
Total Population	2,915		3,503		+ 20.2
Black	15	.5	22	.6	+ 46.7
Hispanic	44	1.5	52	1.5	+ 18.2
Asian, Pacific Islander	70	2.4	58	1.7	− 17.1
White, Other	2,830	97.1	3,423	97.7	+ 21.0

Village; President Werner Perthel, about $840. Incorporated: 1959. The village was built on two golf courses: Acacia and Indian Head. MHV: $166,300.

INVERNESS

	1980	Percent	1990	Percent	% Change
Total Population	4,046		6,503		+ 60.7
Black	3	.1	20	.3	+ 566.7
Hispanic	36	.9	83	1.3	+ 130.6
Asian, Pacific Islander	86	2.1	270	4.2	+ 214.0
White, Other	3,957	97.8	6,213	95.5	+ 57.0

Village; President Donna L. Thomas, $6,000. Incorporated: 1963. Motto: "The Village with a Heritage." Named for Inverness, Scotland, by the original developers, the McIntosh family. Many of the streets have Scottish names. MHV: $365,200.

ISLAND LAKE

	1980	Percent	1990	Percent	% Change
Total Population	2,293		4,449		+ 94.0
Black	2	.1	19	.4	+ 850.0
Hispanic	81	3.5	195	4.4	+ 140.7
Asian, Pacific Islander	3	.1	46	1.0	+ 1433.3
White, Other	2,288	99.8	4,384	98.5	+ 91.6

Village; Mayor Charles R. Amrich, $3,600, plus $75 per special meeting. Incorporated: 1952. The village has a lake with an island in the middle of it. MHV: $95,500.

ITASCA

	1980	Percent	1990	Percent	% Change
Total Population	7,129		6,947		– 2.6
Black	75	1.1	92	1.3	+ 22.7
Hispanic	242	3.4	350	5.0	+ 44.6
Asian, Pacific Islander	176	2.5	224	3.2	+ 27.3
White, Other	6,878	96.5	6,631	95.5	– 3.6

Village; President Shirley Ketter, $4,800. Incorporated: 1890. Motto: "The Village of Irises." The village founder was Dr. Elijah Smith, who came to the area in 1841, purchased land in 1843 and subdivided it. He named the village after he and his wife took a trip to Lake Itasca, Minnesota. MHV: $136,700.

JOLIET

	1980	Percent	1990	Percent	% Change
Total Population	77,956		76,836		– 1.4
Black	15,672	20.1	16,600	21.6	+ 5.9
Hispanic	6,565	8.4	9,741	12.7	+ 48.4
Asian, Pacific Islander	355	.5	742	1.0	+ 109.0
White, Other	61,929	79.4	59,494	77.4	– 3.9

City; Mayor Arthur Schultz, $12,000. Incorporated as the village of Juliet in 1837; as the city of Joliet in 1852. Motto: "City of Champions" because Joliet Township High School band and Joliet American Legion band have won many competitions and because of various high school and grade school championship athletic teams. The settlement first was called Juliet, some say after Romeo and Juliet (Romeoville is nearby) or the daughter of an early settler. It may have been a corrupted spelling of Joliet, since there is a Mound Joliet. At any rate, in 1845, President Martin Van Buren was traveling through and suggested the town be called Joliet after the explorer Louis Jolliet. The state legislature approved the change in 1845. MHV: $64,500.

JUSTICE

	1980	Percent	1990	Percent	% Change
Total Population	10,552		11,137		+ 5.5
Black	1,102	10.4	1,608	14.4	+ 45.9
Hispanic	285	2.7	540	4.8	+ 89.5
Asian, Pacific Islander	81	.8	176	1.6	+ 117.3
White, Other	9,369	88.8	9,353	84.0	– .2

Village; Acting President Edward C. Rusch, Jr., $7,800. Incorporated, 1911. Motto: "Serving the People through Progress." During a meeting on the village's incorporation, early resident William Cronin, Jr., who owned a farm in the area, is said to have slammed his fist down and said, "Let there be justice," hence the name. A street is named for Cronin. MHV: $91,800.

KENILWORTH

	1980	Percent	1990	Percent	% Change
Total Population	2,708		2,402		− 11.3
Black	6	.2	5	.2	− 16.7
Hispanic	27	1.0	25	1.0	− 7.4
Asian, Pacific Islander	37	1.4	48	2.0	+ 29.7
White, Other	2,665	98.4	2,349	97.8	− 11.9

Village; President Stanford Smith, no salary. Incorporated: 1896. Chicago businessman Joseph Sears, seeking a summer home, founded the village around 1889. After a summer trip to England, he chose the name of Kenilworth, England. MHV: $500,000 plus.

KILDEER

	1980	Percent	1990	Percent	% Change
Total Population	1,609		2,257		+ 40.3
Black	0	0.0	4	.2	+ 0.0
Hispanic	11	.7	41	1.8	+ 272.7
Asian, Pacific Islander	10	.6	56	2.5	+ 460.0
White, Other	1,599	99.4	2,197	97.3	+ 37.4

Village; President George L. Welch, no salary. Incorporated: 1958. Named for the Killdeer bird (although misspelled by the village). MHV: $377,500.

LA GRANGE

	1980	Percent	1990	Percent	% Change
Total Population	15,445		15,362		− .5
Black	1,036	6.7	968	6.3	− 6.6
Hispanic	238	1.5	251	1.6	+ 5.5
Asian, Pacific Islander	131	.8	141	.9	+ 7.6
White, Other	14,278	92.4	14,253	92.8	− .2

Village; President William P. Erickson, $3,600. Incorporated: 1879. Motto: "Tradition and Pride Moving Forward." Village founder Franklin D. Cossitt named it after a town in Tennessee. MHV: $166,100.

LA GRANGE PARK

	1980	Percent	1990	Percent	% Change
Total Population	13,359		12,861		− 3.7
Black	19	.1	52	.4	+ 173.7
Hispanic	122	.9	245	1.9	+ 100.8
Asian, Pacific Islander	105	.8	203	1.6	+ 93.3
White, Other	13,235	99.1	12,606	98.0	− 4.8

Village; President Robert Huson, no salary. Incorporated: 1892. Motto: "Village of Roses." Origin of Name: see La Grange. MHV: $141,100.

LAKE BARRINGTON

	1980	Percent	1990	Percent	% Change
Total Population	2,320		3,855		+ 66.2
Black	2	.1	9	.2	+ 350.0

	1980	Percent	1990	Percent	% Change
Hispanic	14	.6	27	.7	+92.9
Asian, Pacific Islander	1	.0	35	.9	+3400.0
White, Other	2,317	99.9	3,811	98.9	+64.5

Village; President Nancy Smith, no salary. Incorporated: 1959. See Barrington for origin of name. MHV: $258,200.

LAKE BLUFF

	1980	Percent	1990	Percent	% Change
Total Population	4,434		5,513		+24.3
Black	24	.5	35	.6	+45.8
Hispanic	27	.6	48	.9	+77.8
Asian, Pacific Islander	44	1.0	55	1.0	+25.0
White, Other	4,366	98.5	5,423	98.4	+24.2

Village; President N. David Graf, no salary. Incorporated: 1895. It's on a bluff overlooking Lake Michigan. MHV: $285,200.

LAKE FOREST

	1980	Percent	1990	Percent	% Change
Total Population	15,245		17,836		+17.0
Black	218	1.4	226	1.3	+3.7
Hispanic	166	1.1	316	1.8	+90.4
Asian, Pacific Islander	198	1.3	465	2.6	+134.8
White, Other	14,829	97.3	17,145	96.1	+15.6

City; Mayor Charles F. Clarke, Jr., $10. Incorporated: 1861; incorporation amended 1869. Motto: "Naturae Et Scientiae Amor," meaning for the love of nature and science. Named for its location. MHV: $493,700.

LAKE IN THE HILLS

	1980	Percent	1990	Percent	% Change
Total Population	5,651		5,866		+3.8
Black	12	.2	5	.1	−58.3
Hispanic	107	1.9	127	2.2	+18.7
Asian, Pacific Islander	10	.2	38	.6	+280.0
White, Other	5,629	99.6	5,823	99.3	+3.4

Village; President Barbara Key, $7,200. Incorporated: 1952. Named for its locaton in a hilly area among four lakes. MHV: $96,600.

LAKE VILLA

	1980	Percent	1990	Percent	% Change
Total Population	1,462		2,857		+95.4
Black	13	.9	20	.7	+53.8
Hispanic	24	1.6	53	1.9	+120.8
Asian, Pacific Islander	14	1.0	18	.6	+28.6
White, Other	1,435	98.2	2,819	98.7	+96.4

Village; Mayor Joyce F. Frayer, $1,500. Incorporated: 1901. Unofficial motto: "Gateway to the Lakes Region." Named for the three lakes in the village—Cedar, Deep and Sun. MHV: $130,400.

LAKE ZURICH

	1980	Percent	1990	Percent	% Change
Total Population	8,225		14,947		+ 81.7
Black	43	.5	125	.8	+ 190.7
Hispanic	348	4.2	565	3.8	+ 62.4
Asian, Pacific Islander	79	1.0	359	2.4	+ 354.4
White, Other	8,103	98.5	14,463	96.8	+ 78.5

Village; President James W. Kay, $5,200. Incorporated: 1896. The village is on Lake Zurich, which was named by 1843 settler Seth Paine. Having been to Switzerland, he named his town for Lake Zurich there. MHV: $161,200.

LAKEMOOR

	1980	Percent	1990	Percent	% Change
Total Population	723		1,322		+ 82.8
Black	0	0.0	4	.3	+ 0.0
Hispanic	9	1.2	31	2.3	+ 244.4
Asian, Pacific Islander	1	.1	6	.5	+ 500.0
White, Other	722	99.9	1,312	99.2	+ 81.7

Village. Incorporated: 1952. MHV: $79,900.

LAKEWOOD

	1980	Percent	1990	Percent	% Change
Total Population	1,254		1,609		+ 28.3
Black	1	.1	1	.1	+ 0.0
Hispanic	11	.9	28	1.7	+ 154.5
Asian, Pacific Islander	0	0.0	11	.7	+ 0.0
White, Other	1,253	99.9	1,597	99.3	+ 27.5

Village; President Scott Breeden, $1,500. Incorporated: 1933. Named because it's on Crystal Lake in a wooded area. MHV: $198,800.

LANSING

	1980	Percent	1990	Percent	% Change
Total Population	29,039		28,086		− 3.3
Black	321	1.1	832	3.0	+ 159.2
Hispanic	598	2.1	779	2.8	+ 30.3
Asian, Pacific Islander	88	.3	124	.4	+ 40.9
White, Other	28,630	98.6	27,130	96.6	− 5.2

Village; Mayor Bill Balthis, $30,000, plus $6,000 expenses. Incorporated: 1893. Motto: "Proud of Our Past, Confident in Our Future." Early settler John Lansing arrived in 1846. The original town was laid out in 1865. MHV: $77,900.

LEMONT

	1980	Percent	1990	Percent	% Change
Total Population	5,640		7,348		+ 30.3
Black	1	.0	6	.1	+ 500.0
Hispanic	111	2.0	181	2.5	+ 63.1
Asian, Pacific Islander	36	.6	52	.7	+ 44.4
White, Other	5,603	99.3	7,290	99.2	+ 30.1

Village; President Joseph Forzley, $4,200. Incorporated: 1873. Motto: "Village of Faith" because of its many churches. The village is on several hills, and "mont" means hill or mountain in French. MHV: $118,400.

LIBERTYVILLE

	1980	Percent	1990	Percent	% Change
Total Population	16,520		19,174		+ 16.1
Black	28	.2	101	.5	+ 260.7
Hispanic	327	2.0	436	2.3	+ 33.3
Asian, Pacific Islander	348	2.1	711	3.7	+ 104.3
White, Other	16,144	97.7	18,362	95.8	+ 13.7

Village; Mayor Jo Ann Eckmann, $5,500. Motto: "Where Commerce and Country Meet." The first settler, George Vardin, settled here in the early 1830s, but the village wasn't incorporated until 1882. It was originally called Vardin's Grove. Independence Day, 1836, the unsurveyed land was opened for settlement, so the settlers decided to change the name to Independence Grove. Since that name was already in use, they agreed on Libertyville. MHV: $188,500.

LINCOLNSHIRE

	1980	Percent	1990	Percent	% Change
Total Population	4,151		4,931		+ 18.8
Black	28	.7	18	.4	− 35.7
Hispanic	41	1.0	109	2.2	+ 165.9
Asian, Pacific Islander	27	.7	133	2.7	+ 392.6
White, Other	4,096	98.7	4,780	96.9	+ 16.7

Village; President Barbara LaPiana, no salary. Incorporated: 1957. Real estate developer Roger Ladd owned most of the land in the area and called it Ladd's Lincolnshire. MHV: $343,900.

LINCOLNWOOD

	1980	Percent	1990	Percent	% Change
Total Population	11,921		11,365		− 4.7
Black	12	.1	13	.1	+ 8.3
Hispanic	254	2.1	368	3.2	+ 44.9
Asian, Pacific Islander	768	6.4	1,770	15.6	+ 130.5
White, Other	11,141	93.5	9,582	84.3	− 14.0

Village; Mayor Frank J. Chulay, $25,000. Settled in 1844 by George Proesel; incorporated in 1911. Motto: "Catch the Pride." Originally called Tessville after an early settler, Johann Tess; name was changed to Lincolnwood in 1936. MHV: $199,300.

LINDENHURST

	1980	Percent	1990	Percent	% Change
Total Population	6,220		8,038		+ 29.2
Black	17	.3	57	.7	+ 235.3
Hispanic	85	1.4	147	1.8	+ 72.9
Asian, Pacific Islander	72	1.2	86	1.1	+ 19.4
White, Other	6,131	98.6	7,895	98.2	+ 28.8

Village; Mayor Paul Baumunk, $6,000. Incorporated: 1956. Motto: "Developing Today for Tomorrow." Most of the village is built on part of what was called the Lindenhurst Farms. MHV: $118,600.

LISLE

	1980	Percent	1990	Percent	% Change
Total Population	13,625		19,512		+ 43.2
Black	402	3.0	562	2.9	+ 39.8
Hispanic	192	1.4	593	3.0	+ 208.9
Asian, Pacific Islander	366	2.7	1,104	5.7	+ 201.6
White, Other	12,857	94.4	17,846	91.5	+ 38.8

Village; President Ronald Ghilardi, $6,000. Settled in 1832; incorporated in 1956. Motto: "The Arboretum Village" (Morton Arboretum is in Lisle). The name was suggested by Alonzo B. Chatfield, who came here in 1835 from New York, where there was a town called Lisle. MHV: $162,800.

LOCKPORT

	1980	Percent	1990	Percent	% Change
Total Population	9,170		9,401		+ 2.5
Black	48	.5	30	.3	− 37.5
Hispanic	156	1.7	276	2.9	+ 76.9
Asian, Pacific Islander	45	.5	48	.5	+ 6.7
White, Other	9,077	99.0	9,323	99.2	+ 2.7

City; Mayor Robert A. Wynveen, $9,200. Platted in 1836; incorporated in 1853. The city is located along the old Illinois & Michigan Canal, built in the 1840s. Lock 1 is in Lockport. MHV: $85,400.

LOMBARD

	1980	Percent	1990	Percent	% Change
Total Population	37,295		39,408		+ 5.7
Black	220	.6	519	1.3	+ 135.9
Hispanic	575	1.5	1,090	2.8	+ 89.6
Asian, Pacific Islander	894	2.4	1,751	4.4	+ 95.9
White, Other	36,181	97.0	37,138	94.2	+ 2.6

Village; President Richard Arnold, $8,400. Platted in 1868; incorporated in 1869. Motto: "The Lilac Village." Named in honor of Josiah P. Lombard, who in the 1860s bought 227 acres in the area and built several houses. MHV: $118,000.

LONG GROVE

	1980	Percent	1990	Percent	% Change
Total Population	2,013		4,740		+ 135.5
Black	7	.3	29	.6	+ 314.3
Hispanic	41	2.0	120	2.5	+ 192.7
Asian, Pacific Islander	31	1.5	131	2.8	+ 322.6
White, Other	1,975	98.1	4,580	96.6	+ 131.9

Village; President George G. Dickson, no salary. First settlers arrived in 1838; village incorporated in 1956. Motto: "Ecology for

Everyone." Name inspired by a long grove of trees and an old Indian trail that ran diagonally through the village. MHV: $430,200.

LYNWOOD

	1980	Percent	1990	Percent	% Change
Total Population	4,195		6,535		+ 55.8
Black	167	4.0	1,017	15.6	+ 509.0
Hispanic	173	4.1	284	4.3	+ 64.2
Asian, Pacific Islander	21	.5	57	.9	+ 171.4
White, Other	4,007	95.5	5,461	83.6	+ 36.3

Village; Mayor Barclay Fleming. Incorporated: 1959. Motto: "Lynwood Positively Our Town." MHV: $96,000.

LYONS

	1980	Percent	1990	Percent	% Change
Total Population	9,925		9,828		− 1.0
Black	2	.0	8	.1	+ 300.0
Hispanic	322	3.2	569	5.8	+ 76.7
Asian, Pacific Islander	89	.9	109	1.1	+ 22.5
White, Other	9,834	99.1	9,711	98.8	− 1.3

Village; President Judith B. Petrucci, $10,000. Incorporated: 1888. Motto: "A Community of Growing Pride." Lyons is the site of a portage through which went French explorers. Named after Lyons, France, which is at the confluence of two rivers. MHV: $89,800.

MANHATTAN

	1980	Percent	1990	Percent	% Change
Total Population	1,944		2,059		+ 5.9
Black	0	0.0	0	0.0	+ 0.0
Hispanic	17	.9	35	1.7	+ 105.9
Asian, Pacific Islander	2	.1	3	.1	+ 50.0
White, Other	1,942	99.9	2,056	99.9	+ 5.9

Village: President Michael R. Naughton, $1,250. Incorporated: 1886. Motto: Memories with Progress. Named for an early resident who came from New York City. MHV: $85,500.

MAPLE PARK

	1980	Percent	1990	Percent	% Change
Total Population	637		641		+ .6
Black	0	0.0	0	0.0	+ 0.0
Hispanic	12	1.9	5	.8	− 58.3
Asian, Pacific Islander	6	.9	0	0.0	− 100.0
White, Other	631	99.1	641	****	+ 1.6

Village. Settled in 1872; incorporated in 1901. MHV: $84,700.

MARENGO

	1980	Percent	1990	Percent	% Change
Total Population	4,361		4,768		+ 9.3
Black	0	0.0	7	.1	+ 0.0
Hispanic	316	7.2	358	7.5	+ 13.3
Asian, Pacific Islander	21	.5	16	.3	− 23.8
White, Other	4,340	99.5	4,745	99.5	+ 9.3

City; Mayor Richard Baker, $3,500. Founded in 1835 by Calvin Spencer. Named for an Indian battle, the Battle of Marengo. Motto: "Home of Settlers' Days." MHV: $88,300.

MARKHAM

	1980	Percent	1990	Percent	% Change
Total Population	15,172		13,136		− 13.4
Black	10,592	69.8	10,040	76.4	− 5.2
Hispanic	217	1.4	193	1.5	− 11.1
Asian, Pacific Islander	24	.2	64	.5	+ 166.7
White, Other	4,556	30.0	3,032	23.1	− 33.5

City; Mayor Evans R. Miller, $25,000. Incorporated: 1925. Motto: "Unity for the Community." Named for Charles H. Markham, president of the Illinois Central Railroad over 100 years ago. The I.C. runs along the border of Markham. MHV: $52,300.

MATTESON

	1980	Percent	1990	Percent	% Change
Total Population	10,223		11,378		+ 11.3
Black	1,266	12.4	5,035	44.3	+ 297.7
Hispanic	333	3.3	365	3.2	+ 9.6
Asian, Pacific Islander	328	3.2	311	2.7	− 5.2
White, Other	8,629	84.4	6,032	53.0	− 30.1

Village; President Mark Stricker, $4,000. Incorporated: 1889. Motto: "Crossroads of Heritage and Progress." Named for Gov. Joel Aldrich Matteson (1853-57), who never lived in the town. MHV: $87,400.

MAYWOOD

	1980	Percent	1990	Percent	% Change
Total Population	27,998		27,139		− 3.1
Black	21,015	75.1	22,733	83.8	+ 8.2
Hispanic	1,893	6.8	1,795	6.6	− 5.2
Asian, Pacific Islander	112	.4	136	.5	+ 21.4
White, Other	6,871	24.5	4,270	15.7	− 37.9

Village; President Donald Williams, $6,302. Incorporated: 1869. Motto: "The Village of Eternal Light." Named for May, the daughter of the village's founder, Col. William T. Nichols, who came from Vermont with six other men in 1868 and started the Maywood Company, a real estate development firm. MHV: $67,900.

McCOOK

	1980	Percent	1990	Percent	% Change
Total Population	303		235		− 22.4
Black	0	0.0	0	0.0	+ 0.0
Hispanic	12	4.0	4	1.7	− 66.7
Asian, Pacific Islander	0	0.0	3	1.3	+ 0.0
White, Other	303	****	232	98.7	− 23.4

Village; Mayor Emil T. Sergo. Incorporated: 1929. Named for John J. McCook, an official of the Santa Fe RailRoad, which ran through town. MHV: $93,300.

McCULLOM LAKE

	1980	Percent	1990	Percent	% Change
Total Population	947		1,033		+ 9.1
Black	1	.1	0	0.0	− 100.0
Hispanic	25	2.6	46	4.5	+ 84.0
Asian, Pacific Islander	2	.2	1	.1	− 50.0
White, Other	944	99.7	1,032	99.9	+ 9.3

Village; President Lois M. Parenti. MHV: $67,500.

McHENRY

	1980	Percent	1990	Percent	% Change
Total Population	10,908		16,177		+ 48.3
Black	5	.0	10	.1	+ 100.0
Hispanic	80	.7	347	2.1	+ 333.8
Asian, Pacific Islander	74	.7	95	.6	+ 28.4
White, Other	10,829	99.3	16,072	99.4	+ 48.4

City; Mayor William J. Busse, $15,000. Founded in 1836; incorporated in 1923. Named for Col. William McHenry, an officer in the Black Hawk Wars. Motto: "A Proud Past and a Progressive Future." MHV: $101,100.

MELROSE PARK

	1980	Percent	1990	Percent	% Change
Total Population	20,735		20,859		+ .6
Black	46	.2	184	.9	+ 300.0
Hispanic	3,060	14.8	6,303	30.2	+ 106.0
Asian, Pacific Islander	308	1.5	491	2.4	+ 59.4
White, Other	20,381	98.3	20,184	96.8	− 1.0

Village; President C. August Taddeo, $32,000. Incorporated: 1892. Named for the Melrose Realty Company, the developers of the village. The company was owned by Allen Eaton and Edward Cuyler. Motto: "Corporate King of the Suburbs." MHV: $99,200.

MERRIONETTE PARK

	1980	Percent	1990	Percent	% Change
Total Population	2,054		2,065		+ .5
Black	0	0.0	30	1.5	+ 0.0
Hispanic	30	1.5	39	1.9	+ 30.0
Asian, Pacific Islander	13	.6	19	.9	+ 46.2
White, Other	2,041	99.4	2,016	97.6	− 1.2

Village; President Madeleon Rogowski, $7,200. Incorporated: 1947. Named for builder J.E. Merrion. Motto: "Friendship, Progress and Citizen Government." MHV: $70,600.

METTAWA

	1980	Percent	1990	Percent	% Change
Total Population	330		348		+ 5.5
Black	2	.6	0	0.0	− 100.0
Hispanic	4	1.2	8	2.3	+ 100.0
Asian, Pacific Islander	1	.3	12	3.4	+ 1100.0
White, Other	327	99.1	336	96.6	+ 2.8

Village; Acting President Julius Abler, no salary. Incorporated: 1960. An Indian name. MHV: $500,000.

MIDLOTHIAN

	1980	Percent	1990	Percent	% Change
Total Population	14,274		14,372		+ .7
Black	25	.2	352	2.4	+ 1308.0
Hispanic	321	2.2	542	3.8	+ 68.8
Asian, Pacific Islander	80	.6	109	.8	+ 36.3
White, Other	14,169	99.3	13,911	96.8	− 1.8

Village; Mayor Thomas J. Murawski, $15,000. Incorporated in 1927 by mostly German settlers. Motto: "The Community that Pride Built." Named for the Midlothian Country Club, founded in 1896, which was named for a borough in Scotland. MHV: $74,500.

MINOOKA

	1980	Percent	1990	Percent	% Change
Total Population	1,565		2,561		+ 63.6
Black	0	0.0	1	.0	+ 0.0
Hispanic	14	.9	27	1.1	+ 92.9
Asian, Pacific Islander	1	.1	14	.5	+ 1300.0
White, Other	1,564	99.9	2,546	99.4	+ 62.8

Village; President Keith Flatneff, $2,000. Incorporated: 1854. In the language of the Potowatomis, it means "contentment, high place and/or place of the maple trees." MHV: $116,200.

MOKENA

	1980	Percent	1990	Percent	% Change
Total Population	4,578		6,128		+ 33.9
Black	0	0.0	10	.2	+ 0.0
Hispanic	43	.9	90	1.5	+ 109.3
Asian, Pacific Islander	13	.3	18	.3	+ 38.5
White, Other	4,565	99.7	6,100	99.5	+ 33.6

Village; President Ronald J. Grotovsky. Incorporated: 1852. Motto: "Planned Progress Pleasant Living." MHV: $115,500.

MONEE

	1980	Percent	1990	Percent	% Change
Total Population	993		1,044		+ 5.1
Black	0	0.0	1	.1	+ 0.0
Hispanic	11	1.1	64	6.1	+ 481.8
Asian, Pacific Islander	1	.1	1	.1	+ 0.0
White, Other	992	99.9	1,042	99.8	+ 5.0

Village; President Richard Wille, $2,400. Incorporated: 1874. Motto: "Indians to Industry." Named for an Indian princess. MHV: $76,600.

MONTGOMERY

	1980	Percent	1990	Percent	% Change
Total Population	3,369		4,267		+ 26.7
Black	64	1.9	91	2.1	+ 42.2

	1980	Percent	1990	Percent	% Change
Hispanic	138	4.1	247	5.8	+ 79.0
Asian, Pacific Islander	11	.3	45	1.1	+ 309.1
White, Other	3,294	97.8	4,131	96.8	+ 25.4

Village; Mayor Raymond C. Kozloski, $9,600. Incorporated: 1835. Named for Mr. Daniel Gray, the first settler, who came from Montgomery County, New York. MHV: $87,300.

MORTON GROVE

	1980	Percent	1990	Percent	% Change
Total Population	23,747		22,408		− 5.6
Black	31	.1	58	.3	+ 87.1
Hispanic	440	1.9	618	2.8	+ 40.5
Asian, Pacific Islander	1,520	6.4	3,370	15.0	+ 121.7
White, Other	22,196	93.5	18,980	84.7	− 14.5

Village; Mayor Richard Hohs, $8,000. Incorporated in 1895; settled in about 1845. Named for Morton, the surname of Levi Parsons Morton, a U.S. vice president under Benjamin Harrison (1889-93) and an official with the Milwaukee Road Railroad, which ran through town. MHV: $150,700.

MOUNT PROSPECT

	1980	Percent	1990	Percent	% Change
Total Population	52,634		53,170		+ 1.0
Black	331	.6	606	1.1	+ 83.1
Hispanic	1,225	2.3	3,411	6.4	+ 178.4
Asian, Pacific Islander	1,490	2.8	3,417	6.4	+ 129.3
White, Other	50,813	96.5	49,147	92.4	− 3.3

Village; Mayor Gerald Farley, $7,000. Incorporated: 1917. Motto: "Where Friendliness Is a Way of Life." The first subdivider of the area, in 1871, gave it the name Mount Prospect to emphasize its relatively high elevation and its prospects for growth. MHV: $155,100.

MUNDELEIN

	1980	Percent	1990	Percent	% Change
Total Population	17,053		21,215		+ 24.4
Black	16	.1	198	.9	+ 1137.5
Hispanic	1,287	7.5	2,867	13.5	+ 122.8
Asian, Pacific Islander	174	1.0	608	2.9	+ 249.4
White, Other	16,863	98.9	20,409	96.2	+ 21.0

Village; Mayor Marilyn Sindles, $10,000. Incorporated: 1909. Named for Cardinal Mundelein, who donated a fire truck to the village. St. Mary of the Lake Seminary is in the town. Motto: "Where Youth Has a Future." MHV: $115,900.

NAPERVILLE

	1980	Percent	1990	Percent	% Change
Total Population	42,330		85,351		+ 101.6
Black	314	.7	1,795	2.1	+ 471.7

	1980	Percent	1990	Percent	% Change
Hispanic	418	1.0	1,527	1.8	+ 265.3
Asian, Pacific Islander	921	2.2	4,133	4.8	+ 348.8
White, Other	41,095	97.1	79,423	93.1	+ 93.3

City; Mayor Sam Macrane, $15,000. Founded in 1831; incorporated in 1890. Named for its first settlers, John and Joseph Naper. MHV: $176,500.

NEW LENOX

	1980	Percent	1990	Percent	% Change
Total Population	5,792		9,627		+ 66.2
Black	2	.0	13	.1	+ 550.0
Hispanic	74	1.3	181	1.9	+ 144.6
Asian, Pacific Islander	18	.3	18	.2	+ 0.0
White, Other	5,772	99.7	9,596	99.7	+ 66.3

Village; President John Nowakowski, $1,500 plus $50 a meeting. Founded in 1830; incorporated in 1946. First called Hickory Settlement, then Tracy. Motto: "Home of Proud Americans." Will County's first post office was opened on June 29, 1833, in New Lenox. Named for the hometown of a section boss building the Rock Island Railroad, Lenox, New York. MHV: $109,200.

NILES

	1980	Percent	1990	Percent	% Change
Total Population	30,363		28,284		− 6.8
Black	63	.2	122	.4	+ 93.7
Hispanic	495	1.6	1,016	3.6	+ 105.3
Asian, Pacific Islander	888	2.9	1,988	7.0	+ 123.9
White, Other	29,412	96.9	26,174	92.5	− 11.0

Village; Mayor Nicholas Blase, $4,000. First settled in 1831 and became a village in 1852; incorporated in 1899. Motto: "Where People Count." Nobody really knows how the town got its name. MHV: $140,700.

NORRIDGE

	1980	Percent	1990	Percent	% Change
Total Population	16,483		14,459		− 12.3
Black	6	.0	12	.1	+ 100.0
Hispanic	148	.9	321	2.2	+ 116.9
Asian, Pacific Islander	158	1.0	234	1.6	+ 48.1
White, Other	16,319	99.0	14,213	98.3	− 12.9

Village; President Joseph Sieb, $25,000. Incorporated: 1948. The name is a combination of Norwood Park the township's name, and Park Ridge, a nearby suburb. Norwood, in turn, took its name from the 1867 novel *Norwood: Or Village Life in New England* by Henry Ward Beecher, the clergyman, orator and writer. MHV: $136,200.

NORTH AURORA

	1980	Percent	1990	Percent	% Change
Total Population	5,205		5,940		+ 14.1
Black	139	2.7	184	3.1	+ 32.4
Hispanic	190	3.7	307	5.2	+ 61.6
Asian, Pacific Islander	45	.9	158	2.7	+ 251.1
White, Other	5,021	96.5	5,598	94.2	+ 11.5

Village; Mayor Alfred Imgrund, $3,480. Founded in 1834 as Schneider's Mill; incorporated in 1905. Motto: "Village with a View to the Future." So called because it is located north of Aurora. MHV: $97,300.

NORTH BARRINGTON

	1980	Percent	1990	Percent	% Change
Total Population	1,475		1,787		+ 21.2
Black	0	0.0	20	1.1	+ 0.0
Hispanic	5	.3	40	2.2	+ 700.0
Asian, Pacific Islander	8	.5	19	1.1	+ 137.5
White, Other	1,467	99.5	1,748	97.8	+ 19.2

Village; President Walter R. Clarke, Jr., no salary. First houses built in 1857. Incorporated: 1959. MHV: $307,000.

NORTH CHICAGO

	1980	Percent	1990	Percent	% Change
Total Population	38,774		34,978		− 9.8
Black	10,495	27.1	12,043	34.4	+ 14.7
Hispanic	1,963	5.1	3,213	9.2	+ 63.7
Asian, Pacific Islander	949	2.4	1,268	3.6	+ 33.6
White, Other	27,330	70.5	21,667	61.9	− 20.7

City; Mayor Bobby E. Thompson, $44,000. Incorporated: 1909. Motto: "City of Vision." Named for its location. MHV: $64,000.

NORTH RIVERSIDE

	1980	Percent	1990	Percent	% Change
Total Population	6,764		6,005		− 11.2
Black	0	0.0	10	.2	+ 0.0
Hispanic	56	.8	173	2.9	+ 208.9
Asian, Pacific Islander	34	.5	63	1.0	+ 85.3
White, Other	6,730	99.5	5,932	98.8	− 11.9

Village; Mayor Richard Scheck, $3,600. Incorporated: 1923. Motto: "Village of Friendly People." So called because it is north of Riverside. MHV: $112,500.

NORTHBROOK

	1980	Percent	1990	Percent	% Change
Total Population	30,778		32,308		+ 5.0
Black	73	.2	68	.2	− 6.8
Hispanic	533	1.7	510	1.6	− 4.3
Asian, Pacific Islander	897	2.9	2,079	6.4	+ 131.8
White, Other	29,808	96.8	30,161	93.4	+ 1.2

Village; President Richard T. Falcone, $1,200, plus $50 per meeting. Incorporated in 1901 as Shermerville. Name changed to Northbrook in 1923, so as to be identified less with a single family. Took its name from its location—along the middle fork of the North Branch of the Chicago River. Motto: "The Village of Friendly Living." MHV: $271,000.

NORTHFIELD

	1980	Percent	1990	Percent	% Change
Total Population	5,807		4,635		− 20.2
Black	18	.3	11	.2	− 38.9
Hispanic	42	.7	53	1.1	+ 26.2
Asian, Pacific Islander	103	1.8	200	4.3	+ 94.2
White, Other	5,686	97.9	4,424	95.4	− 22.2

Village; President Richard M. Rieser, Jr., no salary. Incorporated in 1926 as Wau-bun, an Ojibway word meaning "dawn." But Samuel Insull, the builder of the Skokie Valley Line of the North Shore Railway, which ran through town, preferred the name Northfield for his station at Willow Road, so in 1927 the village name was changed. The first settler was John Happ, a blacksmith from Trier, Germany, who first set up shop in Winnetka in 1843, then moved with his ten children to the Northfield area in 1854. MHV: $296,700.

NORTHLAKE

	1980	Percent	1990	Percent	% Change
Total Population	12,166		12,505		+ 2.8
Black	21	.2	177	1.4	+ 742.9
Hispanic	1,013	8.3	2,028	16.2	+ 100.2
Asian, Pacific Islander	266	2.2	486	3.9	+ 82.7
White, Other	11,879	97.6	11,842	94.7	− .3

City; Mayor Reid Paxon, $20,000. Incorporated: 1949. Named derived from town's location between North Avenue and Lake Street. Motto: "City of Friendly People." MHV: $91,100.

OAK BROOK

	1980	Percent	1990	Percent	% Change
Total Population	6,641		9,178		+ 38.2
Black	21	.3	74	.8	+ 252.4
Hispanic	167	2.5	244	2.7	+ 46.1
Asian, Pacific Islander	507	7.6	1,576	17.2	+ 210.8
White, Other	6,113	92.0	7,528	82.0	+ 23.1

Village; President Karen M. Bushy, $2,500. Founded in 1834 as the town of Fullersburg, in honor of its first settler, Ben Fuller. Incorporated as Oak Brook in 1958, it was named by its developer and leading resident, Paul Butler. Previously, Butler called his home there Oak Brook. The Butler family founded the Natoma Dairy in the Oak Brook area in the 1890s. MHV: $477,000.

OAKBROOK TERRACE

	1980	Percent	1990	Percent	% Change
Total Population	2,285		1,907		– 16.5
Black	16	.7	16	.8	+ 0.0
Hispanic	41	1.8	49	2.6	+ 19.5
Asian, Pacific Islander	48	2.1	102	5.3	+ 112.5
White, Other	2,221	97.2	1,789	93.8	– 19.5

City; Mayor Richard F. Sarallo, $40,000. Incorporated as Utopia in 1958, a name taken from a postal station there in the middle 1800s. In 1959, the village adopted the name of the well known shopping center—Oakbrook Terrace. The shopping center later became a part of the village of Oak Brook. Motto: "Teens are Key to the Future." MHV: $129,700.

OAK FOREST

	1980	Percent	1990	Percent	% Change
Total Population	26,096		26,203		+ .4
Black	522	2.0	158	.6	– 69.7
Hispanic	443	1.7	647	2.5	+ 46.0
Asian, Pacific Islander	253	1.0	387	1.5	+ 53.0
White, Other	25,321	97.0	25,658	97.9	+ 1.3

City; Mayor James A. Malecky, $4,500. Founded in 1892; incorporated as a village in 1947; as a city in 1971. Motto: "Pride in Our Past, Faith in Our Future." Named for the area's oak forests. MHV: $104,300.

OAK LAWN

	1980	Percent	1990	Percent	% Change
Total Population	60,590		56,182		– 7.3
Black	38	.1	66	.1	+ 73.7
Hispanic	753	1.2	1,322	2.4	+ 75.6
Asian, Pacific Islander	525	.9	614	1.1	+ 17.0
White, Other	60,027	99.1	55,502	98.8	– 7.5

Village; Mayor Ernest F. Kolb, $43,000. Incorporated: 1909. Settled in 1858 by John Simpson, who built a home at Ninety-fifth and Central. Originally called the Black Oak Settlement, it was renamed Oak Lawn in 1882. Folks just thought it sounded better. MHV: $108,100.

OAK PARK

	1980	Percent	1990	Percent	% Change
Total Population	54,887		53,648		– 2.3
Black	5,929	10.8	9,804	18.3	+ 65.4
Hispanic	1,364	2.5	1,915	3.6	+ 40.4
Asian, Pacific Islander	1,492	2.7	1,785	3.3	+ 19.6
White, Other	47,466	86.5	42,059	78.4	– 11.4

Village; President John F. Philpin, $9,600. Incorporated: 1902. Various parts of town previously were called Oak Ridge, Harlem and Ridgeland. Motto. "Vision." MHV: $138,700.

OAKWOOD HILLS

	1980	Percent	1990	Percent	% Change
Total Population	1,255		1,498		+ 19.4
Black	0	0.0	2	.1	+ 0.0
Hispanic	11	.9	35	2.3	+ 218.2
Asian, Pacific Islander	2	.2	3	.2	+ 50.0
White, Other	1,253	99.8	1,493	99.7	+ 19.2

Incorporated: 1958. MHV: $112,600.

OLD MILL CREEK

	1980	Percent	1990	Percent	% Change
Total Population	84		73		− 13.1
Black	0	0.0	0	0.0	+ 0.0
Hispanic	0	0.0	0	0.0	+ 0.0
Asian, Pacific Islander	0	0.0	0	0.0	+ 0.0
White, Other	84	****	73	****	− 13.1

Village; President Emory A. Allison, no salary. Incorporated: 1958. Named after the Mill Creek Hunt Club, which was founded there in 1932. And the creek—Mill Creek—is so named because a grain mill was operated there in the 1920s. MHV: $162,500.

OLYMPIA FIELDS

	1980	Percent	1990	Percent	% Change
Total Population	4,146		4,248		+ 2.5
Black	207	5.0	685	16.1	+ 230.9
Hispanic	65	1.6	55	1.3	− 15.4
Asian, Pacific Islander	160	3.9	252	5.9	+ 57.5
White, Other	3,779	91.1	3,311	77.9	− 12.4

Village; President Robert E. Field, $1,200—$50 a meeting, for two meetings a month. Incorporated: 1927. Named after the Olympia Fields Country Club. The club, in turn, was named by its first president, Alonzo Stagg, the famous University of Chicago football coach, who admired the sporting traditions of the ancient Greeks. MHV: $184,400.

ORLAND HILLS

	1980	Percent	1990	Percent	% Change
Total Population	2,784		5,510		+ 97.9
Black	0	0.0	216	3.9	+ 0.0
Hispanic	106	3.8	239	4.3	+ 125.5
Asian, Pacific Islander	19	.7	60	1.1	+ 215.8
White, Other	2,765	99.3	5,234	95.0	+ 89.3

Village; President Lorin Schab, $4,800. Incorporated in 1961 as Westhaven. Changed name to Orland Hills in 1986, associating itself by name to its larger and prosperous neighbor, Orland Park. MHV: $103,500.

ORLAND PARK

	1980	Percent	1990	Percent	% Change
Total Population	23,045		35,720		+ 55.0
Black	24	.1	140	.4	+ 483.3

	1980	Percent	1990	Percent	% Change
Hispanic	328	1.4	826	2.3	+ 151.8
Asian, Pacific Islander	622	2.7	1,273	3.6	+ 104.7
White, Other	22,399	97.2	34,307	96.0	+ 53.2

Village; President Frederick T. Owens, $16,000. Incorporated: 1892. Motto: "Golf Center of the World." The origin of the word "orland" is uncertain, but the most widely accepted explanation is that a group of the earliest settlers were from Orland, Maine. Another theory is that "orland" is a shortened form of the word "overland." MHV: $152,700.

PALATINE

	1980	Percent	1990	Percent	% Change
Total Population	32,166		39,253		+ 22.0
Black	106	.3	370	.9	+ 249.1
Hispanic	618	1.9	1,410	3.6	+ 128.2
Asian, Pacific Islander	506	1.6	1,274	3.2	+ 151.8
White, Other	31,554	98.1	37,609	95.8	+ 19.2

Village; Rita Mullins, $6,000. Incorporated: 1866. Motto: "A Real Home Town." Named for Palatine, New York, the hometown of the town's leading settler, Harrison Cook. MHV: $149,600.

PALOS HEIGHTS

	1980	Percent	1990	Percent	% Change
Total Population	11,096		11,478		+ 3.4
Black	17	.2	37	.3	+ 117.6
Hispanic	87	.8	129	1.1	+ 48.3
Asian, Pacific Islander	272	2.5	299	2.6	+ 9.9
White, Other	10,807	97.4	11,142	97.1	+ 3.1

City; Mayor Eugene G. Simpson, $12,000. Incorporated: 1959. See Palos Park for origin of name. MHV: $160,400.

PALOS HILLS

	1980	Percent	1990	Percent	% Change
Total Population	16,654		17,803		+ 6.9
Black	261	1.6	373	2.1	+ 42.9
Hispanic	452	2.7	575	3.2	+ 27.2
Asian, Pacific Islander	250	1.5	352	2.0	+ 40.8
White, Other	16,143	96.9	17,078	95.9	+ 5.8

City; Mayor Gerald R. Bennett, $12,000. Founded: 1958. Motto: "Pride in Progress." See Palos Park for origin of name. MHV: $125,600.

PALOS PARK

	1980	Percent	1990	Percent	% Change
Total Population	3,150		4,199		+ 33.3
Black	1	.0	7	.2	+ 600.0
Hispanic	14	.4	74	1.8	+ 428.6
Asian, Pacific Islander	43	1.4	97	2.3	+ 125.6
White, Other	3,106	98.6	4,095	97.5	+ 31.8

Village; Mayor Rosemary S. Kaptur, $12,000. Settled in 1830; incorporated in 1914. Takes its name from Palos Township, named about 1850 for Palos, Spain, the city from which Columbus set sail for the New World. The name, village historians say, was suggested by an early settler, Melanchan Powell, who claimed one of his Welch ancestors was among Columbus' sailors. In Spanish, palos means "tall tree," the "mast of a ship" or "promontory." MHV: $206,400.

PARK CITY

	1980	Percent	1990	Percent	% Change
Total Population	3,673		4,677		+ 27.3
Black	52	1.4	220	4.7	+ 323.1
Hispanic	224	6.1	736	15.7	+ 228.6
Asian, Pacific Islander	60	1.6	215	4.6	+ 258.3
White, Other	3,561	97.0	4,242	90.7	+ 19.1

City; Mayor Robert Allen, $1,800. Incorporated: 1958. Motto: "Thanks to God and Our American Constitution that Righteousness and Our American Law Made Park City Possible." Named for the four mobile home parks that joined together to incorporate as a city, so as to avoid annexation by neighboring Waukegan. MHV: $92,700.

PARK FOREST

	1980	Percent	1990	Percent	% Change
Total Population	26,222		24,656		− 6.0
Black	3,178	12.1	6,072	24.6	+ 91.1
Hispanic	626	2.4	769	3.1	+ 22.8
Asian, Pacific Islander	380	1.4	278	1.1	− 26.8
White, Other	22,664	86.4	18,306	74.2	− 19.2

Village; President F. Patrick Kelly, $6,050. Founded and built in 1949 by Chicago builder Philip Klutznick. Motto: "Capture the Spirit." Named for its parks and nearby forests. It is one of America's first post-World War II planned communities. MHV: $58,800.

PARK RIDGE

	1980	Percent	1990	Percent	% Change
Total Population	38,704		36,175		− 6.5
Black	60	.2	48	.1	− 20.0
Hispanic	334	.9	474	1.3	+ 41.9
Asian, Pacific Islander	501	1.3	791	2.2	+ 57.9
White, Other	38,143	98.6	35,336	97.7	− 7.4

City; Mayor Ronald Wietecha, $1,200. Originally called Brickton because of a large brick industry there that supplied bricks to Chicago after the Great Fire of 1871. Renamed Park Ridge in 1873, and incorporated in 1910. The name was inspired by the high glacier-formed ridge running through town. MHV: $185,700.

PEOTONE

	1980	Percent	1990	Percent	% Change
Total Population	2,832		2,947		+ 4.1
Black	0	0.0	1	.0	+ 0.0

	1980	Percent	1990	Percent	% Change
Hispanic	16	.6	17	.6	+ 6.3
Asian, Pacific Islander	1	.0	12	.4	+ 1100.0
White, Other	2,831	****	2,934	99.6	+ 3.6

Village; President R.E. Anderson, $4,000. Founded in 1856 on land bought from the Illinois Central RailRoad and platted by David Goodwille. Peotone is either the name of an Indian chief or a made-up word by an Illinois Central official who, according to village lore, "combined consonants and vowels at random." Motto: Peotone—A Good Place to Live." MHV: $86,000.

PHOENIX

	1980	Percent	1990	Percent	% Change
Total Population	2,850		2,217		− 22.2
Black	2,655	93.2	2,112	95.3	− 20.5
Hispanic	43	1.5	69	3.1	+ 60.5
Asian, Pacific Islander	3	.1	1	.0	− 66.7
White, Other	192	6.7	104	4.7	− 45.8

Village; Mayor January Belmont, $5,000. Incorporated: 1900. Named for the bird of Greek mythology. MHV: $42,800.

PINGREE GROVE

	1980	Percent	1990	Percent	% Change
Total Population	183		138		− 24.6
Black	0	0.0	0	0.0	+ 0.0
Hispanic	5	2.7	5	3.6	+ 0.0
Asian, Pacific Islander	0	0.0	0	0.0	+ 0.0
White, Other	183	****	138	****	− 24.6

Village. Incorporated: 1907. MHV: $73,800.

PLAINFIELD

	1980	Percent	1990	Percent	% Change
Total Population	3,767		4,557		+ 21.0
Black	2	.1	4	.1	+ 100.0
Hispanic	33	.9	65	1.4	+ 97.0
Asian, Pacific Islander	3	.1	24	.5	+ 700.0
White, Other	3,762	99.9	4,529	99.4	+ 20.4

Village; President Mary T. Latta, $3,600. Will County's oldest community, it was founded 1829, platted in 1834 and named for the prairies. The first settler was Rev. Jesse Walker, the pioneer Methodist circuit rider and early settler of Wheaton, who established a sawmill with his son-in-law, James Walker. The settlement became known as Walker's Grove. MHV: $122,100.

POSEN

	1980	Percent	1990	Percent	% Change
Total Population	4,642		4,226		− 9.0
Black	85	1.8	87	2.1	+ 2.4
Hispanic	175	3.8	311	7.4	+ 77.7

	1980	Percent	1990	Percent	% Change
Asian, Pacific Islander	18	.4	21	.5	+ 16.7
White, Other	4,539	97.8	4,118	97.4	− 9.3

Village. Incorporated: 1901. MHV: $60,400.

PRAIRIE GROVE

	1980	Percent	1990	Percent	% Change
Total Population	680		654		− 3.8
Black	0	0.0	1	.2	+ 0.0
Hispanic	22	3.2	22	3.4	+ 0.0
Asian, Pacific Islander	1	.1	3	.5	+ 200.0
White, Other	679	99.9	650	99.4	− 4.3

Village. Incorporated: 1973. MHV: $178,500.

PROSPECT HEIGHTS

	1980	Percent	1990	Percent	% Change
Total Population	11,808		15,239		+ 29.1
Black	218	1.8	262	1.7	+ 20.2
Hispanic	630	5.3	2,190	14.4	+ 247.6
Asian, Pacific Islander	281	2.4	677	4.4	+ 140.9
White, Other	11,309	95.8	14,300	93.8	+ 26.4

City; Mayor Edward Rotchford, $5,400. Founded in 1937 when two young real estate developers, Allen Dawson and Carleton Smith, started building small homes on large lots on Elmhurst Road, north of Camp McDonald Road; incorporated in 1976. The name is a combination of the names of two neighbors—Arlington Heights and Mount Prospect. MHV: $167,300.

RICHMOND

	1980	Percent	1990	Percent	% Change
Total Population	1,068		1,016		− 4.9
Black	0	0.0	4	.4	+ 0.0
Hispanic	19	1.8	14	1.4	− 26.3
Asian, Pacific Islander	0	0.0	0	0.0	+ 0.0
White, Other	1,068	****	1,012	99.6	− 5.2

Village. Incorporated: 1872. MHV: $89,300.

RICHTON PARK

	1980	Percent	1990	Percent	% Change
Total Population	9,403		10,523		+ 11.9
Black	688	7.3	2,335	22.2	+ 239.4
Hispanic	338	3.6	351	3.3	+ 3.8
Asian, Pacific Islander	177	1.9	185	1.8	+ 4.5
White, Other	8,538	90.8	8,003	76.1	− 6.3

Village; President Rudolph A. Banovich, $6,000. Incorporated: 1926. Motto: "Proud Past, Bright Future." Name was given by the Illinois Central Railroad to its milk stops in Rich Township. The town took its name from the station. MHV: $75,300.

RIVER FOREST

	1980	Percent	1990	Percent	% Change
Total Population	12,392		11,669		– 5.8
Black	106	.9	224	1.9	+ 111.3
Hispanic	188	1.5	279	2.4	+ 48.4
Asian, Pacific Islander	195	1.6	309	2.6	+ 58.5
White, Other	12,091	97.6	11,136	95.4	– 7.9

Village; President Robert Jones, no salary. Incorporated: 1880. Motto: "Proud Heritage, Bright Future." Named derived from its location along the Des Plaines River. MHV: $258,900.

RIVER GROVE

	1980	Percent	1990	Percent	% Change
Total Population	10,368		9,961		– 3.9
Black	1	.0	6	.1	+ 500.0
Hispanic	202	1.9	411	4.1	+ 103.5
Asian, Pacific Islander	77	.7	141	1.4	+ 83.1
White, Other	10,290	99.2	9,814	98.5	– 4.6

Village; Thomas J. Tarpey, $12,000. Incorporated: 1888. Motto: "The Village of Friendly Neighbors." Named for its location along both sides of the Des Plaines River. MHV: $100,700.

RIVERDALE

	1980	Percent	1990	Percent	% Change
Total Population	13,233		13,671		+ 3.3
Black	36	.3	5,557	40.6	
Hispanic	321	2.4	460	3.4	+ 43.3
Asian, Pacific Islander	38	.3	29	.2	– 23.7
White, Other	13,159	99.4	8,085	59.1	– 38.6

Village; Mayor Edward L. Kepley, Jr., $5,000. Incorporated: 1892. Motto: "Best Little Village in Illinois." The town's first mayor, Frederick C. Schmidt, named it Riverdale because of its location along the Little Calumet River. One founder of Riverdale, George Dolton— who also founded suburban Dolton—came to the area because he thought Chicago was too swampy, too far north to become a commercial center, and would never make it. MHV: $55,800.

RIVERSIDE

	1980	Percent	1990	Percent	% Change
Total Population	9,236		8,774		– 5.0
Black	0	0.0	2	.0	+ 0.0
Hispanic	133	1.4	243	2.8	+ 82.7
Asian, Pacific Islander	45	.5	85	1.0	+ 88.9
White, Other	9,191	99.5	8,687	99.0	– 5.5

Village; President Joseph DiNatale, no salary. Incorporated: 1875. Motto: "Village in the Forest." The Des Plaines River runs through town. MHV: $176,400.

RIVERWOODS

	1980	Percent	1990	Percent	% Change
Total Population	2,804		2,868		+ 2.3
Black	18	.6	10	.3	− 44.4
Hispanic	25	.9	45	1.6	+ 80.0
Asian, Pacific Islander	47	1.7	98	3.4	+ 108.5
White, Other	2,739	97.7	2,760	96.2	+ .8

Village; President Charles M. Smith, $6,000. Incorporated: 1959. Named for its location along the Des Plaines River. MHV: $407,900.

ROBBINS

	1980	Percent	1990	Percent	% Change
Total Population	8,853		7,498		− 15.3
Black	8,681	98.1	7,367	98.3	− 15.1
Hispanic	59	.7	20	.3	− 66.1
Asian, Pacific Islander	5	.1	4	.1	− 20.0
White, Other	167	1.9	127	1.7	− 24.0

Village; Mayor Irene H. Brodie, $10,000. Incorporated: 1917. Named for three generations of the Robbins family, starting with the developer Henry E. Robbins, who built the town. MHV: $39,500.

ROCKDALE

	1980	Percent	1990	Percent	% Change
Total Population	1,913		1,709		− 10.7
Black	4	.2	7	.4	+ 75.0
Hispanic	235	12.3	232	13.6	− 1.3
Asian, Pacific Islander	3	.2	3	.2	+ 0.0
White, Other	1,906	99.6	1,699	99.4	− 10.9

Village; President Henry T. Berry, $3,000. Incorporated: 1902. It's on rocky ground. MHV: $54,400.

ROLLING MEADOWS

	1980	Percent	1990	Percent	% Change
Total Population	20,167		22,591		+ 12.0
Black	249	1.2	362	1.6	+ 45.4
Hispanic	1,303	6.5	2,522	11.2	+ 93.6
Asian, Pacific Islander	523	2.6	785	3.5	+ 50.1
White, Other	19,395	96.2	21,444	94.9	+ 10.6

City; Carl F. Couve, $7,000. Incorporated: 1955. Motto: "Progress through Participation." Named for the slightly hilly topography. MHV: $127,300.

ROMEOVILLE

	1980	Percent	1990	Percent	% Change
Total Population	15,519		14,074		− 9.3
Black	244	1.6	376	2.7	+ 54.1
Hispanic	1,401	9.0	1,434	10.2	+ 2.4
Asian, Pacific Islander	106	.7	125	.9	+ 17.9
White, Other	15,169	97.7	13,573	96.4	− 10.5

Village; Mayor John Strobbe, $30 per weekly meeting. Incorporated: 1901. Motto: "Right in Romeoville." In pioneer days, Romeoville was a twin city of the early city of Juliet, which in 1845 renamed itself Joliet. In 1895, Romeo was renamed Romeoville. On the Isle a la Cache in Romeoville, the explorers Jacque Marquette and Louis Jolliet stored their collection of beaver furs and pelts. MHV: $73,300.

ROSELLE

	1980	Percent	1990	Percent	% Change
Total Population	16,948		20,819		+ 22.8
Black	141	.8	232	1.1	+ 64.5
Hispanic	312	1.8	550	2.6	+ 76.3
Asian, Pacific Islander	702	4.1	1,110	5.3	+ 58.1
White, Other	16,105	95.0	19,477	93.6	+ 20.9

Village; President James Rak, $8,500. Founded in 1874; incorporated in 1889. Motto: "Grow Together with Us." Named for Col. Roselle Hough, a land developer and railroad promoter. MHV: $124,200.

ROSEMONT

	1980	Percent	1990	Percent	% Change
Total Population	4,137		3,995		− 3.4
Black	20	.5	31	.8	+ 55.0
Hispanic	317	7.7	785	19.6	+ 147.6
Asian, Pacific Islander	132	3.2	180	4.5	+ 36.4
White, Other	3,985	96.3	3,784	94.7	− 5.0

Village; Mayor Donald E. Stephens, $45,000. Incorporated: 1956. Named for the Chicago street that runs into the village, Rosemont Avenue. The street, in turn, was named by developer John L. Cochran for Rosemont, Pennsylvania, a suburb of his hometown, Philadelphia. MHV: $152,600.

ROUND LAKE

	1980	Percent	1990	Percent	% Change
Total Population	2,644		3,550		+ 34.3
Black	11	.4	10	.3	− 9.1
Hispanic	120	4.5	418	11.8	+ 248.3
Asian, Pacific Islander	10	.4	26	.7	+ 160.0
White, Other	2,623	99.2	3,514	99.0	+ 34.0

Village; President James Lumber, $4,000. Incorporated: 1908. Named for nearby Round Lake, which is—as advertised—round. MHV: $84,400.

ROUND LAKE BEACH

	1980	Percent	1990	Percent	% Change
Total Population	12,921		16,434		+ 27.2
Black	28	.2	169	1.0	+ 503.6
Hispanic	985	7.6	2,347	14.3	+ 138.3
Asian, Pacific Islander	57	.4	218	1.3	+ 282.5
White, Other	12,836	99.3	16,047	97.6	+ 25.0

Village; Mayor Carl Schrimpf, $34,000. Incorporated: 1937. It sits on the north and west shores of Round Lake. Motto: "A Total Community." MHV: $73,200.

ROUND LAKE HEIGHTS

	1980	Percent	1990	Percent	% Change
Total Population	1,192		1,251		+ 4.9
Black	1	.1	2	.2	+ 100.0
Hispanic	88	7.4	164	13.1	+ 86.4
Asian, Pacific Islander	6	.5	4	.3	– 33.3
White, Other	1,185	99.4	1,245	99.5	+ 5.1

Village; Mayor Sandra Morris, $3,000. Incorporated: 1960. Motto: "Eyes to Future." Name refers to town's slight elevation and nearby Round Lake. MHV: $65,100.

ROUND LAKE PARK

	1980	Percent	1990	Percent	% Change
Total Population	4,032		4,045		+ .3
Black	2	.0	9	.2	+ 350.0
Hispanic	239	5.9	522	12.9	+ 118.4
Asian, Pacific Islander	12	.3	4	.1	– 66.7
White, Other	4,018	99.7	4,032	99.7	+ .3

Village; President Cole Akins, $7,900. Incorporated: 1947. Motto: "Pride in the Park." Located on the south shore of Round Lake. MHV: $66,100.

ST. CHARLES

	1980	Percent	1990	Percent	% Change
Total Population	17,492		22,501		+ 28.6
Black	78	.4	87	.4	+ 11.5
Hispanic	474	2.7	576	2.6	+ 21.5
Asian, Pacific Islander	82	.5	261	1.2	+ 218.3
White, Other	17,332	99.1	22,153	98.5	+ 27.8

City; Mayor Fred T.L. Norris, $12,000. Settled in 1834; incorporated in 1874. Motto: "Pride of the Fox." Formerly called Charleston, it was renamed St. Charles when it incorporated as a village in 1839 because there was already a Charleston downstate. A lawyer, Steven Jones, suggested St. Charles because many of the settlers were from the St. Charles, New Hampshire, area. MHV: $137,400.

SAUK VILLAGE

	1980	Percent	1990	Percent	% Change
Total Population	10,906		9,926		– 9.0
Black	154	1.4	1,790	18.0	+ 1062.3
Hispanic	830	7.6	964	9.7	+ 16.1
Asian, Pacific Islander	65	.6	77	.8	+ 18.5
White, Other	10,687	98.0	8,059	81.2	– 24.6

Village; Mayor Mark Collins, $7,000. Incorporated: 1957. Motto: "Pride and Progress." Named for the Sauk Trail, blazed by the Indians. MHV: $49,800.

SCHAUMBURG

	1980	Percent	1990	Percent	% Change
Total Population	53,305		68,586		+ 28.7
Black	645	1.2	1,471	2.1	+ 128.1
Hispanic	986	1.8	1,829	2.7	+ 85.5
Asian, Pacific Islander	1,573	3.0	4,454	6.5	+ 183.2
White, Other	51,087	95.8	62,661	91.4	+ 22.7

Village; Mayor Al Larson, $13,657. Incorporated: 1956. Motto: "Progress through Thoughtful Planning." Named for Schaumburg Township, which itself was named in 1850 for the home region in Germany of many early residents. The story is told that the residents were debating possible township names when a prominent German landowner, Frederick Nerge, ended all discussion by slamming his fist to the table and saying, "Ich wende es Schaumburg nennen!" (It will be called Schaumburg!) MHV: $133,500.

SCHILLER PARK

	1980	Percent	1990	Percent	% Change
Total Population	11,458		11,189		− 2.3
Black	72	.6	124	1.1	+ 72.2
Hispanic	751	6.6	1,382	12.4	+ 84.0
Asian, Pacific Islander	158	1.4	439	3.9	+ 177.8
White, Other	11,228	98.0	10,626	95.0	− 5.4

Village; President Edward E. Bluthardt, $20,040. Incorporated: 1914. Motto: "Plowshares to Jet Fields." MHV: $111,100.

SHOREWOOD

	1980	Percent	1990	Percent	% Change
Total Population	4,714		6,264		+ 32.9
Black	29	.6	124	2.0	+ 327.6
Hispanic	59	1.3	117	1.9	+ 98.3
Asian, Pacific Islander	28	.6	96	1.5	+ 242.9
White, Other	4,657	98.8	6,044	96.5	+ 29.8

Village; President Bertha Hofer, $50 a meeting. Founded in 1830; incorporated in 1957. Known as Troy until the Shorewood Beach Association—a group of summer cottage owners who settled the area—changed the name in 1957 because there was already a Troy in Southern Illinois. The new name refers to the village's location along the Du Page River. MHV: $118,800.

SKOKIE

	1980	Percent	1990	Percent	% Change
Total Population	60,278		59,432		− 1.4
Black	613	1.0	1,311	2.2	+ 113.9
Hispanic	1,612	2.7	2,457	4.1	+ 52.4
Asian, Pacific Islander	4,242	7.0	9,253	15.6	+ 118.1
White, Other	55,423	91.9	48,868	82.2	− 11.8

Village; Mayor Jacqueline Gorell, $20,000. Incorporated in 1940 as Skokie, changing the name from Niles Center. "Skokie" is an Indian word, commonly thought to have meant "swampland." Motto: "Village of Vision." MHV: $149,400.

SLEEPY HOLLOW

	1980	Percent	1990	Percent	% Change
Total Population	2,000		3,241		+ 62.1
Black	5	.3	23	.7	+ 360.0
Hispanic	16	.8	41	1.3	+ 156.3
Asian, Pacific Islander	17	.9	48	1.5	+ 182.4
White, Other	1,978	98.9	3,170	97.8	+ 60.3

Village; President Theresa J. Peterson, no salary. Incorporated: 1958. Named by Floyd Falese, who owned and developed much of the land. He may have borrowed the name from the tale by Washington Irving. MHV: $198,800.

SOUTH BARRINGTON

	1980	Percent	1990	Percent	% Change
Total Population	1,168		2,937		+ 151.5
Black	0	0.0	26	.9	+ 0.0
Hispanic	1	.1	14	.5	+ 1300.0
Asian, Pacific Islander	29	2.5	260	8.9	+ 796.6
White, Other	1,139	97.5	2,651	90.3	+ 132.7

Village; President Warren R. Fuller, no salary. Incorporated: 1959. Motto "Thoughtful Progress." So named because it is located south of Barrington. MHV: $500,000.

SOUTH CHICAGO HEIGHTS

	1980	Percent	1990	Percent	% Change
Total Population	3,932		3,597		− 8.5
Black	9	.2	45	1.3	+ 400.0
Hispanic	312	7.9	483	13.4	+ 54.8
Asian, Pacific Islander	5	.1	6	.2	+ 20.0
White, Other	3,918	99.6	3,546	98.6	− 9.5

Village; President David L. Owen, $4,800. Incorporated: 1907. So called because it is south of Chicago Heights. MHV: $59,900.

SOUTH ELGIN

	1980	Percent	1990	Percent	% Change
Total Population	6,218		7,474		+ 20.2
Black	55	.9	178	2.4	+ 223.6
Hispanic	252	4.1	428	5.7	+ 69.8
Asian, Pacific Islander	33	.5	204	2.7	+ 518.2
White, Other	6,130	98.6	7,092	94.9	+ 15.7

Village; President Thomas J. Rolando, Jr., $2,400. Incorporated: 1897. Before that, the area was called Clintonville. A railroad station in town is still called Clintonville. Now called South Elgin because it is located south of Elgin. MHV: $94,700.

SOUTH HOLLAND

	1980	Percent	1990	Percent	% Change
Total Population	24,977		22,105		− 11.5
Black	120	.5	2,564	11.6	+ 2036.7
Hispanic	395	1.6	454	2.1	+ 14.9
Asian, Pacific Islander	308	1.2	398	1.8	+ 29.2
White, Other	24,549	98.3	19,143	86.6	− 22.0

Village; President Harold. J. Gouwens, $,1000. Founded in 1848; incorporated in 1896. Motto: "Community of Churches." When Dutch immigrants came to the Chicago area, they settled in two areas—High Prairie, which is now the Roseland neighborhood in Chicago; and Low Prairie, now called South Holland. MHV: $90,600.

SPRING GROVE

	1980	Percent	1990	Percent	% Change
Total Population	571		1,066		+86.7
Black	0	0.0	0	0.0	+0.0
Hispanic	6	1.1	9	.8	+50.0
Asian, Pacific Islander	2	.4	1	.1	−50.0
White, Other	569	99.6	1,065	99.9	+87.2

Village; John L. Toler, $5,500. Incorporated: 1902. Named for the fresh-water springs in the area. MHV: $146,900.

STEGER

	1980	Percent	1990	Percent	% Change
Total Population	9,269		8,584		−7.4
Black	1,028	11.1	207	2.4	−79.9
Hispanic	640	6.9	595	6.9	−7.0
Asian, Pacific Islander	8	.1	41	.5	+412.5
White, Other	8,233	88.8	8,336	97.1	+1.3

Village; President Louis Sherman, $16,000. Incorporated: 1896. Motto: "Where Progress Is a Fact and Not a Promise." Named for the Steger Piano Factory, the company around which the town was built. MHV: $55,300.

STICKNEY

	1980	Percent	1990	Percent	% Change
Total Population	5,893		5,678		−3.6
Black	43	.7	12	.2	−72.1
Hispanic	146	2.5	392	6.9	+168.5
Asian, Pacific Islander	30	.5	40	.7	+33.3
White, Other	5,820	98.8	5,626	99.1	−3.3

Village; President Frank Baley, $7,200. Incorporated: 1913. Named for Alpheus Beede Stickney, an early settler who died three years after the town's incorporation. MHV: $94,000.

STONE PARK

	1980	Percent	1990	Percent	% Change
Total Population	4,273		4,383		+2.6
Black	7	.2	25	.6	+257.1
Hispanic	1,272	29.8	2,544	58.0	+100.0
Asian, Pacific Islander	189	4.4	153	3.5	−19.0
White, Other	4,077	95.4	4,205	95.9	+3.1

Village; Mayor Robert D. Natale, $38,000. Incorporated: 1939. Named after its developer, H.O. Stone & Co. Motto: "Small Town with a Big Heart." And it is, indeed, a small town—four-tenths of a square mile. MHV: $81,200.

STREAMWOOD

	1980	Percent	1990	Percent	% Change
Total Population	23,456		30,987		+ 32.1
Black	172	.7	616	2.0	+ 258.1
Hispanic	1,213	5.2	2,298	7.4	+ 89.4
Asian, Pacific Islander	536	2.3	1,315	4.2	+ 145.3
White, Other	22,748	97.0	29,056	93.8	+ 27.7

Village; President Billie D. Roth, $6,000. Incorporated: 1957. Named inspired by Poplar Creek, which runs through town. MHV: $107,100.

SUGAR GROVE

	1980	Percent	1990	Percent	% Change
Total Population	1,366		2,005		+ 46.8
Black	0	0.0	8	.4	+ 0.0
Hispanic	14	1.0	35	1.7	+ 150.0
Asian, Pacific Islander	1	.1	4	.2	+ 300.0
White, Other	1,365	99.9	1,993	99.4	+ 46.0

Village; President Mario F. Tolomei, $3,500. Incorporated: 1957. Named for a grove of sugar maples. MHV: $123,100.

SUMMIT

	1980	Percent	1990	Percent	% Change
Total Population	10,110		9,971		− 1.4
Black	1,637	16.2	1,360	13.6	− 16.9
Hispanic	2,022	20.0	3,115	31.2	+ 54.1
Asian, Pacific Islander	84	.8	201	2.0	+ 139.3
White, Other	8,389	83.0	8,410	84.3	+ .3

Village; Mayor Ronald Bragassi, $13,000. Incorporated: 1890. Named for its relatively high elevation. MHV: $70,700.

SUNNYSIDE

	1980	Percent	1990	Percent	% Change
Total Population	1,432		1,529		+ 6.8
Black	1	.1	0	0.0	− 100.0
Hispanic	14	1.0	13	.9	− 7.1
Asian, Pacific Islander	0	0.0	3	.2	+ 0.0
White, Other	1,431	99.9	1,526	99.8	+ 6.6

Village. Incorporated: 1956. MHV: $121,200.

SYMERTON

	1980	Percent	1990	Percent	% Change
Total Population	120		110		− 8.3
Black	0	0.0	0	0.0	+ 0.0
Hispanic	1	.8	7	6.4	+ 600.0
Asian, Pacific Islander	0	0.0	0	0.0	+ 0.0
White, Other	120	****	110	***	− 8.3

Village. Incorporated: 1905. MHV: $48,300.

THIRD LAKE

	1980	Percent	1990	Percent	% Change
Total Population	222		1,248		+ 462.2
Black	0	0.0	3	.2	+ 0.0
Hispanic	2	.9	10	.8	+ 400.0
Asian, Pacific Islander	0	0.0	9	.7	+ 0.0
White, Other	222	****	1,236	99.0	+ 456.8

Village; Mayor Karen McCluskey, $50 per meeting. Incorporated: 1959. One of four lakes in the immediate area. The two to the west are Gages and Druce lakes—Then Third Lake, Then Fourth Lake. MHV: $168,400.

THORNTON

	1980	Percent	1990	Percent	% Change
Total Population	3,022		2,778		− 8.1
Black	6	.2	2	.1	− 66.7
Hispanic	52	1.7	86	3.1	+ 65.4
Asian, Pacific Islander	2	.1	5	.2	+ 150.0
White, Other	3,014	99.7	2,771	99.7	− 8.1

Village; President Kenneth J. Pearson, $3,400. Founded in 1834; incorporated in 1900. Named for Col. W.P. Thornton, a state canal commissioner. MHV: $71,100.

TINLEY PARK

	1980	Percent	1990	Percent	% Change
Total Population	26,171		37,121		+ 41.8
Black	463	1.8	601	1.6	+ 29.8
Hispanic	405	1.5	944	2.5	+ 133.1
Asian, Pacific Islander	213	.8	516	1.4	+ 142.3
White, Other	25,495	97.4	36,004	97.0	+ 41.2

Village; Mayor Edward J. Zabrocki, $7,800. Founded in 1842; incorporated in 1892. Named for Samuel Tinley, Sr., the first stationmaster of the village's Rock Island Railroad depot. The village owes its existence to the railroad. MHV: $115,900.

TOWER LAKES

	1980	Percent	1990	Percent	% Change
Total Population	1,177		1,333		+ 13.3
Black	0	0.0	4	.3	+ 0.0
Hispanic	0	0.0	13	1.0	+ 0.0
Asian, Pacific Islander	2	.2	11	.8	+ 450.0
White, Other	1,175	99.8	1,318	98.9	+ 12.2

Village. Incorporated: 1966. MHV: $283,700.

UNION

	1980	Percent	1990	Percent	% Change
Total Population	622		542		− 12.9
Black	0	0.0	0	0.0	+ 0.0
Hispanic	14	2.3	18	3.3	+ 28.6
Asian, Pacific Islander	0	0.0	0	0.0	+ 0.0
White, Other	622	****	542	***	− 12.9

Village. Incorporated: 1897. MHV: $82,200.

UNIVERSITY PARK

	1980	Percent	1990	Percent	% Change
Total Population	6,245		6,204		-.7
Black	2,764	44.3	4,910	79.1	+ 77.6
Hispanic	116	1.9	114	1.8	- 1.7
Asian, Pacific Islander	40	.6	37	.6	- 7.5
White, Other	3,441	55.1	1,257	20.3	- 63.5

Village; President Vernon Young, $3,300. Incorporated in 1967 as Park Forest South. Renamed University Park, in 1984, because it is home to Governors State University. MHV: $60,600.

VERNON HILLS

	1980	Percent	1990	Percent	% Change
Total Population	9,827		15,319		+ 55.9
Black	107	1.1	259	1.7	+ 142.1
Hispanic	334	3.4	589	3.8	+ 76.3
Asian, Pacific Islander	464	4.7	954	6.2	+ 105.6
White, Other	9,256	94.2	14,106	92.1	+ 52.4

Village; President Barbara Williams, $6,000. Incorporated: 1958. Motto: "People Planning with Pride." Named after Vernon Township, named itself for Civil War Capt. Vernon. There are no hills in Vernon Hills. MHV: $140,500.

VILLA PARK

	1980	Percent	1990	Percent	% Change
Total Population	23,185		22,253		- 4.0
Black	102	.4	252	1.1	+ 147.1
Hispanic	456	2.0	1,125	5.1	+ 146.7
Asian, Pacific Islander	466	2.0	711	3.2	+ 52.6
White, Other	22,617	97.6	21,290	95.7	- 5.9

Village; President Joyce Daly, $2,000. Originally two small towns— Villa and Ardmore. Combined and incorporated as Ardmore in 1915. Changed to Villa Park in 1917. Motto: "The Garden Village." MHV: $109,600.

WADSWORTH

	1980	Percent	1990	Percent	% Change
Total Population	1,104		1,826		+ 65.4
Black	0	0.0	19	1.0	+ 0.0
Hispanic	21	1.9	49	2.7	+ 133.3
Asian, Pacific Islander	7	.6	25	1.4	+ 257.1
White, Other	1,097	99.4	1,782	97.6	+ 62.4

Village; Mayor Don Craft. Incorporated: 1962. Motto: "The Village of Country Living." MHV: $170,100.

WARRENVILLE

	1980	Percent	1990	Percent	% Change
Total Population	7,519		11,333		+ 50.7
Black	78	1.0	215	1.9	+ 175.6
Hispanic	103	1.4	345	3.0	+ 235.0
Asian, Pacific Islander	134	1.8	362	3.2	+ 170.1
White, Other	7,307	97.2	10,756	94.9	+ 47.2

City; Mayor Vivian M. Lund, $1,290. Incorporated: 1967. Named for Col. Julius Morton Warren, a native of Chautauqua County, New York, who became the first settler of the Warrenville area in 1833. MHV: $112,200.

WAUCONDA

	1980	Percent	1990	Percent	% Change
Total Population	5,688		6,294		+ 10.7
Black	1	.0	0	0.0	− 100.0
Hispanic	135	2.4	250	4.0	+ 85.2
Asian, Pacific Islander	18	.3	29	.5	+ 61.1
White, Other	5,669	99.7	6,265	99.5	+ 10.5

Village; Mayor James Keagle. MHV: $100,000.

WAUKEGAN

	1980	Percent	1990	Percent	% Change
Total Population	67,653		69,392		+ 2.6
Black	12,484	18.5	13,772	19.8	+ 10.3
Hispanic	9,253	13.7	16,443	23.7	+ 77.7
Asian, Pacific Islander	1,228	1.8	2,123	3.1	+ 72.9
White, Other	53,941	79.7	53,497	77.1	− .8

City; Mayor Haig Paravonian, $64,400. Incorporated: 1859. Motto: "Envisioning New Horizons." Waukegan is a Potowatomi name, meaning "Little Fort." The town was an Indian settlement and early French trading post. MHV: $72,600.

WAYNE

	1980	Percent	1990	Percent	% Change
Total Population	940		1,541		+ 63.9
Black	0	0.0	3	.2	+ 0.0
Hispanic	1	.1	22	1.4	+ 2100.0
Asian, Pacific Islander	3	.3	21	1.4	+ 600.0
White, Other	937	99.7	1,517	98.4	+ 61.9

Village; President Ed Berry, no salary. Incorporated: 1958. Named for General Anthony "Mad Anthony" Wayne, who in the Treaty of Greenville on Aug. 4, 1795, forced the Indians to cede land for three midwestern forts, including Fort Dearborn. MHV: $300,800.

WEST CHICAGO

	1980	Percent	1990	Percent	% Change
Total Population	12,550		14,796		+ 17.9
Black	202	1.6	270	1.8	+ 33.7
Hispanic	2,094	16.7	4,510	30.5	+ 115.4
Asian, Pacific Islander	132	1.1	190	1.3	+ 43.9
White, Other	12,216	97.3	14,336	96.9	+ 17.4

City; Mayor Paul Netzel, $24,000. Incorporated: 1906. Motto: "Where History and Progess Meet." First settler was Alonzo Harvey in 1842. Originally called Junction, and then Turner Junction, the name was changed to West Chicago in 1896. MHV: $94,200.

WEST DUNDEE

	1980	Percent	1990	Percent	% Change
Total Population	3,551		3,728		+ 5.0
Black	4	.1	10	.3	+ 150.0
Hispanic	56	1.6	76	2.0	+ 35.7
Asian, Pacific Islander	24	.7	15	.4	− 37.5
White, Other	3,523	99.2	3,703	99.3	+ 5.1

Village; President Calvin Grafelman, $3,996. Incorporated: 1890. Originally part of Dundee, but the town split down the middle of the Fox River with development. West Dundee is west of the river. MHV: $124,100.

WESTCHESTER

	1980	Percent	1990	Percent	% Change
Total Population	17,730		17,301		− 2.4
Black	14	.1	144	.8	+ 928.6
Hispanic	182	1.0	315	1.8	+ 73.1
Asian, Pacific Islander	222	1.3	467	2.7	+ 110.4
White, Other	17,494	98.7	16,690	96.5	− 4.6

Village; President John J. Sinde, $2,000. Incorporated: 1925. Motto: "A Good Place to Live." Developed by Samuel Insull, the Chicago traction magnate, who developed the first 2,200 acres beginning in 1924, running an L line out from Chicago in 1926. He dreamed up the English-sounding town name, saying he hoped Westchester would offer "the best in small-town English life." MHV: $127,200.

WESTERN SPRINGS

	1980	Percent	1990	Percent	% Change
Total Population	12,876		11,984		− 6.9
Black	19	.1	19	.2	+ 0.0
Hispanic	115	.9	127	1.1	+ 10.4
Asian, Pacific Islander	98	.8	76	.6	− 22.4
White, Other	12,759	99.1	11,889	99.2	− 6.8

Village; President Edmund B. Driscoll, no salary. Incorporated: 1886. Motto: "Queen of the Western Suburbs." Name inspired by the mineral springs that flowed there, including eight in the area of Spring Rock Park. MHV: $195,800.

WESTMONT

	1980	Percent	1990	Percent	% Change
Total Population	16,718		21,228		+ 27.0
Black	293	1.8	710	3.3	+ 142.3
Hispanic	328	2.0	731	3.4	+ 122.9
Asian, Pacific Islander	715	4.3	1,721	8.1	+ 140.7
White, Other	15,710	94.0	18,797	88.5	+ 19.6

Village; Mayor Frank H. Bellerive, $6,000. Incorporated: 1921. Motto: "The Progressive Village." So called because it's west of Chicago and one of the highest points along the Burlington Northern Railroad. Originally called Greggs Station, the town was a milk station on the train line and the site of brickyards to provide bricks for the rebuilding of Chicago after the 1871 fire. MHV: $129,200.

WHEATON

	1980	Percent	1990	Percent	% Change
Total Population	43,043		51,464		+ 19.6
Black	1,068	2.5	1,304	2.5	+ 22.1
Hispanic	615	1.4	1,051	2.0	+ 70.9
Asian, Pacific Islander	742	1.7	1,945	3.8	+ 162.1
White, Other	41,233	95.8	48,215	93.7	+ 16.9

City; Mayor Gwendolyn Henry, no salary. Settled in 1839 by Jesse Wheaton, incorporated as a village in 1859 and as a city in 1890. MHV: $148,700.

WHEELING

	1980	Percent	1990	Percent	% Change
Total Population	23,266		29,911		+ 28.6
Black	188	.8	504	1.7	+ 168.1
Hispanic	1,282	5.5	2,508	8.4	+ 95.6
Asian, Pacific Islander	487	2.1	1,376	4.6	+ 182.5
White, Other	22,591	97.1	28,031	93.7	+ 24.1

Village; Mayor Sheila H. Schultz, $4,000. Incorporated: 1894. Motto: "A Great Place to Be." Possibly named for Wheeling, West Virginia, although nobody knows for sure. MHV: $113,400.

WILLOW SPRINGS

	1980	Percent	1990	Percent	% Change
Total Population	4,147		4,509		+ 8.7
Black	2	.0	10	.2	+ 400.0
Hispanic	59	1.4	128	2.8	+ 116.9
Asian, Pacific Islander	63	1.5	48	1.1	− 23.8
White, Other	4,082	98.4	4,451	98.7	+ 9.0

Village; Mayor James Rizzi, $1,500. Incorporated: 1892. Motto: "Progress with Tradition." Named for its willows and springs. MHV: $141,700.

WILLOWBROOK

	1980	Percent	1990	Percent	% Change
Total Population	4,953		8,598		+ 73.6
Black	44	.9	97	1.1	+ 120.5
Hispanic	80	1.6	186	2.2	+ 132.5
Asian, Pacific Islander	398	8.0	814	9.5	+ 104.5
White, Other	4,511	91.1	7,687	89.4	+ 70.4

Village; President Eugene Noose, $50 per twice-monthly meeting, plus $2,600 as liquor control commissioner. Incorporated in 1960 with 167 residents, weeks before a state law would take effect that required a population of 400 for incorporation. The homeowners association president, Anton Borse, forced to come up with a name for the new town immediately, looked out his window at a clump of willow trees along a creek and decided on Willowbrook. MHV: $191,300.

WILMETTE

	1980	Percent	1990	Percent	% Change
Total Population	28,229		26,690		- 5.5
Black	95	.3	130	.5	+ 36.8
Hispanic	337	1.2	449	1.7	+ 33.2
Asian, Pacific Islander	763	2.7	1,843	6.9	+ 141.5
White, Other	27,371	97.0	24,717	92.6	- 9.7

Village; President John Jacoby, $3,000. Incorporated: 1872. Named for Antoine Ouilmette, an early French explorer whose Indian wife, Archange, was awarded the land on which the town is located (see Geography chapter). MHV: $280,800.

WILMINGTON

	1980	Percent	1990	Percent	% Change
Total Population	4,424		4,743		+ 7.2
Black	15	.3	12	.3	- 20.0
Hispanic	17	.4	54	1.1	+ 217.6
Asian, Pacific Islander	11	.2	10	.2	- 9.1
White, Other	4,398	99.4	4,721	99.5	+ 7.3

City; Mayor Robert P. Weidling, $13,100. Founded in 1836; became a village in 1854; incorporated as a city in 1865. Originally called Winchester, but changed to Wilmington in 1838. Motto: "The Island City," because a portion of this coal-mining town is on an island bordered by the Kankakee River and the Mill Race Canal. MHV: $83,400.

WINFIELD

	1980	Percent	1990	Percent	% Change
Total Population	4,422		7,096		+ 60.5
Black	16	.4	67	.9	+ 318.8
Hispanic	22	.5	147	2.1	+ 568.2
Asian, Pacific Islander	42	.9	121	1.7	+ 188.1
White, Other	4,364	98.7	6,908	97.4	+ 58.3

Village; President John R. Walde, $1,250. Incorporated: 1921. Settled in 1849 by John Hodges and originally known as Frederickburg. Named today for a general in the 1832 Black Hawk War, Winfield Scott. MHV: $145,600.

WINNETKA

	1980	Percent	1990	Percent	% Change
Total Population	12,772		12,174		- 4.7
Black	62	.5	45	.4	- 27.4
Hispanic	120	.9	105	.9	- 12.5
Asian, Pacific Islander	151	1.2	347	2.9	+ 129.8
White, Other	12,559	98.3	11,782	96.8	- 6.2

Village; President Jeanne Bradner, no salary. Incorporated: 1869. Winnetka is an Indian word meaning "beautiful land." MHV: $483,500.

WINTHROP HARBOR

	1980	Percent	1990	Percent	% Change
Total Population	5,438		6,240		+ 14.7
Black	2	.0	7	.1	+ 250.0
Hispanic	85	1.6	137	2.2	+ 61.2
Asian, Pacific Islander	60	1.1	124	2.0	+ 106.7
White, Other	5,376	98.9	6,109	97.9	+ 13.6

Village; Robert Marabella, $2,700. Incorporated: 1901. Motto: "The Cornerstone of Illinois." Named for the Winthrop Harbor and Dock Company, which laid out the town and operated a dock. MHV: $91,700.

WONDER LAKE

	1980	Percent	1990	Percent	% Change
Total Population	752		1,024		+ 36.2
Black	0	0.0	0	0.0	+ 0.0
Hispanic	7	.9	11	1.1	+ 57.1
Asian, Pacific Islander	0	0.0	3	.3	+ 0.0
White, Other	752	* * *	1,021	99.7	+ 35.8

Village. Incorporated in 1975. MHV: $94,600.

WOOD DALE

	1980	Percent	1990	Percent	% Change
Total Population	11,251		12,425		+ 10.4
Black	11	.1	27	.2	+ 145.5
Hispanic	611	5.4	870	7.0	+ 42.4
Asian, Pacific Islander	248	2.2	381	3.1	+ 53.6
White, Other	10,992	97.7	12,017	96.7	+ 9.3

City; Mayor Jerry C. Greer, $3,400. Incorporated: 1928. Named for the local woods and dales. MHV: $122,400.

WOODRIDGE

	1980	Percent	1990	Percent	% Change
Total Population	22,322		26,256		+ 17.6
Black	864	3.9	1,599	6.1	+ 85.1
Hispanic	516	2.3	1,078	4.1	+ 108.9
Asian, Pacific Islander	719	3.2	1,617	6.2	+ 124.9
White, Other	20,739	92.9	23,040	87.8	+ 11.1

Village; Mayor William F. Murphy, $4,800. Incorporated: 1959. Motto: "Pride in Progress." Name inspired by the many trees. MHV: $120,500.

WOODSTOCK

	1980	Percent	1990	Percent	% Change
Total Population	11,725		14,353		+ 22.4
Black	23	.2	56	.4	+ 143.5
Hispanic	392	3.3	1,114	7.8	+ 184.2
Asian, Pacific Islander	62	.5	201	1.4	+ 224.2
White, Other	11,640	99.3	14,096	98.2	+ 21.1

City; Mayor James D. Shoemaker. Founded in 1845, it originally was called Centerville because it is located in the geographic center of

McHenry County. Renamed Woodstock when incorporated in 1845, at the suggestion of civic leader Joel E. Hohnson, who had been born in Woodstock, Vermont. MHV: $92,300.

WORTH

	1980	Percent	1990	Percent	% Change
Total Population	11,592		11,208		– 3.3
Black	4	.0	18	.2	+ 350.0
Hispanic	180	1.6	315	2.8	+ 75.0
Asian, Pacific Islander	32	.3	72	.6	+ 125.0
White, Other	11,556	99.7	11,118	99.2	– 3.8

Village; President Daniel A. Kumingo, $28,600. Motto: "The Friendly Village." Named after the Township of Worth, which was named for a Col. Worth. Incorporated: 1914. MHV: $94,900.

ZION

	1980	Percent	1990	Percent	% Change
Total Population	17,861		19,775		+ 10.7
Black	3,146	17.6	4,304	21.8	+ 36.8
Hispanic	665	3.7	1,253	6.3	+ 88.4
Asian, Pacific Islander	244	1.4	332	1.7	+ 36.1
White, Other	14,471	81.0	15,139	76.6	+ 4.6

City; Mayor Billy McCullough, $12,000. Incorporated: 1900. Established by evangelist John Alexander Dowie as the headquarters of his Christian Catholic Church. The town name, like the street names, comes from the Bible. MHV: $68,000.

Sources: Elizabeth Novickas; Northeastern Illinois Planning Commission; U.S. Census Bureau; Mediamark Research, Inc.; information on salaries, mottos, dates of founding, and the stories of the town names were obtained from the suburbs themselves; *Local Community Fact Book Chicago Metropolitan Area Based on the 1970 and 1980 Censuses* edited by The Chicago Fact Book Consortium; U.S. Census Bureau.

CEMETERIES

FIRSTS

■ Early settlers first buried their dead right next to their houses, which accounts for the occasional unearthing of skeletons during downtown excavations for developments. Since early settlements hugged the river, many bones have been found along its path. But burials there created other problems. As a March 12, 1849, *Chicago Daily Democrat* story read, "During the spring freshet, two coffins were seen floating down the river."

■ The city's first official cemeteries probably were established in 1835: Ten acres east of Clark near Chicago Avenue (Protestant) and sixteen acres at Twenty-third and Lake Michigan (Catholic). But as early as 1830, a map showed a fort cemetery just south of Fort Dearborn, which was on the south bank of the Chicago River.

■ Jack Johnson, the first black ever to win the world heavyweight championship, was buried in Graceland Cemetery in 1946.

Rent-a-graves: Temporary graves or rent-a-graves were sold in the Chicago area during the Great Depression. The graves were sold for forty years, after which they could be used or sold by the cemetery again. In 1975, the practice of reselling these graves was attacked by the Illinois Attorney General's Bureau of Consumer Fraud because the used graves were sold to unsuspecting customers. This was made particularly apparent when a family went to visit a recently deceased grandmother only to find other bones scattered about the gravesite. Normally a new arrival was placed in the used grave with the old bones on the bottom.

EXTREMES

■ The oldest Chicago area cemetery is probably the parish cemetery of St. James, Sag Bridge at 107th and Archer in Lemont, which is dated at 1837. The next oldest could be the now inactive St. Stephen Cemetery in Carol Stream, where the first burial was in 1854.

■ Two designated Chicago landmarks contain bodies: The Thirty-fifth Street tomb of Stephen A. Douglas (1865), onetime presidential rival of Abraham Lincoln; and the Getty Tomb (1890) in Graceland Cemetery designed by Louis Sullivan.

The Getty Tomb, designed by Louis Sullivan, contains the remains of steel executive Henry Getty, his wife and his daughter.

Caddy-comb: Willie "The Wimp" Stokes made national news after he was murdered in 1984. Not because of the murder, but because of his wake. Stokes, the son of a a South Side drug dealer, who later was murdered himself, was propped up in a coffin made to look like a Cadillac and his fingers were stuffed with $1,000 bills.

■ Former Chicago Mayor Long John Wentworth has the largest single lot in Rosehill Cemetery at two-thirds of an acre. It also has the tallest monument—a seventy-two foot granite obelisk. By his wish, he originally had no inscription on his monument so when people would see it, they would ask who it was and then learn more about him. (See Politics for burials of Chicago mayors.)

Stealing Scarface's Stone: Al Capone's 125-pound grave stone in Mt. Carmel Cemetery has been stolen at least twice.

■ The last king of Yugoslavia is buried in Libertyville. Relatives of King Peter II, who was also the grandson of England's Queen Victoria, wanted Peter to be buried in Queen Victoria's royal plot. But through his will, the king insisted on Libertyville. King Peter II died in 1970 at age forty-seven and was buried at the St. Sava Orthodox Monastery—headquarters of the Serbian Orthodox Diocese of the

United States and Canada. He became king in 1934 at age eleven after his father Alexander I was assassinated. His uncle Prince Paul took over, signed a deal with the Nazis and was ousted. Peter took control at age seventeen. But he fled one month later when the Germans invaded. The king worked for a savings and loan in California.

> **Triangle of Tragedy:** On Dec. 1, 1958, a fire at Our Lady of the Angels School, 3820 W. Iowa, killed ninety-two children and three nuns. Three rows of graves for twenty-five children killed in that fire were laid out in a triangular section of the Holy Innocents Shrine of Queen of Heaven Cemetery in Hillside.

■ The Tower of Remembrance in Shalom Memorial Park in Palatine is one of the largest, if not the largest, Holocaust memorials in the Midwest. The eighty-foot-high monument with a gold leaf eternal flame was dedicated in 1988 in memory of the estimated 6 million Jews who died in Nazi concentration camps.

> **Parking Lot Graves:** There's a half-acre cemetery in the Yorktown Shopping Center parking lot in Lombard. It was put there in 1880 by William Boeger for his family and members of the Church of St. Paul at Butterfield and Myers roads. The church closed in 1906 but the cemetery lives on, although now it is flanked on three sides by parking lots.

LIST OF TEN LARGEST CEMETERY TRUST FUNDS IN ILLINOIS
(As of the End of 1989)

1. General Care Foundation Jewish Cemeteries, Forest Park, $16.6 million.

2. Rosehill Cemetery and Mausoleum, 5800 N. Ravenswood, Chicago, $7.1 million.

3. Woodlawn Cemetery, 7600 W. Cermak, Forest Park, $4.3 million.

4. Evergreen Cemetery Mausoleum & Crematory, Evergreen Park, $3.1 million.

5. Lincoln Cemetery, Blue Island, $3 million.

6. Montrose Cemetery and Crematorium, 5400 N. Pulaski, $2.8 million.

7. Randhill Park Cemetery Association, Inc., Palatine, $2.8 million.

8. Central Cemetery Company of Illinois (Memorial Park), Skokie, $2.6 million.

9. Mt. Greenwood Cemetery Association, Chicago, $2.5 million.

10. Oakridge Cemetery, Mausoleum, Chapel and Crematorium, Hillside. $2.4 million.

Circus Graves: Woodlawn Cemetery in Forest Park has a burial ground for performers. Called Showmen's Rest, this area is maintained by the Showmen's League of America. Fifty circus performers killed in a train accident near Hammond, Indiana, in June 1918, were buried there. Most headstones bear just their nicknames like "Baldy" and "Six Horse Driver." Five stone elephants mark their graves.

PAYING FOR THE DEAD

■ More than 4,500 cemeteries are registered with the state. Cemeteries offering perpetual care must be licensed with the state. A cemetery selling perpetual care must deposit 15 percent of the sales price of an interment into a trust fund to produce income for the care of the gravesite and cemetery; or 10 percent of an entombment; or 10 percent of an inurnment. The annual earnings of these trusts must be used to care for the cemetery and the principal must remain intact.

NUMBER OF CEMETERIES BY COUNTY

	Licensed	Other*	Total
Cook	44	177	221
Du Page	14	16	30
Kane	16	35	51
Lake	20	12	32
McHenry	23	32	55
Will	25	61	86

*non-private cemeteries, such as religious and municipal cemeteries are only required to be registered.

Death in the Park: The south part of Lincoln Park used to be a cemetery. Some 20,000 bodies were buried there. In 1870, it was turned into a park and the bodies were moved to other Chicago-area cemeteries. But the Couch mausoleum, which holds at least the body of Ira Couch (1806-1857), proprietor of the old Tremont House Hotel, stayed. In 1871, park district officials decided it was too difficult and expensive to move it. As for other remains in the park, they still pop up. In 1970, bones were unearthed when the Chicago Historical Society built an addition.

CHICAGO'S OLDEST CEMETERIES

Oak Woods Cemetery: 1035 E. Sixty-seventh St., founded: 1853, first burial on May, 20, 1865.

Buried here are: Ida B. Wells (civil rights leader); Jesse Owens; Kennesaw Mountain Landis (baseball's first commissioner); Jesse Binga (Chicago's first black banker); Mayor Harold Washington; Bernard Epton (Washington's unsuccessful Republican opponent); Paul Cornell (founder of Hyde Park); the parents of General J. Pershing; Adrian "Cap" Anson (player and manager of the Chicago White Stockings, predecessors of the Cubs); "Big" Jim Colosimo (mob boss); Clarence Darrow; Enrico Fermi (physicist who engineered the first controlled nuclear reaction).

A Rose to Remember: A red rose is left every week at the grave of Harold Washington in Oak Woods Cemetery.

Rosehill Cemetery: 5800 N. Ravenswood Ave., established: 1859.

Buried here are: Charles Gates Dawes (U.S. vice president from 1925-29 under Calvin Coolidge); Avery Brundage (president of U.S. Olympic Association and International Olympic Committee); John G. Shedd; Maurice L. Rothschild (merchant); Milton Florsheim (shoe manufacturer); James Scott Kemper (insurance); A. Montgomery Ward; Robert S. Scott (of Carson, Pirie, Scott); Ignaz Schwinn (bicycle manufacturer); Julius Rosenwald; Frances E. Willard (Women's Christian Temperance Union); Charles Hull (donated house to Jane Addams); Major Gen. Thomas Ransom (Civil War hero).

Calvary Cemetery: Evanston, established: 1859

Buried here are: Lawrence Kelly (co-founder of Chicago Lyric Opera); John M. Smyth (furniture); Edward Hines (lumber); Ferdinand Henrotin (Henrotin Hospital); John Cudahy (meat packer); Charles Comiskey (owner of White Sox); James T. Farrell (author); Ald. Michael "Hinky Dink" Kenna (corrupt 1st Ward politician).

Landmark of Death: Chicago businessman Henry Harrison Getty commissioned Chicago architect Louis Sullivan in 1890 to build him a family tomb in Graceland Cemetery. The square tomb with its clean lines and artful yet subtle decoration prompted the City Council to give the tomb landmark status in 1971. As for Sullivan himself, he, too, was buried in Graceland, but not with the same amenities. Sullivan died broke in 1924, and for several years after his burial he didn't even have a headstone.

Graceland Cemetery: 4001 N. Clark, dedicated: 1860, chartered: 1861.

Buried here are: Mies van der Rohe, Daniel Burnham, Louis Sullivan (all architects); John Kinzie (early Chicago settler); boxing champions Jack Johnson and Bob Fitzsimmons; George Pullman (Pullman railroad car); Phillip D. Armour (meatpacker); Cyrus McCormick (inventor of the reaper); John Jones (prominent early black politician in Chicago); Marshall Field; Potter Palmer (Palmer House) and wife Bertha (onetime queen of Chicago society); Victor Lawson (founder of the *Daily News*); Gov. John Peter Altgeld; Melville Fuller (Chief Justice U.S. Supreme Court); Allen Pinkerton (detective); Timothy Webster (hanged in Virginia as a Union spy).

Death Moves: The body of John Kinzie was moved four times. He was first buried north of the river, then moved to old North Side Cemetery, then to City Cemetery and finally to Graceland Cemetery.

BIZZARE, FAMOUS AND UNIQUE MONUMENTS OF CHICAGO'S OLDEST CEMETERIES

■ The statue of "Eternal Silence," often called the "Statue of Death," by Lorado Taft, is a haunting, hooded figure that marks the Graceland Cemetery grave of early Chicago hotel owner Dexter Graves, who died in 1844.

■ George Pullman's family was afraid his workers still held a grudge after the 1894 Pullman strike, so when Pullman was buried in 1897, in Graceland Cemetery, his coffin was sunk inside a block of concrete the size of a small railroad car with railroad ties and more concrete piled on top.

Flowers for Big Jim: A mason jar filled with flowers is periodically left on the steps of the mausoleum of crime boss Big Jim Colisimo, who was murdered in 1920.

■ William A. Hulbert, co-founder of baseball's National League, is buried beneath a granite baseball, seams and all, in Graceland Cemetery. When conditions are just right, you can hear the roar of the crowd at nearby Wrigley Field.

■ George S. Bangs, who designed the first railway mail car, is buried beneath a small-scale granite replica of one in Rosehill Cemetery.

■ Famed Lincoln sculptor Leonard Volk's last work in Rosehill Cemetery was a life-sized statue of himself. Volk's other works in Rosehill include the Volunteer Fireman's Monument showing a fireman with a coiled hose and a megaphone standing on top of a thirty-six-foot column.

■ A popular stop in Rosehill cemetery is the statue of Lulu E. Fellows, who died in 1883 at age sixteen. The statue, encased in glass, is of a girl sitting. The inscription: "Many hopes lie buried here."

■ The Rosehill Cemetery crypt of fourteen-year-old Robert E. Franks, who was murdered in 1924 by two university students, Richard Loeb and Nathan Leopold, bears the words: "Life is because God is infinite, indestructible and eternal."

■ A towering monument of Georgia granite and aged brass name plates is topped by an unarmed Confederate soldier in Oak Woods Cemetery. This marks the Confederate Mound, where about 4,275 Confederate soldiers are buried. They died in Camp Douglas, a prisoner-of-war camp once on the South Side.

■ A railroad wheel, lantern and smokestack made of sandstone mark the grave of Cale Cramer, a New York Central engineer who lost his life in an 1887 train wreck while saving his passengers.

How Deep Do You Go: A corpse in Illinois has to be buried at least eighteen inches below the surface of the ground. There is no state law that demands that a body be buried in a vault or coffin, but few, if any, cemeteries would allow a burial without one. A primary purpose of the vault is to avoid sinkholes. The top of the vault must be a minimum of eighteen inches below the surface of the ground by state law. The eighteen inches is really just to allow a good root system for the grass. With a vault, a grave is usually about five feet deep.

Sources: *Chicago Sun-Times* and *Daily News*, *Chicago Sun-Times* reporter Mark Brown, Cook County Forest Preserves; Office of the Cook County Medical Examiner; Office of the Comptroller, State of Illinois; Oak Woods Cemetery, Graceland Cemetery, Calvary Cemetery; Rosehill Cemetery; Diocese of Joliet Catholic Cemeteries; Catholic Cemeteries, Archdiocese of Chicago.

GHOSTS

TEN TOP GHOST STORIES

1. **Resurrection Mary.** They say she was buried in her dancing shoes. But nobody is sure who she is or was. Blonde and beautiful, she is said to appear now and again on Archer road near Resurrection Cemetery, 7200 S. Archer Road. She hitchhikes a ride to the nearby Willowbrook Ballroom and Restaurant in Willow Springs, dances the night away with a young man, and leaves with him. But as they pass the cemetery, she screams, jumps out of the car, runs through the tombstones and disappears. "Resurrection Mary," folks say, was a young Polish woman killed in a car crash in 1931 after leaving a dance at the Willowbrook. And it's said there are three Marys fitting her description, all killed in car crashes, buried in Resurrection.

2. **Fort Sheridan.** Ghost sightings at Fort Sheridan include "a lady in orange" who showed up at a brunch at the community club; an old stockade with the sounds of a conversation in German; footsteps in a locked area; a man in a white robe appearing in a photo of Christmas lights in the 1970s (some call it a double exposure); a phantom blacksmith; a ghostly soldier; a phantom radiator-tapping custodian; and a woman in a library window.

3. **The Two Altar Boys at Holy Family Church.** It is said two altar boys, brothers who drowned together in 1874, haunt the aisles of Holy Family Church at 1080 West Roosevelt. In his autobiography, Father Arnold Damen, the church's founder, reported he was awakened by the boys one night in 1890. He said they were wearing cassocks and holding candles and led him to a dying woman, their mother. And then they disappeared. Two statues of the boys were carved, one for each side of the altar. Some worshipers used to swear that the wooden eyes followed them.

4. **The Flapper.** Dressed in Roaring Twenties attire, a woman with jet black hair occasionally has been sighted on Des Plaines Avenue near Waldheim Cemetery in Forest Park. Men supposedly have

picked her up and taken her dancing, just like Resurrection Mary. The men also seem to get treated like Mary's dates. They drop the flapper off at Waldheim's old caretaker's cottage and she vanishes.

5. **St. James, Sag Bridge Cemetery.** Even in daytime, St. James, Sag Bridge Cemetery in southwest Cook County can make you feel uncomfortable. It is the oldest cemetery (1837) in the county. Many of those buried beneath the faded white tombstones died while digging the Illinois and Michigan Canal in the 1830s and 1840s. It's also said to be near an Indian burial ground. A priest, it is rumoured, once saw the ground rise and fall as if it were breathing. And a county policeman, it is said, once chased several figures in monk-like hooded robes until they vanished.

6. **Mary Alice Quinn.** Mary Alice Quinn was fourteen when she died in 1935. Shortly before her death, Mary Alice supposedly told her parents she would someday help suffering people and promised to "shower roses on the world." People have credited her with miracle cures, and some say they have smelled the scent of roses in her bedroom in Calumet City. Others claim to smell roses—even in the dead of winter—at her gravesite in Holy Sepulchre Cemetery, 6001 W. 111th St., Worth.

7. **Bachelor's Grove.** Along the road leading to this Midlothian cemetery, it is said, there is a ghost house—but you can't always see it. A pale blue light has been spotted flickering across tombstones and through the marsh surrounding this abandoned churchyard. Some people also say they've seen a farmhouse, complete with a front porch, railings, a swing and an indoor light. Sometimes the house is on one side of the road, sometimes it's on the other.

8. **St. Valentine's Day Massacre.** The garage is gone, but the memory lingers. On Feb. 14, 1929, seven men were gunned down— reputedly by Al Capone's boys. The killing garage at 2122 N. Clark is gone and a senior citizens' project has been built in its place, but a few trees on a grassy spot in the middle of the lot is said to be the killing spot. Dogs, it is said, move away from these trees, sometimes whining. And late at night some residents have said they hear crying and moaning.

9. **Drumbeats in the Night.** Robinson Woods, a county forest preserve at Lawrence Avenue and River Road, holds the family graves of Alexander Robinson, an Indian chief of mixed blood. The cemetery plot is part of the land granted Robinson through the treaty of Prairie du Chien in 1829. But when one of Robinson's ancestors, a welfare recipient named Herbert Boettcher, died in 1973, the forest preserve district refused to allow him to be buried there, allegedly for "sanitary reasons." Ever since then, it is said, drumbeats have been sounding from the graves in the woods. Some say they have even recorded the drumbeats.

10. **Calvary Cemetery.** The ghost of a drowning young man, folks say, now and again pops up near Calvary Cemetery, on the lakefront in Evanston. As the story goes, the young man is spotted drowning in Lake Michigan. He struggles and yells for help. Then he crawls out of the lake, across Sheridan Road and into the cemetery.

INDEX

Chicago Sun-Times   Sundays Free Offer

Sign me up for 8-weeks of the Chicago Sun-Times! I want daily and Sunday delivery (Sundays FREE)

___ Please bill me for daily and Sunday delivery of the Chicago Sun-Times at 2.25 per week (Sundays FREE). (PC660)

Name _____

Address _____ Apt. ___

City/State/Zip _____

Phone _____

After 8 weeks, home delivery will continue at the regular rate unless the Chicago Sun-Times is notified otherwise. Valid only for new subscribers and valid only where home delivery is maintained. Not valid with any other discounted offer. Phone number is required to process order. Offer expires 12/31/91.